To Lee Burress

Steadfast beacon of intellectual
freedom for all of us.

N.J.K. and J.M.K.

Censored Books

Critical Viewpoints

edited by
Nicholas J. Karolides
Lee Burress
John M. Kean

The Scarecrow Press, Inc.
Lanham, Maryland, and London
2001

PS
65
.C46
C46
2001

SCARECROW PRESS, INC.

Published in the United States of America
by Scarecrow Press, Inc.
4720 Boston Way, Lanham, Maryland 20706
www.scarecrowpress.com

4 Pleydell Gardens, Folkestone
Kent CT20 2DN, England

"Anne Frank: The Diary of a Young Girl" © 1993 by Katherine Paterson; "Blackballing"
© 1993 by John A. Williams; "A Farewell to Arms" © 1993 by James A. Michener;
"Take the Tortillas Out of Your Poetry" © 1993 by Rudolfo A. Anaya
First paperback edition 2001

British Library Cataloguing-in-Publication Information Available

The hardback edition of this book was previously cataloged by the Library of Congress
as follows:
Library of Congress Cataloging-in-Publication Data
Censored books : critical viewpoints / edited by Nicholas J. Karolides, Lee   Burress,
John M. Kean.
      p.   cm.
    Includes bibliographical references.
    ISBN: 0-8108-2667-4 (acid-free paper)
        1. American literature—History and criticism. 2. American literature—
Censorship. 3. Censorship—United States.
    I. Karolides, Nicholas J. II. Burress, Lee. III. Kean, John M.
    PS65.C46C46   1993
    810.9—dc20   93-349

ISBN 0-8018-4038-3 (pbk. : alk. paper)

∞™ The paper used in this publication meets the minimum requirements of
American National Standard for Information Sciences—Permanence of
Paper for Printed Library Materials, ANSI/NISO Z39.48-1992.
Manufactured in the United States of America.

CONTENTS

II. CHALLENGING BOOKS 49

ACKNOWLEDGMENTS

We are indebted to Maxine Burress, Inga Karolides and Carol Kean for their editorial advice with regard to language sensitivity and response to clarity of content. They each read every essay and provided invaluable insights. In addition, Maxine Burress prepared the biographical summaries of the contributors.

We acknowledge with gratitude the Wisconsin Council of Teachers of English which released to us the copyright of our previous text, *Celebrating Censored Books*, 1985, edited by Nicholas J. Karolides and Lee Burress. A number of articles in this volume first appeared in the earlier one.

INTRODUCTION

Lee Burress
Nicholas J. Karolides
John M. Kean

> Congress shall make no law respecting an establishment of religion,
> or prohibiting the free exercise thereof; or abridging the freedom of
> speech or of the press; or the right of the people peaceably to
> assemble, and to petition the government for a redress of grievances.
> (U. S. Constitution, the Bill of Rights).

This collection of essays has been prepared to provide assistance to
the growing number of students, teachers, librarians, and parents who
find themselves confronting a censorship situation. The pressure of
censorship is an increasingly burdensome characteristic of the world of
students and teachers.

Even though there were celebrated censorship cases such as the
Scopes Trial (arguing about the teaching of evolution), prior to World War
II, censorship was an infrequent problem of school life in the United
States. *The Merchant of Venice* was challenged on a few occasions by
parents because of the belief that it taught an unflattering and stereotypical
picture of Jews. Several social science texts, especially the books of Harold
Rugg, were driven out of the schools in the 1930s on the false grounds that
the books taught communist ideas. English departments were, however,
essentially free of challenges to the materials in use before 1950. Their
materials were largely British, or nineteenth century American in nature.
Very little twentieth century American literature was in the school
curriculum before 1950.

After 1950, a number of changes in public school practices may be
cited to explain, in part, the growth in censorship pressures. First, the

standard English curriculum moved away from a 19th century British emphasis toward a more twentieth century American-focused curriculum. The paperback revolution of the postwar period spurred this transition. When it became possible to purchase a set of books for the classroom at twenty-five or fifty cents apiece, many teachers began to teach fairly current books, and to teach the whole book, not an excerpt from an anthology.

Before 1950, relatively few schools had libraries. Along with changes in the curriculum, many schools developed increasingly complex libraries, which made a greater number and variety of books more available to students and teachers. A survey of a national sample of school libraries in 1988 indicated that the median number of books for use by elementary schools was 8,773, for middle schools, 9,148, and for high schools, 14,153 (Censorship update, NCTE, 1988).

The school population has increased significantly, decade by decade across this century. By 1950 most of the grade school population was in school, with prominent exceptions for impaired children or minority group children. However, before 1940, only approximately one-half of the high school age group was in high school. By 1980, 90% of the students of school age were in the elementary and secondary grades. The substantial increase in the high school population came from the lower middle class and working class children, whose parents, for the most part, were not high school graduates. The increasing numbers of and diversity of the public school population and increased diversity of materials have created new tensions in what had been an essentially white, middle class institution. Today, the high school attempts to serve all socio-economic levels and all ethnic groups in our multi-cultural society. Whether it does its job well or not is under continual debate.

The public schools' current critics frequently assert that the schools do not teach values. Other critics object to the values that they think are being taught. The schools do teach values--the values of critical inquiry and diversity, values that enable students to measure the degree to which this society is becoming fully democratic, as envisioned by at least some of our forebears.

One of the basic values explicitly taught in the schools is the equal worth of all persons. This is also a major or minor theme in a high proportion of the challenged books discussed in the following essays. The schools teach highly idealistic attitudes toward life and toward our society, more so perhaps than is justified by reality. Certainly not all segments of this society believe in the equality of all persons. The democratic virtue of self-reliance is another value which is explicitly taught, though not all parents embrace this particular virtue as one of their own. It would be difficult to find much American literature that did not contain these two themes: self reliance and the equal worth of all persons.

It seems likely that the relative success of the schools in teaching the attitudes above, along with the great success of the schools in producing what one recent study describes as the most literate generation of young Americans yet (recognizing the "savage inequalities" that Jonathan Kozol described in his book of that title), is responsible for much of the recent censorship pressure (Kirsch & Jungeblut). If students, along with the general public, were not reading the books discussed in this volume, there would of course be no complaints.

Several studies report that book sales have increased in recent decades at a rate significantly higher than population growth, four times greater by one report. These increases have continued throughout the postwar years in spite of the growth of TV viewing. In 1947, the U.S. published approximately 7,000 different titles. Currently, the U. S. publishes over 50,000 different titles. Magazine sales have increased at about twice the population growth. Library use increased at almost twice the rate of population growth. Prior to 1964 by one estimate, about one-fourth of Americans had no access to a public library. Today, in many states every citizen has access to a library. For a full discussion of this point, see L. Burress, *The Battle of the Books: Literary Censorship in the Public Schools: 1950-85* (79-81).

While the schools cannot claim credit as the only agency responsible for this great growth in literacy, they surely have played a significant role in this major social change. In fact, a reasonable conclusion is that the public schools are the most efficient, least corrupt, most successful public institution in the United States.

Several other factors have probably played a role in the continuing rise of censorship pressures. The increase in costs of education, especially heavy reliance on property taxes in many states, is one. The need for a scapegoat for various social ills such as the rise in teenage pregnancy and the use of drugs is a second. Third, the rise of fundamentalism, as Joan DelFatorre points out in her forthcoming book, *What Johnny Shouldn't Read: Textbook Censorship in America,* has had a vigorous impact on the public schools.

Our reasons for including a book in a public school curriculum or library will differ according to its proposed use. One book may be included in our curriculum because it is considered a classic of American literature. The same book may be included in other classrooms because it illuminates an historical period, or because it provides an entry into the study of foreign cultures. The same book may again be used because it mirrors contemporary social issues, or because it reflects upon value questions which arise in our students' journeys toward maturity. Or a book may provide an alternative perspective for individual readers.

There are always new books and books that have been around for years which will need to be justified for school use. Authors are constantly writing books that will challenge contemporary parameters or provide fresh insights of what is acceptable, while older books are reexamined within the context of constantly changing perspectives from religious leaders, psychologists, politicians and many others concerned about the welfare of children and/or the content of the curriculum.

One welcome factor has been the increased willingness of citizens to ask questions about the conduct of public institutions. This provides an opportunity for the schools to encourage more parental involvement than has sometimes been true in the past. As June Berkeley discovered while teaching in a small town in Southern Ohio, it is possible, when teachers and parents work together, to develop support for the best possible set of educational materials. We should note that in rare cases, the schools have been insensitive to the concerns of parents and have generated hostility where it is not necessary. If on occasion the schools have in fact used materials not appropriate to the grade level in question, they should be quick to remedy mistakes.

Many organizations are engaged in the efforts to preserve intellectual freedom in the schools. The American Library Association (ALA) and its Office for Intellectual Freedom are the most well-known advocates for intellectual freedom. For over forty years, ALA has published the *Newsletter on Intellectual Freedom*. This newsletter, published six times a year, provides regular updates on censorship, censorship challenges, court cases, legal decisions, and other information useful to anyone who wishes to keep abreast of U.S. Constitutional issues relating to freedom of speech and the press. Organizations such as the National Coalition Against Censorship, People for the American Way, and the American Civil Liberties Union also regularly provide help for school personnel when issues of censorship arise. The National Council of Teachers of English and the International Reading Association, both of which have long standing commitments to intellectual freedom, have formed a joint task force to encourage and assist schools in fighting censorship. The statement from the joint task force adopted by both groups argues that

> All students have the right to materials and educational experiences that promote open inquiry, critical thinking, diversity in thought and expression, and respect for others in the public school classroom. Denial or restriction of this right is an infringement of intellectual freedom.

The task force is currently working to produce a document that would heighten sensitivity about censorship concerns and provide a resource for communities facing challenges to intellectual freedom.

Many publications have articulated the importance of intellectual freedom in schools. *The Students' Right to Read* and *The Students' Right to Know*, both published by the National Council of Teachers of English in 1982, addressed specifically the need to combat censorship in English language arts classrooms. Their rationale could be applied to other curriculum content as well. In 1988, the American Association of School Administrators and the American Library Association published *Censorship and Selection: Issues and Answers for Schools*, a publication which speaks to a broader range of challenges. These publications are a place to start our study of issues related to intellectual freedom, but they do not provide the specific support that is required for particular titles.

Before we can begin to write a book rationale for our classroom or school library, two conditions should apply: (1) we know the book extremely well, and (2) we believe that this book makes a significant contribution to our curriculum and to students. Writing a rationale for why a book ought to be in the curriculum requires a knowledge of the goals and objectives of the curriculum, the skills, abilities and interests of students, a knowledge of students' literary and popular culture backgrounds, and a knowledge of the broader area of study in which the book is to be used. It is also helpful to know how frequently the title is used in similar situations, what reviewers have had to say about it in professional journals and in the popular press, and what awards the title has won, if any. Much of this material should be available locally; for example, in the school's curriculum guides. Much of the information, however, must be culled from a variety of sources such as textbooks, monographs and journals related to teaching or educational materials. *The Book Review Index*, published by Gale Research Company since 1965, provides an index of reviews appearing in more than 200 periodicals. Readers who are particularly concerned about children's and young adult literature should consult the annotated list of reference and bibliographical resources described in "Familiarity with Reference" (Kenney 48-54). All of these sources add to the rationale writer's own justifications for using a specific title. And since rationales frequently don't get written until a work has been challenged, the rationale writer should also be familiar with the concerns that have been expressed about the work in the local community. This information should be available in a written complaint filed by a local community member but may also need to be acquired through an interview. The local newspapers are another obvious source for community viewpoints on the controversial material. At the state and national level, the rationale writer should consult the *Newsletter on Intellectual Freedom* which keeps track of what titles have been challenged and why they have been challenged.

A rationale explains why a title is valued in the curriculum. It provides reasons for having a book in the public school library or for using it in the classroom. It does not provide all of the support that is needed. A book may be attacked for reasons that are not included in an essay. For support, teachers and librarians should consult with their local educational association or union, their local, state, and national subject matter organization and one or more of the anti-censorship coalitions or committees mentioned earlier. Most state professional organizations have such committees. A number of states also have intellectual freedom coalitions made up of union representatives, subject matter organizations, librarians, and school administrators.

The titles that are discussed in this book were chosen on the basis of frequency of challenge. Lee Burress listed over 800 titles that were challenged between 1950 and 1985, in *The Battle of the Books*. That list came from 17 surveys of censorship pressures carried out by various scholars. In addition, several titles were added to the list of frequently challenged books from more recent reports, especially from the ALA *Newsletter on Intellectual Freedom*. One person who was asked to write an essay complained because his favorite censored book was not on the list. The reason is fairly clear; that book is very rarely assigned in the schools, so it is almost never challenged. We could not practically provide essays on 800 or 900 titles, so we chose the books that are most often reported by teachers or librarians as objects of attack. Indirectly, therefore, this list of titles is an index of books that are used in the schools.

If we examine the list of challenged titles, it is clear that most are twentieth century books, that most are by American authors, and that a disproportionate number are by non-Caucasian writers and deal with non-Anglo Saxon characters (disproportionate, that is, in comparison with the total number of books published in the U.S.). There is a strong suggestion here that racism lies behind the challenges. It is frequently disguised under charges that the books contain obscene or pornographic language. So far as the present writers know, no book used in the public schools has been found by a court to be obscene.

Another reasonable conclusion that may be drawn from the list is that good books are more likely to be challenged than are books of little value. Every library, bookstore and supermarket contains many books with the same kind of language as may be found in the challenged list of books. The great majority of those books are ephemeral or superficial. There is little in them, therefore, to question the values of this society, to challenge readers to question their own values or way of life. The essays in this collection provide specific support for a rather select list of titles which are frequently challenged. They also serve as models for the development of rationales for use in the public schools.

The present volume is different from our earlier collection, *Celebrating Censored Books*, in two significant ways. It is expanded. The earlier volume focused on the so-called "dirty thirty." This volume doubles the number of works discussed and includes a selection from the earlier volume. In addition to essays written by teachers and professors of literature, *Censored Books: Critical Viewpoints* includes essays by poets, novelists and dramatists- -authors of adult and adolescent literature.

The central charge to these reviewers was direct and simple: Why should anyone read this book? Why should it be recommended? They were asked to express their impressions of the text, of the concepts and emotions that readers might experience, of the personal and social understandings that might be achieved. A second concern addressed the question, Why is this book under attack? The reviewers were asked to consider the censorial challenges to the text in relation to its perceived merits. Another consideration suggested to reviewers was pedagogic, that is, classroom application.

The essays included in *Censored Books: Critical Viewpoints* provide, in effect, a defense of these frequently challenged books, a rationale for ensuring access to them for readers and support for teaching them. This collection does not, however, propose a curriculum for the English language arts classroom nor is it a cultural literacy list. The editors are not arguing that everyone must read all of these books. Rather, we strongly advocate the right of readers to select literary materials in an open marketplace of ideas and of teachers to select classroom materials in keeping with appropriate teaching objectives.

The collection is organized in two sections. The first, "Perspectives: Censorship by Omission and Commission," offers six author's views. Arthur Miller considers historical attempts to "revise" Shakespeare's *King Lear* in conjunction with current omissions of segments of his plays from school texts. He reflects on current censorship practices against an international backdrop. John Williams focuses on acts of omission—

publishers censoring, that is, not publishing—works by African-American authors. The nature and force of censorship attacks and their impact on authors is revealed by Norma Fox Mazer. She introduces censorship by commission, that is, the act of self-censorship, encouraged by publishers so as not to offend the public. Similarly, Rudolfo Anaya reflects on cultural discrimination that proscribes Hispanic-American writers and the effect of self-censorship on the expression of their life experiences. The last two essays in this section, by Mary Stolz and Lee Bennett Hopkins, encourage broad understanding of censorship challenges. They illustrate their insights with a wide selection of diverse fiction and poetry that has been challenged, from picture-story books to mature adolescent novels.

The second section, "Challenging Books," provides responses and defenses of individual books. Arranged alphabetically by the title of the text, they provide a varied perspective. Some are oriented to social issues, others to personal transactions with the text, and others to teaching concerns. They provide diverse, thoughtful approaches, suggesting that there is no one best way to prepare a rationale for a book or a particular situation. The array is enlightening.

But as these essays enlighten, we hope that they will stir the reader to take a deeper look at the whole question of intellectual freedom for our youth. We, as educators and parents, must constantly remind ourselves and our students that the constitutional guarantees of separation of church and state, freedom of speech and of the press, even the right to congregate to exchange ideas are not given by God but must be won anew with each generation. With the ever escalating calls for accountability in public education, the growing diversity in the school population and the concomitant rise in controversial materials designed to address the needs of all of our youth, (and let's not forget the increasingly organized religious right) we cannot expect or even hope that the number of censorship attempts directed to our public schools will diminish anytime soon. Our future depends upon our youth having the opportunity to grapple with ideas in their reading, their viewing and their interactions with each other and their adult mentors. We can opt for no less if we are to have an educated public capable of dealing with the culturally pluralistic and diverse nature of our world.

WORKS CITED

Burress, Lee. *The Battle of the Books: Literary Censorship in the Public Schools, 1950-85.* Metuchen, NJ: Scarecrow Press, 1989.

DelFatorre, Joan. *What Johnny Shouldn't Read: Textbook Censorship in America.* New Haven, CT: Yale University Press, Forthcoming.

Karolides, Nicholas J. and Lee Burress, Eds. *Celebrating Censored Books.* Racine, WI: Wisconsin Council of Teachers of English, 1985.

Kenney, Donald J., Ed. "Familiarity with Reference." *The Alan Review* 19 (Fall 1991): 48-54.

Kirsch, I. S. and A. Jungeblut. *Literacy: Profiles of America's Young Adults, Final Report.* Princeton, NJ: Educational Testing Service, 1986.

Kozol, Jonathan. *Savage Inequalities: Children in American Schools.* New York: Crown Publications, Inc., 1991.

PROLOGUE

A friend who is reading his way through all the issues of *The New Yorker* found this piece in the July 2, 1927 issue (27-28), and called it to our attention. It illustrates several principles. One is the French proverb, "The more things change, the more they stay the same." Another is the "banned in Boston principle"; the phenomenon that often occurs that when a book is attacked, it then becomes quite popular and the publishers have to rush additional copies into the market. Unfortunately, it does not always occur, as the case of "The Lottery" demonstrates. Attacks on that story have driven it out of all literature anthologies. However, the "banned in Boston principle" is illustrated by the case of the attack on *The Magician*, by Saul Stein, at Montello, Wisconsin in 1981: when a book is attacked, very often the sales increase dramatically. In his satiric advice beneath, Upton Sinclair explains how the principle could be put to good use in the 1920s.

How to Be Obscene[1]

Upton Sinclair

I have made a discovery almost priceless to authors. If I were a selfish author, I would keep it to myself and live on it the rest of my life. Being an altruist, I pass it on for my colleagues to make use of.

You spend a lot of time writing a book, and then maybe no one pays any attention to it. The season is dull, and there are mountains of books on

---

[1] Reprinted by permission: c 1927, 1955 *The New Yorker Magazine*, Inc.

the desks of the literary editors; you have got lost in the mob, your book is dead, and your wife and kids can't go to the seashore this summer.

But then some good angel puts it into the head of a Boston preacher to read your book and take it to the Boston police, and the police go and arrest a bookclerk for selling your book, which is obscene. Instantly the press agencies flash the name of your book to every town and village in the United States, and your publishers get orders by telegraph from Podunk and Kalamazoo. The literary editors grab the book out of the pile they had set aside to be turned over to the second-hand dealers. The printers of your book have to telegraph to the mill for a carload of paper for a new edition, and the royalties from the first three days' sales pay your expenses while you travel from California to Boston, to enter a protest against the action of the censor, and ensure the sale of the new edition before it has gone to press.

Last week I was a guest of the Kiwanis Club of Boston. They gave me a very nice luncheon of cold meats and potato salad and ice cream and cake, and we saluted the flag, and sang songs about it, and then I told them about this wonderful situation--using the Kiwanis dialect, which, as you may know, is closely related to the Rotary and Lions' languages. I said: "Under this arrangement we authors are using the rest of the United States as our selling territory, and Boston as our advertising headquarters."

If it were necessary to write really obscene books, I wouldn't recommend this plan, because real obscenity is altogether foreign to my interests. But the beauty of the plan is that you don't have to write anything really harmful; all you have to do is to follow the example of the great masters of the world's literature, and deal with the facts of life frankly and honestly. That is what the Boston police call "obscenity," and as soon as the rest of the country understands that, it will be an honor to have the Boston advertisement. So far they have conferred it upon H. L. Mencken, Percy Marks, Sinclair Lewis, Theodore Dreiser and myself. I am now engaged in trying to get them to confer it upon William Shakespeare and the author of the Book of Genesis, but they say these classics don't need advertising.

You don't have to give very much space in your book to the forbidden subjects. Under the Boston law, they can pick out a single paragraph, or even a single sentence which they do not like, and on the basis of this, they can advertise an entire book, which may be otherwise quite all right from the prudish point of view. Nobody has to read the whole book save a Boston police clerk; he picks out the passages which tend to corrupt his sensitive religious nature, and marks them. These passages are sworn to in a complaint, and after that they are the "evidence," and if you try to read any other passages, you are out of order.

This matter is of such great importance to authors that I am sure they will want full particulars, seeing that I am here on the ground, and have got all the data. Just what must one say in order to annex this free Boston advertising? In the case of my novel "Oil!" which they are now boosting for me, they specify nine pages out of a total of 527--and you can see how easy that makes it for any author.

To begin with, one must not mention that such a thing as birth control exists. In Boston they have arrested Margaret Sanger several times, and they make desperate efforts to keep all knowledge of contraception from the masses of the people. Boston also has its Watch and Ward Society, whose purpose is to keep you from mentioning the passionate aspects of love in any place but a medical treatise. This was explained to me by Mr. Fuller, proprietor of the Old Corner Book Store, and chairman of the committee of the booksellers which is trying to persuade the police to arrest the authors instead of the booksellers. Mr. Fuller talked very eloquently to me for an hour, to persuade me that it was my duty to get arrested. I tried to oblige him, but the courts wouldn't let me. They thought I had had my share of advertising.

It is very simple, after all, to get this Boston police advertisement; all you have to do is to take any book of the great standard literature of the world, pick out the passages dealing with love and courtship, write something of the same sort in your book, and then mail a few copies to members of the Boston society. Get "The Ordeal of Richard Feverel," for example, or "Tess of the D'Urbervilles."

Don't write anything really obscene, of course, and don't think that I mean any such thing. I have never written anything of the sort in my life, and police advertising couldn't tempt me. Not for a million dollars would I put into a book of mine any words as vile as those *Hamlet* addresses to

Ophelia in one passage of that play. (I think some cheap actor wrote it into
the script, but there it is, a part of standard English literature, taught in all
high schools.) And not all the wealth in New York could hire me to write
a story as foul as the tale of what Lot's daughters did to their drunken old
father in Genesis XIX, 30-38.

PART I

PERSPECTIVES:
CENSORSHIP BY OMISSION AND COMMISSION

ON CENSORSHIP
Arthur Miller

What a strange irony it is that at the very moment when all over
Europe and Latin America repressive regimes have been driven out of
power and with them their censors from office, that we Americans should
be increasingly discovering the uses of censorship over our own writers
and artists. The devil, as was once said, has many disguises; defeated in
one place he pops up somewhere else.

Evidently there are many Americans who still do not understand
why censorship and democracy cannot live happily together. What so
many seem to forget is that a censor does not merely take something out,
he puts something in, something of his own in a work that does not belong
to him. His very purpose is to change a work to his own tastes and
preconceptions.

Many forget that when they read a work that has passed through
censorship, they are putting themselves in the hands of an anonymous
person whose name appears nowhere and cannot be held responsible for
what is published.

Perhaps we can appreciate what censorship really means by looking
at a strange story that took place in Britain at the end of the 18th Century.

A teenager named William Henry Ireland, illegitimate son of a
wealthy London antique dealer, desperate to get into his father's good
graces, came home one day claiming to have been given various papers in
Shakespeare's hand, as well as a lock of hair of Shakespeare's wife, by a
stranger whose carriage had nearly run him down on the street. Following
the near-accident, he and this stranger had become friends, according to
young William, and as a token of the man's regard for him he had been
given these invaluable papers and the lock of hair.

The elder Ireland immediately had the handwriting on the papers checked by the authorities who pronounced it Shakespeare's, and the ink and paper were without question of the Elizabethan period, nearly two centuries old. All London was agog, and the boy and his father became overnight sensations. Naturally, young Ireland, until now utterly ignored by everyone, got enthusiastic and announced that his new friend had a whole trunkful of Shakespeare's original manuscripts which he promised he might let the boy have one day.

After producing various forged snippets of Shakespeare's lovenotes, and a few of the Bard's "lost" verses, young Ireland (would-be poet and idolizer of the late Thomas Chatterton, another young forger-poet), proclaimed that his benefactor had decided to give him nothing less than the original manuscript of "King Lear," but only in due time. And sure enough, after some weeks young Ireland showed up with that very manuscript. A gathering was instantly convoked in the Ireland living room where the new discovery was read to a dozen of the most authoritative literary critics, noble patrons of the arts, and cultural leaders of the time.

At the end, James Boswell, the famous biographer of Samuel Johnson, fell to his knees before the manuscript to thank God that at long last the true Shakespeare had been revealed to the world, a Shakespeare who was positive and cheerful rather than brooding and dark and defeatist, a Shakespeare who scorned foul language and never brought up sex or bodily functions, a Shakespeare who was clearly a true Christian gentleman rather than the barbaric, foul-mouthed rotter whose works had always embarrassed decent people with their obscenities and blood-covered view of mankind and the English nation.

Of course what young Ireland had done was to clean up "King Lear" to suit the narrow middle-class tastes of his time. It was a time when revolution was gathering in France, threatening to British stability, if not the idea of monarchy itself. Ireland's major fix was to brighten up the end so that the aged King, rather than raving on the heath, swamped in his madness and abandoned by the world, was reunited with his daughters in a comforting sentimental scene of mutual Christian forgiveness, whereupon they all lived happily ever after. The paper on which this version was written was indeed authentic, the young forger having snipped off sheets of it from the blank ends of Elizabethan wills and deeds in the files of the London law office where he worked as a clerk. The antique ink he had produced himself after months of lonely experiment.

Only one critic, Edmund Malone, saw through the forgery, but he did not expose the fraud by analyzing ink or paper but rather the mawkishness of the "newly discovered" alterations, the shallow naivete behind their versification. But as important as any technical doubts was his conviction that the spirit behind this "new-found authentic King Lear" was pawkey, narrow-minded, fearful of sexuality and the lustiness of the English tongue, and fearful too of the play's awesome image of human judgement's frailty, and the collapse of the very foundations in reason of government itself. The real "King Lear" reduces man to his elemental nature, stripping him of rank and money and his protective morality, in order to present a vision of the essence of humankind with no ameliorating illusions. In place of these challenges the "newly discovered" play was a story of reassurance fit for family entertainment, one that offers comfort by turning a far-ranging tragedy into a story of misunderstandings which are pleasantly cleared up at the end.

In a word, young William Ireland did what censorship always attempts to do—force a work to conform to what *some* people want life to look like even if it means destroying the truth the work is written to convey.

Had the Ireland forgery been left uncontested, we can be sure that "King Lear" as a play would never have survived the hour. Many critics then and since have thought it a nasty work with an improbably black estimate of humanity, but succeeding generations have come to treasure it precisely for its truthfulness to life's worst as well as its best.

What Ireland did was erase the doubts about life that were in the original play and were so discomforting to the upper class of Britain at the time.

Censorship is as old as America. The Puritans forbade the reading of novels—or, indeed, anything but scripture—as one of the condemned "vain pursuits." A reader nowadays would find it impossible to recognize in those novels what could possibly have aroused the Puritan fathers to such fury against them. But closer to our time, there is hardly a master writer who has not felt the censor's lash, from James Joyce to Gustave

Flaubert to D.H. Lawrence to Hemingway and Fitzgerald, to William Faulkner and a long, long list that just about comprises the roster of world literature. Someone somewhere could doubtless find reasons for moral outrage in a MacDonald's menu or a phonebook.

Of course there is no denying that there are people who misuse freedom to appeal to the sinister in us, our brutality, scorn for justice, or concealed violence and lust. By exploiting our suppressed feelings people with no interest in anything but making an illicit buck can prosper, for example, by exploiting human sexual curiosity even if it victimizes children.

But the problem, clearly, is that when we legitimize censorship of what we agree is anti-social art we come very close to legitimizing it for real art. For example, right now some three hundred and fifty lines of *Romeo and Juliet* are customarily removed from American school textbooks because they are about sex. There is a similar emasculation of the two other most commonly taught Shakespeare plays, *Julius Caesar* and *MacBeth*. In other words, lines of very high poetry are forbidden American students who, it is assumed, will think that much less often about sex. Of course this is ridiculous; all this censoring does is deprive them of realizing that there is something sublime and beautiful in sex and that it is not merely dirty. It throws them entirely to the mercies of suggestive videos and rock lyrics and really raw pornography which apparently nothing will stop, and will certainly not be slowed by censoring *Romeo and Juliet*.

The purported aim of censorship is always to preserve public morality but we ought not forget that for those who advocate censorship pornography is by no means necessarily the only kind of immoral communication. If it becomes established policy that blotting out certain sexual images in art is acceptable, then there is nothing in principle to stop the censoring of other "immoral" expression.

I have had some experience with "moral" censorship myself. In 1947, my play *All My Sons* was about to open in the Colonial Theatre, Boston, for its first performances before coming to Broadway. The Catholic Church at that time exercised censorship over the Boston theatres and threatened to issue a condemnation of the play unless a certain line were eliminated from it. I should add that the raunchiest burlesque shows in

America were playing on the Boston "Strip" at the time, but these apparently were not bothersome to the moral authorities. What troubled them terribly was the line, "A man can't be a Jesus in this world!" spoken by Joe Keller, a character who has knowingly shipped defective engine parts to the Air Force resulting in twenty-odd fighter planes crashing and who is now pleading for his son's forgiveness. The name of Jesus was forbidden utterance on the Boston stage, no matter that in this case it was used to indicate Jesus' high moral standard. I refused to change the line, as much because I could not think of a substitute as anything else, but the hypocrisy of the complaint was painful to contemplate, given the level of entertainment of the Boston "strip" a few blocks from my theatre.

In 1962, when my film "The Misfits" was previewed by religious censors, the gravest displeasure was expressed with a scene in which Marilyn Monroe, in a mood of despair and frustration—fully clothed, it should be said—walks out of a house and embraces a tree trunk. In all seriousness this scene was declared to be masturbation, and unless it was cut the picture would be classified as condemned and a large part of the audience barred from seeing it. Once again it was necessary to refuse to oblige a censor, but I would not have had that privilege had I lived in a different kind of country. Experiences like these have helped me to stand against censorship.

Life is not reassuring; if it were we would not need the consolations of religion, for one thing. Literature and art are not required to reassure when in reality there is no reassurance, or to serve up "clean and wholesome" stories in all times and all places. Those who wish such art are welcome to have it, but those who wish art to symbolize how life really is in order to understand it and perhaps themselves, also have a right to their kind of art.

I would propose to censors and their supporters that they write the stories and paint or shoot the pictures they approve of, and let them offer them to the public in open competition with the stories and pictures of those whose works they want to suppress.

Let them write a new *Romeo and Juliet* that is wholesome and unoffending and put it on a stage and invite the public to come and enjoy it as millions have enjoyed Shakespeare's play for three hundred years.

Who knows?—maybe they will win out.

But of course they cannot accept this challenge; censorship is an attack on healthy competition. It comes down to a refusal to enter the arena and instead to wipe out the competitor by sanctions of suppressive writs and the police power.

I write this as one who is often disgusted by certain displays that call themselves art and are really raids on the public's limitless sexual curiosity, purely for the purpose of making money. As an artist I sometimes wonder at my having to compete with this easy and specious way of attracting attention and gaining a public following. And I will not deny my belief that there may ultimately be a debasement of public taste as the result of the incessant waves of sexual exploitation in films and other media.

But bad as this is, it is not as bad as censorship, because the censor is given a police power no individual ought to have in a democracy—the power not only to keep bad art from the public, but good art, too; the power not only to protect people from lies but from uncomfortable truths. That way lies not wholesomeness, not community values, but the domination of the many by the few acting in the name of the many. Nobody said it was easy to be a free people, but censorship not only makes it harder, it makes it in the end impossible.

Probably because we in general enjoy freedom to express ourselves we are unaware of not only the power that a censor takes but the hypocrisy that inevitably accompanies it. In the winter of 1965 I interviewed a lady in her Moscow offices, one Madame Elena Furtseva, then head of all culture of the Soviet Union. In theory and often in practice this woman and the committee she headed had the power to shut down any play before or during its run in a theatre, or to cancel a film or suppress a novel or book of poems or whatever. She could also promote certain books if she so pleased. She had been Kruschev's special friend and when he was ousted she cut her wrists but was saved and restored to her job.

Behind her chair was a long table piled high with at least a hundred books lying on their sides. Each volume had a few slips of paper sticking out of its pages which I deduced marked passages of censorable writing which her assistants were submitting to her to decide upon.

She looked quite exhausted and I remarked sympathetically on this.

"Well I have so much I must read, you see," she said, and gestured toward the possibly offending books behind her.

With nothing to lose—my U.S. Passport snug in my pocket, I ventured: "You know, I have never met writers anywhere who are as patriotic as your Russian writers. Whatever their criticisms, they have a deep love of country. Why don't you make an experiment; don't tell anybody but let's say for one month just don't read anything. See what happens. Maybe nothing will happen. Then you won't have to be reading all this stuff every day."

She tried hard for a sophisticated smile but it came out looking hard and painful. And then she said something interesting: "The Soviet worker cannot be asked to pay for the paper and ink to print ideas that go counter to his interests and his moral ideas of right and wrong."

I can't help thinking of that statement when I hear people saying that the American taxpayers ought not be asked to pay for artworks that offend their tastes or their ideas of right and wrong. The fundamental fallacy in such a statement is quite simple and inexorable; how did Madame Furtseva know what the Soviet worker thought was right and wrong, moral or immoral? How *could* she know when no one but her and her assistants were allowed to read possibly offending works?

Indeed, for nearly three-quarters of a century Soviet writing has been kept remarkably chaste, with very strict rules about depicting sex, while at the same time the Soviet abortion rate was rising to the highest in the world. It was also very strict about barring negative pictures of Soviet conditions in all the media and forbade any genuine attack on the system. After three-quarters of a century of such censorship the Soviet system appears to have collapsed. Why? Because reality does not go away when a censor draws a line through a sentence or tears a page out of *Romeo and Juliet*.

If there is a way to curb pornography, if there is any possibility of preventing people from lathering after obscene material, it can only be the result of changing their tastes. If they don't want the stuff it won't be profitable and it will vanish. I doubt that day will ever come, no matter what, but surely cursing the darkness never brought light. Through education raising the intelligence level of the population, sensitizing people to real rather than cosmetic feeling, enhancing mutual respect between the sexes and between races—these are the paths to decency, not calling in the cops to drive out the bad guys.

There is an analogy here to the narcotics problem. We spend tens of millions on planes to spot smugglers, more millions to wipe out Peruvian coca crops, more millions on narcotics police; but of course the narcotics keep coming in because Americans want dope. Meantime, an addict who wants to get rid of the habit has to wait as long as a couple of years to get placed in a rehabilitation clinic because these are underfunded.

Censoring Shakespeare won't make us good and may possibly make us a little more stupid, a little more ignorant about ourselves, a little further from the angels. The day must come when we will stop being so foolish. Why not now?

BLACKBALLING
John A. Williams

It seems I have spent much of my professional life writing about censorship. Writers, readers, publishers and educators today seem more concerned than in the past about the current threats to intellectual freedom.

I believe that is only because, for the first time perhaps, they have reason to feel that their views are being seriously challenged by local, state and federal governments and by the growing numbers of "Art Vigilantes" who first came out of the woodwork years and years ago over books and had a resurgence during the Mappelthorpe controversy. The possibility that artists may have to sign pledges that they will not produce works without "redeeming social value" to receive needed funding also threatens the future of artistic freedom, however one defines that freedom.

Curiously, the "anti-artists," raising their hue and cry, seem to share a vision with me and it is that all art is political. They, however, are far more capable of doing something about their opinions than I could ever be.

A black American writer, I cannot recall when my views were *not* challenged, indeed, even censored in one manner or another, *most* especially when I discussed how racism and censorship complement each other. I have worked with educators on the college level who themselves, by dismissing or ignoring the works of minority writers, cannot see this as a vigorous kind of censorship. The American literary canon reeks of a censorship that is only compounded when its caretakers will not for a moment consider additions to its lists and go to extraordinary lengths to denigrate those who will.

American publishers themselves have always been "Gate-keepers," refusing African-Americans publication though the black American literary tradition is older than the nation; it began in the mid-eighteenth century. For a hundred years thereafter black authors were published in England or not at all. Today, publishers and editors decide, on the basis of canonical and financial demands it increasingly appears, not only which books to publish, but which books to *keep* publishing. (There was also a time, not too long gone, when most publishers would not publish books by black authors if they thought these books would offend white readers in the South.) From time to time I work with the English and social science teachers in the public school system in the town where I live, modifying curricular needs to be more inclusive, more global. Ninety-eight percent of the books we wish to use are out of print, and letters to specific publishers and the American Booksellers Association about this situation have never been answered.

As a result, the portrayals of black Americans in the books that are readily at hand no longer are the ones black parents want their children to study because most of the portraits are not positive. (The works of Richard Wright are an example. He is one of the very, very few listed in the literary canon, but black parents do not want their children to read *only* Wright's *Black Boy* or *Native Son*, unless they also read other works by black Americans that are unmistakably positive.) I don't believe this situation has much to do with the black parents protesting *The Adventures of Huckleberry Finn*. Most people have no idea that Twain was the muckraker he was, and the failure of schools to teach the *complete* Twain, or more of him than is now taught, has led to the present impasse.

My membership in writers and academic organizations never brought forth any real concerns from my colleagues about the levels of censorship encountered by minority writers. Indeed, they sometimes seem to have been angered by my persistence in calling it to their attention. (I no longer hold membership in any academic organization.) It seems, however, and I have written about this elsewhere, they are more concerned with censorship in its familiar uniform abroad than with the button-down, old boy/old girl censorship here at home. Nothing illustrated this more than the uproar over Salman Rushdie's situation, wherein not only was he put under a sentence of death, but his publishers and the bookstores were reluctant to handle *The Satanic Verses*.

At once artists, especially writers, leaped to Rushdie's side, holding marches, meetings and rap sessions in support of his right (which I, of course, support) to write whatever in the world he wished. Other, closer and perhaps less visible victims of censorship, continued to be ignored.

In 1984 The New York Public Library held a four-month exhibit, *Conflict: 500 Years of Censorship*. A part of the exhibit, *Censorship and Black America* was held uptown in the NYPL branch, The Schomburg Center for Research in Black Culture. Therefore, not nearly as many people who saw the exhibit downtown saw the one uptown. (My sense is that this arrangement itself smacked of censorship.)

In the "uptown catalogue" Langston Hughes (whose multitudinous works seemed not to move so fast after his questioning by the McCarthy Committee in 1953) said in 1957, "Censorship, the black list: Negro writers, just by being black have been on the blacklist all our lives." He noted that there were libraries that would not carry books by black writers, that there existed American magazines that had *never* published anything by or about black people and film studios that had never hired a black writer. These situations have only barely changed today. Chester Himes was kicked off the Warner Brothers lot in the late 1940s by Jack Warner, after he'd been hired by the head of the reading department to read scripts for $47.00 a week. Warner did not want, Himes said, "any niggers on his lot." Today one finds a black writer now and again at one of the major studios; Maya Angelou, for example, did a "development" stint at 20th Century in 1978, and undoubtedly there have been several others since then, but not so anyone could notice real changes in Hollywood.

The magazines that published black writers were overwhelmingly *not* the early incarnations of the popular magazines, those in the Hearst chain like *The Cosmopolitan* and *Redbook*, and the Curtis publications like *The Ladies Home Journal* and *Holiday*, or *McCall's* or *Liberty*. Barriers did fall to a measurable degree in the late 1950s and early 1960s. This was all but too late for writers like Hughes, Wright, Himes and William Attaway who had frequently been published by *New Challenge, New Masses, The New Republic,* organs then on the Left, and sometimes *The Saturday Review, The Atlantic Monthly,* and far less than sometimes in *The Saturday Evening Post,* another Curtis Publication. *Mademoiselle,* daringly, I suspect, even published in 1945 a section of Richard Wright's "American Hunger." Overall, though, the publications, even in the "more receptive" magazines were rare.

 Hughes also said there were areas of America where "Negro newspapers and magazines cannot be sold except surreptitiously."

Those papers from the north, *The Chicago Defender, The Pittsburgh Courier, The Afro-American,* were carried into the Deep South by Pullman porters and waiters. They *smuggled* the papers into a hundred and fifty towns and cities because white people did not allow them to be sold openly nor, in most cases, did they deliver them when they came in the U.S. mail. And Richard Wright documented in *Black Boy* how he had to pretend to have been sent by a white person to secure a book from the library in order to get it for himself. Over 25 years ago when I worked with some frequency in Africa, I noticed that most of the U.S. Information Services Libraries did *not* carry many books by black American authors, James Baldwin and Ralph Ellison being the notable exceptions. Carl Rowan, a black journalist then head of the organization, instead of responding to me about my complaint, contacted my New York office. He wanted to know who I was to be raising so much hell. The situation, however, remained unchanged.

In Africa itself, the works of its "elder" writers such as Peter Abrahams who had been publishing since 1942, Ezekiel Mphalale, Cyprian Ekwensi, Amos Tutuola and Camara Laye, and somewhat later, Chinua Achebe and Wole Soyinka, were usually published in Europe and only occasionally made their way back home to Nigeria or Senegal, but never to South Africa. The Nigerian government forbade Ekwensi's *Jagua Nana* to be made into an Italian film for fear the movie would portray Nigeria in a bad light.

Back in the U.S. there is, we find, censorship within censorship. In 1988 (paper, 1989) Herbert Mitgang published *Dangerous Dossiers: Exposing the Secret War Against America's Greatest Authors.* The war was being conducted by the FBI. *Publishers Weekly* said of the book: "Mitgang's damning indictment of government interference with freedom of expression is a blockbuster, an important, brave, chilling expose." I had earlier read in the paper of record, *The New York Times,* Mitgang works for that he was writing the book. I knew Mitgang somewhat; we'd served on The Authors Guild council at one time and I'd had occasion to send him a note or two about something he'd written in the *Times*. I sent him another note when I read he was doing the book. I reminded him that Richard Wright had been heavily and constantly monitored by several different U.S. government agencies prior to and long after the publication of *Native Son* in 1940. There was no response from Mitgang, which was not unusual. When his book was published, I was appalled to see that Wright or his work (like James Baldwin with two mentions) was noted only in passing five times; he was never placed in any of the 13 category/chapters Mitgang had set up. Among the American Nobel Prize Laureates, Pearl Buck's dossier had the most pages, 203, data obtained by Mitgang through the Freedom of Information and Privacy Act. Richard Wright, according to one of his biographers, Addison Gayle, had 227. All other American Nobel writers cited in Mitgang's book (Lewis, Faulkner, Hemingway, Steinbeck, Mann) had far fewer pages.

I recently learned from British writer James Campbell, who was writing a major article on Wright and James Baldwin for the *London Independent* (and who confirmed the number of pages in Wright's FBI dossier), that James Baldwin had over 1,700 pages in his file. Such omissions reinforce "official" censorship, not only in the case of minority writers but white as well. My colleague at Rutgers, H. Bruce Franklin, for example, whose latest book is *War Stars* (Oxford, 1988) shares with his wife an FBI file—not up-to-date—of over 5,000 pages.

Within the academy, where we are finding almost daily displays of racism, it is not unusual to find extra-legal censorship ceaselessly at work. To provide another personal example (black writers do not sit around comparing with each other the incidents of racism-censorship, so I am generalizing with the absolute certainty that censorship for us is perhaps the most completely shared experience), over 30 years ago a story of mine, "Son in the Afternoon," was rejected by a magazine editor with a particularly vicious racist note to my agent. Some time later I managed to get the story published in a "little magazine" based in the Village edited by the late Seymour Krim. The story was much anthologized during the late 1960s and early 1970s.

X. J. Kennedy used it in his 1976 Little, Brown *Introduction to Fiction* and in his *Literature: An Introduction to Fiction, Poetry and Drama*, first and third editions. In both texts the story was dropped from the second editions because a number of teachers and their students complained that it made them uncomfortable, but it was restored (with a caution) in the third edition, because other teachers wanted it. The story also appears in the Langston Hughes anthology, *The Best Short Stories by Negro Writers from 1899 to the Present* (Little, Brown, 1967), a work composed of 48 authors that has been on several lists of censored books. After 1958, however, I wrote only novels and essays, never again stories.

All books that are censored are proscribed on the basic ground that they will alter something perceived to be imbedded deeply within the foundations of a society, some belief, some habit, some possession, intangible or not. Those officiating at the censoring ceremonies do not, of course, say that, possibly because books usually were deemed in most societies to be powerful tools of learning. That is why for most of human history, they were created and written by special groups numbering very few people. That has changed. The world is more accessible, and ideas are abundant, because there are far more writers of every kind and persuasion. But censorship tends to close doors to many of them. Readers, especially student readers, ought to sample what they think they fear, or what is unknown or even only partially known to them. In the case of the Hughes anthology, noted above, the book was often dismissed out of hand because of "revolutionary tendencies." How I *wish* every African-American writer *was* a revolutionary!

Collections similar to *The Best Short Stories by Negro Writers*, once read, tend to reveal that the "outsiders" have more in common with all peoples than not. And that may be why some individuals and groups, including U.S. government agencies, insist on censorship. "Differences" are exploitable in ways that we may not even have considered.

No teachers are ever sure which novel or story or essay they assign to students will open a door to some great arena for that student and in the process create another thinker, hopefully for the good of all. For "...books," John Milton says in his *Areopagitica*, "are not absolutely dead things, but do contain a potency of life in them to be as active as that soul whose progeny they are; nay, they do preserve as in a vial the purest efficacy and extraction of that living intellect that bred them. I know they are as lively, and as vigorously productive, as those fabulous dragon's teeth; and being sown up and down, may chance to spring up armed men." Milton saw licensing as censorship. Today there is no first, obvious step, such as the licensing of printed work; we have arrived directly at the point.

The value of any banned book or story is that each provides some information as to how we live and what we are, as opposed to what we *say* we are. Even bad—that is to say—anti-humanist—books reveal how much travel we have yet to do, but most of the censored works are not bad books as much as literature that challenges us to be better than we now are. It would be facile to suggest that, had the academic and artistic communities raised 100 years ago, as much hell as they are now attempting to do over the censorship of black literature (and, subsequently, other minority literatures), they would not now be fighting to preserve works produced by their own communities; facile, but who can successfully argue that this is an untruth?

But it is almost too late for argument; we shelter in the same boat. Silences must be replaced with action and sound. Names ought to be named. Organizations and communities ought to be brought into the light. And perhaps teachers should consider offering courses using books that have been or are still banned, by discussing the ideas in such works when the works themselves are completely unavailable for closer study. "Almost too late" because, here and there are signs that something *may* be changing. Literature textbook editors are requesting a more complete ethnic representation in the texts. A major American publisher tied in with the Before Columbus Foundation to publish two anthologies, one of poetry, the other of fiction, consisting of works published by the Foundation's American Book Award winners from 1980-1990. (The BCF has been heads and shoulders above any other organization in seeking out and publishing ethnic literary works.) The first black anthology of contemporary fiction in at least a decade, *Breaking Ice*, was published in 1990.

When I was young and shuffling back and forth across the Pacific Ocean on various troopships during World War II, the pockets of my fatigues filled with paperback books, I believed these little packages, so filled with the world and its peoples, would soon create a universe of literate and informed folk. But in the 40-plus years I've been a writer, I've seen that dream not deferred, but done in. I wish it back to life as Mary and Martha wished Lazarus life once more. There is no single savior who can accomplish that. There is only us.

NOT LAUGHABLE, BUT LETHAL
Norma Fox Mazer

Breathes there a writer for young adults with soul so dead that he or she doesn't have a file marked CENSORSHIP? Mine holds articles about the subject, plus records of my own books that have been censored. One is a letter from a woman whose daughter had read *Up in Seth's Room*. This book about a girl in love with an older boy, sprang from the impulse to let girls know that they could say no and still have love.

"I am appalled," my correspondent wrote, "that you think no more of our younger generations than to put such filth into a book.... Surely you have never encountered true love as such or you wouldn't intentionally mislead the teenagers of America into thinking this lustful drive has any connection with love.... I feel for these children who doesn't have the correct teaching at home and get in contact with a writing such as yours.... I'm praying you won't write any more of this type and that eventually you will withdraw these from the press." She signed, "A Christian, Phyllis Hodges, R.N."

My favorite thing about this letter is that it was written on stationery that showed a fat, friendly frog sitting on its pink lily pad under the equally friendly notation FROM MY PAD TO YOURS.

Not in my file, but on my bookshelf is a marked copy of this same book from a Salt Lake City Librarian who sent it back to me with a sincere plea for me to write "nicer" books in future. Some of the words circled for my benefit throughout the book were "love," "make love," "kiss," and "breasts," plus "I saw him kissing you," "What business of theirs was it if she kissed someone?" and "I love you."

My first reaction on receiving this marked copy of my book was laughter. It wasn't the first or only time I had this reaction. The censorious are so often silly.

Mike Royko, a columnist for the *Chicago Sun Times*, wrote a book about the late Chicago Mayor Richard Daley. The book was well praised. It was on *The New York Times* best seller list. But when a senior high school student in a small town in New York showed her parents a passage in the book in which the word "hell" was used, they were offended and shocked. Her father said flatly that when he was in high school, "I never saw the word hell printed in a school book." And he and his wife began to raise hell to have Royko's book banned from their daughter's high school.

Royko's response was to call the family and promise them his support in their attempts to have his book banned. "It is," he told another reporter, "a rare and wonderful opportunity to have someone try to ban a book these days. These people want to succeed because they feel the book is harmful to young minds. I want them to succeed because if people think the book is harmful to anyone's mind it will stimulate prurient interest in the book. And any time you can stimulate prurient interest you probably sell a lot of copies."

He went on to say that he felt fortunate that his book which has "absolutely no sex and only a few quotations containing swear words, should have a chance to be banned." He also wrote to the family, telling them that he now had another book out, and if there was anything at all they could do about getting that one banned, too, he'd really appreciate it.

This is one of my favorite stories, containing, as it does, laughter and true irony, which we see little enough of these days. It's twisting the tail of the beast. It's springing headlong into the eye of the storm instead of fleeing in terror from it. It's using laughter to thwart the censors. Ah, what a world it would be if laughter were enough to stop them.

It isn't. After the laughter comes the indignation. Censors are too often not laughable, but lethal. I don't laugh when books are burned. As they have been in nice clean little mid-western towns. I don't laugh when the censors drive a dedicated, energetic, thoughtful teacher out of the school system. As I know they have in Florida. I don't laugh when, because one parent has a fit about a book, all kids in a school are denied the right to read that book.

In Vermont, one year, two mothers in a small town called the Police

Chief after their daughters brought home *Saturday the Twelfth of October*. This is a combination time travel, utopian, feminist adventure novel. As usual, when I wrote it, I had something serious in mind. The parents didn't bother reading the book, but saw enough, they felt, by skimming it for "bad words" to be convinced of its dire effects on their teenage children. The Police Chief obligingly photocopied the front and back cover and the pernicious pages. He arrested the book, took it away, but whether manacled or not I never did find out. The whole episode reminded me nostalgically of Arlo Guthrie's Alice's Restaurant and his saga of garbage removal in Vermont.

Some of the words in my book considered criminal by the parents were "snot," "piss," and that scourge of the western world, "penis." Written complaints using such words as "sickening," "obscene," "profanity," "loathsome impression," "perverted views," plus the more colloquial "turned my stomach" and "junk reading" were filed.

The Attorney General of Vermont was sent the book in hopes that he would make a finding of its being obscene under Vermont law. The A.G. weighed in with a letter saying the novel had "serious literary value...thus not a violation of...the infamous obscenity statute." And, he added, "I trust that none of the complainants have read Shakespeare, Chaucer, Salinger, Mailer, Updike, Cheever, Twain, Faulkner and Hemingway, to name a few."

I can never resist telling my Vermont and Salt Lake City stories gleefully, although I know a proper demeanor would be one of sober outrage. Indeed, on another level, I am outraged. Who are these people trying to tell everyone what to read and me what to write?

Appalling as this censorship is, in a certain sense it's easy to deal with. The monster is in the daylight, its face exposed. There is another sort of censorship that hides its face. It's pre-censorship. It's the *I don't want to get in trouble so I won't buy this book* kind of censorship. How many schools have I been in where I was told, "We love your books, but..."? But what? "We don't have this one on the shelves because..." Because? "Because the parents here are sort of backward." Or "The principal is impossible." Or "It's this community...the kids are unsophisticated." I was in a middle school, talking to kids. The librarian took me aside. "I love *Up in Seth's*

Room, I think it has something important to say to the kids." Oh, wonderful. I haven't noticed it around, though. "No, I don't have it here." Oh. Why not? "I don't think these kids are ready for it." Oh. The kids aren't ready for it? Or the parents? "Yes, that's right. The parents aren't ready for it." And she beamed at me, as if we two understood things.

Censors come in all shapes, sizes, varieties. The ones we all know are the rampaging self-righteous, the bad word seekers, the noisy would-be purgers and banners, who too often put teachers and librarians on the defensive, forcing them into justifying their professionalism, their judgement, their selections. Then comes pointing to the excellent reviews, the usefulness of the book, the high literary quality, and so on, as if every book must pass these tests. And what if a book isn't useful, hasn't garnered excellent reviews, and has no particular literary quality? What if it's just fun to read? In all this hullabaloo, we sometimes forget that one of the nasty side effects of censorship is to make reading seem a ponderous occupation to be approached with an awed seriousness.

I heard this week that one of my short stories along with several others in the short story collection *Sixteen* is the object of a censorship attempt in Connecticut. My story, "I, Hungry Hannah Cassandra Glen..." is about two kids who, not having enough to eat at home, talk themselves into an after the funeral feast. They honor the death of their deceased adult acquaintance by satisfying their hunger. The objecting parent calls the children in the story "pathetic." Her objections to other stories in the collection included "no good role models," "the story was about death," and "the story was about pregnancy."

Again I laugh. But not so hard. The censors have moved from language to character. And why not? Isn't it a logical progression? Give the censorious an inch and they certainly will take a mile. To bend to the slightest, silliest point the censors make is not to placate them, but to hand them power, which they will use. Does it not make sense that if they can tell us "penis" is a forbidden word not only to their children but to all children, then, next, they will tell us that our character's thoughts are bad, their attitudes are bad, and in fact the whole story is bad and should not be read and should never have been written?

Censors are slow death to the writer. They seek to corral and bind and tie down exactly that which the writer seeks to make free, to unfetter, unfurl, unleash: imagination. What else do we writers have but this mysterious thing which is not a "thing" at all, lacking, as it does, physical reality? Imagination can not be held, touched, measured or weighed. Like apes probing with a stick into the ant hole to pull out one or two ants for the delicious taste, we writers use language to probe into our imaginations and pull out the tiny ants of language in the hope that enough will emerge for a meal, or a story.

Imagination is infinite, but words are finite. Over and over, we must use the same ones in different combinations. How to make the music, the color, the sense, the imagery that fills our minds apparent to the reader? How to create pictures in the readers' minds, how to engender emotion? These are our problems, and for problem solving, words are our tools. We tell stories, grope for meaning and for ways to infuse our stories with that meaning. Never are words thrown down on the page randomly. When the would-be censors ask "Why can't you use nice words?" do they really think that this or that word is thrown into the text because the writer needed a snappy, attention getting four letter word to break up all those dull six and eight letter words?

Censors apparently feel called upon to tell other people what to think, how to feel, how to live, what to read. Sometimes I'm furious when I consider that it was just to escape this sort of thing (and worse: the worse that follows upon censorship) that my grandparents and millions of others uprooted themselves from their homelands and traveled to this country. And sometimes I'm simply and purely amazed by the censors' confidence in their own righteousness. To me, it seems difficult enough to thread my own way through this complex world with honesty, without taking on the task of directing other people.

I love writing and I love reading, and I resent and fear any attempt to prevent me from doing this freely. I believe in my right and the right of everyone else to read what we choose. It's clear to me that the attacks on children's and young adult books are only the beginning. It makes sense. Again, it's the logical progression. Why stop with kids? Aren't the stores full of unlovely books? Soon, somewhere in this country, someone is going to be energized by the idea that we adults are being polluted by the books we read. It has happened, of course, already in the case of Salman Rushdie and *The Satanic Verses*. But that's not our country, we think. We could never be like that!

Think about it. Do you ever find language and ideas offensive in books? Certainly, I do. The recipe begins—mix in a little holy indignation, a drop of self righteousness, a cup of blind certainty....

Listen! We must defend the right of authors to hold and express views that are not ours. We must defend the right of our children to read books other parents don't approve. It's not just their battle we're fighting. It's ours. And is this not what our country is all about? Those who hold views different from others must be heard: yes, and this includes the censors, themselves. Let them speak their piece. They are a minority with loud voices. But we can not allow these voices to frighten us. We can not allow these people to gnaw away at our freedoms. That way lies deprivation. That way lies conformist, non-thinking children. That way lies the demise of the beautiful and sacred right to think and choose for ourselves.

We are lucky, we Americans, but should we fall in with the threatening voices that want us to conform, that would cleanse our libraries and schools of more than their narrow, rigidly approved ideas, then we will no longer be distinguished from so many other sad places in the world.

TAKE THE TORTILLAS OUT OF YOUR POETRY

Rudolfo A. Anaya

In a recent lecture, "Is Nothing Sacred?", Salman Rushdie, one of the most censored authors of our time, talked about the importance of books. He grew up in a household in India where books were as sacred as bread. If anyone in the household dropped a piece of bread or a book, the person not only picked it up, but also kissed the object by way of apologizing for clumsy disrespect.

He goes on to say that he had kissed many books before he had kissed a girl. Bread and books were for his household, and for many like his, food for the body and the soul. This image of the kissing of the book one has accidentally dropped made an impression on me. It speaks to the love and respect many people have for them.

I grew up in a small town in New Mexico, and we had very few books in our household. The first one I remember reading was my catechism book. Before I went to school to learn English, my mother taught me catechism in Spanish. I remember the questions and the answers I had to learn, and I remember the well-thumbed, frayed volume which was sacred to me.

Growing up with few books in the house created in me a desire and need for them. When I started school, I remember visiting the one room library of our town and standing in front of the dusty shelves. In reality, there were only a few shelves and not over a thousand books, but I wanted to read them all. There was food for my soul in the books, that much I realized.

As a child I listened to the stories of the people, the cuentos the old ones told. Those stories were my first contact with the magic of storytelling. Those stories fed my imagination, and later, when I wrote books, I found the same sense of magic and mystery in writing. In *Bless Me, Ultima,* my first novel, Antonio, my main character who has just started to school, sees in them the power of the written word. He calls books the "magic of words."

For me, reading has always been a path toward liberation and fulfillment. To learn to read is to start down the road of liberation, a road which should be accessible to everyone. No one has the right to keep you from reading, and yet that is what is happening in many areas in this country today. There are those who think they know best what we should read. These censors are at work in all areas of our daily lives.

Censorship has affected me directly, and I have formed some ideas on this insidious activity, but first, I want to give an example of censorship which recently affected a friend of mine, a Chicano poet and scholar, one of the finest I know. For some time I have been encouraging Chicano writers to apply for the National Endowment for the Arts literary fellowships. A number of poets who use Spanish and English in their poetry applied but did not receive fellowships; they were so discouraged they did not reapply. This happened to my friend. He is an excellent poet, mature, intelligent, and he has an impressive academic background. He knew that when you apply for a fellowship you take your chances, so he did not give up after being turned down twice. He also knew, we all knew, that many of the panels which judged the manuscripts did not have readers who could read Spanish or bilingual manuscripts. In other words, the judges could not read the poetic language which expresses our reality. My friend rightfully deduced that his poetry was not receiving a fair reading.

"You know," he told me, "if they can't read my bilingual poetry, next time I apply I'm sending them only poems I write in English. My best poetry is bilingual, it reflects our reality, it's the way we speak, the way we are. But if I stand a better chance at getting a fellowship in English, I'll send that. But the poems I write only in English are really not my best work. It's just not me."

I was dismayed by my friend's conclusion. How he coped with the problem has tremendous cultural implications, implications which we may call self-imposed censorship. My friend was censoring his creativity in order to fit the imposed criteria. He sent in his poorer work because that was the work the panelists could read, and therefore consider for reward.

My friend had concluded that if he took his language and culture out of his poetry, he stood a better chance of receiving a fellowship. He took out his native language, the poetic patois of our reality, the rich mixture of Spanish, English, pachuco and street talk which we know so well. In other words, he took the tortillas out of his poetry, which is to say he took the soul out of his poetry. He still has not received a fellowship, and many of those other poets and writers I have encouraged to apply for the fellowships have quit trying. The national norm simply does not want to bother reading us.

I do not believe we should have to leave out the crucial elements of our language and culture to contribute to American literature, but, unfortunately, this is a conclusion I am forced to reach. I have been writing for a quarter century, and have been a published author for eighteen years. As a writer, I was part of the Chicano Movement which created a new literature in this country. We struggled to change the way the world looks at Mexican Americans by reflecting our reality in literature, and many eagerly sought our works, but the iron curtain of censorship was still there.

Where does censorship begin? What are the methods of commission or omission which censorship employs? I analyze my own experiences for answers. Many of my generation still recall and recount the incidents of censorship on the playgrounds of the schools when we were told to speak only English. Cultural censorship has been with us for a long time, and my friend's story suggests it is with us today.

If we leave out our tortillas—and by that I mean the language, history, cultural values and themes of our literature—the very culture we're portraying will die. Publishing has often forced us to do just that. Trade publishers who control publishing in this country continue to have a very narrow view of the literature of this country. At a time when multicultural diversity is challenging the literary canon, the major publishers still are slow to respond to the literary output of Chicano writers. After twenty-five years of contemporary Chicano writings, there are still only three or four Chicano writers who publish with the big trade publishers.

The alternative presses of the 1960s were created to contest the status quo. The views of ethnic writers, gay and lesbian writers, and women writers had been consistently censored out of the literary canon. Most of us grew up without ever seeing our identity reflected in the books we read; we knew that had to change.

Twenty years ago when Chicano writers began to create poetry and stories which reflected our contemporary reality, we were met with immediate hostility. The arbiters of literary acceptance immediately branded our works as too political. They complained it wasn't written in English. Does it speak to the universal reader? Of course the work of the Chicano writers was universal, because its subject was the human condition. The problem was that in the view of the keepers of the canon, the human condition portrayed in our literature was Chicano and the keepers knew nothing about us. And, yes, it was political. All literature, especially poetry and fiction, challenges the status quo. Our literature introduced a different history and heritage to American literature. There was a new rhythm, music, and cultural experience in our works, and a view of an ethnic working class which performed the daily work but which was invisible to those in power. Yes, there was a political challenge in the work; it could be no other way. The country had to change, we insisted.

Many refused to listen. Censorship is fear clothed in the guise of misguided righteousness. Censorship is a tool of the powerful who don't want to share their power. Of course, our poetry and literature reflected to our communities our history and our right to exist as a distinct culture. Look at the plays of Luis Valdez and the changes they brought about in the agricultural fields of California. Look at the generation moved to pride and activism by "I am Joaquin." Even my "non-political" novel, *Bless Me, Ultima*, has moved people to explore the roots of their agrarian, Mexicano way of life. And the healing work of Ultima, a curandera, illustrated to my generation some of our holistic, Native American inheritance.

Free at last! each of our works proclaimed. Every Chicano poem or story carried within it the cry of a desire for freedom and equality. That is what literature should do: liberate. But the status quo does not like liberation. It uses censorship as a tool. As I have suggested, in some cases, it is a thinly veiled censorship. Let me provide another example.

Just two years ago, the editor of a major publishing firm asked me to submit a story for a middle school reader. Those readers have the power to shape how thousands of children think about Mexican Americans. The criteria were: "It can't have religion in it; it can't be mystical; it can't have Spanish in it." Everything that was in *Bless Me, Ultima* was rejected out of hand before the publisher would look at a manuscript. Needless to say, I did not submit a story. Like my friend applying for the fellowship, I was censored before I got to first base.

In other cases, the censoring has been direct and brutal. On February 28, 1981 the morning newspaper carried a story about the burning of my novel, *Bless Me, Ultima*. The book was banned from high school classes in Bloomfield, New Mexico, and a school board member was quoted as saying: "We took the books out and personally saw that they were burned."

Obviously, my novel did not meet the criteria of the status quo. Using a technique censors often use, they zoomed in on one detail of the novel, the so-called bad words in Spanish, and they used that excuse. Had they read the novel they would have discovered that the novel is not about profanity. That was never the novel's goal. The novel was a reflection of my childhood, a view into the Nuevo Mexicano culture of a small town. I looked at values, I looked at folkways, I created heroic characters out of poor farmers. I wrote about old healing remedies used by the folk to cure physiological and psychological illness. I elevated what I found in my childhood, because that's the way I had experienced my childhood. Poverty and suffering did not overwhelm us; they made us stronger. My novel was my view of the human condition, and it reflected the Mexicanos of New Mexico because that was the community I knew.

What was its threat, I've asked myself over the years. Why did the censors burn *Bless Me, Ultima*? I concluded that those in power in the schools did not want a reflection of my way of life in the school. The country had not yet committed itself to cultural diversity. Fifteen million Chicanos were clamoring at the door, insisting that the schools also belonged to us, that we had a right to our literature in the schools, and the conservative opposition in power fought back by burning our books. That narrow-minded, conservative opposition is still fighting us.

The burning of my novel wasn't an isolated example. Every Chicano community in this country has a story of murals being attacked or erased, poets banned from schools, books being inaccessible to our students because they are kept systematically out of the "accepted" textbook lists. This is still the case. There is a well-organized, well-funded group in this country which threatens publishers by keeping their books out of schools if the editors publish the work of multicultural writers.

The 1990 attack on the NEA by fundamentalist censors has created a national furor and discussion. Those of us who believe in the freedom of expression have spoken out against this infringement on our right to know. But as Chicanos who belong to a culture still existing on the margin of the mainstream society, and as a community that has struggled to be heard in this country, censorship is not new to us. We have lived with this vicious attack on our freedoms all our lives.

For us, taking your tortillas out of your poetry means taking your history and way of life out of the poems and stories you create. That is what the censors who burned *Bless Me, Ultima* were telling me. Your literature is a threat to us, we will take it out of the classroom and burn it. We'll say it's the profanity we don't like, but what we really fear is the greater picture. Your view is a multicultural view of this country, and we don't like that. We will not share our power.

The threat to keep us subservient did not abate. The English Only movement continued the old censorship of the school playgrounds, but now the game had moved into the state legislatures. This threat continues to be used against our language, art and literature.

The struggle for liberation continues. This summer a magazine from New York advertised for subscriptions. Here are quotes from their letter: "There is only one magazine that tells you what is right and what is wrong with our cultural life today." The next quote: "Do you sometimes have the impression that our culture has fallen into the hands of the barbarians?" And, finally, "Are you apprehensive about what the politics of 'multiculturalism' is going to mean to the future of civilization?"

The editor is telling us that he knows what is right or wrong with our cultural life, then goes on to call those that do not fit into his definition, barbarians. He then identifies the barbarians as those of us who come from the multicultural communities of this country. We are supposed to have no culture, and so they assign themselves the right to censor. This dangerous and misguided attack of the status quo on our creativity continues.

This type of censorship was focused against the National Endowment for the Arts in the halls of Congress in 1990. The censors of the far right attacked two or three funded projects because they objected to the content of the works. The censors assumed the right to keep these creative works away from all of us. Censors, I have concluded, are afraid of our liberation. Censorship is un-American, but the censor keeps telling you it's the American way.

Let me return to the theme of bread and books. Tortillas and poetry. They go hand in hand. Books nourish the spirit, bread nourishes our bodies. Our distinct cultures nourish each one of us, and as we know more and more about the art and literature of the different cultures, we become freer and freer. Art is a very human endeavor, and it contains within its process and the objects it produces a road to liberation. The liberation is significant not only to the individual artist; it is a revelation for the community. It is not we who are the barbarians; it is those who have one narrow view which they are convinced is the only right view. Multiculturalism is a reality in this country, and we will get beyond fear and censorship only when we know more about each other, not when we know less.

I don't know anyone who doesn't like to sample different ethnic foods, the breads of many many groups; just as many of us enjoy sampling books from different areas of the world. I travel to foreign countries, and I know more about myself as I learn more about my fellow human beings. Censorship imposes itself in my path of knowledge, and that activity can be justified by no one.

WHITE-OUTS AND BLACK-OUTS ON THE BOOK SHELVES

Mary Stolz

Those of our ancestors who cowered under the joyless preachings of Cotton Mather are not without descendants. Then, ideas not consonant with his moral and religious strictures were punished and proscribed. A man or woman who persisted in independent thought or behavior was banished, hanged, or pressed to death. Today, arbiters of the actions of others form joyless, presumptuous moral vigilante groups, many of them in fact sufficiently powerful to dictate what is and is not acceptable viewing, reading, and listening for the rest of us. In a sense, they call for the banishment, hanging or pressing to death of the work of artists and writers unacceptable to them.

In order to impose subjective standards of "decency" and "americanism," they urge the boycotting—if not the actual closing— of museums displaying art they deem offensive. (That they lost their case in Cincinnati will not prevent their pressing on with the "cause.") These groups also consider themselves invested with the right—the duty—to picket bookstores, and to raid libraries (school or public) that offer matter contrary to their concept of what is allowable in print.

The state of Florida, never in the cultural vanguard, has made itself ridiculous, at least in Clay County, where irate parents have actually forced school principals to remove the lovely book, *My Friend Flicka*, because in it a female dog is properly referred to as a bitch. They would, perhaps, prefer "lady" dog, as in "lady" doctor or "lady" lawyer? Possibly "mama dog"? Difficult to think what euphemism would satisfy their querulous taste.

In Florida, too, Joyce Kilmer's verse, "Trees," can no longer be included in a school poetry class, as it contains the suggestive word *breast*, which might give rise to impure thoughts on the part of students.

In Owensboro, Kentucky, by order of John Settle, the director of elementary school education, and as a direct result of parental pressure, the novels of Judy Blume are no longer to be bought for school libraries. Words used in a serious context as expressions of frustration on the part of children, are occasionally to be found in her work. "Dammit" is one example. This is sufficient, in Owensboro, to sweep her books out the door.

Many years ago I was the bewildered object of a localized boycott. In the book, *Belling the Tiger*, a cat exclaims, "Bless me!" A religious group in Utah wrote to Harper & Row—then Harper and Brothers—to protest this "blasphemy." I had used it as a common expression of surprise. It could, on the other hand, be a call to sanctify. But blasphemy? Logic and dogmatism will forever be incompatible.

On the other—happier—hand, in Manatee County, Florida, librarians receiving complaints and demands for exorcism of books displeasing to the sensibilities of individuals receive a letter in which the following paragraph appears:

> It [the library] also recognizes that many library materials are controversial and may offend some patrons. However, it is not the library system's responsibility to practice censorship.... Censorship is purely an individual matter and while anyone is free to reject for himself materials of which he does not approve, he cannot exercise censorship to restrict the freedom of use and/or access to others. The responsibility for the materials selected by minors rests with the parents and/or legal guardians.

So far, no books have been taken from the shelves of Manatee County public libraries at the request of fanatics.

A fine victory!

But—back to the first, and heavy, hand—Nat Hentoff reports how, in Montello, Wisconsin, a group calling itself "Concerned Citizens" actually *removed* (another word for *stole*) volumes from school libraries, replacing them with tracts of their religious persuasion. In a stunning rebuttal to criticism of the action, one "citizen" said, "It is not censorship to replace one book with another." Fortunately, this calamity was reversed by the Montello school board.

Nonetheless, such groups, countrywide, have intimidated teachers, librarians and school boards. Or, alternatively, they have got themselves *onto* school boards, from which vantage they can more easily censor by pre-selection, simply leaving books they find unacceptable out of the budget. The encroachment they have successfully made into the right—and the duty—of public and school librarians to offer volumes that, in their view, are controversial, is a form of mental vandalism shocking to people whose faculties and sensibilities are in reasonable order. Literary merit does not enter into their thinking, nor does the guarantee to freedom of expression contained in the First Amendment of our Constitution. Indeed, these are the people who would highhandedly alter various other amendments to the Constitution according to their individual views—without regard to the rights, ideas, dreams, aspirations, imaginings or hopes of anyone other than themselves, and without respect for the Constitution itself, a mighty document framed by intelligent, forward thinking statesmen—a breed lacking in today's political comedy.

In his essay on Nathaniel Hawthorne, Henry James relates that, as a child, Hawthorne, for reading matter, "was constrained to amuse himself, for want of anything better, with *The Pilgrim's Progress* and *The Faery Queen*. He goes on to say that a boy may have worse company than Bunyan and Spenser. It seems to the modern sense a stern and limited library for a youthful mind. James also says that, "'Juvenile literature' was but scantily known at that time," and that "the enormous and extraordinary contribution made by the United States to this department of human happiness was locked in the bosom of futurity." A charming and complicated Jamesian compliment to the children's book writer.

That "futurity" was arrived at about a century ago, with Louisa May Alcott's decision to become a writer. *Little Women* caused a happy sensation with its portrayal of a Massachusetts family behaving like ordinary and very real people. It was highly decorous without being, in the fashion of other children's books of the time, menacingly minatory. It was an immediate success.

But hold!

A group of New Englanders condemned this seemly tale because the March girls left their blinds up at night, thus enabling Laurie (next door neighbor, and *male*!) to "peep in and espy them at their evening pursuits." Mind, these were living room blinds, and the girls were writing letters, embroidering samplers with homely mottoes, absorbing Marmee's gentle counsel. The Victorian mentality that put bloomers on piano legs and began an earnest campaign to be-bloomer all barnyard animals not decently veiled with feathers or fur attempted to suppress *Little Women*! In the confusion that passes for human cerebration, a kernel of sense is sometimes to be found (or regained), and now pianos and animals are permitted their natural nakedness, and *Little Women* is securely beyond the reach of puritanical censors.

It is interesting that the present-day monitors of our virtue appear to be absent from the barricades where television and films are concerned, and display no outrage, mount no picket lines to ban the visual portrayal of ungovernable violence, of appalling cruelty to man and beast alike, of unconscionable vulgarity in speech and action, of satanism and necrophilia, of sexual congress with accompanying sound effects. They remain complaisant about what comprises most of modern filmed "entertainment." In my view, (I prefer to qualify, so as not to be associated with the view of Concerned Citizens that there is but one side to any question—theirs) in my opinion, then, watching the average television fare is tantamount to ingesting an emetic. It has been claimed that many shows are dangerous to immature and biddable minds, and that seems all too likely. But it is no part of my duty to darken the screen for people who find their gratification there. I only wonder why the moralists are not heard from? Possibly they are watching, so haven't leisure to mount a protest. [Recently, I was informed that an effort has been mounted to curb the violence and vulgarity increasingly evident in films and on television. That it is having no observable success, a glance at the listings of a TV guide or a movie log will immediately make clear.]

But you take nakedness in *books* now—and that's another matter altogether.

About the great Maurice Sendak, unparalleled interpreter to children of their inner world, much has been written. He understands, is a partner in, their terrors and triumphs, dreams of glory and retribution, in the sappiness and solemnity, innocence and knowingness, generosity and meanness, goodness and villainy of their natures, of their age.

Though it seems improbable that a single person could do it, Sendak has created a mythology. A mythology of monsters that began with *Where the Wild Things Are.* I remember the day Ursula Nordstrom, peerless children's book editor of Harper & Row, showed me the advance art work for this book. "Heavens to Betsy," said I, a pretty tame children's book writer. "This is heady stuff indeed." And indeed it was. Some of Miss Nordstrom's fellow editors, and many librarians and parents, were certain the book would send little minds clean around the bend in terror. Sendak knew better. Ursula Nordstrom knew better. The children knew better. They took the book to their hearts and to bed. And now we have a world peopled (if that's the word) with amiable grotesques of whom the genesis is fading, which is what happens with myth.

Sendak has ruffled sensibilities on other occasions. His splendid *In the Night Kitchen* contains some pictures which include a perky penis. It's a small part, as it is a small boy levitating in the night kitchen and out over the city. Groups of concerned citizens (lower case) took one look, scurried about like dislodged ants, clapped hands to mouths, whimpered, *"Oh, oh, oh! How dreadful, how—how—how NAUGHTY!"*

Then they went to work.

The book was banned. It was removed from many public and school libraries that had bought it. Listen further! In many libraries where the book had been purchased, the offending organ was either carefully whited-out, or equipped with a diaper. How anyone could do this without folding over the desk laughing is a wonder. But what an attention getter! Since the little boy is drifting overhead in a state of nakedness—one most children like to be in—and since most children are aware of how little boys are genitally endowed, it would seem that the absence of the part would be more troubling than its inclusion. Unless led to see it otherwise, children take the book for what it is, the tale of a glorious, nutty night adventure. Perhaps it requires experience to recognize the strange and marvelous artistic worth of this book, but children don't need a critical sense to know that there is something wonderful here. As both logic and the critical sense are lacking in the thought processes of book moralists, they decided that the floating boy either be fig-leafed or, better yet, sent into literary exile. Doubtless, in human history, genius has often blushed unseen and wasted its fragrance on the desert air. But once seen and scented, nothing afterwards can smother it. *In the Night Kitchen* soars above the inanity of prudes.

Not sex alone flutters the hencoop where these birds roost. There's the matter of pigmentation. Not the animal kind. *Our* kind. Humankind's. (The repetition of the word "kind" strikes me as ironic in this context, but let it stand.)

Years ago, Garth Williams wrote *The Rabbits' Wedding*, a gentle tale of two rabbits, modestly placed in the world's scheme, and most loving toward each other. He created a tempest in the brier patch by presenting, in words and pictures, one white rabbit and one black rabbit. This was clearly for the fine painterly contrast, like those oriental screens which use a light and a dark animal for dramatic effect. It's a beautiful book.

But, alas.

These two little bunnies, who wanted to live together forever in peace and affection, went and *married* each other. With dandelions in their ears, they came over the hill to the spot where all the other forest animals joined uncritically in the wedding dance. (The so-called "lower creatures" do not concern themselves with physical appearance.)

Miscegenation the cry went up, and the shy married couple found themselves at the center of a maelstorm. They were written up in newspapers and news magazines. They were denounced from pulpits! They didn't only get themselves talked about, written about, preached about, they got themselves banned from bookstores and seized from library shelves, and not just in Dixie. It was a farrago, it was startling, it was consummately silly.

It remains a beautiful book.

The overseers of literary sanitation have also attempted to proscribe access to *The Learning Tree*, by the eminent photographer, Gordon Parks. It contains some of the finest, most affecting writing of any novel of our time. Mr. Parks is black. His story is of black families in a small Kansas town in the 1920s. It is about, especially, thirteen-year-old Newt Winger, as appealing a boy as Huck or Tom or Holden, with unspeakably greater afflictions and griefs and humiliations to face, and face down, and to the extent possible, overcome. It is about the stamina it takes to grow up black in America and remain reasonably sane. It is full of love and rage and pain and beauty, glows with family communication and loyalty and tenderness. It bristles with vulgarity, with violence, with the confusion that comes from aroused young hormones. It is about prejudice and pride, and is a book of truth. As such, it has been attacked, as have so many other truthful books, by those (by now I'm finding them tiresome even to write of) self-appointed dictators of public morality.

This is not a unilateral outrage. Blacks have attempted to get *Huckleberry Finn* permanently banned from public access. They do not take into account the time at which Mark Twain wrote, the extraordinary regard and balance he showed in his portrait of Jim, in his depiction of a friendship, that took no account of race. They seem not to care that it is one of the glories of American literature. It offends them, so off with its head.

The self-interested (and devil take the rest of you) we have always with us, as we have the prim, the prudish, the priggish, the prurient. If they were of no more consequence than 19th century fulminators against naked piano legs, or 20th century starters-back-in-horror at the sight of a naked little boy, who would care? Unhappily these latter-day self-anointed, self-appointed, self-righteous and often vicious busy-bodies have made inroads—overt *and* surreptitious—into the rights of us who would happily leave them alone if they'd do the same in turn.

They will not. Nor will they abandon efforts to find and uncover and suppress what is, to their impure minds, impure.

We might have hoped to find leadership from those in positions to lead. But no. Far from trying to stimulate and elevate the minds and imagination of the people who entrusted them with the first office of the land, Ronald Reagan, and now George Bush, preoccupied with gladiatorial posturings and extravagance, have dealt arts and intellect in the United States a grievous, perhaps mortal, wound. Reagan, with his gummy mentality, his hostility toward evidence of creative or unorthodox thought, slashed school and library budgets and art endowments that Mr. Johnson, with his Title IV program, had significantly helped. George Bush, despite his patently cynical campaign pledge to be the "education president," has made no slightest effort to help the children of this country up a single rung on the ladder of literacy, let alone scholarship. So far as education is concerned, the United States squats just about on the bottom. With underequipped schools and underpaid teachers, with wholesale cuts in endowments to the arts, we are steadily becoming a nation of ignoramuses. Tests reveal that high school graduates, and college students, speak ungrammatically, are unable to locate Europe on a map, cannot do simple fractions, can't say in which century Franklin Roosevelt was president, can't even *name* three presidents in office before Ronald Reagan, can't say who Joseph Conrad was, either haven't read a book since leaving school, or, as at Princeton, name Stephen King as their favorite writer. Grade school children put in a working week looking at television, and are permitted to do so by their parents, who can doubtless chalk up an impressive hourly record themselves.

Reagan and Bush, who might have bestowed enormous benefits, were catastrophically unable to make the connection between good education (education is reading) and a society of individuals able to think clearly, contribute skills and unearth genius, dream grandly, lead examined lives that would benefit themselves and the country. Mention must be made of the reluctance of the people themselves to further education, if it means taxation. School bond issues are regularly voted down, and I have heard otherwise fairly rational persons say, "Why should I pay school taxes? I have no children in school."

Even without the assistance of these two intellectually enfeebled presidents, one might have felt hopeful of reversing the upsurge of literary and artistic bigotry were the public troubled by it. There is little sign that this is so. Much is heard from those enraged by what they consider evil, but those who value their children's right to read, to think, to make their own decisions, are—through laziness, indifference, or complacence—very nearly mute. ("I'll see to it that *my* child is not victimized by these untutored gangs...you look after your own.")

Education, culture, cannot flourish under such conditions, and without cultivated, educated citizens, a nation cannot flourish.

One of those semi-literate peers of the realm in 18th century England said to the great Samuel Johnson: "But what is the *use* of books?" To which Dr. Johnson replied: "Sir, they are to teach us to enjoy life and help us to endure it."

No one has the right to tell others in which books they will find enjoyment, and in which find help to endure existence in our terrifying and unjust world.

"SHUT NOT YOUR DOORS": AN AUTHOR LOOKS AT CENSORSHIP

Lee Bennett Hopkins

> Shut not your doors to me proud libraries,
> For that which was lacking on all your well-fill'd shelves,
>   yet needed most I bring,
> Forth from the war emerging, a book I have made,
> The words of my book nothing,
>   the drift of it every thing.
> A book separate, not link'd with the rest
>   nor felt by the intellect,
> But you ye untold latencies will thrill to every page.
>
> Walt Whitman
Leaves of Grass/1865

I chose this verse to begin my collection *Voyages: Poems by Walt Whitman* for it is incredible to me that this sentiment was expressed over 125 years ago. Yet, some libraries still are shutting their doors on Walt Whitman. They are also closing out a multitude of writers being censored by non-writers. In the world of children's literature, countless titles are being scrutinized, then banned, in every genre—fiction, non-fiction, even poetry!

I am astonished at what I find in journals and newspapers. Imagine, for example, that a Superintendent of Schools in Panama City, Florida, announces "a three-tier book classification system," banning such acclaimed novels as Robert Cormier's *I Am the Cheese* about a teenager who becomes involved in a spy-like web, and Susan Beth Pffefer's novel, *About David*, dealing with teenage suicide—one of the major problems children in our country face today. Other headlines have blared: "Alabama

Textbooks Banning Threatens School Librarians"; NEA Files Brief in Tennessee Textbook Case"; "Censor's New Aim: Limiting Study of *Ideas in Schools.*"

Where are we going? What are we headed for?

Indeed, censorship is a rampant disease that makes it difficult to reach readers. James J. Jacobs states: "...most of us realize if every book which makes someone unhappy were torched, we could operate the city library from the trunk of a Japanese import."

Each and every book is under scrutiny. Shel Silverstein's popular volumes of light verse, *Where the Sidewalk Ends* and *A Light in the Attic* are constantly under attack due to lack of "moralism." One parent fought to have *A Light in the Attic* banned from a North Dakota school library because the eight-line verse, "How Not to Have to Dry the Dishes," encourages children to break dishes so they won't have to dry them. Yet, if one carefully observes Mr. Silverstein's body of work, one will find humane messages contained within his verses, more so than any current writer of verse today. The renowned poet, Myra Cohn Livingston, states: "Silverstein's genius lies, of course, in finding a new way to present moralism, beguiling his child readers with a technique that establishes him as both an errant, mischievous and inventive child as well as an understanding, trusted, and wise adult" (95).

Following another parent-complaint in North Kansas, Missouri, William Cole's anthology, *I'm Mad at You*, was placed on "a restricted shelf for teacher use only" because it contains Eve Merriam's "Mean Song," a verse filled with delightful word play, which originally appeared in her book of poems, *There Is No Rhyme for Silver*. Published in 1962, the verse has since been widely anthologized without protest.

Still another parent from Lancaster, Ohio, asked that two books by poet Jack Prelutsky be removed from library shelves. *Nightmares: Poems to Trouble Your Sleep* and *The Headless Horseman Rides Tonight: More Poems to Trouble Your Sleep*, because she complained that her seven-year old daughter required medical care from stomach problems after hearing one of Mr. Prelutsky's selections read aloud.

Censors hit the minds and hearts of writers whose major audience is children and adolescents. In a speech on censorship held at the International

Reading Association Annual Convention in May 1987, Myra Cohn Livingston reported: "Several years ago I received word from an editor of a major textbook publisher that a limerick of mine scheduled for use in a textbook had to be dropped." The five-line verse, titled "Fourth of July" in Mrs. Livingston's book *Celebrations* deals with lighting fireworks with a *match*.

The editor told Mrs. Livingston: "We can't have anything about children playing with matches."

"But how do you light fireworks?" Mrs. Livingston queried. She had become familiar with the restrictions about "junk food, about witches, about proper English, Black dialect, brandnames, violence, Negative and Positive images." Should she now add "children playing with matches" to the list of forbiddens?

Judy Blume, one of the most popular, yet most banned authors in the country, has talked about her view of censorship:

> Several years ago, while writing *Tiger Eyes*, my editor asked me to delete a few lines because, as he said, that passage would surely make the book a target for censors. I deleted the passage and I've regretted the decision ever since. I think my editor does too. I have vowed not to be intimidated again. But what about all the other writers? If I were that young writer today, I might not write for and about children at all. I might find it impossible to write honestly about them in this climate of fear. Because I don't know how to get into the mind and body of a character without allowing his or her sexuality to come through. Sexuality is an important part of life. It's healthy, not sick. (144, 176)

Richard Peck, another well-acclaimed author of young adult books, has been criticized for being "too realistic." On the basis of "community standards" his young adult novel, *Are You in the House Alone?* has been removed from the shelves of classrooms and libraries in many towns. Mr. Peck relates that he wrote the book "because the typical victim of rape is a teenage girl in our country. That's a very hard truth. Yet, I wanted my readers to know some things about this crime, that our laws are stacked against the victim and in favor of the criminal. I wanted them to know what it's like to be a victim...I had to deal only in the truth. I couldn't put a happy ending on this story because we don't have any happy endings to this problem in our society" (65).

Censors hit the hearts and minds of educators, too. Misha Arenstein, a veteran teacher in Westchester County, New York, a true advocate of children's books relates:

> Over twenty years have elapsed since I entered the teaching profession—one I still adore. The echo of a myriad of changes fills my head. I remember early on as an elementary teacher, formally requesting my Board of Education's approval for the use of Judy Blume's pioneer novel, *Are You There God? It's Me, Margaret*. The President and the Board laughed at my timidity, thinking I was too intimidated by so-called controversial books!
>
> In later years, I recall a parent complaining about my use of M. E. Kerr's, *Dinky Hocker Shoots Smack*. Was I *advocating* the use of heroin? The criticism vanished as I asked the parent whether she had read the book. The parent judged the entire content of Kerr's work by the title alone.
>
> Today, a seasoned and literate reader of children's literature, past and present, I fear most the reactionary atmosphere surrounding all of us. I indulge in self-censorship—a practice widely prevalent in many schools. Coming across a mild expletive, an off-color word, or a situation involving realistic sexual interest, I often set a book aside. Will my administrators welcome the chance to defend my academic freedom, I silently ponder? Will parents influenced by years of negative comments about teachers and teaching understand my fervent attempt to get children to read? Censorship and its silent effect on us all must present the answers.

Unheard of decades ago, college professors of children's literature devote chapters in textbooks to censorship. Their concerns are voiced in texts that are worth reading, each providing sound guidelines to educators as to what to do when the censors do come.

The distinguished educator, Charlotte S. Huck, includes a discussion of censorship in her volume, *Children's Literature in the Elementary School,* reiterating what Misha Arenstein feels in these troubled days. "A more subtle and frightening kind of censorship," Dr. Huck states, "is that kind practiced voluntarily by librarians and teachers. If a book has come under negative scrutiny in a nearby town, it is carefully placed under the librarian's desk until the controversy dies down" (38).

Arethea J. S. Reid echoes this phenomenon in her text, *Reaching Adolescents: The Young Adult Book and the School.* She begins the chapter, "Censorship and the Young Adult Book" with: "Censorship sends terror up and down the teacher's and the librarian's and the administrator's spine. No educator has failed to reexamine the materials used in the classroom or library when well-publicized cases of censorship, book-banning, and book-burning have occurred. No creative teacher feels safe from the censor's wrath when he or she reads about teachers who were fired for using particular books in their classrooms" (422).

In Zena Sutherland's, *Children and Books,* Alice Naylor devotes eleven pages (615-625) to the issue of censorship, including excellent listings of "Anti-Intellectual Freedom Organizations" and "Pro-Intellectual Freedom Organizations" and a fine bibliography.

Distinguished editors of children's books such as Jean Karl, feel the effects also. In her article, "Calm Down, Squirrels," Ms. Karl relates: "These days, I look at *damns* and *hells* and *gods and pisses* and all the other four letter words that spell realism to many. And in many cases they are realism. They are exactly the way the characters that use them would talk, and so they must talk that way, no matter what the censor might believe. To create books that lie about speech or about any aspect of life is to create distrust in readers, to say that we cannot depend upon books. It is to doom the book as a part of common life.... Every aspect of language, and of incident, in books being edited is considered with an eye to what must be there and what might simply be fodder for the censor" (77).

So many writers have felt the impact of the censor's arbitrary bite in America: Maurice Sendak, Ezra Jack Keats, Norma Klein, Carl Sandburg, Langston Hughes, E. B. White. The list could fill a volume! But one thing is certain. In fifty years or fewer, those people banning books will be long gone. But the *books* such as Sendak's *In the Night Kitchen,* Keat's *The Snowy Day,* Klein's *Mom, the Wolf Man, and Me,* the poetry of Sandburg and

Hughes, the verses of Merriam and Livingston, and the classic tales spun by White will live on and on and continue to be loved long after the censors' knives are dutifully blunted.

It is time to *stop* shutting those doors and open new ones—open young minds to the feasts that only books can bring—to life and language that can be found nowhere else except on printed pages.

"We need those books that reflect every aspect of our cultural diversity," Jean Karl states. "And if we can no longer picture teen-age sexual explorations, the trauma of abortion, their terrors of drug addiction after its initial pleasures, the things that are really wrong with our society, and lives that are not lived in a perfect suburb, then we are lying to our children and forcing them into cultural blindness that could eventually shatter the fabric of the nation. For democracy is based on trust and understanding, on acceptance, and when these are missing, the diversities that will continue to exist will fragment, rather than enrich the commonwealth" (77).

We *do* need these books. We need to light *more* bulbs in *more* attics, not turn them off. We need to start *opening* more library doors. And we need to do it *now*!

REFERENCES

Arenstein, Misha. Conversation with author. April, 1987.

Blume, Judy. *Newsletter of Intellectual Freedom.* (September, 1986): 144, 176.

Huck, Charlotte S. *Children's Literature in the Elementary School.* 4th ed. New York: Holt, Rinehart & Winston, 1987.

Jacobs, James J. "Making Kids Safe for Books." *The People,* (October, 1985).

Karl, Jean. "Calm Down, Squirrels." *The Advocate.* (Winter, 1982): 77.

Livingston, Myra Cohn. *Climb Into the Bell Tower: Essays on Poetry.* New York: HarperCollins, 1990.

Naylor, Alice P. "Censorship." in *Children and Books.* Ed. Zena Sutherland and Mary Hill Arbuthnot. 7th ed. New York: Scott Foresman and Co. 1986.

Peck, Richard. *From Writers to Students: The Pleasures and Pains of Writing*, ed. M. Jerry Weiss. Newark, DE: International Reading Association, 1979.

Reid, Arethea J. S. *Reaching Adolescents: The Young Adult Book and the School*. New York: Holt, Rinehart & Winston, 1985.

PART II

CHALLENGING BOOKS

A RATIONALE FOR TEACHING *HUCKLEBERRY FINN*

John M. Kean

> It is by the goodness of God that in our country we have those three unspeakably precious things: Freedom of speech, freedom of conscience, and the prudence never to exercise either of them. Mark Twain's Notebook (Geismer 243)

The *Adventures of Huckleberry Finn* is more often caught than taught. It has become, with *The Adventures of Tom Sawyer*, such a staple of the American literary tradition that many, if not most adults "know" the story even though they often confuse it with *Tom Sawyer*. Recently I asked a class of college students, average age twenty-six, to write briefly on what they thought *Huckleberry Finn* was about. Of forty-five people in the class, two admitted to never having read the novel, but they thought it was about "a boy who gets into many mischievous adventures, how he handles them and grows through them." Several seemed to have a global view: "Boy takes raft trip, encounters raffish characters, learns real meaning of friendship." "Huckleberry Finn was about a boy and how he related to people. The story was about his adventures as he grew up, and about his relationship with those around him." "Huck Finn was about a white boy who helped a Negro to gain freedom. He stood up for what he believed in rather than following the norms of his time." Others clearly remembered major themes and often specific incidents in the book which related to that theme: "...whenever Huck really tries to figure something out he compares how he sees things to how society sees things; he always thinks he is wrong (i.e., should he send the letter informing Miss Watson about Jim's whereabouts); but really society is wrong and Huck is right. This is especially true of racism." While still others saw many themes as represented by this student: "Huckleberry Finn is a million things: the story of a boy's moral growth; he does what he thinks is right instead of what society expects; a fictional account of the life and language of people in that historical period; an excellent geographical description of the Mississippi area; adventure, excitement; an often sarcastic, clever portrayal of people."

The range of responses from college-educated adults to this novel probably approximates their responses to many classics of literature. Time had fuzzed their memories and softened their responses to Huck Finn and had fused them with other reading experiences and contemporary issues. None of these students had read it since finishing high school. Some of them remembered reading it as junior high school students, some in a senior high school social studies or an American literature class. No trends were evident in when they had first been exposed to it. None of them could remember how it had been taught, although most of them believed that they had been required to read it.

Huckleberry Finn is a teachable novel that should be included in the school curriculum. It should and can be included in numerous places within the humanities and social science curricula. The reasons for including *Huckleberry Finn* in the curriculum are many and varied:

1. Mark Twain (Samuel Langhorne Clemens) is one of America's greatest authors.
2. *Huckleberry Finn* is believed by many to have truly started an American literature tradition.
3. The novel is an historical fictionalized description of the antebellum South with a particular emphasis on class and race.
4. It presents a classic portrayal of a youth's "rites of passage."
5. It is an exciting adventure story.
6. It provides a means to study literary elements used by the novel writer.

MARK TWAIN

Sometime between 1860 and 1900, the dominant emphasis in American literature began to change from romantic to realistic. Writers, to be sure, were sometimes romantic, as Twain was in *Personal Recollections of Joan of*

Arc, and sometimes realistic, as he was in *Old Times on the Mississippi* and *The Adventures of Huckleberry Finn.* Writers didn't identify themselves this way but in effect, as they dealt with their genres, they tended to insist on "veritism," the truthful presentation of material. The major American realistic writers during this period were Mark Twain, William Dean Howells, and Henry James.

And of these Mark Twain "had more qualities that Americans like to think of as American than any other writer this country has produced. [His] stature...is recognized not merely in the way in which he reflected the multiform aspects of American life, but also in the way his nature more and more rebelled against that life--its commercialism, its easy optimism, its essential shallowness." (Wann 14)

Mark Twain is considered unique among American authors. No study of American literature would be complete without a study of his work.

HUCKLEBERRY FINN AS LITERARY MASTERPIECE

Although it would be an injustice to represent Mark Twain's contributions to literature with *Huckleberry Finn* only, it stands as one of his most significant contributions to American literature. Ernest Hemingway praised it: "All modern American literature comes from one book by Mark Twain called *Huckleberry Finn.*" T.S. Eliot pronounced it a masterpiece, and Lionel Trilling recognized it as "one of the world's great books and one of the central documents of American culture" (Hearn 37-8).

There were other accolades as well by Robert Louis Stevenson, Rudyard Kipling, William Morris and George Bernard Shaw. Shaw wrote Twain that "the future historian of America will find your works as indispensable to him as a French historian finds the political tracts of Voltaire" (Ibid). Critics, scholars, and, yes, the student, and the adult reader of literature have read and studied and written about *Huckleberry Finn* since it was published. It has remained popular, its many messages never diminished by those who would let the author explain himself.

HUCKLEBERRY FINN AS A HISTORICAL DOCUMENT

As pointed out by Trilling and Shaw, *Huckleberry Finn* is a central document of American culture and an indispensable document for understanding our cultural heritage. Twain was a journalist, river boat pilot, traveler, writer, lecturer, publisher, capitalist, and humanitarian. He brought all of this background to his novels, but he also brought his boyhood years growing up in Hannibal, Missouri, to which he and his family came in 1839 when he was four years old. It was all of these experiences that somehow crystallized in *Huckleberry Finn*. As he himself noted, "If you attempt to create a wholly imaginary incident, adventure or situation, you will go astray and the artificiality of the thing will be detectable, but if you found on a *fact* in your personal experience it is an acorn, a root, and every created adornment that grows up out of it, and spreads its foliage and blossom to the sun will seem reality, not inventions" (Ibid).

It is possible to read *Huckleberry Finn* as an adventure. In fact, Twain himself referred to it as "another boy's" book. He himself, however, sometimes equivocated: "Part of my plan has been to try to pleasantly remind adults of what they once were themselves, and of how they felt and thought and talked, and what sheer enterprises they sometimes engaged in" (Geller 245). But what Twain of course did do, within the context of an adventure story, was to draw a picture of Middle America in the pre-Civil War period in such a way as to make clear the hypocritical, self-centered, simple-minded blindness of much of our society. He draws a stark picture of the American code of life and conduct that is often so close to us, the issues so painfully not resolved even today, that some people claim that the book is too sensitive to be read by credulous readers who may too easily read Twain's indictment of the right/wrong morality of the old South as approbation of that morality. This is particularly true of slavery. All of the characters in *Huckleberry Finn* accept the slave code. The racist bias in the novel is of course one aspect of Twain's pervasive irony on racism in our society. The moral crisis in Huck's deciding to break the code is perhaps one of the best scenes in the novel: "students who cannot take a serious stand on a moral question and at the same time realize that this stand can be supported in more ways than one are not intellectually ready for this novel" (Miller 103).

One study completed in 1983 at Pennsylvania State University, examined the effects of reading *Huckleberry Finn* on the racial attitudes of ninth-grade students. The data from that study indicated "that students who read the novel as part of an instructional unit demonstrated both a deeper sensitivity to the moral and psychological issues central to the novel (a number of which deal with issues of race) and a more positive attitude on matters calling for racial understanding and acceptance" (21). The committee that produced the report did, however, recommend that the book be moved from ninth grade to eleventh or twelfth grade since many ninth graders interpreted it as an adventure story and missed the elements of satire critical to understanding the novel. They suspected that much of the satire when directed at Black characters was often misperceived as caricature. The committee also noted that there did not appear to be any program providing instruction in minority group concepts in the school system and that *Huckleberry Finn* was the only novel in the curriculum to present "a segment of the Black experience."

The concern over racism, over religion, and politics in *Huckleberry Finn* only reinforces its importance to the understanding of our own culture and our own literary background. If Mark Twain had chosen to set this story in King Arthur's England or Homer's Greece, undoubtedly the culture could be studied with detachment. Students would not be committed to their own religious, cultural, or political views and hence would be able to separate Twain's sharp focus on people, institutions, and relationships from the historical structure that he chose to use in the novel. It is precisely because Twain shows us our own cultural background, however, that the novel can do so much to inform us about our own cultural biases. To read *Huckleberry Finn* is to see how we have thought and acted in our own time, own towns and counties. As Huck and Jim witness society, its values, its traditions, and indeed as they participate (albeit on the fringes of others' lives throughout their sojourn), so we too come to witness and perhaps to question our observations. Or, even if we do not question, we at least note the similarities and differences between then and now, note the growing and even the withering of our national spirit. Examples abound in the novel. Many of them, of course, need explication if the student is to fully appreciate them. Huck's time with the

Grangerfords and Shepherdsons in Chapters 17 and 18 is a case in point. In these chapters, Twain devastatingly describes the pointless bloody vendetta between these families, ties it to eternal struggles on the frontier between farmers (grangers) and herders (shepherdsons) and at the same time attacks the rank, caste, and pedigree system that dominated the South prior to the Civil War. In Chapter 22 Twain speaks out through Sherburn about mobs and individual courage. Mobs and the lack of independence is important in *Huckleberry Finn* and echoes in fiction Mark Twain's own position in his essay "The United States of Lyncherdom": "...the increase [in lynching] comes of the inborn human instinct to imitate--that and man's commonest weakness, his aversion to being unpleasantly conspicuous, pointed at, shunned, as being on the unpopular side" (Geismer 37).

He abhors the mob and pokes fun at it in other places in the novel as the gullible townspeople along the Mississippi are duped by the "King" and the "Duke." The conflict between individual courage and doing what everyone else does has already been noted in Huck's wrestling with his own conscience concerning Jim, but it is evident elsewhere as well. Shortly after rescuing the King and Duke from their pursuers in Chapter 19, Huck recognizes "that these liars warn't no kings nor dukes, at all, but just low-down humbugs and frauds. But I never said nothing, never let on; kept it to myself: it's the best way; then you don't have no quarrels, and don't get into no trouble." Huck and Jim harbor these humbugs and frauds until finally Huck in desperation risks personal misadventure to rescue the Wilks sisters' inheritance by hiding the money in their deceased father's coffin. His personal courage in action had, at that point, not been accompanied by personal courage in voice, until of course he is faced with Mary Jane Wilks' desolation at the separation by sale of Black children from their mother. Huck finally begins to "study it out." Should he tell the truth? What will he risk? He decides for truth.

HUCKLEBERRY FINN AS A YOUTH NOVEL

Huckleberry Finn is also a classic adolescent "rite of passage" novel. The themes of initiation, death, and rebirth recur throughout. "You don't know me, without you have read a book by the name of 'The Adventures of Tom Sawyer,' but that ain't no matter." And it isn't any matter. For the character of Huck is fully developed in his own story. It is the story of a boy perhaps fourteen years old, son of the town drunkard, one of the first drop-outs in our history, an identified delinquent who must escape from "home" and his father. He eventually decides to do this by disappearing in such a way as to be presumed dead, a trick which he uses several times during the novel. It is from this point in Chapter 7 that Huck embarks on his journey, his growing up time. His journey with Jim down the Mississippi is a time when he begins to develop an understanding of another human being in a non-stereotypic way. No other human being contributes so much to his growth as does Jim. Although Huck never completely transcends the stereotypic notions of his society, he does change attitudes toward other people as his experiences with Jim force him to confront his views about Black people. He rejects the notion of people as property, recognizes the feelings of others, and learns to respond to the individual rather than the role.

From each adventure that he and Jim have, Huck grows and learns about humanity. He begins to think for himself, going beyond what he has been told and what he has observed in his own home town. He begins to search for meaning, the self that can stand alone under pressure, and for significant others. But the process is slow. It is a long time from his rejection of "Pap" to his acceptance of Jim as his father, guide, protector, and teacher. Huck must decide between society's rules and his friend. He must decide what rules to follow. "...somehow I couldn't seem to strike no places to harden me against him." In this situation, as well as others, (e.g., the King and the Duke against the Wilks), Huck seems to be showing a degree of moral development far superior than one would expect for an adolescent. He deals with moral problems not from the competing rights position that one would expect in a simplistic law and order society but from a contextual inductive relativistic position that Carol Gilligan in her study of psychological theory and women's development would probably judge as a feminist position since Huck seems to worry about helping others when he can, never mind the deviousness in the way he chooses to help them.

It is not unexpected that a boy's book of the nineteenth century would not deal with sexual awakening, but Twain certainly deals with all other aspects of adolescent development: emotions, family relationships, social adjustment (or perhaps the lack thereof in this case), religion (if only in the strong symbolism of the river and the almost complete failure of Christian religion to respond to the violence and duplicity of the period), initiation and identity. Huck swings wildly from childish follies to social sensitivity and back again. Huck's misbehaviors and eccentricities only highlight the terrible turbulence of adolescence. Current adolescents can recognize and deal with Huck's crises even if they find difficulty identifying with them in the setting of the violent American antebellum frontier which was the Mississippi.

The book, again, is an exciting adventure story with a typical plot of the young boy who breaks with the past and sets off on a journey to find himself--a journey filled with adventures that test him physically, psychologically, and intellectually. The journey is filled with many narrow escapes and sometimes satisfactory resolutions. Huck is a bewildered, not always willing, witness to the baser side of humanity and the grandeur of the river and the countryside. One can only speculate about how the boy will assimilate these experiences, for he still has much growing to do as he considers "light[ing] out for the Territory."

LITERARY ELEMENTS IN *HUCKLEBERRY FINN*

We can delight in the humorous and varied escapades that Huck has, yet develop a deeper vision of the world as Twain saw it and described it. But if our students are to understand the world as Twain viewed it, they need to begin to understand the literary elements that Twain used to describe this world. Many of Twain's themes become evident in the novel and in the discussion of it. His themes deal with the issues of freedom, human dignities, and personal responsibility, trickery and deceit, respect and compassion, complacency about evil, bigotry, avarice, optimism, shallowness--the essential problems of human beings learning to respect and care for others.

The unique style of Twain presents an excellent opportunity to examine the structure of the novel, the use of satire, realistic characterization, point of view, sensory description of people and places, literary allusion, the use of language, humor and pathos, tragedy, and romance. Some of these have already been described above and space here is too limited to examine in detail how these might be treated. Some are more critical than others. Understanding satire is critical to the comprehension of Huckleberry, but satire probably should not be introduced using *Huckleberry Finn*. Satire as a concept can better be introduced through the study of modern satirists such as political cartoonists or columnists (e.g., Art Buchwald) where students have access to other descriptions of the human vices and follies that the satirists ridicule or scorn. This is also true of dialect. Twain's use of dialect is important to the authenticity of his characters, but his dialect should not be the first written dialect to which students are exposed (although it certainly was a first to Twain's readers when the novel was officially published). Students unused to dialects other than their own are much too likely to associate the difference with lack of intelligence and to use it to belittle others out of ignorance of the ways that language works.

In an adolescent novel called *The Day They Came to Arrest the Book*, Nat Hentoff has one of his black student characters, Steve Turney, express it this way: "In this book, those words—particularly 'nigger'—are not intended by the author, Mr. Clemens. . .to insult or humiliate *me* or any other black person. They are intended to rebuke and bring scorn to those ignorant, so-called grown-up white people in the book who use those words.... Huckleberry Finn uses that word because the way he grew up and where he grew up it was the natural thing to do.... He doesn't see black people as niggers, even though he uses the word. He sees Jim as a *man*, a man who should be free, and he tries hard to help him keep free" (162-3). Hentoff's novel would make an interesting preface to the study of *Huckleberry Finn* in the high school curriculum.

Huckleberry Finn has much to teach us about ourselves as developing human beings, our culture and our history. As his creator put it in a presentation copy of the novel:

This is Huck Finn, a child of mine of shady reputation. Be good to him for his parent's sake. (Hearn 1)

Steve Turney in Hentoff's novel understood this well.

WORKS CITED

The Effects of Reading Huckleberry Finn. A cooperative study of the State College Area School District and the Forum on Black Affairs of the Pennsylvania State University. State College, PA: Pennsylvania State University, 1983.

Geller, Evelyn. "Tom Sawyer, Tom Bailey, and the Bad Boy Genre." *Wilson Library Bulletin* 51.3 (November, 1976): 245-250.

Geismer, Maxwell, ed. *Mark Twain and the Three R's: Race, Religion, Revolution and Related Matters.* Indianapolis: The Bobbs-Merrill Company, 1973.

Gilligan, Carol. *In a Different Voice.* Cambridge: Harvard University Press, 1982.

Hearn, Michael Patrick. *The Annotated Huckleberry Finn.* New York: Clarkson H. Potter, Inc., 1981.

Hentoff, Nat. *The Day They Came to Arrest the Book.* New York: Dell Publishing Company, 1982.

Miller, Bruce. *Teaching the Art of Literature.* Urbana, IL: National Council of Teachers of English, 1980.

Wann, Louis, ed. *The Rise of Realism: 1860-1900.* New York: MacMillan Company, 1961.

THE ADVENTURES OF HUCKLEBERRY FINN: REVIEW OF HISTORICAL CHALLENGES

Arlene Harris Mitchell

Writing *The Adventures of Huckleberry Finn* was evidently a challenge for Samuel Clemens (Mark Twain). He began the book as a sequel to *The Adventures of Tom Sawyer* (1875), put the book aside for several years, and completed the more serious novel *Huckleberry Finn*, in 1883. A different challenge awaited Twain, however. His problems with the censors and the book challengers began shortly after the American publication of the book in 1885. (There was a British publication in 1885.)

Ken Donelson makes the point that there are two problems with censors. "Censors see evil in so many places for so many reasons that there's no way of satisfying all their objections" (214). Surely *Huckleberry Finn* has been challenged for a variety of reasons. In 1897 Brander Matthews of the London *Saturday Review* praised *Huckleberry Finn* and T.S. Perry of the *Century Magazine* commented favorably. These reviews, however, were in the minority. Most of the early critics either attacked the book or ignored it.

Despite its favorable critique, the *Century*, which had serialized several sections prior to publication, had already done some censorship of chapters to be included. The paper had excluded the shooting of Boggs and the attempted lynching of Col. Sherburn, as well as the line placed by the duke to draw an Arkansas audience to their Royal Nonesuch show: "ladies and children not admitted (DeVoto 1932). A superintendent of schools wrote to the *Century* claiming that *Huckleberry Finn* was "destitute of a single redeeming quality." Gilder, the editor, responded that Twain "is not a giber at religion or morality" but is a good citizen. He has faults and "at times he is inartistically and indefensibly coarse" (DeVoto 213).

In 1885 the *Boston Advertiser* dismissed the book as a failure and criticized Twain for his "spirit of irreverence" while the *Springfield Republican* compared *Huck Finn* and *Tom Sawyer* to the dime novels of the "blood-and-thunder reading population" stating that the "moral tone is low and their perusal cannot be anything less than harmful" (*Critic* 155). *Life*, a comic magazine in 1885, condemned *Huckleberry Finn* as unsuitable for children and stated that it "contained one blood curdling scene after another." The *Critic* quoted novelist Louisa May Alcott as saying, "If Mr. Clemens cannot think of something better to tell our pure-minded lads and lasses, he had better stop writing for them" (*Critic* 155). She referred to his use of dialect as the "language of the gutter" (Kaplan, Mr. Clemens 268).

In 1889, the St. Louis *Republican* reported that a survey for children's books revealed a "healthy and hopeful" standard in juvenile reading but that a few books were of "harmful tendency." Included among the worst books were *Tom Sawyer* and *Huckleberry Finn.*

In addition to the press criticisms, the Concord Library in Massachusetts, probably the first library to ban the book, called it "trashy, vicious, and unfit to be placed next to books by Emerson and Thoreau." The *Boston Transcript* (1885) reported that the library charged that *Huckleberry Finn* was more "suited to the slums than to intelligent, respectable people." Twain wrote a letter to his editor Webster, dated March 18, 1885, wherein he called the library ban a "rattling tip-top puff which will go into every paper in the country...and sell 25,000 copies for us sure" (Smith & Gibson 525). Sales were high and the novel was among the best sellers of its time (Brooks 1948).

In 1902, the Denver Public Library banned *Huckleberry Finn* (Budd 1982), and in 1905, both *Tom Sawyer* and *Huckleberry Finn* were excluded from the Brooklyn Public Library as "bad examples for ingenious youth" and Huck was described as a "deceitful boy" (Dickinson 183). One of the librarians, Asa Don Dickinson, voted against the decision and wrote to Twain about the matter. Twain responded, "I wrote Tom Sawyer & Huck Finn for adults exclusively, & it always distresses me when I find that boys and girls have been allowed access to them." The explanation in the beginning seemed sincere as Twain continued, "The mind that becomes soiled in youth can never again be washed clean." It was at the end of the letter that Twain's sarcasm which permeated his responses to the newspapers' criticisms and to the Concord Library seventeen years earlier became evident.

"I cherish an unpleasant bitterness against the unfaithful guardians of my young life, who not only permitted but compelled me to read an unexpurgated Bible through before I was 15 years old" (Paine 1280).

Eventually, the negative criticisms of the late nineteenth century gave way to a more positive analysis of the novel. Literary critics began to praise *Huckleberry Finn* as a masterpiece and to recognize Mark Twain as a social critic. Foner is one of the few published critics who referred to this censorship stating the significance that was probably the underlying generator of the early censorship. Foner submitted the premise that while the reasons advanced by the authorities were

> the book's endemic lying, the petty thefts, the denigration of respectability and religion, the bad language, and the bad grammar, it was clear...that the authorities regarded the exposure of the evils of slavery and the heroic portrayals of the Negro characters as hideously subversive (209).

During the hundred years after its publication, critics have exclaimed the worthiness of *Huckleberry Finn* as literature even though there is question over the structure of the last chapters. Lionel Trilling, in his "Introduction" to the book, asked "Wherein does (Huck Finn's) greatness be?" and answered, "Primarily in its power of telling the truth." Kenneth Lynn, in the *Yale Review*, spoke highly of the novel and the "intense relationship" of Huck and Jim. Lynn referred to the bewilderment Jim feels while confiding to Huck. Jim had hit his child for disobeying him (chapter 23). "De Lord God Almighty forgive po' ole Jim, koze he never gwyne to forgive hisself as long's he live!" Lynn considered this moment as possibly the most poignant in the novel.

T. S. Eliot in his "Introduction" to *Huckleberry Finn* stated "Huck would be incomplete without Jim, who is almost as notable a creation as Huck himself. Huck is the passive observer of men and events. Jim the submissive sufferer from them; and they are equal in dignity."

In the 1980s *Huckleberry Finn* placed third on the "must read" list by the National Endowment for the Humanities and ninth on the list of the most challenged books. In a 1989 report from the Center for the Learning and Teaching of Literature *Huckleberry Finn* was third (70%) in public schools, first (76%) in Catholic schools and third (56%) in independent schools surveyed (a total of 498 schools). There had been a significant increase in its popularity in school districts since 1960 while it remained among the top challenged books (Applebee).

The challenges of 1984 were different from the challenges of 1884. The social norms have changed. There is little or no controversy over the pranks of Huck and Tom, or over Huck's lack of knowledge of standard English. The references to feuds, near lynchings, and ornery preachings can be explained away as satire and drawing on local color. People often leisurely duplicate the setting out on a raft for the sheer sportsmanship or adventure of it.

As times changed, however, the situation of African American people changed. Even the use of the term Negro had been replaced with more descriptive terms of Black and African American. Although literary critics have praised Twain as a social critic, and Jim as a character with dignity, it is the portrayal of Jim that has precipitated the challenges to *Huckleberry Finn* in the latter years of the nineteenth century. The controversy continued in different ways for different reasons. African Americans were no longer newly freed slaves, unsure of a place in society, struggling for sheer existence and substance for life. But the shackles, though invisible, and the cruelties of slavery, though historical, are still very real in their history and their minds. Gains in economic, political, educational, and social status have caused African Americans to take exception to *Huckleberry Finn* based primarily on the portrayal of Jim and the profuse use of the word "nigger." A cursory reading of the book shows Jim, a slave, as illiterate, superstitious, gullible, and as Eliot pointed out a "submissive sufferer." Jim's dialect is difficult to read and to understand. In addition, the word "nigger" is used whenever there is a reference to slaves, Black people in general, and to Jim in particular—over 160 times. The consistent use of this derogatory term and Jim's seemingly inferior traits are the focus of the objection to *Huckleberry Finn* today.

On June 25, 1982, in a 5-4 decision, the Supreme Court ruled that "local school boards may not remove books from the school library shelves simply because they dislike the ideas contained in those books and seek their removal to prescribe what shall be orthodox in politics, nationalism, religion or other matters of opinion." Nonetheless, there have been nearly one thousand attempts to have over one hundred different books removed from schools and public libraries in thirty- four states. Books by or about minorities are challenged most frequently. According to the Office for Intellectual Freedom of the American Library Association, *Huckleberry Finn* is at the top of the list of books found to be offensive by African Americans. During the nineteen eighties, *Huckleberry Finn* came under challenge in classrooms of Davenport, Iowa; Houston, Texas; Winnetka, Illinois; Montgomery County, Maryland; Fairfax County, Virginia; Warrington, Pennsylvania; State College, Pennsylvania; and in 1990 in Plano, Texas.

In Fairfax County, Virginia, a racially balanced group, called the Human Relations Committee of Mark Twain Intermediate School, challenged the book because it is "poison," anti-American, works against the melting pot theory, and is in conflict with the Fourteenth Amendment and the Preamble. John Wallace, an African American assistant principal in Fairfax County, stated that he would rewrite the book, deleting the use of "nigger" and other "negative references" (Nelson 25).

In 1981, in Warrington, Bucks County, Pennsylvania, *Huckleberry Finn* was removed from the Tamanend Junior High School curriculum and placed in the tenth grade curriculum. Parents had wanted it banned from the required reading throughout the district (Hilferty, "Huck Finn" B03). The principal of Tamanend, in an interview with John Hilferty of the Philadelphia *Inquirer*, stated that if one boy was embarrassed, there are others who are embarrassed also, but would remain quiet. "Junior high school kids can be terribly cruel to each other," he commented. Parents argued that students in eighth grade were not mature enough to understand Twain's "subtle attack on slavery" and responded to the word "nigger" by abusing black students ("Parents" B01).

In State College Pennsylvania, parents demanded "that this book *(Huckleberry Finn)* be immediately discontinued as a regular part of the

English curriculum." A parent's objection included the profuse use of the term "nigger" in the book, the stereotyped image of Jim, and said that her son (the only African American student in the classroom) suffered "social and emotional discomfort throughout the instructional unit" (*Effects of Reading Huckleberry Finn* 1). An extensive review was made by an interracial committee composed of teachers, administrators, and parents of students in State College Area School District, along with faculty members and graduate students from Pennsylvania State University's Forum on Black Affairs. I served on this committee which used quantitative and qualitative measures to ascertain racial attitudes and the effects the reading of the book had on the ninth grade students. The decision was made to move the book to the eleventh or twelfth grade literature curriculum where the broader aspects of literature and Twain's satire could be understood and appreciated by the readers.

In an editorial, *The Cincinnati Enquirer* reported that in the small Texas town of Plano, a City Councilman objected to the "epic as 'racist and degrading' in its treatment of blacks. To protect black students from classroom embarrassment, he said, the school board should take the epic off the required reading list. The board put the book on the optional-reading list" ("Mark" 11).

Lee Burress reported that many editors and publishers have concern with the word "nigger" and have omitted it or replaced it. A Singer anthology substituted the word "slave,"McGraw-Hill replaced it with the words "servant," "folks," or "hand." Scott, Foresman omitted the word "nigger" from a passage and rewrote the line. It was originally printed as "'Betsy!' (this was a nigger woman), 'you'." The publisher changed it to "'Betsy, you fly around'" (95).

Mark Twain, in his autobiography, confessed, "In my schoolboy days, I had no aversion to slavery. I was not aware that there was anything wrong with it. No one arraigned it in my hearing; the local papers said nothing against it; the local pulpit taught us that God approved it...if the slaves themselves had an aversion to slavery, they were wise and said nothing" (Clemens 6). Nonetheless, *Huckleberry Finn* makes a statement against slavery. Michael Hearn claimed that "no work of American literature exposes the corruption of the 'peculiar institution' more eloquently than does Mark Twain's novel" (117).

Hearn and Trilling are rare in that they have addressed the use of "nigger." Most scholars of Twain address the slavery issue but not the term. Hearn explained that Huck uses the word "nigger" because he is a "child of his time" (117). Lionel Trilling expressed that

> (nigger) is the only word for a Negro that a boy like Huck would know in his place and time—that is, an ignorant boy in the South, before the Civil War.... It is right beyond question that the word should be driven out of the language, together with all the other words that have been used to express hostility and contempt for certain ethnic groups in our country.... And it is a part of the consciousness of themselves of each of the ethnic groups who have had to endure one or another degree of social disadvantage; it is something to be confronted and dealt with, not evaded or forgotten (American 509).

This certainly is a statement based on truth and circumstance and should not be ignored. But it must also be acknowledged that the term "nigger" historically had been and currently remains a word used in contempt and condescension. The *Oxford English Dictionary* defines "nigger" as "a Negro...(colloquial and usually contemptuous). The word has been used to mean colored persons; to separate 'colored persons' from Negroes; to distinguish a despicable deed or person whether white or black."

The *Interracial Books for Children Bulletin* included an historical overview "About the Word Nigger." In part it reported that "one might conclude from the way Mark Twain used "nigger" in *Huckleberry Finn* that during slave times it was an acceptable term without derogatory implications...although widely used, its sense was then, as it is today, pejorative and its purpose was to demean the black person.... Following the Civil War the term came into increasingly frequent use, as one way to constrain the freed slaves" (9).

In *Huckleberry Finn*, it is the word used always in relationship to "Negroes."

The major problem may be not only in Huck's use of the term, but in the accepted triteness that pervasive use of the word seems to create. Is "nigger" so commonplace in the novel that it has created an insensitive or subconscious reaction. Teachers often refer to "Nigger Jim." Even scholars of Twain, including DeVoto, Leacock, and Paine, have called Jim, "Nigger Jim,"—an adjective that Twain never used as Jim's name in the novel.

Nat Hentoff wrote a young adult novel *The Day They Came to Arrest the Book*, wherein *Huckleberry Finn* is highlighted as the controversial book, and the use of the word "nigger" as the dominant problem. In the novel, Steve Turney, an African American youth, explained that the word "nigger" was not intended "to insult or humiliate me or any other black person"(162). But the term does cause problems in real life situations.

In my dissertation study, eleventh grade students kept journals recording their reactions while reading *Huckleberry Finn*. Several comments stand out. A white student in an interracial class wrote, "Twain's attitude toward Huck and Jim is probably the same as most people of that time. People had a lot of racist feelings during the period in which the novel took place. Twain did not have an attitude of hate against Jim but didn't always consider the way he might have felt" (Mitchell 176).

An African American student wrote, "Last night I read the first six chapters of Huck Finn. I was appalled and embarrassed by the 1st few chapters by the repeated use of the nigger. On one page alone it was used six times. I didn't see the purpose of the use of the word.... I was embarrassed as (teacher's name) read from the book" (89). (The teacher referred to is white.)

The following comment also exemplifies the discomfort expressed by several African American students: "While studying Huckleberry Finn, think that they have some nerve calling somebody a nigger if you know what I mean..." (89). This particular student added, "but in spite of that I still liked the book."

This is the crux of the dilemma. Twain has created a complex story that is acknowledged by scholars as a masterpiece which portrays and criticizes the historical society in which he lived. It is satirical in nature and unique in style. Huck's maturation is an important experience in the novel and Jim's role in that realization must be acknowledged. The many levels on which the novel can be read keeps it as one that offers a wide range of possibilities to a wide range of readers. And it is enjoyed by young adult readers. But so long as it is the choice of districts, not only self selected by its readers, it must also be understood by its readers. Studies have shown that the novel is too complex for junior high readers to appreciate, and the attitudes they may carry from the book on a superficial level may be devastating.

Experiencing with literature in the classroom is a social activity. The sharing of ideas, both written and oral, serve as springboards for the cognitive processes that help to prepare students for adulthood. Reflections on culture, values, and traditions are communicated to peers and made public. In sharing ideas on *Huckleberry Finn*, African-American students, especially, often feel alienated and sometimes hostile. White students may view the term "nigger" as acceptable just as they accept on surface the novel only as an adventure story.

Reading *Huckleberry Finn* places demands on the reader and on the teacher. It is not enough to consider what students should read because it is on "the required-reading" list or because teachers like to teach it. Considerable thought must be given to the students' past experiences and current academic and emotional maturity. Most of the controversy of teaching *Huckleberry Finn* in schools has occurred when the book has been used in classes below the eleventh grade, has been used in lieu of or in the absence of literature by African-American writers, or has been taught without placement in an appropriate historical or literary context. These considerations must be made carefully and consciously by teachers and school boards.

Justin Kaplan makes the comment that Huck and Jim are "just too good for us, too truthful, too royal, too passionate, and, in a profounder sense than the one we feel easy with, too moral. Banning is one way of dealing with this profound affront. Another is denial" (Born 18). Surely, *Huckleberry Finn* has a place and purpose in the literary canon. Perhaps that place and purpose should be revisited as we look at the complexity of the novel and its effect on young adult readers. It appears that 1885 is not so long ago; the feud continues and *Huckleberry Finn* remains one of the controversial books in our schools.

WORKS CITED

Applebee, A. N. *A Study of Book-length Works Taught in High School English Courses.* New York: State University of New York at Albany, 1989.

Boston Transcript, 17 March, 1885.

Brooks, V. W. *The Ordeal of Mark Twain.* New York: E. P. Dutton, 1948.

Budd, L. J. *Critical Essays on Mark Twain, 1867-1910.* Boston: G. K. Hall & Co., 1982.

Burress, L. *Battle of the Books: Literary Censorship in the Public Schools, 1950-1985.* Metuchen, NJ: Scarecrow Press, 1989.

Clemens, S. L. *The Autobiography of Mark Twain.* New York: Harper & Row, 1959 ed.

Critic, 3 (March 28, 1885): 155.

DeVoto, B. *Mark Twain's America.* Cambridge: Houghton-Mifflin, 1932.

Dickinson, A.D. "Huckleberry Finn Is Fifty Years Old--Yes; But Is He Respectable?" *Wilson Bulletin* (November 1935): 183.

Donelson, K. "Six Statements/Questions from the Censors." *Phi Delta Kappan* (November 1987): 69.

Effects of Reading Huckleberry Finn on the Racial Attitudes of Ninth-grade Students. State College Area School District, Fall, 1983.

Eliot, T. S. "Introduction." *Adventures of Huckleberry Finn.* New York: Chanticleer, 1950.

Foner, P. S. *Mark Twain Social Critic.* New York: International Publishers, 1958.

Hearn, M. P. "Expelling Huck Finn." *The Nation* 235 (Aug 7-14, 1982): 117.

Hentoff, N. *The Day They Came to Arrest the Book.* New York: Dell Publishing, 1982.

Hilferty, J. "Huck Finn Won't Be Taught at Bucks School." Philadelphia *Inquirer* 24 Sept 1981: B03.

_____. "Parents Protest Huck Finn on Racial Ground." Philadelphia *Inquirer* 9 Sept 1981: B01.

"Huck Finn Is Banned in Bucks School." Philadelphia *Daily News* 24 Sept 1981: 2.

"Huckleberry Finn and the Minstrelsy Tradition." *Interracial Books for Children Bulletin.* 15.1 (1984).

Kaplan, J., Ed. *Mr. Clemens and Mark Twain.* New York: Simon and Schuster, 1966.

_____. "Born to Trouble: One Hundred Years of Huckleberry Finn." The Center for the Book Viewpoint Series No. 13 (Sept 11, 1984).

Leacock, S. *Mark Twain.* New York: D. Appleton & Co. 1933. *Life* 5, Feb 26, 1885.

Lynn, K. S. "Huck and Jim." *Yale Review.* 67 (Spring 1988): 421-431.

"Mark Twain: Once Again, His Masterpieces Are Attacked as Racist Works." Editorial. *The Cincinnati Enquirer.* 10 Dec 1990: 11.

Matthews, B. "Mark Twain–His Work." In L. J. Budd, ed. *Critical Essays on Mark Twain, 1867-1910.* Boston: G. K. Hall & Co., 1982.

Mitchell, A. H. "A Study of the Literary Understanding of *The Adventures of Huckleberry Finn* and the Attitudes of Students Toward the Characterizations and Language Used in the Novel." Diss. The Pennsylvania State University, 1987.

Neider, C., ed. *The Autobiography of Mark Twain.* New York: Harper and Row, 1917.

Nelson, N. "Raft of Controversy Over Huck Finn." Philadelphia *Daily News* 14 July 1982: 25.

Paine, A. B. *Mark Twain's Autobiography.* New York: Chelsea House, 1980.

Smith, H. N., and W. M. Gibson. *Mark Twain--Howells Letters.* Cambridge: Belknap Press of Harvard University Press, 1960.

Trilling, L. "Introduction." In *Adventures of Huckleberry Finn.* New York: Rinehart, 1948.

_____. In *American Literature.* New York: Ginn and Co., 1964.

ANNE FRANK: THE DIARY OF A YOUNG GIRL
Katherine Paterson

As every mother knows, the diary of an adolescent is sacrosanct. In *The Diary of a Young Girl*, Anne Frank, like young people the world over, was trying to deal with the "little bundle of contradictions" she found herself to be. In her diary, which she called "Kitty," she could confide her feelings, those that flamed with the idealism of youth and those that betrayed its fears, angers, and confusions.

Ordinarily, Anne's diary, too, would be inviolable, but hers was written under extraordinary circumstances. And so it is her very private revelations that for the last more than forty years have given a winsome, human face to one of the most brutal, least humane chapters of history.

As I write these words, war continues around the world. For us in America, after the Persian Gulf War, a war of missiles and machines, it is all too easy to forget the human cost of this mass destruction. No one wants to dwell on the cruel annihilation of innocent people that war always causes.

Even now, nearly fifty years after Anne wrote her diary, it is almost more than we can conceive, that during World War II, from 18 to 26 million "undesirable" men, women, and children were "put to death by the Germans through hunger, cold, pestilence, torture, medical experimentation and other means of extermination in all the camps of Germany and the occupied territories," to quote an official post-war French government document (*Britannica* 86). It is hard for many to believe that six million of this number were "undesirable" simply because they were of Jewish descent. But we have no choice but to believe. The atrocities in France alone fill 13 official Allied volumes. The Nazis themselves kept documents and photos. The first Allied troops to invade the occupied areas tell stories of the horrors they found when they liberated the death camps. And there were survivors—eye-witnesses to the holocaust—whose psyches were permanently branded by the hellish experience even as their bodies bore the tattoos of the camps.

How could this have happened? How could the country that produced Martin Luther and Beethoven and Goethe, also produce, not only a Hitler, but a society who rallied to his support or simply did nothing while these millions of persons, whose only crime was that the Nazis found them "undesirable," suffered and died?

"All that is required for evil to triumph," someone has said, "is for good people to do nothing."

But there were good people who refused to numb their consciences. Putting their own lives on the line, they openly protested the anti-Semitism of the Nazis or secretly hid Jews from the Gestapo. "My story," says Miep Gies, one of the small group who hid the Frank family in Amsterdam, "is a story of very ordinary people during extraordinarily terrible times. Times the like of which I hope with all my heart will never come again. It is for all of us ordinary people all over the world to see that they do not" (Gries 12).

It was Miep and Bep (called Elli in the published Diary) who picked up the notebooks and scattered pieces of paper off the floor of the hiding place after the "Green Police" had taken away the eight occupants of the "Secret Annexe" and the two supervisors of the company in whose back building the Franks and their friends were hiding.

Miep did not read the papers she hid away in her desk. She was sure they were written in Anne's writing and feared they might contain information about other Jews or the persons who were helping them. It was the feeling of those involved in this dangerous opposition to the German authorities that the less information any one individual possessed, the less could be obtained from him or her under torture. So the first person to read Anne's writings was her father, Otto Frank, the only survivor of the eight occupants to return from the death camps after the war.

"I want to go on living after my death!" Anne had written on April 4th, 1944, "And therefore I am grateful to God for giving me this gift, this possibility of developing myself and of writing, or expressing all that is in me."

I can shake off everything if I write; my sorrows disappear, my courage is reborn. But, and that is the great question, will I ever be able to write anything great, will I ever become a journalist or a writer? I hope so, oh, I hope so very much, for I can recapture everything when I write, my thoughts, my ideals and my fantasies... (Frank 177-78).

"In any case," Anne had written on May 11, 1944, "I want to publish a book entitled *Het Achterhuis* after the war. Whether I shall succeed or not, I cannot say, but my diary will be a great help."

Otto Frank took the notebooks and loose sheets upon which Anne had written and set about fulfilling his daughter's dream of living on through her writing. His first thought was simply to share the "essence" of her writings with relatives living in Switzerland and close friends. It was not a simple task. He found, for example, that Anne had begun to revise her original diary, perhaps with an eye to publication, so that some of the loose sheets contained a second version of the original diary entries, expanding or condensing accounts of the same events. She had also included a list of pseudonyms for the occupants of the hiding place and their protectors which, out of consideration for survivors and their relatives, Mr. Frank chose to use in the eventually published diary.

In the epilogue of the published diary, he also allowed the publishers to include this statement, "Apart from a very few passages, which are of little interest to the reader, the original text has been printed." In light of the fact that Mr. Frank's selected text was taken from two versions of the same events and included, as well, writings from Anne which were not part of either version of the diary proper, this statement led to a great deal of misunderstanding. Critics, some with not so secret pro-Nazi leanings began to maintain that the diary had not been written by Anne at all, but by Otto Frank or someone in his employ.

The allegations became serious and were repeated in respectable journals. At length the Dutch government undertook to settle once and for all the questions about *The Diary of Anne Frank* which were being circulated.

Were the documents the work of Anne Frank herself and written by her in the years 1942-1944 as claimed? The Netherlands State Forensic Laboratory did extensive investigations of the paper and ink on the original documents supplied by the estate of Otto Frank and compared the handwriting in both versions of the diary and in the other writings from the "Secret Annexe" reputedly written by Anne, with letters, postcards, and a poem in an autograph album which had been written by Anne and dated during the period from June 30, 1940 to July 5, 1942, before the Franks went into hiding.

These samples, which served as standards of Anne's handwriting, both cursive and handprinting, were gathered from friends and relatives as well as from the Otto Frank estate. The postmarks, censorship marks, paper and ink of these samples, or standards, were carefully examined for authenticity. They were scientifically compared with paper, ink and markings known to come from the period 1942 to 1944 and found to be the same. Having established the standards as authentic, the forensic laboratory then went on to compare the standards with the notebooks (paper, bindings, glue) loose sheets, ink and handwriting which comprised the writings from the "Secret Annexe."

The report of the State Forensic Science Laboratory "has convincingly demonstrated that both versions of the diary of Anne Frank were written by her in the years 1942 to 1944. The allegations that the diary was the work of someone else (after the war or otherwise) are thus conclusively refuted." A detailed summary of this report can be found in *The Diary of Anne Frank: The Critical Edition*, prepared by the Netherlands State Institute of War Documentation and published in English by Doubleday in 1989.

This critical edition is an invaluable resource for persons who wish to see the historical documents which became, largely through the selections made by Otto Frank with minor corrections and changes by others, the literary document which we know as *The Diary of Anne Frank*.

In comparing the three versions, two from Anne's handwritten diaries and loose sheets, and the one which Otto Frank typed up and which was eventually published, the reader is struck with how relatively few corrections and changes were made in the editing process. The published diary, while selected from both versions of Anne's own, and adding, from time to time, passages from the loose sheets that weren't strictly speaking a part of the formal diary, is Anne's own work. It is her voice we hear, her words we read—not a parent's or an editor's rewriting.

In *The Diary of a Young Girl*, we do certainly have the "essence" of Anne's literary bequest.

The omissions from the original documents, are not, however, what I would call "a very few passages, of little interest to the reader." For example, the original documents contain more details of the squabbling that went on between the residents of the annex, instances of what Anne felt to be proof of the selfishness of the other residents. No one changes character by these omissions, but it seems obvious, that out of regard for his dead wife and the feelings of those who had survived, Otto Frank felt that it was unnecessary to include all the stories which documented Anne's complaints against the other residents. He understood, as any good parent would, that the diaries served as a safe place for Anne to vent a lot of feelings that in those close quarters she would have had to keep bottled up otherwise.

As noted earlier, Frank's original typing from his daughter's notebooks and papers was done to share with relatives and friends "the essence" of his daughter's accounts of their life in hiding. It was some of these friends who persuaded him that he must seek to publish this manuscript.

Ironically, finding a publisher proved very difficult. The Dutch publisher that finally agreed to take on the project asked that certain passages be deleted, most notably references to menstruation and Anne's recollection of wanting to touch her friend's developing breasts. It is noteworthy that the English publishers included these same passages, and, indeed, it would be hard to imagine that a young girl entering puberty would have no curiosity about her changing body, or would have failed to record in her diary such an important, life changing event as menstruation. The Dutch publisher also suggested the deletion of certain "offensive remarks" about Anne's mother (*Critical Edition* 69) and probably eliminated other passages simply to shorten the book to make it fit in the series for which they had chosen it (Ibid.).

There were also, as usually occurs, editorial changes, spelling, for example, or changes in wording when the publisher thought the Dutch readership might not understand. Anne's first language was German, so sometimes her Dutch was inaccurate or strained.

The Dutch publisher obviously did not know what it had in hand, for the initial run was for 1,500 copies. But *Het Achterhuis* (The House Behind) attracted immediate, favorable attention. Soon afterwards, the book was translated into German by another German emigre to the Netherlands who had taught Margot literature and had known Anne. The choice was made by Otto Frank, but was, apparently, not the best choice, as he himself later admitted. "She was too old for the job, many of her expressions were pedantic and not in a youthful enough style. In addition she...misunderstood many Dutch expressions" (*Critical Edition* 71). It was probably this teacherish translation which gave credence to the rumor in German intellectual circles, that the book could not have been the creation of a teenager. The German translation also omitted several passages apparently thought to be incomprehensible or particularly offensive to German readers. Thus, for example, the rule that required people in the annex "to speak softly at all times, in any civilized language, therefore not in German," was changed to read: "All civilized languages...but softly!!!" (*Critical Edition* 73)

The English version of *Het Achterhuis*, renamed *The Diary of a Young Girl*, was first published in 1952. Again it was greeted with critical acclaim. "A truly remarkable book," said the reviewer in *The New York Times.* "One of the most moving personal documents to come out of World War II," reported *The Philadelphia Inquirer.* But perhaps more important than the critical reception was the response of young people to the book. Anne was one of them—another teenager, concerned about her looks, about school, about friends, about her somewhat rocky relations to her parents. She pasted the pictures of film stars on her wall and wondered how it would feel to be kissed. Anne was bright, articulate, and funny. She could be marvelously idealistic and downright catty. She was an absolutely real adolescent living through an unreal nightmare.

Years after the war, the girlfriend, who is called Lies in the book, was asked about the Anne she remembered. "Anne and I were very close friends," she said, "you must understand that, and yet no one suspected that she could write. With Margot it would have been different. We thought Margot terribly talented and capable of anything. But Anne, you see, was just my friend..." ("Lies P." quoted in Schnable 36).

But Anne's wise father knew, that even with her many friends, Anne needed a diary—a place where she could confide her most intimate thoughts. "It's odd for someone like me to keep a diary," Anne observes six days after her father has given her one for her thirteenth birthday, "not only because I have never done so before, but because it seems to me that neither I—nor for that matter anyone else—will be interested in the unbosomings of a thirteen-year-old schoolgirl. Still what does that matter? I want to write, but more than that, I want to bring out all kinds of things that lie buried deep in my heart" (20 June, 1942).

The other occupants and their protectors knew that Anne spent a lot of time writing—it would be hard to keep any activity a secret in the confined space of the annex. Miep tells of surprising Anne at the task and of Mrs. Frank's gentle intervention in what was at first an awkward scene. "Her voice was ironic, and yet kind. 'Yes, Miep, as you know, we have a daughter who writes'" (Gies 186). And Anne would, from time to time, read excerpts from her writing to amuse the others, but for the most part, her diaries served, as she had intended from the first, as a "great support and comfort" as she confronted the challenge of growing up and the terror that she might not be allowed to.

How is a work like a diary to be judged? The book is certainly well-written, but it is (despite the author's revisions) the fresh work of a bright, sensitive adolescent. It is precisely the most censured passages in the book that give it its freshness, its reality as the work of a child struggling to become a woman, physically and psychically. It cannot be judged, therefore, as a novel by a mature writer might be judged. As to style, it is artless. With reference to composition, it was left tragically uncompleted.

To judge a diary is, in a sense, to judge the person who wrote it, and what right have we to do that? Some critics have complained that Anne does not "set a good example" for young readers. They feel that her concern for sexual matters is inappropriate reading matter—that her unhappiness with her mother and her rude comments on the adults in the annex tend to undermine adult authority. But Anne is an adolescent. And if she cannot be allowed to sort out her feelings about herself, her body, her relationships in the privacy of her diary, where on earth could she do so? Certainly to expunge these passages would destroy the book's credibility as a diary written by a normal, if intellectually precocious, teenager.

There are, however, in Anne's writing, passages which burn with youthful idealism. The most quoted one is probably the most heartbreakingly naive: "It's really a wonder that I haven't dropped all my ideals, because they seem so absurd and impossible to carry out. Yet I keep them, because in spite of everything I still believe that people are really good at heart." Usually, those who quote Anne Frank stop there, but to do so, is to retain only the naivete of the adolescent and fail to see the strong young woman she has become after two years in hiding.

"I simply can't build up my hopes on a foundation consisting of confusion, misery, and death." She continues in that same passage. "I see the world gradually being turned into a wilderness, I hear the ever approaching thunder, which will destroy us too, I can feel the sufferings of millions and yet, if I look up into the heavens, I think that it will all come right, that this cruelty too will end, and that peace and tranquility will return again.

"In the meantime, I must uphold my ideals, for perhaps the time will come when I shall be able to carry them out" (15 July, 1944).

Especially in these days when the thunder is still roaring in our ears, all of us, young and old, need to hear this voice which has survived the horror of Hitler's holocaust and continues to speak life and light and hope to a world afraid of the dark.

WORKS CITED

"Anti-semitism." *Encyclopaedia Britannica:* Vol. 2. 1969 ed.

Frank, Anne. *Diary of a Young Girl.* Trans. B. M. Mooyaart. New York: Pocket Books, 1972.

Gies, Miep. *Anne Frank Remembered.* New York: Simon and Schuster, 1987.

Netherlands State Institute of War Documentation. *The Diary of Anne Frank: The Critical Edition.* New York: Doubleday, 1989.

Schnable, Ernst. *Anne Frank: A Portrait in Courage.* Trans. Richard and Clara Winston. New York: Harcourt, Brace and Company, 1958.

ANNIE ON MY MIND BY NANCY GARDEN
William Sleator

To begin by demolishing what will almost certainly be a basic
misconception about this book: *Annie on My Mind* does not idealize or
encourage homosexuality. On the contrary, it is an often painful account
of the very serious problems that can result from a homosexual experience.
These problems are not only encountered by the teenage protagonists, but
also by two adults involved in a long-term homosexual relationship. No
one can argue that this book might influence readers to experiment with
homosexuality. The book will instead make it very clear to readers that
homosexual behavior often causes great suffering.

I also want to dispense right away with what will probably be another
cause for concern: there is no explicit sex in this book. No one reading this
book will learn anything about actual sexual practices. It is important to
emphasize that most teenagers—whether parents realize it or not—have
already learned about such things from conversations with their friends,
and of course from movies and television. They will not learn about them
here.

I must quickly add that although *Annie on My Mind* does not paint a
rosy picture of homosexuality, it doesn't condemn it either. The gay
people in this book are not pathological misfits. These characters are
different from heterosexuals in only two essential ways: they love members
of their own sex; and to live in a manner that is natural for them they must
deal with a society that often brands them as freaks—and punishes them
severely.

The three-dimensional and mostly positive portrayal of gay characters
may be one of the most difficult aspects of the book to defend to some
people. But I can only point out that if the book were moralistic or preachy,
if it were an obviously slanted tract depicting homosexuals as either

virtuous martyrs or evil sickos, then it would have no credibility or interest for teenagers, who tend to be skeptical by nature. The fact that gay characters are depicted realistically and often sympathetically only emphasizes, and makes more compelling and moving, the point that homosexual behavior means risking harsh consequences.

The story is a highly believable account of what happens to two teenage girls who begin to realize, with great difficulty and hesitation, that they have feelings of love for one another. Liza, the protagonist, meets Annie, a girl her own age who goes to a different school, at a museum. Their common interest in art and the middle ages is the initial basis for their friendship. Liza's parents are affluent, her father a professional; she attends a private school. Annie's family are Italian immigrants with menial jobs; she goes to a large inner-city school. They both learn a great deal from the differences in their backgrounds.

Much of the plot concerns the situation at Liza's private school, Foster Academy. The headmistress is a stern and forbidding woman who believes that students should be disciplined for minor infractions of often arbitrary rules, and also that students should report such infractions, even when they are innocent mistakes that cause no real harm to anyone. We learn quickly that Liza, who is student council president, is a highly-principled young woman who is willing to put herself on the line for what she believes, even at the risk of getting in trouble herself.

Foster Academy is in financial difficulties. A fund drive is in progress. Any hint of scandal at the school could result in the failure of the fund drive, and the closing of the school.

The affection between the girls progresses very, very gradually. Liza does not even realize what her feelings mean until well into the book. Nothing physical happens until it is clear to them both that they love each other emotionally. In fact, both girls have great difficulty even admitting to these feelings, aware of the great stigma attached to them which adds to the credibility. The physical contact is very tentative at first—a touch, a hug. It is also entirely mutual—neither "seduces," or puts any kind of pressure on, the other. Implicit here—though never stated directly—is the fact that nothing would happen if *both* girls did not want it to. No one can "make" someone else gay if the inclination is not there already. Eventually both girls are able to admit that they very much want to express their feelings completely. But there is, of course, no place where they can make love.

Ms. Widmer and Ms. Stephenson are two of the most popular and accomplished teachers at Foster Academy. They share a house, but no student has ever been there until the headmistress asks the teachers to "volunteer" their house for a student council meeting. At the meeting, Liza learns that the two teachers are going away over spring break, and the boy who usually takes care of their cats is not available. Liza feels comfortable in the house, it is not far from where she lives, and without thinking much about it offers to feed their cats herself. Not until the first day that Annie goes to the house with Liza to help her feed the cats do they realize that now they do have a place.

The lovemaking, as I've already said, is handled with great delicacy and no explicit details. What is emphasized is that it is an expression of love, not merely sex, and is entirely mutual. It is beautiful for both of them.

From books they find in the master bedroom, and because of the way the bedrooms are furnished, the girls realize that the two teachers are lovers and seem to have been together for quite a long time. The vacationing teachers, of course, do not know about Annie, have not influenced Liza in any way, and have no idea what is going on in their house.

Liza and Annie are discovered by the prying school secretary and another student, under conditions that make it obvious they were in bed together. An uproar ensues. The headmistress is terrified that if a scandal occurs it will kill the fund drive and the school will have to close. She tells Liza's parents, which is of course a very painful situation for Liza. For the first time in her life she lies to her parents, telling them that she and Annie were merely "experimenting," and that there was no "real" sexual contact between them. Annie, who goes to a different school and is not involved in the scandal, does not tell her parents, not wanting to hurt them. Liza is suspended from school. She and the two teachers are required to attend, separately, a disciplinary meeting of the school board of trustees. The board will decide if the incident should go on Liza's permanent record, and whether or not MIT, which has accepted Liza as an architecture student, will be informed of it. Not only is the experience itself humiliating, it is also possible that her relationship with Annie will have a disastrous effect on her entire life.

It is decided that no disciplinary action will be taken against Liza. When she returns to school, many of the students avoid her, others make nasty remarks—though a few of them are understanding and treat her no differently than before.

The two teachers do not get off so easily. It is naturally assumed— erroneously—that they influenced the two girls. They are fired from their jobs and the incident is put on their records, meaning they will never be able to teach again. They are excellent teachers who have inspired many students. Though completely innocent, their lives are now irrevocably changed. Yet the two teachers do not blame Liza and Annie for their misfortune. They tell them that bad things often happen, they can deal with them—it would only be unbearable if they couldn't stay together.

During her first semester at MIT Liza thinks about Annie all the time. Annie, who is studying at Berkeley, has written Liza a letter, but Liza is unable to answer it. Finally, after going through the whole experience in her mind, and knowing that she still loves Annie, she telephones her. The book ends on a positive note; the two of them will be together over Christmas vacation.

It's a curious phenomenon that many parents believe the only way teenagers will find out that sex exists is by reading about it in books. They seem to feel that if they keep books that mention sex away from kids, then kids will never think about sex or want to experience it. The real truth, as anyone who understands teenagers knows, is that peer pressure, the media, and especially adolescent biology itself all combine to guarantee that teenagers will naturally be curious about, preoccupied or even obsessed with sex—even if they never read a single word about it.

So why are some parents so afraid of books? One reason is that these people are aware of the power of literature. They are correct that literature is powerful, but in my opinion they are incorrect as to the nature of its power. They're afraid that literature will influence behavior, when in fact it is peer pressure, and the attitudes of society as reflected in the popular mass media, that have the strongest influence on the way teenagers want to appear, the way they dress and talk, the way they behave with others.

The power of literature is not that it directly influences behavior (except perhaps for political tracts) but that it conveys information. And good literature, by which I mean the kinds of books we are discussing here, conveys accurate information. TV commercials and music videos aren't interested in accuracy—they're interested in selling products any way they can. Other teenagers aren't interested in accuracy—they're interested in coming across as cool and with it. They want to appear to be knowledgeable about the world—and about sex—and to create this impression they often convey information to their peers that is full of dangerous misconceptions.

This is why it is so important that young readers have access to books that will give them a true and accurate picture of the world. But that is not necessarily a line of reasoning that will change the minds of people who want to ban books. In fact, the opposite is often true: it is the information in books that many concerned parents feel is so dangerous.

Since they don't seem to be thinking about the fact that kids are *already* being bombarded with information from so many other sources—remind them. Make it very clear to people who want to protect kids from books that all kids are constantly being fed details about sex, and other controversial subjects, from the media and from their friends. And it is this irresponsible and often false information, *not* the information in good books, that can be truly dangerous to them. Even the most protective parents must realize that they can't isolate their kids from Madonna videos, or from other kids at school who will encourage them to experiment with sex. It is the accurate and unbiased information found in good books that will help to counteract these influences, and give kids a basis for making wise and responsible decisions.

But this line of reasoning may still not have much effect on people who want to ban *Annie on My Mind* because of its specifically homosexual content. Homosexual behavior is highly stigmatized in this society—*especially* among teenagers. Derogatory slang words for homosexuals are just about the worst insults teenagers can inflict on each other. Unlike drugs and heterosexual behavior, which are often regarded as glamorous by young people, teenagers see homosexuality as a brand of shame, probably the most potent reason for being cruelly ostracized. Everyone knows how obsessed adolescents are with peer approval and acceptance. To imagine that reading a book might be enough to motivate a teenager to experiment with behavior that is already so powerfully stigmatized by much more pervasive and controlling influences is so illogical that it verges on the fantastic.

How can you get this fact across to adults who want to keep this book off the shelf? You could just point it out to them, but they may still resist the logic of it. I can suggest several other strategies. However, first I must emphasize that I have far less contact with people who want to ban books than do librarians and teachers. I'm just throwing out ideas for you to think about.

But it seems to me that simply *asking* adults if reading this book would influence *them* to change their sexual orientation might give them pause for thought. If they argue that teenagers are more susceptible to suggestion, then ask them to consider this question in the context of how they felt as teenagers. Would this book have compelled them to engage in behavior they found personally repugnant, and that would cause most people to treat them as outcasts?

Perhaps this strategy is too personal and direct. Much more important questions to ask are: Why would anybody—especially teenagers—*want* to be gay? What is the attraction of homosexuality? Anyone who seriously considers these questions will have to admit that our society views homosexuality as unattractive, for the reasons given above—which are also emphasized in *Annie on My Mind.*

The fact is that the attraction and rewards of *hetero*sexuality are so overwhelming and undeniable that there can be only one reason anyone would risk losing them—and that is if the risk is inevitable. If it were possible to choose between being straight and being gay, faced with society's sanctions, most people would not choose to be gay. Reading *Annie on My Mind* will do nothing to alter that fact.

What this book *will* do is tell readers a story involving lesbian characters who may be quite different from what they have probably heard about lesbians from their peers or other unreliable sources. The gay characters in this book are ordinary fallible people who have no choice but to express their love in a way that makes many people hate and fear them.

To lead satisfying lives under these conditions requires strength and courage. But the book is not a diatribe proclaiming that all gay people are innocent victims who behave perfectly in every situation; they make mistakes, and with luck they can learn from them. Like all good novels, *Annie on My Mind* is more than anything else a believable story about particular individuals.

I have so far said nothing about what effect this book might have on the very small percentage of young readers who do have homosexual feelings. I don't know whether bringing up this issue in defense of the book will help to keep it on the shelf or have the opposite effect (it is not up to me to make that decision) but it should be mentioned here. *Annie on My Mind* will be a blessing for teenagers who are becoming aware that they may be homosexual, and terrified because of it. Once again, it will not encourage them to be actively gay; the book is very clear about the problems gay people must resolve. But it will also let them know that being gay does not necessarily mean one is depraved or mentally ill or condemned to a life of misery and humiliation—which are the messages they have probably heard from other sources. It will show them that gay people can have loving, long-term relationships, that they can have satisfying lives and be productive members of society—that they are different from other people only because of whom they love. It is not an overstatement to say that this information may well save some teenagers from much anguish and self-hatred, and perhaps even do a little to help them adjust successfully to their sexual orientation. But gay readers are not the major issue here.

I'm not sure *any* book can convey to teenagers the astonishing concept that being exactly like everybody else may not be the most important thing in life. But this book might possibly stimulate them to take another look at peer pressure, and to begin to question the validity of judging people on the basis of arbitrary opinions. Whatever readers of this book choose to believe about homosexuality, in a broader sense they will see an example of what it means to be different and experience how it feels to be treated as an outcast. And if they do gain an inkling of compassion from reading this book, then that can only improve their own lives and the lives of those around them.

IN DEFENSE OF: *ARE YOU THERE, GOD? IT'S ME! MARGARET, DEENIE,* AND *BLUBBER*— THREE NOVELS BY JUDY BLUME

Robin F. Brancato

"My mother says God is a nice idea..."

"I don't even believe in God!"
(from *Are You There God, It's Me, Margaret*)

I turned away from the kitchen door and ran back to my room. As soon as I got into bed I started touching myself. I have this special place and when I rub it I get a very nice feeling. (from *Deenie*)

Caroline and Wendy started another game of Tic Tac Toe while Bruce went to work on his nose. He has a very interesting way of picking it. (from *Blubber*)

These are some of the lines, obviously taken out of context, that are most likely to raise the hackles, the blood pressure, and the eyebrows of Judy Blume's critics. Those who are disturbed by America's most popular author of books for young readers include religious conservatives, parents worried about sexual precocity in their children, and certain academics who say Blume lacks taste and/or literary merit. These critics range from rabid censors who would love to see all Blume's books banned, to middle-of-the-roaders who object primarily to her book *Forever*, to mild-mannered skeptics who merely wonder if certain Blume titles might trouble children who read them at too young an age. Judy Blume's critics are numerous, but the number is negligible when compared to the hordes of kids who buy and devour her books as if they were Big Macs (over 50 million Blume books sold!), or even when compared to the number of kids who write to Blume without a parent ever suggesting, or a teacher assigning, such an active response. To find out what Judy Blume is up to, especially in *Are You There God? It's Me, Margaret* (1970), *Deenie* (1973), and *Blubber* (1974), what it is that her critics fear, and what can be said to calm those fears...read on.

Are You There God? It's Me, Margaret, is about twelve-year-old Margaret Simon's attempts at coming to terms with her interreligious background and her entrance into puberty. The candor with which Judy Blume describes Margaret's feelings and experiences shocked some people back in 1970 and continues to unsettle certain readers even now, when Margaret, if real, would be a thirty-something yuppie. The novel deals with such universal concerns as dislocation (moving and readjusting), family tensions (grandma interferes), and preoccupation with physical maturation, boys, and sex (Margaret practices kissing her pillow; Margaret exercises to increase her bust and pretends she has gotten her menstrual period before she actually gets it). After seeking, by way of a school project, to learn about comparative religion, Margaret doesn't come to any easy decision about her own religious identity. The novel, which concludes with Margaret's resuming her talks with God and thanking him that she had finally gotten her first menstrual period, is not primarily about physical changes in puberty but about an adolescent's personal relationship with God.

Deenie has to do with complications in the life of beautiful Wilmadeene Fenner, seventh grader, when she discovers that she has scoliosis. This trial is intensified by the fact that Deenie's mother has had her heart set on Deenie's becoming a successful model. In addition to the theme of learning to cope with a physical handicap, *Deenie* deals with additional adolescent concerns, such as sibling rivalry, peer acceptance and sexuality. (The references that have created the greatest stir have to do with masturbation. The first-person narrator tells the reader that she sometimes touches a "special place," and then later, in a sex-education class in school, Deenie's gym teacher assures the students, as part of a question-and-answer session, that "...it's normal and harmless to masturbate.")

At the end of the novel, which is mainly about the discomforts, physical and emotional, that Deenie suffers as a result of scoliosis, she is still confined most of the time to her restricting body brace but is on her way to accepting her temporary disability. She is also on her way to becoming sensitized to others who have to live with handicaps or disfigurement.

Blubber gives us a picture of a typical fifth grade, where Jill Brenner and her classmates have taken to tormenting an easy victim, overweight Linda Fischer. Jill participates in the teasing, not knowing that her classmates will soon turn the tables and pick on her instead. As a sufferer Jill comes to realize, though not through any great epiphany or with any great remorse, that kids are cruel and fickle and that today's Miss Popularity can be tomorrow's outcast.

Before examining why each of these three books has had censorship attempts made against it, let's consider what it is in general about Blume's works that her critics object to. First, some fear that her frankness about sex and her nonjudgmental position will "give kids ideas," or that this frankness will cause hangups where none existed previously. Some critics are primarily concerned with the marketing of certain Blume books—the fact that Forever (about the premarital sexual relationship of a senior girl, who is seventeen at the outset) and Blume's adult novels, Wifey and Smart Women, have sometimes attracted the same pre-teen readers who know Blume through her much less controversial Tales of a Fourth Grade Nothing or Superfudge. These two objections will be rebutted by kids, by sympathetic adults, and by Judy Blume herself in the pages ahead.

In addition to these complaints about references to sexuality and about marketing methods, some critics are offended, as well, by what they perceive as Blume's general permissiveness, by her so-called simplistic resolutions, by her so-called stereotyped characters, and by her language (a sprinkling of words such as "damn," and "ass"). Others deplore the so-called nastiness of some of her main characters, such as Jill in Blubber; or the unwillingness of many of her adult characters to stand up to children; or the everybody-speaks-in-the-same-voice quality of her protagonists, regardless of their age or sex. Still others say that Blume doesn't challenge young readers enough and that she creates a narrow view of the world in her focus on the affluent suburbs. One such opinion comes from John

Garvey, writing in *Commonweal* (in July, 1980):

> There is something dismal about teaching children to cope, where in previous generations books for children encouraged a larger imagining, a thrill at the size of the universe they might encounter.

Let's take a look at these criticisms and come back with a defense for each:

Permissiveness—Is Blume really so permissive, or is she merely inviting kids to think for themselves? According to Robert Lipsyte in *The Nation* (1981), Blume "asks more questions than she answers, gently nudging her readers toward a healthy skepticism."

Easy resolutions—Each of Blume's heroines confronts a critical experience, and it's true that each comes to tolerate, accept, or embrace his or her life, but so do Alcott's Little Women, so does Laura Ingalls Wilder's Laura, so does Anne Frank in her diary. Jack Forman in *The Horn Book Magazine* (January-February 1985) reflects on this point in the following statement that agrees with the criticism but still praises Blume:

> Her characters almost always survive heavy personal, family, and school problems by turning to their own internal resources, absorbing any temporary discomfort or hurt, and getting on with their lives. They learn from their mistakes, and become more self-reliant. Very little attention, however, is given to how others are affected by the resolution of problems, and rarely does Blume confront the lingering pain and hurt which characters might feel after resolving the problems.... Unquestionably, children and teenagers need to believe in themselves and carve a niche for themselves in their society; they need the reassurance of a life after problems. Judy Blume gives them this. But they also need to know that there are consequences to their actions affecting other people and that there is a price paid for their mistakes—even if they learn the right lessons.

Stereotyped characters—Blume characters, admittedly, are pretty ordinary people, says John Gough (*The School Librarian*, May 1985).

Most of the famous modern teenage characters in children's books are not ordinary. They are extremely bright or talented or difficult or sensitive or tough or eccentric.... These characters are very easy to be interested in; but we should not rush to dismiss more ordinary characters, such as Blume's. They are human, too, and probably more like most readers than their more extreme and critically acceptable counterparts.

Everybody-speaks-the-same, limited focus, and wimpy adults—First of all, it's not true that Judy Blume's adult characters are always weak. Margaret's grandmother, for instance, is strong-willed, caring, and feisty. Second, if the characters often speak alike and if the focus is "limited," then consider the fact that all Blume's books are about twentieth century, middle class, mostly suburban life, which she's showing more honestly than most other writers of books for children. Is it possible that if there is a sameness among the characters and a limited focus, that this says more about middle-class America than about Judy Blume's limitations?

Language—In an age when, sad as it is to admit, harsh, unseemly, abusive language is often the lazy norm, rather than the refined, original, truly expressive language that most of us would prefer, in an age when a President of the United States was widely quoted as threatening to "kick ass" in the Middle East, Judy Blume is a model of discretion. She's simply trying to suggest how kids really speak. Although standards differ from one community to another, surely the sprinkling of "bad words" used by her characters puts them in the conservative camp almost anywhere in this country today. If Blume's characters don't think and talk like real kids, why should readers put any stock in their feelings, hopes, and dreams?

No literary merit? Let's wrap up these allegations with two summary statements. Though Blume's style is simple, according to Jack Forman, it's "an attractive simplicity and a very natural sense of humor." "She's an underrated writer," says John Gough "critically abused or neglected, who deserves close attention and stands up to scrutiny very well."

This is the nature, then, of the literary criticism of Blume's books. As for the meaner critics, the ones who yearn to censor her, who are they, and where do they come from? Some are reviewers or educators, but most, let's assume, are parents, alarmed at the thought of their children nibbling at the apple on the Tree of Knowledge. These parents are vocal and geographically diverse. In Leesburg, Florida, in 1981 (according to an Associated Press story in the *St. Petersburg Times*) a Baptist minister led "a movement to purge school libraries of novels by Judy Blume, saying some of the stories amount to a sexual "how-to" lesson for young students." Other censors tried to ban *Margaret* and *Blubber* in Xenia, Ohio in 1983. *Margaret* was accused of being anti-Christian and against parental and school authority, and *Blubber* was pulled off the shelves for containing the word "bitch" in connection with a teacher.

In Peoria, Illinois, in 1984 the ACLU urged school officials to rescind a ban on three Blume novels, but the officials subsequently found three others to be unsuitable. Objections were to language and to descriptions of sexual coming of age. A director of elementary education in Daviess County, Kentucky instructed elementary librarians in 1990 to avoid purchase of additional Blume titles. Although attempts at banning Blume have often been resolved, eventually, in favor of the author, her books are sometimes assigned to a shelf where they may be read only by children who bring a note from home. Here's a sampling of additional places where censorship attempts were made against Judy Blume during the 1980's: Brigham City, Utah; Gilbert, Arizona; Dedham, Massachusetts; Tuscaloosa, Alabama; Fond du Lac, Wisconsin; and DesMoines, Iowa. There are undoubtedly many unreported cases, as well, of Blume books not being purchased in the first place, or being quietly removed from library shelves, or being kept in libraries under wraps.

Why is this censorship of Blume so inappropriate, so misguided, so unfair? Let's look at statements for the defense, first from Blume's staunchest supporters—kids; then from adults sympathetic to what she is doing; and finally from Judy Blume herself. This is what kids say (according to Barbara Ann Porte in *The Advocate*, University of Georgia)—and, by the way, *kids should know*, because unlike many would-be censors who have read only selected passages thought to be provocative, young defenders have read the books from cover to cover:

"She writes about people I would like to know."

"She knows what I am like.
"Her books are funny."
"Her books are sad."
"Your books help me not to be afraid."

A typical reader comment begins like this one, from *Letters to Judy*, a collection of some of the nearly 2,000-a-month pieces of mail received by Blume and published by Putnam's and by Pocket Books in 1987, royalties from which go to Kids Fund, a foundation that finances projects intended to enhance the lives of kids:

Dear Judy,
Whenever I have a fight with somebody I sit right down and write a letter to you. I don't always send it but it makes me feel better just to write it.
Jennifer, age 11

The volume of an author's fan mail and the willingness of young readers to bare their souls to a famous stranger may not be the measure of that writer's literary merit, but surely in an age when most adolescents look at the world and feel confusion, anxiety, or even terror, Judy Blume should be regarded as a national treasure. She provides comfort ("I thought I was weird for doing and thinking some things but your books make me feel okay."); she fills a need ("My mom never talks about the things young girls think most about."); she offers hope ("The main reason I am writing is I want your advice."). Emily Dickinson wrote: "If I can stop one heart from breaking, I shall not live in vain...." Judy Blume's candid novels may not be exactly what Emily Dickinson had in mind, but let the censors consider for a minute the thousands of appreciative responses from Blume's readers, and let those censors weigh all the hearts stopped from breaking, the lives saved from aching, and the pains cooled by Blume, against the unlikely possibility of a child's being damaged by a so-called unpleasant word, an unholy thought, or a grim truth in one of her books.

Adult supporters of Blume admire in her books the same things that kids admire—her authentic contemporaneity and, mainly, her honesty.

As a supplement to the decorous fiction of the past, from *Little Women* to Nancy Drew, as an alternative to fantasy and science fiction, as a giant step up from the sanitized fluff of Sweet Dreams and The Babysitter's Club, let there be Judy Blume, whose realism, it's true, brings with it some "unpleasant details," says Faith McNulty in a 1983 assessment of Blume in the *New Yorker*, some "things we all notice but usually don't mention," in books of "mesmerizing intimacy," that give us a "feeling of reading a secret diary." Let librarians spend the bulk of their shrinking budgets, if they must, on the challenging, ennobling classics, on books that, according to Garvey in *Commonweal*, encourage a larger imagining, so long as they save a few dollars for Judy Blume books, books that show young people who are, according to critic John Gough, "surviving, finding themselves, growing in understanding...."

Here are some testimonials from mothers, as reported by Barbara Ann Porte:

1) "My gynecologist recommended Margaret to me for my daughter."
2) "I wish I'd had books like that when I was thirteen."
3) "They (Blume's books) help me talk with my children about subjects I could otherwise not bring up."

This last comment is a recurring one, and is probably the basis of the strongest argument in favor of Blume's works. How many parents, through the ages, have languished in uneasy silence, waiting for a child to take the initiative in asking the big question? How many other parents have, in embarrassment, thrust a sex-ed book at their offspring and then hurried out of the room, or else bumbled into an artificial monologue about "Now that you're growing up..."? Even John Garvey of the "larger imagining" school, writes ". . .if parents and schools won't tell their children about sex, better they should learn from Judy Blume than not learn at all."

But what better recommendation can there be for a book, any book, than that it served as a catalyst for fruitful discussion, especially discussion between parent and child? Whether the parent gives the child the Blume book as a present or catches him or her reading it under the bedcovers, the odds are much more favorable for a natural exchange of ideas and opinions than in the "Here, read this article" approach. How relatively easy to talk about fictitious characters: "Do you know anybody like Margaret?" "I understand that some people are embarrassed by certain references in *Deenie*...." "Whose fault do you think it is that Blubber gets picked on?" Teachers can ask these questions, too, of course, but ideally it is parents who will do the asking. There may be parents who will still shy away from such discussions, even under the protective cloak of fiction. And there will be parents who don't have the time or interest to read the books, let alone to initiate a friendly book talk. So be it. Let them have their selfish silence. Just don't let them deny their own children, and other people's children, access to books that may inform, or comfort, or sensitize. As Judith Goldberger says in the *Newsletter on Intellectual Freedom* of May 1981,

> ...an adult's agony over discussing these matters with children is nothing when compared to the personal agony the young experience when faced with the actual situations. And that is one reason why young people devour Judy Blume's books. They deal with matters of primary concern to their readers, with which many of those readers' parents can't or won't help them. Often, rather than talking *with* their children about touchy subjects, parents talk *at* them. Or they don't talk at all.

Let's look for a moment now at the three specific Blume titles and see what each has to recommend it.

Are You There God? It's Me, Margaret—According to Judith Goldberger, "*Margaret* is not about a girl who wants a bra any more than *Hamlet* is about a man who is in love with a woman who goes crazy...." In addition to Margaret's concern with her first menstrual period, with playing a kissing game called "Two minutes in the Closet," and with looking at her friend's father's anatomy book, she is also concerned with exploring the nature of religious faith, with trying to get along with friends, parents, and grandparents, and with worrying, as most young people do, whether she is normal. Says Faith McNulty, "Except perhaps in *Forever*, Blume imparts no illicit knowledge but merely fills in an area of adolescent experience usually left blank in print."

Deenie—In addition to being a book often recommended by orthopedic surgeons to patients who have scoliosis, *Deenie* is the story of a down-to-earth teenager, who deals surprisingly well with her mother's pushiness and insensitivity. By the end of the book Deenie arrives at a better understanding with her older sister; she realizes that the people she cares about most accept her, body-brace and all, and she convinces the reader that a condition such as scoliosis doesn't have to stand in the way of normal psychological and sexual development. The two or three brief references to masturbation are an understated, realistic minor motif in a novel that is about an adolescent's wish to be accepted.

Blubber—*Blubber* is a book that is sometimes used by teachers in the upper elementary grades to sensitize students to the cruelty of scapegoating. In New Zealand the book is used in teacher training. Although some critics object to Blume's nonjudgmental stance, this gives the book the ring of truth. Bullying is a given in the world Blume has created. Whereas in other books, and often in the real world, adults step in, in a crisis, and absolve children of responsibility, in *Blubber* the adults are too preoccupied, or unsuspecting, or ineffectual, just as they sometimes are in life. This leaves the young people to take charge themselves, and to learn, the hard way, that allegiances shift quickly among kids, and that (without a word about religion) the Golden Rule is a worthwhile principle to uphold.

In addition to the sympathetic critics already cited, Judy Blume, in her own defense, makes the following points about her books (in a speech sponsored by the National Coalition Against Censorship, May 17, 1990, and elsewhere):

1) She purposely takes no moral stand, because there are usually no purely "right" answers to difficult questions and to act as though there were is unrealistic.

2) The cause she aligns herself with is the child's right to know. "If children ask," she says, "they're entitled to an answer. These people (censors) want to go back to not being honest with children, but you can't go back, and you can't make the rest of the world go back with you."

3) Communication is everything. When children and parents talk, fear is diminished.

4) "Kids are their own best censors," she says. "Children don't read books, including mine, until they're ready." Bookstores support Blume in this claim.

In an age when we have serious reason to wonder whether books and reading will continue to attract young people who have grown up with television, we clearly need Judy Blume. Thousands of young readers who are hungry for understanding and affirmation particularly need her. "More than any other author, before or now," says Dorothy Broderick of Voice of Youth Advocates, "(Blume) knows that our real lives are first and foremost internal; only when we get ourselves together can we begin to share life with another person." Can anyone be against books that help us understand ourselves and each other?

THE *BIBLE*: SOURCE OF GREAT LITERATURE AND CONTROVERSY

Edward B. Jenkinson

"No other collection of books has influenced Western culture more than the Old Testament. No other collection has been printed in as many languages and in as many editions. No other collection is more worthy of study in the schools."

I first wrote those words 18 years ago in the Introduction to *Teaching the Old Testament in English Classes*. At that time, elective courses on the *Bible* as literature flourished in the public schools. James Ackerman, Thayer Warshaw, and others conducted summer institutes on, and wrote books about, teaching both the Old and New Testaments *as* and *in* literature. As they acquainted teachers with the rich and varied literature of the *Bible* that they considered appropriate for English classes, they also explained potential controversies and problems that might accompany such courses in the schools. For example, in the Introduction to the 1973 volume, I wrote:

> The writers have chosen the familiar term "Old Testament" for the literature to be covered. This is a Christian term for what is called simply "the *Bible*" (or *Tanach*) within the Jewish community. Whereas many Christians see the events recorded here (Abraham, Moses, Prophets) as culminating in the New Testament, Jews do not accept the implication that their sacred literature is "old" in the sense that it is superseded by a new revelation. Similarly, the commonly used B.C. (Before Christ) and A.D. (In the year of our Lord) are Christian terms; Jews, and many Christian scholars, prefer B.C.E. (Before the Common Era) and C.E. (Common Era). Teachers should be aware that all these terms are controversial; they would do well to explain their choices to their classes.

Choice is a key word for teachers to consider as they teach the *Bible* as literature in public schools. Although they might select a particular edition of the *Bible* as the class text, prudent teachers permit students to bring their own, or their families' *Bibles* to class. And although their courses might be entitled "The *Bible* as Literature," teachers can choose to include approaches to the *Bible as, in, and* literature, as well as the *Bible* and its *contexts,*

In *Handbook for Teaching the Bible in Literature Classes,* Warshaw illustrated how teachers might deal with the book of Job with each of the four approaches:

For the *Bible as* literature, the main activity would consist of analyzing the framing, characterization, recurring images and motifs, and the irony—verbal and situational—in the book of Job itself.

For the *Bible in* literature, the reading would consist of the book of Job and, for example, MacLeish's *J.B.* The class would analyze both, perhaps with an emphasis on the latter, and discuss the relationships between the two selections.

For the *Bible and* literature, the class might compare the book of Job with another literary treatment of the subject of unmerited suffering, such as Wilder's *The Bridge of San Luis Rev* or Voltaire's *Candide.*

For the *Bible* and its *contexts,* one might relate the book of Job to the historical and cultural climate of postexilic Israel, when many scholars think the book was put into its present form. (Warshaw then noted that he felt that any of the first three approaches is more appropriate for the teacher of English than the last.)

Teachers in the seventies prepared phase-elective courses that focused on the literature primarily of the Old Testament: the origins of humankind, the patriarchal legends, the story of Joseph, Moses and the Exodus, the fall of Jericho, Deborah, Gideon, Samuel, David, Solomon, Job, Ruth, Jonah, Esther, Daniel, proverbs, love songs, and psalms. Those selections represent a wide range of writing: folk tales, legends, history, fables, sagas, riddles, songs, laments, philosophy, short stories, and biography—and the list is not complete.

Several teachers told me that, while they recognized both the impact of the New Testament on Western civilization and the merits of its literature, they felt far more comfortable teaching the literature of the Old Testament because they thought they would be less likely to be challenged for their selections. A few said that they believed it would be difficult to teach New Testament literature without crossing the sometimes wavy line that separates church and state.

Elective courses on the *Bible* as literature began disappearing as phase-elective English programs fell victim to budget cuts and the back-to-basics movement. The rise in schoolbook protests in the early eighties also contributed, I believe, to the waning interest among teachers of English in Biblical literature. Many new and not just a few veteran teachers, and their school administrators, misinterpreted Supreme Court rulings on prayer and *Bible* reading in the schools. And their attitudes toward Biblical literature are sometimes reflected by their students. For example, it is not uncommon for a few pre-service teachers in my classes to believe that the *Bible* may not even be mentioned, let alone taught, in public schools. When I quote this passage from *Abington v. Schempp*, some students are shocked:

> It might well be said that one's education is not complete without a study of comparative religion or the history of religion and its relationship to the advancement of civilization. It certainly may be said that the *Bible* is worthy of study for its literary and historic qualities. Nothing we have said here indicates that such study of the *Bible* or of religion, when presented objectively as part of a secular program of education, may not be effected consistent with the First Amendment.

As I lecture throughout the nation about the schoolbook protest movement, I am no longer surprised when a few teachers tell me that they studiously avoid teaching any literature—Biblical or otherwise—that mentions God, Jesus, and prominent Biblical characters or that describes Western religions. Those teachers and their administrators have not read the Supreme Court decisions in their entirety and/or they have listened to ministers who denounce the teaching of comparative religion and of the *Bible* as literature. In one of a dozen debates I had with one of the founders of the Moral Majority, the minister told the audience that he read the first 346 pages of the book I wrote with Ackerman and Jenks and found 353 errors. In the rebuttal, I noted that he may have found 353 differences of interpretation or opinion. He then told the audience that no matter what I said about the *Bible* that I was wrong, giving as one example the fact that my co-authors and I had a section on "The Two Stories of Creation" in Genesis. He scoffed at my error while explaining to the audience that any true Biblical scholar recognized that there was only one story of creation in the *Bible*. He then chastised me for helping to write a book on teaching the Old Testament as literature, declaring that the "*Bible* should only be taught as the Word of God—never as anything else."

And the battle continues. The very people who condemn the schools for the literature that is taught also denounce the teaching of the *Bible* as literature—because they do not want it taught except from their point of view. They and other opponents of the *Bible* have intimidated some teachers and librarians to the extent that the mere presence of a *Bible* in a school library caused one young librarian to panic. She called a state librarian to announce that she had just found a copy of the *Bible* in the school library. "Whatever should I do with it?" the frantic librarian asked. The state librarian responded: "Catalog it and then read it."

Students can profit greatly from a close reading of Biblical literature. Not only will they become familiar with what many scholars call the most influential writings in the Western world, they will also become acquainted with the sources of many allusions and symbols in classical and contemporary literature. The *Bible* has been instrumental in shaping the content and style of imaginative writing from Caedmon, in the seventh century, through Milton in the seventeenth, to Faulkner, Golding and others in the twentieth.

But prominent writers are not the only ones who call upon the *Bible* for allusion, symbol, and metaphor. Many people compare friends and enemies to Biblical characters in everyday conversations. It is not uncommon to hear persons in a community compared to Samson, David, Goliath, Delilah, Cain, Abel, Deborah, or Jezebel. Nor it is uncommon for ordinary citizens as well as prominent writers to season their writings and conversations with Biblical quotations or references such as the following:

forbidden fruit (Gen. 3:1-6)

my brother's keeper (Gen. 4:9)
scapegoat (Lev. 16:8)
the apple of his eye (Deut. 32:10)
the voice of the people (I Sam. 8:7)
give up the ghost (Job 3:11)
Spare the rod and spoil the child. (Prov. 13:24)
Pride goeth before a fall. (Prov. 16:18)
Eat, drink, and be merry. (Eccel. 8:15)
Turn the other cheek. (Matt. 5:39)
Go the second mile. (Matt. 5:41)
crystal clear (Rev. 22:1)

The *Bible* continues to influence language, thought, the arts, and letters. Its importance *as* and *in* literature cannot be denied. Therefore, I repeat part of what I wrote at the beginning of this essay: "No other collection is more worthy of study in the schools."

WORKS CITED

Ackerman, James S., Alan Wilkin Jenks, and Edward B. Jenkinson. *Teaching the Old Testament in English Classes*. Bloomington: Indiana University Press, 1973.

Warshaw, Thayer. *Handbook for Teaching the Bible in Literature Classes*. Nashville: Abingdon, 1978.

THE *BIBLE* AND THE CONSTITUTION
Robert M. O'Neil

The use of the *Bible* in school and college courses presents distinctive problems of Church and State. It is of course a unique literary work, the study of which surely needs little justification. At the same time, the *Bible* is of course a book of scripture, with deep religious meaning for some (though not all) students. Not surprisingly, a separate body of law has evolved affecting the use of and teaching about the *Bible*.

We might begin our analysis of those legal issues with the school prayer and *Bible* reading cases of the early 1960s. One could go back further, for this was not the first time the Supreme Court dealt with religion and schools. But the pre-1960 cases—upholding reimbursement of parents for the cost of bussing children to parochial schools, and dealing with released and shared time programs—are not helpful on the issue before us. Thus we do best to begin with what seems the Supreme Court's first direct commentary on these questions.

The central issue in the 1962 cases was whether public schools could start the day with prayers and readings from scripture. That a majority of the Court said they could not, since such practices violate the Establishment Clause of the First Amendment and represent unwarranted governmental support of religion. But the Justices felt compelled to say something in passing about the role of religion.

Justice Clark, writing for the Court, observed that "the *Bible* is worthy of study for its literary and historical qualities" and added that a liberal education would be incomplete without some exposure to scripture. Justice Brennan, in a lengthy concurring opinion, was anxious to acknowledge that the Court had not barred all uses of religion in the schools. He reassured readers that "it would be impossible to teach meaningfully many subjects in the social sciences and humanities without some mention of religion."

Some states seized this invitation all too eagerly. A few months after the Court had spoken, Alabama decreed that devotional *Bible* study should be built into the curriculum as a regular course of study. That policy was challenged at once, and state courts found it to be a transparent violation of the spirit of the Supreme Court judgments. Other states adopted subtler measures—units or courses on comparative religion, or including a study of the role and content of the *Bible*, or increased emphasis on the role of the *Bible* in courses on world history and literature.

Only one early challenge reached a court high enough to yield a reported opinion. Curiously the case came from higher education. It involved an elective course on the *Bible* as Literature in the English Department at the University of Washington. A conservative religious organization, one of whose members had taken the course, sued the University claiming in part that such a course should not be offered at a public institution of higher learning. They also argued that the approach taken in the course collided with their religious views.

The Washington state courts upheld the University's inclusion of such a course in a broad curriculum. That would seem so easy a judgment as not to deserve much analysis—and so it would have been but for a 1931 Washington case holding that the state constitution forbade giving academic credit for any courses offered under religious auspices. It was thus necessary to distinguish the University elective from the situation to which the earlier case had been addressed—and that could be rather easily done by reconciling the Washington cases with the Supreme Court's approach to prayer and *Bible* reading.

It was not until the late 1970s that the issue returned to the courts in a relatively pure form. Two cases from Chattanooga offer valuable insight. Since 1922, the public schools had offered a *Bible* study course. Special *Bible* teachers had been assigned and paid by religious groups to go into the schools for this purpose. The courses were elective, and students took them only with parental approval. No grades in such courses were entered on any official transcripts. Proponents of the program argued that the emphasis in these courses was on the historic, literary and social content of the *Bible*. But since the teachers were sponsored by outside religious organizations, the federal courts found that religion was excessively intruded into the curriculum, and that the whole program therefore violated the Establishment Clause.

The court did, however, suggest that the religious impetus might be removed in such a way as to preserve the program. The school board took the hint, and redesigned the program as a public school offering. The teaching was now done by regular school teachers, and not by teachers sent in from outside. Six months later the issue came back to the court, and this time the program was upheld.

A somewhat similar case from Bristol, Virginia, reached the federal courts about six years ago, and seems to offer the latest word on *Bible* study in the schools. Since the Bristol course was virtually identical to that in Chattanooga, it met a similar fate in the courts. The judge did go on to suggest a framework within which a constitutionally valid program might be designed.

The suggested elements were essentially these: control and supervision of the course must be under public school auspices; teachers must be employed by the public schools on a regular basis; no inquiry could be made into the religious beliefs of the teachers; the curriculum and teaching materials must be selected by the school board; the course must be elective, with an alternative for all children not electing the *Bible* course; any private funds must be received unconditionally; and the course must be taught "in an objective manner, with no attempt made to indoctrinate the children as to either the truth or falsity of the biblical materials."

In these cases the issue is not so much that of special *Bible* courses, but rather the role of religion in the mainstream of the curriculum. In order to address that issue, we should now turn to several other settings in which the courts have been quite active during the last quarter century. Surely something must be said of creationism in the schools, and to that thorny question I would now like to turn.

We all know about the *Scopes* case. What we do not always appreciate is that the validity of the Scopes-type laws remained in doubt for some forty years thereafter. It was not until 1968 that the Supreme Court finally held that states may not bar the teaching of evolution. In fact the Arkansas law in question forbade teaching at all levels—including graduate courses at the University of Arkansas—that "mankind ascended or descended from a lower order of animals."

Even though teachers were subject to criminal sanctions for violation, the state courts upheld the law. A decisive majority of the Justices reversed that judgment, and found such a law to be in clear violation of the Establishment Clause. Its impetus and purpose were so plainly religious as to leave no doubt. There was simply no possible secular justification for a law that banned all references to the Darwinian theory of the origins of human life. The sole aim of such a law, said the Court, "is to blot out a particular theory because of its supposed conflict with the biblical account, literally read."

There matters stood until the last few years. Several states, notably Arkansas and Louisiana, passed so-called equal time or balanced treatment statutes. These laws required that if evolution is taught in the public schools, then equal time or balanced treatment must be given to something called "creation science." The new Arkansas law was wholly invalidated by a federal district judge in 1983, and the state did not appeal.

Louisiana did not give up so easily. That state took all the way to the Supreme Court the question whether it could require balanced treatment, and could offer something called creation science. The Justices gave the answer most observers had expected, with only Chief Justice Rehnquist and Justice Scalia dissenting. Justice Brennan, writing for the Court, called the legislature's claim of a secular purpose a "sham"; the law in effect required the teaching of a religious belief, and not a scientific study: "The preeminent purpose of the Louisiana legislature was clearly to advance the religious viewpoint that a supernatural being created humankind." There apparently ends the saga of creationism in the schools—although it is barely possible that proponents will devise yet another and more ingenious approach to including such material in the curriculum.

Between the Arkansas and Louisiana creationism cases the Supreme Court fashioned a more complex theory for determining when a practice violates the Establishment Clause. The test emerged in the parochial school aid cases, but applies here as well. It has three elements: First, a judgment of the purpose of the law or program; if the purpose is religious, then a court need look no further. The second criterion is that of effect;

even if the purpose is secular, a religious effect may still invalidate the law or program. A third hurdle remains.

Even if the purpose and effect are both secular, the law may still be shown to create excessive entanglement between religious and secular institutions—for example, through supervision of religious practices, or through involvement of religious personnel in an otherwise valid secular school program. It is the application of these three tests to practices and activities in the schools that has produced the litigation of the last two decades, and it is with these tests that we are still concerned.

Several issues remain for our consideration. One is the curiously perplexing question of what is in fact "religion." The cases are surprisingly few. Perhaps the most intriguing involved a pilot New Jersey program in the 1970s to bring into the public schools a unit on Transcendental Meditation—which, after careful review, the federal courts found to be religious in nature and thus not admissible to the curriculum.

Even when we know what "religion" is—and usually we do—other issues complicate deciding whether the use of religious material in public schools crosses the constitutional line. Let me illustrate briefly with one of the most important but neglected cases the Supreme Court has ever decided in this area. Ten years ago a citizen group in Kentucky took up a collection to post copies of the Ten Commandments in every public school classroom in the state. There was to be no public expense, and no special attention drawn to framed copies of the Commandments.

Another group of citizens went to court to enjoin this program, and eventually prevailed in the Supreme Court. The Justices did not even set the case down for oral argument, taking the rather unusual approach of reversing the lower court without argument, so clear did the issues seem to them. The discussion bears centrally on the topic before us, and thus may be worth quoting since it is relatively brief and sheds much light on the questions that concern us here:

> The pre-eminent purpose for posting the Ten Commandments on schoolroom walls is plainly religious in nature. The Ten Commandments is undeniably a sacred text in the Jewish and Christian faiths, and no legislative recitation of a supposedly secular purpose can blind us to that fact.

This is not a case in which the Ten Commandments are integrated into the school curriculum, where the *Bible* may constitutionally be used in an appropriate study of history, civilization, ethics, comparative religion or the like.... Posting of religious texts on the wall serves no educational function. If the posted copies of the Ten Commandments are to have any effect at all, it will be to induce the school children to read, meditate upon, perhaps to venerate and obey, the Commandments. However desirable this might be as a matter of private devotion, it is not a permissible state objective under the Establishment Clause.

One might conclude by returning to the cases most closely in point, those dealing with prayer and *Bible* reading. I would underscore the passing reference in those decisions to the *educational* role of scripture.

What emerges from this analysis is a sense that regular members of the instructional staff—curriculum-developers and teachers—may treat religion in their classes under three conditions: (a) if the emphasis is entirely secular and not sectarian; (b) if the materials are part of the regular instructional process of the school or the district; and (c) if the classroom experience could not be said in any other way to advance or inhibit religion. Whether as an educational matter these are reasonable and workable criteria is a judgment that must be left to experts close to the classroom and to pedagogy in the schools.

BLACK BOY (AMERICAN HUNGER): FREEDOM TO REMEMBER

Maryemma Graham and Jerry W. Ward, Jr.

CENSORSHIP. The word evokes the shouting down of speakers whose ideas are somehow ideologically incorrect, the destruction of printing presses, the spectacle of parents angry that school texts contain language and ideas pernicious to underaged Dick and Jane (which they already think of as ancient), bans on the exhibition of Mapplethorpe photographs, the Inquisition, special markings for motion pictures and rap compact discs, and the pyramid of books aflame. Ideas and images deemed offensive must be suppressed or hidden or destroyed. The censoring agents are either "legally" constituted policies regarding heresy, obscenity, and sedition, or instant spokespersons for community values. On the other hand, there is no reason censorship should not also bring to mind the idea of taking a census, of counting heads and thus accounting for population, for in classical Latin *censor* refers to one of two officials who took the census. It is profitable for readers of Richard Wright's *Black Boy*, either the first edition of 1945 or the unexpurgated Library of America edition of 1991 to consider options in positioning Wright's autobiography. The book might be suppressed in public school curricula on the grounds that it is morally (and politically) "dangerous." The greater danger is nurturing cultural illiteracy by denying students the opportunity to learn why *Black Boy* might free the mind to remember what the hypocrisy of censorship would conceal.

Recognizing the ambiguous reception that might be accorded *Black Boy*, we accepted the invitation to prepare a rationale or defense of the book. That the book is an autobiography, a record of childhood and youth, is crucial. Recreating and inscribing himself in a particularized moment of American history from angles available to an African American male, Wright did not intend to corrupt, scandalize, or blaspheme but rather to illustrate how obscene was denial of access to full participation in the democratic process by law, custom, and the practice of race. One need not prepare, except as a supplement, a rationale for *Black Boy;* the autobiography embodies its own defense.

Discovering the book's rationale against censorship does require the effort to understand that the primal causes in the making of the book were Wright's analytic intelligence and the cultivated hell the United States was for black Americans between 1900 and 1945, and to some extent continues to be despite the illusion of progress. The rationale for the autobiography is the same we attribute to any work we conclude is liberating; it provides a necessary language for the mysteries of *human existence* that manifest themselves in the rhetoric of dream and nightmare.

The claim that *Black Boy* is liberating, even mythical, is not to be taken as an assertion that the book explains much more than the universal potentials of the person who is socialized to be black and male in a racist society. Richard Wright selected those he deemed most representative of his own life experiences from a range of such potentials. At the risk of being simple, we must remind readers that *Black Boy* speaks specifically for Wright. And Wright speaks specifically for a very distinct community, a fact that he made explicit in his January 26, 1940 acceptance speech before the Springarn Award Committee. At the beginning of the speech, Wright said:

> It is with a deep sense of responsibility that I accept the Springarn Medal. I accept it in the name of the stalwart, enduring millions of Negroes whose fate and destiny I have sought to depict, in terms of narrative and scene, in imaginative fiction. It cannot be otherwise, for they are my people, and my writing—which is my life and which carries my convictions—attempts to mirror their struggles for freedom during these troubled days.
>
> [from a typescript of the speech given to Maryemma Graham by Julia Wright]

These were and still are powerful words, and they should remind us that

Wright, saw the world through his own terrifying set of experiences, just as most writers relate to their experiences.

The significance of the book as commentary on other black American males changes according to a reader's affinities, social experiences, associations and knowledge of literary conventions. As Ralph Ellison informed readers, *Black Boy* is Richard Wright's blues. Attempts to condemn or censor Wright's autobiography for its negative portrayal of black males and females are perhaps misreadings of a hypertextual kind, insufficiently attentive to genre and to the "facts" of race and gender at the time of the book's composition. To remove the book from the material complexity in which it was formed serves to further conceal the dynamics of the specific historical and intellectual processes which inform the work's production and transmission. It is precisely the "facts" of race and gender in the United States that help us probe the sociohistorical matrix of this important work.

On the other hand, autobiography is not sociology, however rich its sociological implications might be. The abused male, playing subject to his own objectification, has the options of *accommodating* oppression, *becoming* the destructive and self-destructive rebel, or *resisting* through a spiraling quest for the safe space where integrity, balance, and wholeness might be achieved. In Wright's first published novel, *Native Son*, Bigger becomes the destructive and self-destructive rebel, whose quest for wholeness is accomplished through means more criminal than rational. In *Black Boy* is a record, one man's record, partially authentic and partially fictional, of the achievement of the safe space, with integrity and balance intact; it is a wholeness based on self-control and discipline. Wright exercises other options for the recorded memory of his own life than those he had chosen for *Native Son.*

The rather graphic portrait of an abused male child, together with his presentation of his parents' failure to fulfill their responsibility, creates sufficient justification for Wright's predisposition toward extreme individualism, self-reliance, and non-conformity. His growth experiences stress the need for self-discovery, about himself, as the representative voice of all black boys and girls, and about the society in which he lived. It can be argued that as an artist Wright highlighted the negativity of *accommodating* and *becoming* in order to strengthen the act of *transcending resistance* that is *Black Boy*.

The book is a trace of Wright's exploitation of outsideness, Wright's prowess in manipulating language and its codes. Part of the success of this manipulation is demonstrated by his ability to subvert the discourse of the dominant culture and bring it under the terms of his own control. Nowhere is this clearer than in his strategy for borrowing books from the segregated public library in Memphis. Not only does he "forge" (the dual meaning seems intentional) his own notes to borrow the books, but he names himself "nigger" to insure his success:

> That afternoon I addressed myself to forging a note. Now, what were the names of books written by H. L. Mencken? I did not know any of them. I finally wrote what I thought would be a foolproof note: Dear Madam: Will you please let this nigger boy—I used the word "nigger" to make the librarian feel that I could not possibly be the author of the note—*have some books by H. L. Mencken?* I forged the white man's name. (235)

Using quite personal angles, Wright insured that readers would honestly confront what is endemic in a closed society.

Black Boy establishes its one justification in the sense that George Orwell's *1984*, Aldous Huxley's *Brave New World*, and Ray Bradbury's *Fahrenheit 451* do. These books invite us to imaginatively recreate the experience of living within closed systems. It tells us much about social breakdown and disorder in American life with a vividness sociological writing cannot provide. It valorizes the enduring importance of slave narrative, for example, as a genre for understanding the insights and aspirations of the oppressed, a genre that has always named the lie upon which American society has and continues to batten: the beautiful and truly noble democratic theories of life, liberty and the pursuit of happiness. The reality for a substantial number of Americans has been death, unfreedom, and the flight from despair. *Black Boy* performs the Latinate role of accounting.

Black Boy is a critique of American optimism betrayed. In the context of Wright's autobiography, the myth of optimism in democracy and what some members of the democratic state decide it is important for other members to never know and experience. What is it in *Black Boy* that is so horrible that the book should be censored? The accusing finger directed at democratic principles that failed?

The reaction of Pete Trussell of Jackson, Mississippi to *Native Son* provides clues for anticipating reactions to *Black Boy*. Let us assume that Trussell is one of a growing body of parents who make censorship challenges, part of a movement well documented in the American Library Association's Office of Intellectual Freedom survey of secondary school librarians for the years 1986-89. In his letter to the editor of *The Clarion-Ledger* (February 24, 1992), Trussell is concerned that the National Endowment for the Humanities awarded a grant to the Mississippi Authority for Educational Television to produce a documentary on Wright's life. Wright, after all, authored books that included "profanity and racially offensive language," "accounts of fornication and adultery," "alcohol abuse by minors," and "sympathy toward the Communist Party." And Trussell feels "very strongly about our underage children being required to read material of this type in public schools." The scenario of attempted censorship ended well, according to the *Clarion-Ledger* of May 19, 1992.

> Pete Trussell...objected to *Native Son*, by Richard Wright, being required reading for all 10th-graders because of foul language and violence.

> Trussell, whose daughter, Jennifer, attends Wingfield High School, first objected to the novel in November. Since then, a committee of parents, students, teachers and principals have reviewed the book and recommended it remain on the required reading list but that it be taught in the 11th grade.

> Trussell was told [by the Jackson School Board] that district policy allows students to choose an alternative to a book they find offensive.

In this instance, all freedoms—the freedom to read, the freedom to object, the freedom to choose—were preserved. Jennifer may have chosen to read

Gone With the Wind.

What is potentially offensive in *Black Boy* may be profane language and violence, but the function of profanity and violence is a double-edged sword, wounding the "self" in the autobiography as it pierces a reader's consciousness of racism's systemic operations. At one level, these cultural dynamics preclude the book's being a proper target of censorship. In writing *Black Boy,* Wright intended, among other things, to exercise his First Amendment rights. He did so with such power that his book is internationally acknowledged as a classic among American autobiographies, particularly in its depiction of the forces in American society that participated in constructing, to borrow James Baldwin's marvelous phrasing, "a low ceiling of actual possibilities" for young black males. That which can be verified by the traditional, rigorous procedures of historical and sociological scholarship does not warrant censorship. It is not far afield to speculate that those who would wound Richard Wright symbolically through the censorship of *Black Boy* share some values with those who wounded the author more directly in his lifetime.

The Trussells of our world are not driven by any passionate attention to literature that may lead to the discovery of a "truth." They would have tremendous difficulty understanding that what may be profane and violent in the text of *Black Boy* is an objective correlative of the very conditions the book seeks to address. For example, Wright would not have conveyed the autobiographical truth had he written "Crush that Negro boy's testicles, Harrison!" rather than "Crush that nigger's nuts, nigger!" (Chapter XII). Instead, the Trussells of the world proceed as naive readers with God on their side, confusing parts with wholes, the surface features of a text with the thick descriptions being evoked, what is only a reference to immorality with what is genuinely so. Their motives are not literary, but they are nevertheless embroiled with interpretation and the political economy of which literature is a part. They are not seeking out proper targets for censorship (if indeed any symbolic expression can be legally censored after the 1992 Supreme Court ruling on a St. Paul, Minnesota ordinance on hate speech and its 1989 decision regarding the Flag Protection Act), but rather any material which they deem offensive or disagreeable. Their concern is very noticeable if the material in question is used in publicly funded activities, especially in education. Those who appoint themselves guardians of public morals and social values will always provide us with occasions for justifying the potentially redemptive value of such books as *Black Boy*.

As we suggested earlier, much of the value of *Black Boy* is located in its providing engaging ways for us to think about how our lives are shaped by law and custom, by interracial encounters and intraracial negotiations, by desire and psychological defeat and intrepidity, by American dreams and nightmares. The entire text of *Black Boy (American Hunger)*, now available in the Library of America edition, challenges our stereotypical thinking about South and North. In Part I, "Southern Night" (Chapters I-XIV), the autobiographical self learns that his people "grope at noonday as in the night," believing in a better world up North. In Part II, "The Horror and the Glory" (Chapters XV-XX), Northern exposure results in the self's "knowing that all I possessed were words and a dim knowledge that my country had shown me no examples of how to live a human life" (364-365). There is no hiding place in regional differences. But what perhaps touches us most deeply, whether we are tender students or hardened adults, are the concluding words of *Black Boy:*

> I would hurl words into this darkness and wait for an echo and if an echo sounded, no matter how faintly, I would send other words to tell, to march, to fight, to create a sense of the hunger for life that gnaws in us all, to keep alive in our hearts a sense of the inexpressibly human. (365)

In the humanistic affirmation of this conclusion is a foreshadowing of the charge several decades later to ask not what our country could do for us, but rather what we might do for our country. If *Black Boy* is read and taught intelligently as the affirmative *literary and social* critique that it is, valid reasons for wanting to censor the book will indeed be far to seek, despite the unholy alliance between the racism of the radical right and the political correctness of the conservative left. *Black Boy* is a catalyst for the freedom to remember.

WORKS CITED

"Jackson Public School Action." (Jackson, Mississippi) *Clarion-Ledger*, 19
    May 1992: 5B.

Trussell, Pete. "Letter to the Editor." (Jackson, Mississippi) *Clarion-Ledger*,
    24 February 1992: 6A.

Wright, Richard. "Acceptance Speech—Springarn Award Committee."
    January 26, 1946.

Wright, Richard. *Black Boy (American Hunger)* in *Richard Wright: Later
    Works*. New York: Library of America, 1991.

BLACK LIKE ME:
IN DEFENSE OF A RACIAL REALITY
Walter C. Farrell, Jr.

John Howard Griffin's *Black Like Me* took America by storm in 1960. For it was the first, and to date only, book in which a white American "literally" entered the skin of a Negro and articulated to the world the Negro's struggle for freedom, equality, and dignity. Griffin's personal odyssey in several states of the old Confederacy was unique in that it enabled a white person to view the race problem from the "inside looking out" instead of from the "outside looking in." He was able to capture the raw, genuine feelings of both Negroes and whites as they were buffeted by the peculiar system of "Jim Crow" segregation. His experience served to strip an unjust situation of all of its pretensions and rationales.

However, during the two previous decades, black and white writers had objectively explicated the race problem via fiction and sociological and anthropological inquiries. Beginning in 1940, Richard Wright pricked the national conscience with his riveting tale of a Negro protagonist's (Bigger Thomas) birth, degradation and execution in the classic novel, *Native Son*. This was followed in 1941 by *Deep South*, by Allison Davis, et. al., a socioanthropological study that showed how the Negro adapted to the mandates of the southern caste system while still striving to maintain a sense of self-worth and a modicum of hope for the future. In 1944, Gunnar Myrdal, the Swedish economist, produced the magnum opus, *An American Dilemma*, which was touted as the most comprehensive study of the totality of the Negro's problem in American Democracy. Finally, Ralph Ellison's award winning *Invisible Man* (1952) fictionalized the Negroes' virtual invisibility in their adopted land—their inability to get white America to recognize or to accept their essential humanity.

This was the backdrop against which *Black Like Me* was conceived.

For by 1959 both black and white writers had established the parameters of the race problem in all of its statistical and human complexity. Griffin, at first intent on conducting a research study, decided instead to transform his pigmentation from white to brown so that he might personally endure the pain and suffering of his Negro brothers. When first released, *Black Like Me* was hailed by the critics and damned by many segments of the public. In 1960 many white Americans were still trying to hold on to the status quo. The 1954 *Brown* decision, which ushered in school desegregation, was still limited in its impact. Martin Luther King, Jr. was only then beginning to establish a national and international reputation, and the freedom riders had not entered the South. Black was not yet beautiful, and the cauldrons of northern and southern ghettos had not yet boiled over. In short, there were few manifestations of national concern about racial discrimination. *Black Like Me*, in its poignant portrayal of the absurdity and injustice inherent in southern black/white relations, forced America to look at the problem anew. No longer could it be said that liberal whites and angry blacks had overstated the case or that "egghead" scholars did not really understand the uniqueness of southern race relations. The traditional defenses had been laid bare since a southerner had captured the incongruity of racial discrimination.

White readers who considered themselves decent, godfearing citizens were embarrassed by the stark, authentic revelations. Those who had psychologically constructed a harmonious world of blacks and whites living happily in their castle-like places were faced with a discomforting state of dissonance. Therefore, it is obvious why someone who endorses censorship would object to *Black Like Me*.

The most frequent objections to Griffin's work have been that it did not accurately reflect the reality of the southern social situation and that its publication only served to create and to inflame racial antagonisms and was, perhaps, inspired by radicals, communists or agitators.

Upon entering the Negro world as a Negro, Griffin was struck by the overwhelming immediacy of second-class citizenship. As a Negro, he found that his primary concern was the white man and how to get along with him. Somehow, he had to find a way to hold his own as a man and to raise himself in the esteem of whites without for one moment letting them think that they had any God-given rights that he did not also possess. The reality of the Negro's plight was that he was not really treated "as a second-class citizen, but as a tenth-class one" (47). Nowhere was this more evident than in the pattern of economic injustice. Even when Negroes prepared themselves, they could not get jobs commensurate with their education or capabilities. College graduation still left them with a long hard pull as most had to take postal, teaching or preaching jobs. Many came to accept the fact that they were not going to ever quite manage. Consequently, a lot of them just gave up. They learned to take what they could, often in pleasure or wild gestures, because they had absolutely nothing to lose.

At the same time whites used these behavior patterns as a *raison d' etre* for denying Negroes first-class citizenship. Negroes were consigned to the lowest stratum of society and then blamed for being at that point in the social order. This oppressive circular reality worked to depress individual initiative and fostered intraracial conflicts as Negroes, disillusioned by their lack of progress, often turned on each other. The Negro, as a consequence, encountered a double problem. "First, the discrimination against him. Second, and almost more grievous his discrimination against himself; his contempt for blackness that he associat[ed] with his suffering; his willingness to sabotage his fellow Negroes because they [were] part of the blackness he...found so painful" (44).

To be a Negro, Griffin discovered, required the continual sufferance of a series of small, incremental indignities, whose cumulative weight seared one's very soul. One had to adjust to maintaining a genial countenance so as not to offend any white who might equate sullenness with a breach of the deferential status assigned to the Negro. If hungry, one had to be certain that he was always in close proximity to a Negro establishment or risk being rebuffed at any other. In public one had to stay constantly on the move, unless permitted to remain idle by a white, to avoid being monitored or harassed by the police. And if one mastered all of these balancing acts on his daily tightrope of life, he had to always reconcile himself to the fact that any white reserved the right to simply "cut the rope" for no good reason.

Thus, the Negroes' only respite from utter hopelessness was their belief—the belief of their forebears—that these insults and degradations were not directed at them personally, but directed against Negroes in general. "His mother or aunt...long ago...prepared him, explaining that he as an individual [could] live in dignity, even though he as a Negro [could not]" (48). Nevertheless, these assaults on the Negroes' personhood had a wrenching impact for they gave them a view of the white man that the white man never understood. Although the Negro was part of the black mass, the whites were always individuals and had sincerely felt that they had been fair and kind. Moreover, they were surprised and "offended to find Negroes suspicious of them, never realizing that the Negro [could not] understand how...whites as a group [could]...contrive to arrange life so that it destroy[ed] the Negro's sense of personal value...deaden[ed] the fiber of his being" (48).

And when Negroes or whites dared to question the injustice of it all, they were immediately branded as traitors, communists or agitators. Any enlightened move toward racial justice was viewed as "Zionist-inspired, Satan inspired, Illuminati-inspired...part of some secret conspiracy to overthrow Christian civilization" (43). If one wanted to be a good southern Christian, one dared not act like one. It was felt that the very first time Negroes were given the right to vote, to have decent employment, to have a decent home and to receive a quality education that this would lead to a mongrelization of civilization and thus prove to be the ruination of America. People were afraid that doing the right and decent thing was in effect aiding the communist conspiracy. Good white people who harbored no ill will against the Negro were cowered into tacitly supporting this insane contradiction. The system fed on itself.

But Griffin does not offer this odyssey as an indictment against southern peers but only to facilitate the coming together of good and decent persons of both races who were trying to bridge this abyss of hate and despair with understanding and compassion. By lancing this boil of racial distrust and enmity and allowing the contents to spew into the public consciousness, Griffin sought to enhance communication, at a peer level, across racial lines.

Black Like Me is one of the thirty most frequently censored books throughout America (Robinson 10). Referred to as the "dirty thirty" by several scholars, these books have been banned based on objections to the moral values, religious ideas, violence and racial ideas that they examine. *Black Like Me,* in its explication of the viscera of the Southern racial situation in the late 1950s, provides an appropriate baseline from which to assess racial progress during the past quarter century. Griffin's rendering of this unsavory part of the American past is sensitive and balanced. The picture he draws, although graphic in its detail, neither paints all blacks as saints nor all whites as sinners; he does an excellent job of capturing the hopes, fears and stereotypes of both groups.

In the Stygian night of racial intolerance, Griffin is able to provide us with beacons of racial progress. This work's primary value is that it is able to uncover—often in obtuse and indirect ways—the humanity of both blacks and whites. While the Negro was locked in racial bondage, whites were constrained by psychological shackles, often not knowing why. Though the book presents elements of pessimism and numerous human tragedies, it is uplifting in the sense that it does present hope for the future. As fact, the book's purpose is to articulate the contradiction and irrationality of racist behavior in order to stimulate change. Its appeal to the essential decency of white Americans was, in part, reinforced via the non-violent resistance against racial discrimination led by Dr. Martin Luther King, Jr. Griffin, simply, was advocating only "that this country rid itself of the racism that prevented some citizens from living as fully functioning men and as a result dehumanized all men" (185). He poked holes in the shields of patriotism, religion and innate racial inferiority that many Americans had used to justify the Negro's oppression. Moreover, the long suffering heroes in this book emerge from both the victim and oppressor classes. While many Negroes succumbed to the weight of subjugation, numerous whites were destroyed socially and financially for just being fair.

What Griffin shows us throughout his odyssey is a consistent "conspiracy of resistance" by Negroes and whites, as well, to the mandated system of racial inequality. The reader is presented on the one hand with a poor black sawmill worker, living on the financial edge and ensnared in the trap of discrimination, holding on to his dignity and aspirations for his family and, on the other, with a white newspaperman who refused to prostitute his conscience or his paper in defense of racial injustice. Both these men, unknown to each other, were engaged in their own little conspiracies against the system of segregation. These parallels and others throughout the book offer the most compelling reason for the inclusion of *Black Like Me* in our school libraries and on reading lists throughout our nation. We are shown passionately, but without hyperbole, that America's historical struggle with the race question has been a biracial one, that in the depths of "inhumanity and indecency" there are sterling examples of "humanity and decency"—those tenets of our experience by which we define ourselves and become whole. But even more important is the opportunity for the reader to understand the tortuous complexity of racial injustice. White bigots, moderates and liberals are shown to be as much victims of the process as are the Negroes. To the extent that this work can assist readers in understanding that America's racial problems are more than the contrast of good against evil, we shall all have been better served.

In addition, since all is not yet equal in the body politic, *Black Like Me* provides valuable lessons as to how we can proceed in general to make equality a reality. The specific examples that Griffin presents can aid all Americans in being more sensitive about racial stereotypes, well-meaning paternalistic initiatives and the destructive social and psychological impact of assessing people solely on the basis of their skin color, whether it be black, white, brown, red or yellow. The structure of the book, a diary/journal format, also makes for easy reading; high school students, in particular, should find this approach easy to follow, especially the slow readers. Unlike the situation in many of the books examining America's racial problems, racial epithets—nigger, ofay, etc.—are used sparingly and do not intrude upon the narrative, and the writing is simple, direct and devoid of excessive jargon. The early arguments against teaching this book, racial inaccuracy and inflammation of racial passions, have paled over time. In the years since the book first appeared, there has been substantial, if not herculean, progress in American black/white relations. This fact in itself offers a solid justification for the reading and teaching of *Black Like Me* as it reminds us of from whence we have come and where we might wish to go in the area of societal equity.

Black Like Me can be profitably utilized in high school social science and literature classes in a focus on the human condition. In an increasingly desegregated American school system as compared to that at the time of the writing of this book, black and white youngsters can be guided in an honest exploration of the society in which they have lived and of the one which they will shape themselves. Black and white students can use this work as a prism through which to assess and refine their own views of American race relations. Most will find the vast majority of the racial injustices foreign to their personal experiences, and this can only bode well for the future of our country. Furthermore, the virulent indignities and injustices outlined by Griffin can be compared to and contrasted with the often subtle, insensitive racial slights of today. Students can come to appreciate the need to be respectful of individual, social and cultural differences. Are most whites racist? Are most blacks too defensive about their racial background? Has discrimination been almost eliminated? These are the questions that can be addressed in group discussions attendant to the reading of this book.

The most significant and productive use of *Black Like Me* is to apprise the reader of our ability to move forward in our national life. Social and racial progress subsequent to Griffin's experience has resulted in the dismantling of many of the barriers between the races. Several vestiges remain, however, and *Black Like Me* affirms the *irreversibility* of movement toward equality. There is really greater hope now for all Americans to have the opportunity to pursue the fullness of life, liberty and happiness. At the time of Griffin's sojourn into the black experience, despair was the modal outlook of the Negro; that feeling has been replaced, in large measure, by "something solid on which to build" (208), a basis which says that black people will continue to move toward being an integral part of our nation in every aspect of its life.

The often harsh realism of *Black Like Me* enables its readers to grapple with and learn from a personal experience that encompasses what the late W.E.B. Dubois labeled one of the most trenchant problems of twentieth century America—the problem of the color line. Finally, it is exceedingly important that both minority and majority citizens allow the maximum freedom for racially uncomfortable books and other materials. Whites have to be as tolerant of *Black Like Me* as blacks have to be of *The Adventures of Huckleberry Finn*. Both groups will have to fight "what they perceive" as inappropriate stereotypes, and distortions of reality, *not* by suppression but "by presenting counterviews with vigor and clarity" (O'Neil 10). Books that present uncomfortable racial ideas *must* be fully explored in the classrooms of our nation so that we can understand them in the context of American history (Editorial 6). We have to be inordinately careful in circumscribing any aspect of any American's access to allegedly controversial materials if we are desirous of maintaining freedom for ourselves.

NOTES

In order to remain faithful to the context of *Black Like Me* (1960), the term Negro is often used instead of black. It is recognized that the latter term (or the label, African-American) is the preferred contemporary designation for Americans of African descent.

WORKS CITED

Davis, Allison, Burleigh B. Gardner, and Mary R. Gardner. *Deep South*. Chicago: The University of Chicago Press, 1941.

Ellison, Ellison. *Invisible Man*. New York: Random House, Inc., 1952.

Griffin, John Howard. *Black Like Me*. Boston: Houghton Mifflin Company, 1960.

"Missing Huck Finn's Message." Editorial. *Milwaukee Journal* 30 Sept 1984: 6 (Accent on the News).

Myrdal, Gunnar. *An American Dilemma*. New York: Harper and Row Publishers, 1944.

O'Neil, Robert M. "Some Second Thoughts on the First Amendment," *Sims Lecture*. University of New Mexico (Feb 25, 1982): 10.

Robinson, Lorin R. "Scholars to Defend 'Dirty 30' Books." *Milwaukee Journal* 28 Aug 1984: 2, 10.

Wright, Richard. *Native Son*. New York: Harper and Row, Publishers, 1940.

BLESS THE BEASTS AND CHILDREN BY GLENDON SWARTHOUT

Sue Ellen Bridgers

From the first paragraph, indeed the first sentence, of Glendon Swarthout's *Bless the Beasts and Children*, the reader is aware of the writer's enormous literary gifts. A novel of such psychological impact and emotional intensity as this one must rely on the writer's technical skills as much as on the story itself. Swarthout, a successful novelist before the 1970 publication of *Bless the Beasts and Children*, proved himself more than adequate to the task of bringing this tale to life. *Bless the Beasts and Children* is beautifully constructed.

It is the story of six teenage boys, rich kids sent to an expensive summer camp in Arizona which advertises "Send Us a Boy—We'll Send You a Cowboy" for a price of $1600 which is steep for the economy of the late 1960s. These boys, ranging in age from fifteen to twelve, are at Box Canyon Camp for a variety of reasons: John Cotton's mother, who is in her fourth marriage, doesn't want to be reminded by a teenage son that she's not so young anymore; Lawrence Teft who hot-wires cars and tries to open the plane's emergency exit at 3500 feet is expected to profit from the rigid, rule-oriented atmosphere; Sammy Shecker, compulsive eater and nailbiter with a famous Jewish comedian for a father, is described as "the screech of chalk on slate"; Gerald Goodenow suffers from panic attacks and wets his bed, symptoms of emotional problems about which his step-father is unsympathetic; and the Lally brothers, Stephen and Billy, dislike each other intensely and have parents who don't want children interfering in their cyclical split-ups and reconciliations.

The boys' past histories are described in short vignettes interspersed in the action and defined by italics. Since the action of the book occurs over one night during the seventh week of camp, other pertinent information about camp life and the boys' experience during the seven weeks are also revealed in italicized flashbacks. This technique, while not frequently used in literary works, has advantages for the book's teenage readership. The transitions are simplified by the italics and the lyrical quality of the book, which makes it of higher literary quality than most boys are used to reading, is consistently maintained.

There can be no question about the literary merits of this book. The language is rich, metaphorical and lyrical. Swarthout is a serious writer with a serious subject. There is no sloth here and so the demands on the reader are strenuous and yet the story itself is so compelling that a decent but reluctant reader could find himself or herself caught up in the action and willing to embrace the rich language they might, in a lesser story, find problematic. This book will improve a young person's reading skills.

The story itself is compelling. The day before the action, the boys have been on an overnight camping expedition and on the way back to camp, they talk their young supervisor into stopping at a buffalo preserve near Flagstaff. While there they watch with horror while three buffalo at a time are herded into a pen and shot by amateur hunters who have paid a registration fee for the opportunity to shoot big game. This is a method of thinning the herd but it is abjectly unsportsmanlike in its application. The boys watch as the trapped animals are maimed by the inept "hunters" and then shot over and over again, dying agonizing, graphically described deaths. They learn that ninety buffalo will be slaughtered over a three day period and that this is the second day. Swarthout's description of the deaths of these animals is painfully vivid, leaving no doubt of the boys' identity with the animals, these most majestic and indigenous of all the species. Swarthout writes in what can be called a Song for the Buffalo:

> There was more here than mere destruction. The American soul was involved, its anthropology.... We are born with buffalo blood upon our hands. In the prehistory of us all, the atavistic beasts appeared. They graze the plains of our subconscious, they trample through our sleep, and in our dreams we cry out our damnation.... A living buffalo mocks us. It has no place or purpose. It is a misbegotten child, a monster with which we cannot live and which we cannot live without.

The boys don't really plan the ensuing expedition to free the thirty remaining buffalo but when the youngest among them, twelve year old Billy Lally, takes off alone in the night, they follow him and eventually decide to join him. Through the italicized flashbacks the reader learns of the indignities of camp life that have brought them to this moment. They are all rejects from home and from their original camp cabins as well. In a camp hierarchy exemplified by cabin names like Apaches, Navajo, and Sioux, they are the Bedwetters, the lowest of the low, and their trophy which is to be kept until another cabin drops below them in camp skills, is a chamber pot. Is there any doubt they will sympathize with the buffalo? What is at once surprising and reasonable is that they would in the course of their overnight expedition become a coherent group, a band of boys aware of each other's individual strengths, pulling together for the common good. As their ragged band coalesces, each of them becomes whole.

Why is this book in question for young adult readers? The explicit language is quite mild, nothing like what teachers assure me they are apt to hear in the halls of their schools. Cotton, the group's inadvertent leader, thinks to himself early in their quest, "They were crazy as hell" and then thinks: "He must quit swearing. He no longer needed it, nor did they." The implication is, of course, that swearing is a sign of weakness inappropriate for men intent on such an undertaking as theirs.

Authority is defied. In flashbacks, the reader learns that the Bedwetters eventually obtained the other teams' trophies by tricking them, and they also took horses and rode to a drive-in movie they'd been denied because of the rigidity of the camp system. This is not a camp that achieves success by inspiring good will and confidence in its campers. Its atmosphere is demeaning at best. A reader with almost any level of sensitivity would support the Bedwetters' attempts at achieving dignity.

Their greatest adventure is, of course, letting free the buffalo and the bulk of the book involves achieving this goal. They take horses and a .22 rifle from the camp. They steal a truck. They shoot out the tire of some men who harass them along the way. They trespass. They also walk many miles without food or rest; they find unexpected courage in themselves and they accomplish their goal at great personal sacrifice. They free the beasts.

This story could be a fable were it not for the facts. In the sixties, some western states did thin their herds by this inhumane method. But this story is not about the buffalo; it's about the boys and about how they become something larger than themselves. In acknowledging their individual strengths and their need for others, they became a support system that will sustain them in times to come. None of these boys can hope for a happy life immediately following this night. At the very least, they are in serious trouble with the camp management, their parents, and perhaps the law. The writer leaves them there on the Mongollon Rim in Arizona, one of their number lost forever, the authorities closing in and yet the courage they have shown portends the potential for continuing courage, for adult lives well lived.

Perhaps more important than the reason for the boys' quest is the growth experiences that occur along the way. This is a quixotic adventure. These kids don't intend to change the world or even change the regulations that make such an atrocity possible. They just want to free thirty buffalo.

Perhaps Swarthout intended this quest as a metaphor for the personal journey each boy takes. From my own writing experience, I can say that frequently the writer is aware of such connections only subconsciously. Whatever Swarthout's intention, the metaphor is there for the reader. Ironically, because the boys find something that matters beyond themselves, they begin to discern their own worth. They start casting off the anti-social, neurotic, self-defeating behavior that has plagued them.

The attempt to prove themselves that began when they successfully finished a hike in the Grand Canyon and Cotton heaved the chamber pot over the edge of the canyon is completed when Cotton himself is hurled over the rim of the Mongollon Rim in the last moments of the book. If he purposefully drove the truck over the edge or if the brakes failed, they would never know. The buffalo were free, the boys were free, too, except for the knowledge that Cotton was lost to them. It "cracked their hearts even as it freed them, too, forever."

I first read this book when it was published in 1970 and I have remembered it all these years because of the richness of the language, the poignancy of the lives revealed, and the story itself which is startlingly refreshing even today. In the *Library Journal* of March, 1970, Charles Pipes wrote this "unusual novel is one of the best fictional studies of adolescence this reviewer has read in some time." In the *Saturday Review* of May 2, 1970, reviewer Brian Garfield wrote: *"Bless the Beasts and Children* is a compassionate book, a true book, a book of the heart.... Glendon Swarthout has added something fine and important to the literature of our age." *The New York Times Book Review* and *Booklist* offered high praise and the editors of *School Library Journal* listed it as one of the Best Books of the Year in 1970. Twenty years later, it remains a book of timely importance.

Bless the Beasts and Children is a valuable reading experience for the young adult reader. The writing itself, the gifts of language and sustained tone, make it a wonderful study of style. The story is compelling and if, for some, shocking, I would remind you of Proposition Four of the American Library Association's Freedom to Read document:

> We cut off literature at the source if we prevent serious artists from dealing with the stuff of life. Parents and teachers have a responsibility to prepare the young to meet the diversity of experience in life to which they will be exposed as they have a responsibility to help them learn to think critically for themselves.

Bless the Beasts and Children is an opportunity for critical thinking and for exciting, insightful dialogue. The merits of style should outweigh any protestation concerning selective wording. The characters and the compelling events that changed their lives will challenge young people to think about the choices they make in their own lives. *Bless the Beasts and Children* offers the reader a study of humanity that can enrich personal perspective and increase reading skills at the same time. What more can we ask of a book?

THE RELEVANCE OF *BRAVE NEW WORLD*
Robert M. Adams

When he published *Brave New World* in 1932, at the depths of the great depression, Aldous Huxley was cutting sharply across several different social currents. At a time when the world's economic machinery had broken down entirely, he ventured to show that even if it worked perfectly, the society it produced would be a nightmare. He held up to withering scorn the sacred cow of science—or at least the applied scientism of mill and marketplace. He, the grandson of the great Victorian biologist, T. H. Huxley, showed that the vision of a rationally planned society would lead to a heartless, hypocritical swindle; the very idea of a world designed for the greatest comfort of the greatest number was a recipe for mindless mediocrity. Indeed, the sexual promiscuity of society in the sixth century After Ford was an important part of the book, a spot of color even more gaudy than the technology; but the actual scenes of sexual practice were very much muted—at least by today's standards. (We are over half a century into the After Ford era, and already reality has surpassed satire in this respect at least.) When one adds that there's a strong religious streak in the book—the emptiness of a world without God, the horror of a society without supernatural sanctions being repeatedly emphasized—an exploratory reader may well wonder what censorship could find to object to in so conservative and moralistic a book.

In fact, Huxley underwent a common fate of moralists; by describing too vividly the awful corruptions of an existence centered on physical pleasure, he made that existence unduly attractive. How intentional this exaggeration was is hard to say. Undoubtedly the fleshpots of a civilization far in the distant future were highlights that his fictional composition demanded. Herds of identical girls all trained from conception to total promiscuity and equipped with contraceptive cartridge belts provided striking features of the New World landscape—more so in some respects than soma-holidays, feelies, glittering skyscrapers, and helicopter-taxicabs. To heighten the lush exoticism of this decadent civilization, much of it was to be experienced by a particularly innocent observer—a savage brought up amid New Mexican primitives on a diet of Shakespeare's most violent and jealous plays, but with a number of ascetic and masochistic hangups of his own. His mother being promiscuous after the "brave new" fashion, he and she have been brutally ostracized by their Indian neighbors on the Reservation; in addition, he has picked up some attitudes from the sect of Penitentes. (They are of course particularly devout Catholic Christians, but in Huxley's undiscriminating mind they are Indians as well—the Penitentes of Acoma, the Zunis, the residents of Malpais, and for some reason Athapascans from the Yukon Territory, all mixed together.) From this heterogeneous background, intensified by a very selective reading of Shakespeare, the Savage is understood to have picked up a particularly virulent form of sex-disgust; and this contributes largely to the traumatic violence with which he reacts to the pleasure-fixated society of the Brave New World. It is the hinge on which the book's entire action is hung.

Thinking over his unexpectedly successful fiction some years later, Huxley decided that he had made the alternatives much too stark, by forcing the Savage (his only real, viviparous human being) to choose between a squalid clan of hostile primitives and a civilization of manufactured robots. Among other afterthoughts, he reflected that he might have brought his hero into contact with some humane and thoughtful philosophers, who might have offered him a way of life based on individual freedom, respect for others, and some kind of spiritual aspiration dimly indicated as "Man's Final End," the unifying knowledge of the Tao or True Way.

No doubt such a book would have represented Huxley's full views better than the book he actually wrote, but it would have been a less amusing, a less provocative book. It could hardly have avoided being much talkier (talky though the book is in its present form), and it's doubtful that people would still be reading it and thinking about it. *Brave New World* as he wrote it is a shocking book, and deliberately so. The civilized inhabitants of the new society snicker and smirk at the words "father" and "mother" as at ultimate obscenities; their objurgations, "Oh Ford!" and their titles of honor, "Your Fordship," come parodically close to modern locutions. The only respectable way to come into the world is to be incubated in a bottle and preconditioned to ultimate conformity on an assembly line. In these and many other ways, Huxley exercised himself to scandalize not only the Savage (whose ideas about matrimony are not only old-fashioned but in some respects positively medieval), but also the readers of 1932 and even those of the present day, sixty years later.

Among the ways he controlled the tone of his story, so as to tease and provoke, but not to oppress, was to keep the tale light and quick, to skip over practical necessities, and populate his narrative exclusively with caricatures. The inhabitants of the Brave New World are not people, they are products or rather objects; the inhabitants of the New Mexico Reservation are nameless unpersons; even the three partial outsiders (Marx, Helmholtz, and John the Stranger) are allotted only two or three sparse traits apiece. Behind the comic capering of his marionettes, creatures of the sixth century After Ford, Huxley is pointing a satiric finger at practices of the modern world which he represents only in exaggerated outlines. The New World has been communist for so long that the names of its founders have been domesticated in everyday first names. The impersonality and smug uniformity of self-appointed groups are capitalist as well as socialist; the conditioned reflexes which take the place of thinking, the universal reliance on *soma* which stands for all varieties of narcotics, the fetish made of games and passive entertainments, all these are real and present aspects of modern society, which we see in Huxley's book mainly by indirection. Sexual promiscuity is the one practice that he represents for the most part straightforwardly.

Time, as one might expect, has played its tricks with the more gadgety features of the Brave New World. For many of them we have already developed less spectacular surrogates. We don't have "feelies" yet, but X-rated movies, three-D imaging, and the promised wonders of virtual reality are bringing an equivalent ever closer. We don't, so far, condition embryos from the instant of fertilization to be Gammas, Deltas, and low-grade Epsilons, but perhaps we don't need to. What with mass epidemics and mass undernourishment, festering slums and massive illiteracy, society as presently constituted seems capable of producing all the stunted minds of which there's any foreseeable need. As for the brave new program of planned promiscuity, we don't have women wandering around with bandeliers of contraceptive cartridges slung over their shoulders, but a pill a day or an implantation every five years can produce the same result, and more discreetly. In its casual sexual contacts, quickly undertaken and just as quickly forgotten, the Brave New World does little more than mirror the everyday routine of today's singles bars.

Thus the Fordization of society has overtaken and in many respects surpassed what Huxley's nightmare Utopia envisaged. Much of the "ideal" society's daily operation is too routine and boring to be useful in a fiction; so is the routine of almost any society. Huxley gives us no inkling of what life is like for the conditioned morons who dig coal, forge steel, dispose of trash and sewage, and fix the plumbing. Dishwashers and sewer-dredgers have to exist in the Brave New World, but we're not encouraged to think of them. The dreary quality of things, which George Orwell made predominant in his vision of Utopia, 1984, largely drops out of Huxley's book. Yet it's the routinization of life that's the focus of Huxley's satire, and which the quick interplay of his glistening surfaces prevents the reader from confronting directly.

As for those who censor, or would like to censor, *Brave New World*, I think it's mainly the vision of a systematically promiscuous society that most bothers them. Even though it's held up to contempt and derision, even though much of it is only marginally exaggerated from modern practice, there are districts of our cultural landscape, where sex outside marriage is a hateful thought in itself. As a matter of fact, sex in the Brave New World is an anachronism; most of the population are whitmartins (eunuchs), and the reproductive needs of the society are taken care of by sperm-banks, gene-pools, and other artificial-insemination arrangements, about as exciting erotically as the operation of a toilet plunger. The entire reproductive apparatus of the new civilization is arranged to turn out fractional people with the regularity and uniformity of a cookie-cutter. Slight variations in the level of mediocrity are required to keep people complacently in their assigned slots, but nothing more. Even though the supreme manager of civilization's mechanism has to be given a tad more intelligence than any of his products, so that he can explain things, he is no less coldly mechanical than the least of his victims. Huxley saves for his late chapters an account of the Violent Passion Surrogate treatment by which the patient is purged, when necessary, of any emotional excesses. Passions that society can't soothe away it allows to overflow every so often in harmless and socially approved channels. One couldn't ask for a more succinct and efficient demonstration of a model mechanism for censorship.

Perhaps that is what the censors who point disapproving fingers at *Brave New World* object to—that it holds up a cruelly accurate mirror to their own righteous proceedings, mocking the sort of mind-control machinery they would like to establish. But I think this may be giving them too much credit; it presumes that they have read the book through to its last chapters. Much more likely, they didn't get past the Solidarity Service (Unit V, part 2) in which twelve *soma*-stupefied sex partners celebrate total blind ritual togetherness. This is the most bitter of Huxley's satiric sexual images; it is the most offensive to traditional moralists; and it is the most revolting to an imaginative reader. Satirically, it illustrates the crushing of human spontaneity into the mold of a quasi-military collectivist regime. It ruins the very idea of personal relations when people are forced to make love, as if in close-order drill, with anonymous grotesques obeying instructions issued over a loudspeaker. And when one recalls that the basic principle of the brave new community is stability, so that society's rituals and routines are doomed to be repeated over and over again to infinity, one sees how this regime of enforced voluptuousness exactly resembles the agonies of Dante's "Inferno." For in Hell the sinners are doomed to repeat forever an act that was at least originally their own. But here in "Utopia" the choice is already made for them; they are forced to go through with an act that is supposed to be pleasant and is actually, down to the roots of their being, disgusting—at least for a lonely few.

In strict logic the three adventurers—Marx, Helmholtz, and the Savage—ought all to be sent to the lethal chamber at the end of the book; but for two of them some convenient last-minute islands are discovered, and the Savage, saved for an "experiment" which is a mere narrative pretext, wanders off to commit his despairing, solitary suicide. It's a bleak and desolate view of the world—or would be if it didn't occur in the midst of a capering fictional frolic, told with a sharp eye to many tendencies in the modern world that are certainly comic and perhaps grotesquely sad as well. The only thing that censoring *Brave New World* can accomplish is to make the world—such as it is—a little more drab and a little more complacent about matters on which it shouldn't be complacent at all.

HUXLEY'S *BRAVE NEW WORLD* AS SOCIAL IRRITANT: BAN IT OR BUY IT?

Richard H. Beckham

It is obvious why someone who believes in censorship might choose to object to *Brave New World*. This world is a world of sexual promiscuity, a world with a drug culture in the most literal sense of that expression, a world in which the traditional family—in fact, any family at all—has been vilified and rendered taboo, a world in which religion has been reduced to orgiastic rituals of physical expression. It is a world in which art panders to the sensations of mass communications and a world in which the positive values of Western democracy have been ossified into a rigid caste system, in which the members of each caste are mass produced to the specifications of assembly line uniformity.[1]

Readers who have strict standards of sexual behavior, who believe in chaste courtships and monogamous, lifetime marriages confront in this novel a society in which sexual promiscuity is a virtue and in which the sole function of sexuality is pleasure, not reproduction. Since reproduction is achieved by an elaborate biogenetic mass production assembly line, the citizens of *Brave New World* do not need normal human sexual activity to propagate the species. In fact, such activity is discouraged by the state so that the carefully monitored population controls are not disrupted. Women are required to wear "Malthusian Belts"—convenient caches of birth control devices—in order to forego pregnancies. The sole function of sex in this society is pleasure, and the sole function of pleasure is to guarantee the happiness of *Brave New World* and thus assure a stable, controllable population. State encouraged promiscuity assures that loyalty to one's lover or family will not undermine one's loyalty to the state. Thus, "Everyone belongs to everyone else," and the highest compliment a man can offer a woman is that she is "very pneumatic"—a euphemism suggesting that her movements during sexual intercourse are especially pleasurable. Unlike Orwell, who in the novel *1984* placed severe taboos on sexual activity, since as private and personal act it might permit or encourage rebellion against the state, Huxley prophesizes that in the future the state will use sex as a means of population control on the basis of the psychological truism that men and women condition themselves to avoid pain and to seek pleasure.

Lest the pleasure of frequent and promiscuous sexual activity not be sufficient to distract the population and dissuade them from rebellion, Huxley foresees a culture in which widespread and addictive use of drugs offers a second means of assuring a frictionless society. "A Soma in time saves nine,"—a hypnopaedic slogan drilled into the heads of Brave New Worldians from nursery days on—conveys the message that individuals are to protect themselves from normal pain by frequent doses of this widely available and socially acceptable narcotic.

One of the most important uses for Soma is to insulate people from the effects of rapid aging which afflict *Brave New World* inhabitants after an artificially induced period of extended youth. In this "perfect" society— the future as heaven—most of the human qualities of life have been altered and adapted so that they are devoid of crisis and pain. Just as the inhabitants of this world age only during a brief period shortly before death and just as the drug which eases them through this period has no unpleasant side effects, so they are insulated against the normal stresses and tensions of family life. They have no parents to contend with since in Huxley's inspired anticipation of the consequences of biogenetic engineering, they are conceived through artificial insemination, carried in assembly line placentas made of sow's peritoneum, and decanted rather than born. *Brave New World* inhabitants spend their nursery years in state-run institutions where they are conditioned for future life. Those normal mortals who recall the pain of adolescence would be spared such in *Brave New World*; there is no adolescence. As adults, the inhabitants enjoy youth and vitality until near the time of their deaths. People never have to contend with the stress of accommodating themselves to the authority of parents, nor do they know the stress, pain, heartache—nor the joy—of nurturing and raising children.

The birth and childhood of *Brave New World* inhabitants is greatly reduced from the human world in which we daily live. After perusing the early chapters of this novel, the sensitive reader becomes aware that reduction is one of its recurrent themes, and that this reduction usually involves those attributes of life which make us most human. The purpose behind these reductions is to make all existence subservient to the state. Such subservience requires that even such basic institutions of human civilization as religion and art be sapped of their vital force.

With lives so devoid of pain and so concentrated in the physical and the immediate present, the Worldians have little need for the comfort or solace of religion. If religion is that aspect of man's culture which speaks to the spirit, then Worldians have an absence of spirit of which they are unaware. The reduction of religion is symbolized in the icon which replaces the cross as the dominant religious image—a T. The worship of a supernatural savior has been supplanted by worship of a lord of the assembly line, Henry Ford, and the sign of Our Ford is taken from the model name of one of his early cars. The four arms of the cross have been reduced to the three arms of the T.

Religion lends continuity to civilization, and so does art. Each is an important constituent of the emotional component of human life. But, like religion, art in *Brave New World* has been reduced to trafficking in sensation—slight, transitory, physical responses as opposed to the profound, sustained, psychological responses of emotion. The "Feelies"— *Brave New World's* multi-sensory version of the movies—well illustrates this pandering to sensation; rather than celebrating the ideas and emotions of human life, the "Feelies" are designed to give its participants a sensory overload of neural stimulation—the sight and feel of bare flesh on a bearskin rug, for example.

Thus art and religion are controlled by the state and subordinated to the support of the state, but the nature of that state is quite different from what a contemporary reader might expect. In the 1990s, citizens of Western Democracies see their form of government as the best form yet developed by man. As Huxley projects this important facet of human life into the future, he foresees neither Western Democracy nor its historical competitor, Eastern Communism, as the most likely political system. Instead of either he sees a five-tiered caste system occasioned through the perfection of biogenetic engineering and other modern devices of social control. Every man is created biologically equal to all others in his caste. The leisured classes are conditioned to consume, and the working classes are conditioned to manufacture what those other classes consume. Society functions almost as simply as the physical law of equal and opposite reactions.

If Huxley had perversely set out to oversimplify and reduce the most important philosophical and scientific ideas of modern times to a facile society representing a serious projection of what the world will surely become, then one might at least understand the objections of those who seek to censor the book. Neither Marx nor the founders of Western Democracy prevail. The Worldians seem to extrapolate from some of the world's great religions—Islam, Christianity, Judaism—such belief as is useful for their purpose. Freud's insights into family relationships are read only in their negative connotations, and these connotations then become the basis for social organization. Darwin's discoveries about adaptation and heredity are seen not as patterns for understanding how nature works but rather as patterns for manipulating nature to nefarious ends. The history of modern technology culminates in a culture where man eases his way through life on drugs, is free of painful involvement with other human beings, and is sustained by the state's manipulation of mass consumption and mass communication.

But Huxley does not offer *Brave New World* as an ideal. Neither does he render it as an idle fantasy portraying what life might be like in the future. *Brave New World* is a satire, and the pleasurable perfection of society in A.F. 689 is measured against the norm of Twentieth Century society in general and against the norm of a particular primitive society still currently extant. Brave New World has its critics both from within and without. The critic from within is Bernard Marx. Because of some abnormality in his birthing process, he is not a perfect Alpha specimen, which suggests that human imperfection and mechanical malfunction have not been completely eliminated in this brave new world. The critic from without is John Savage. As the child of Linda from the dominant culture and the adopted son of a Native American on a reservation in the American Southwest, he is a half-breed belonging to neither the progressive nor the traditional societies in the book.

Marx introduces some of the universal human norms in the book. He is in the society, but not of it. He is physically smaller than other members of his caste—the dominant Alphas—and this physical distinction seems to generate in him envy and alienation, which are uncommon in the society. He rebels against his superior, and when he finds Linda and her son on the reservation and discovers her past association with his superior, he brings them back to the "World" in order to humiliate his boss. Though he has a professional, psychological interest in the two, he is so flattered by the attention he receives because of his connection with the famous pair that he begins to pander to the society of which he has previously been so harshly critical. Marx is important in a technical sense because it is from his point of view that we see the activities of the society—activities which he both participates in and criticizes.

John, or the savage, articulates the values of both a minority culture, the Native Americans and of the culture of the past. To the degree to which he has assimilated the culture of the Native Americans, he is a child of nature communicant with the earth, sky, wind and water. He is free of the artificial and urban environment in which Bernard spends his life. Though his mother is from the dominant society, John is born outside that society and thus escapes its state-supported brainwashing nurture and its prescriptions against artifacts of earlier times. His education he obtains from the *Bible* and Shakespeare—two of the most important cultural forces in modern Western civilization. It is by the norms of this literature that he executes his criticism of this "Brave New World."

Bernard and John convey to the reader the dilemma of modern life which Huxley expresses in the novel. Through their knowledge humans gain greater and greater control over their environment. As they gain control and are better able to manage their own destiny, they also greatly increase the danger of losing their humanity—the sum total of those facets of life by which people define and know themselves. This point is literally and symbolically illustrated through the tragic conclusion of the novel. John falls victim to that most human of human emotions—love. Yet he cannot reconcile his love for Lenina Crown in a satisfactory way. John cannot accept her as "pneumatic," as "belonging to everybody else," after the fashion of his mother's culture. Nor can he remold her into the image of the beloved he holds from the Biblical and Shakespearean cultural guides he learned in his childhood. John is caught out of time. He cannot go back to his old culture, nor can he assimilate the new. His only option in a world where he has become a freak to be gawked at is suicide. As his body swings from the rope gyrating toward all points of the compass, Huxley suggests that we too may be creating a world in which ironically there is no place for human life and for human emotion.

One of the objectors to this novel comments on its pessimism and tragedy as reasons why it should not be taught. Such an objection overlooks the tone of the book. As satire, the book's purpose is to examine the failings of human behavior in order to encourage reform. Such examinations are painful when we recognize our faults through them. But pain and growth and regeneration are part of the human condition and prove that Huxley's prophesy has not yet come true. And certainly if we try to prevent people—especially young people—from being exposed to the tragic, we would have to eliminate much world literature which has been universally proclaimed great.

Any valid arguments against teaching this book seem to be aesthetic and pedagogical rather than moral. Particularly at the high school level one might opt not to teach the book to some students because of its vocabulary, its form, or its genre. Since the book touches on some important scientific and philosophical ideas, the vocabulary is sometimes academic and abstract. The specific detail with which Huxley describes biogenetic processes requires one to become familiar with a few scientific terms not current in the general vocabulary. The form of the book, especially the opening pages, may discourage a slow or naive reader. Huxley uses a film-montage type of narration to cut back and forth between several conversations that are taking place in different locations. Until one understands this technique the opening passages seem chaotic and unintelligible. The genre of science fiction requires that students use their imaginations. Unless readers are prepared to suspend their disbelief and be ready to accept the givens of a world in which the modes of social and economic behavior are quite different from those of the real world, then they may not want to read very far.

Having stated these caveats, I find far greater justification for reading and teaching *Brave New World*. Many of the cultural concerns discussed in this novel are still matters of great importance to thinking people in general and to young people in particular. In the sixty plus years since Huxley first published this book, some of his prophesies seem far more plausible than they did in 1932. The greater reliability and increased availability of contraceptives, for example, has radically changed sexual attitudes and behavior. A study of the novel might lead to an examination of the concepts of romantic love set forth by John as opposed to the promiscuity practiced by the inhabitants of *Brave New World*. The drug culture of *Brave New World* could be compared to and contrasted with the problems of drug abuse and addiction in contemporary society. Is Soma acceptable because it has no bad side effects? Do people sacrifice their human potential when they subject themselves to mind or mood altering drugs? Do humans deny life when they resort to artificial means to avoid pain?

The most significant and fruitful vehicle for discussion that the novel offers is biogenetic engineering. In this regard more so than any other, Huxley's prophesy seems to be coming true. What are the consequences of man's efforts to control the genetic composition of human offspring? Do we gain or lose by knowing the sex of a child before it is born? What are the moral considerations in prenatal testing of fetuses? In *in vitro* fertilization? In test tube babies? What are the long range social, economic, and political consequences of continued experimentation in biogenetic engineering?

Such questions as these suggest the potential of the novel to provoke discussion about events within the novel and their relationship to events in the lives of its readers.

NOTES

[1] A report in the *Newsletter on Intellectual Freedom* summarizes most of the objections to this book raised over the last twenty years. In this instance,

the complaining parents claimed that "the book is depressing, fatalistic, and negative, and that it encourages students to adopt a lifestyle of drugs, sex and conformity, reinforcing helpless feelings that they can do nothing to make an impact on their world." See the *Newsletter*, September 1981, p. 127.

"ALAS, ALAS, THAT EVER LOVE WAS SIN!" MARRIAGES MORAL AND IMMORAL IN CHAUCER

Margaret Odegard

In September, 1987, *The Washington Post* carried a story about a school superintendent in Panama City, Florida, vigorously removing books from classroom use. Superintendent Hall ordered teachers to examine those texts closely and to separate them into three categories. In the first would be books without "vulgar, obscene or sexually explicit material." In the second would be books with "very limited vulgarity and no sexually explicit or obscene material." In the dread third category would be books with quite a bit of vulgarity or obscene and/or sexually explicit material." Among the titles in this third category was Chaucer's *Canterbury Tales*. According to a 1989 compilation of seventeen national surveys, Chaucer's work is one of the most frequently challenged books in public schools between 1950-1985 (Burress 227-228).

Like those superintendents and parents who find *The Canterbury Tales* threatening to morals, those of us who admire Chaucer believe stories can indeed affect us morally. What we as readers admire, and what we find ridiculous or wrong can be clarified, and enriched by wise and perceptive writers like Chaucer, or cheapened and debased by shallow ones, pandering to our worst impulses. As readers, parents, teachers and citizens our common ground is recognition that stories exert immense power to enchant and persuade. We must choose well; why should we choose Chaucer?

As a writer, Chaucer claimed a dual allegiance, to morality and to observed life. Unless the tales reflect life, they mislead. In the General Prologue, Chaucer begs us not to consider him unmannerly if he gives an account of the pilgrims' words and dealings "using their very phrases as they fell." One way we judge his characters is by their language.

> For certainly, as you all know so well,
> He who repeats a tale after a man
> Is bound to say, as nearly as he can,
> Each single word, if he remembers it,
> However rudely spoken or unfit,
> Or else the tale he tells will be untrue.
>   (CT, 11. 730-735)

However, the prize for the best tale will go to the pilgrim who gives "the fullest measure/ Of good morality and general pleasure" (CT 11. 798). Chaucer places himself in the tradition claiming that literature best persuades us to morality by inviting us to enjoy a good tale. His ethical system is traditional as well: he admires those who live by Christian ethics, like the knight, the parson, and the clerk; he invites us to think about the moral practice of others who often violate those ethical principles.

In the General Prologue portraits of each character provide Chaucer's readers with a rich ethical context in which to place the twenty-nine pilgrims on their way to the shrine of St. Thomas Beckett at Canterbury Cathedral. Those sketches may well serve to introduce students to active and ethical reading. Chaucer does not tell us directly what he thinks of a character; rather he gives us evidence by which we infer which he admires and why, or which he smiles at for their human departures from the ideals they profess. Readers can determine who cheats an employer, who cheats his customers, who cheats in the church courts, and who cheats by selling falsely divine pardon for sins. They can think about which practices are worse than others and why.

Another context Chaucer provides is that of all the other kinds of stories included in *The Canterbury Tales*. Most especially, Chaucer recognizes in "The Knight's Tale" aspects of human nature the Miller knows nothing of—our idealism, our desire for a noble life of honorable action, public service, and courtly love without adultery. The Knight tells his tale first; the Miller's immediately follows. In Chaucer's plan the visions of each are true; the juxtaposed visions of both are more true than either considered by itself.

Further, as we expect morality of our writers, so we expect a comparable ethical obligation of ourselves as readers. To take one component, such as adultery, as the defining distinction between moral and immoral stories, without considering context, is unjust to the writer and the tale, and so immoral. Awareness of religious, literary, social, and sexual contexts is part of our ethic as readers.

Those school superintendents and school boards who object to parts of a story, words, or actions, without considering their place in the whole know that immature readers are apt to do the same. But where will such readers learn to read in context if not in school, where open discussion explores such relations? Obscenity is secret and private; a class reading the Miller's Tale, joined in laughter at human folly, is social and public.

The two most widely anthologized tales are those of the Miller and the Wife of Bath. Both have been charged with obscenity and immorality; both are also claimed as two of Chaucer's masterpieces. What moral issues appear in these characters and their tales?

When we know the characters, we will expect each to tell a tale fitting his or her character. That, too, is part of Chaucer's morality. So, knowing the Miller from the General Prologue we know what sort of a tale he will tell. He cheats those who bring their flour to be ground; he has a golden thumb. He's a wrestler; he can knock a door off its hinges with his head. He has a red beard, like that of a sow or a fox; his nostrils are black and wide; his mouth is like a furnace. Such a man will choose a tale to his liking; we expect, then, one displaying aggression, physical energy, and coarseness, and we will have it. Chaucer, however, provides the Miller with a tale of more acute observation of character, more ingenuity in comic plotting, and a more exact match of comic flaw to comic fate than we have a right to expect.

Chaucer's "The Miller's Tale" is superb comedy. It is also one singled out as obscene because the story is about adultery. Some may regard a recognition that adultery occurs as undermining the ethic of fidelity in marriage. However, morality in literature includes a truthful report of experience; both fidelity and adultery exist. Literature recognizes that good and evil grow in this world together, and as John Milton said, we must learn to distinguish one from the other, and one by way of the other. One moral issue that could well be explored with student readers is why adultery occurs. John, the carpenter, in "The Miller's Tale," is a rich old codger, married to Alison, a young eighteen year old. Chaucer clearly regards such marriages, very common at a time when women had little choice of a marriage partner and were usually married by age fifteen, as unnatural, improper, and unethical criteria for marriage. The comic fate of ridicule is entirely proper for such a husband. Perhaps loveless marriages between a middle-aged man and a young girl, sanctioned by church, state, and family, are the real obscenity. An older man who deludes himself that a young woman will prefer him to a young man of her own age is blinded by his pride and so is due to fall.

The type of story was familiar: a fabliau, a bawdy tale, where proximity is destiny, if those near to one another are of the same age, of opposite sexes, and if the wife is married to a man old enough to be her father. The plot is in the form of a practical joke, carried out for love or revenge or both. But in such a tale, we as readers identify not with the characters, but with the storyteller whose use of the characters' dominant traits is beautifully married to an inventive and just revenge. No one who reads "The Miller's Tale," no matter how immature, can wish to be any of the characters. No one who reads the tale as it is written can avoid wishing she or he could have written it.

John is the very image of bourgeois complacency in his pride in marrying Alison. He has two additional flaws, dangerous when combined and frequently seen together; he is both deeply suspicious of book-learning and credulous, believing what he is told. Both traits gloriously contribute to his comic fate.

What of the other characters—here not a triangle, but a quadrangle? Two young men hope to receive favors from Alison. Nicholas is a clever university student, renting a room in John's house. He uses his wits in an elaborate scheme to gain Alison, who is eager to welcome him. Telling John that his astrological studies prophesy a second flood like Noah's, Nicholas advises John to prepare to save himself, Alison and Nicholas by rigging up ropes to suspend three wooden tubs from the roof of the barn. When the flood comes, each will climb into a tub, cut the ropes, and float away safely. On the prophesied night Nicholas will join Alison, and John will be none the wiser. John, at the mercy of Nicholas' learning and his own credulity, accepts this preposterous prophecy unquestioningly and prepares the scaffolds for his own cuckolding.

But a second young lover, Absalon, a parish clerk, is also courting Alison. Imitating the fashionable young courtly lovers of the day, Absalon serenades her at the waist-high window of her house, sweetening his breath with licorice so his kisses will be welcome. But Alison will have none of him; he is sentimental, effeminate, and infantile, "crying for her as a lamb does for the teat." Absalon is persistent. As Nicholas and Alison are enjoying one another while John sleeps above in his tub, Absalon comes to the window, in the dark of night, for a kiss. His comic fate is to be rewarded with her rear. Rubbing his lips "with sand, with straw, with cloth, with chips," Absalon is determined to be revenged. He obtains a red hot coulter from the blacksmith and returns, telling Alison he has a ring to exchange for a kiss. Unable to resist improving on the joke, Nicholas goes to the window, and offers his rear to Absalon, who this time offers not his lips, but a red-hot branding iron. Mad with agony Nicholas cries, "Help! Water! Water! Help!" Whereupon John, waking from his sleep, cuts the rope, the tub falls to the floor; John faints. When he revives, John insists the second flood has come. Nicholas and Alison run through the streets, telling the townspeople that John is mad.

The comic fate of each of the men matches the flaw of each. Absalon's fastidiousness and his persistence in wooing Alison when he's been told he's unwelcome is rewarded by the misplaced kiss. Nicholas' pride in his cleverness is not content with triumph over John but must offer a second cheek to Absalon. That overreaching pride results in his being branded by Absalon's hot coulter, in turn evoking Nicholas' yell for water, in turn causing John to cut the rope of his tub suspended from the ceiling. We have forgotten John as we see Absalon's and Nicholas' fate; that sudden coming together of all three comic reproofs is wonderful fun. What about Alison? Why is she not punished? We may infer that she is little more than a sex object; surely she has so little freedom of choice that she is scarcely regarded as responsible. That attitude could be regarded as immoral, denying ethical responsibility to the woman in the tale. John's mistake in marrying a woman half his age and his superstitious belief in Nicholas' prophecy are punished by Alison's infidelity and the townspeople's refusal to believe his tale.

The story includes immoral actions. It also includes youthful vitality, and cleverness triumphing over an aging husband. There is no purity; neither is there malice. "The Miller's Tale" invites us to see all three men as ridiculous. There is no fate a young high school reader is more eager to avoid.

Dame Alison, the Wife of Bath, is Chaucer's most famous character, no doubt startling, unnerving, and amusing Chaucer's contemporaries as she continues to do in the twentieth century. No other character in *The Canterbury Tales* is so richly portrayed; no other is more attractive. She is the first woman to speak in her own voice dramatically since Lysistrata, Antigone, and Medea in Greek drama nineteen centuries earlier. Her speech, non-stop, compulsive, social, and self-revealing, has the energy to break up nineteen centuries of icy silence.

Since Chaucer was writing largely for a courtly audience, one of his ethical triumphs is to portray characters—women as well as men—of all social classes as worthy of attentive understanding. The typical courtly romance celebrated the beauty and valor of the well-born. With the Wife, Chaucer includes a member of the rising prosperous middle-class, and a woman, and most revolutionary of all, allows her to speak in her own voice. To recognize artistically those who have hitherto been ignored or treated with condescension is itself one ethical dimension of art.

To appreciate the ethical import of her self-defense, an ethical reader should be aware of the theological, ecclesiastical, legal, and social authority arrayed against her. Medieval anti-feminism, or sexism as we now term it, derives from a Western cultural tradition, both classical and Christian, that is still powerful today, one that engages our current struggle for equality of women, itself a major ethical issue for us.

That tradition depends upon our inveterate habit of identifying the good as the opposite of evil and, in this instance, identifying the distinctive excellence of human nature, as men have understood it, as the good, and women as the opposite, the Other. The classical tradition, from Aristotle for example, identifies the distinctive excellence of human nature as rationality—the power we share with God. But Aristotle's unwarranted leap is that human nature at its best is male. Since women bear children, and consequently spend much time in caring for them, women do not have the leisure necessary for rationality. Women, then, are misbegotten males.

The most powerful component of that tradition is distrust of women's sexuality, naming women as underminers of male thought, religion, and ethic by using their sexual powers. The stories we tell embody those values of the culture; one story we all know is that of Adam and Eve. This story seemed to many at the time Chaucer wrote, and to some now, to present irrefutable evidence of women's essentially inferior intellectual and moral stature. Women religious scholars in recent years have seriously studied the telling and re-telling of the tale. Rosemary Reuther explained that the bodily principle was seen as so intrinsically demonic that the high road to salvation demanded the spurning of the bodily life altogether in ascetic virginity. The medieval cult of the Virgin, she argues, arises not as a reaction against the low status of women, but as a denigration of fleshly maternity and sensuality. The love of the Virgin Mary does not correct but presupposes hatred of real women (Reuther 57).

More recently, Elaine Pagels has studied the history of interpretation of the Adam and Eve story. She discovered that early Christian writers, in the first through the fourth centuries, focussed on issues of freely chosen obedience, exploring the relation of divine commandments to human free will. St. Augustine, in the fifth century, shifted the issue to sexuality, blaming Eve for the fall of man. Tormented by guilt about his earlier sexual life after his conversion, he placed the stamp of original sin on sexuality, where it remained for centuries (Pagels 105-106). "Alas, alas, that ever love was sin!" exclaims the Wife of Bath; ages of anxiety and guilt are caught up in that lament.

Other elements of the Biblical tradition were combined with the story of Adam and Eve. In the New Testament the most striking anti-feminine texts are St. Paul's who based his theological assertions on his understanding of the story of Adam and Eve. "For a man ought not to cover his head, since he is the image and glory of God; but woman is the glory of man. For man was not made from woman, but woman from man.

Neither was man created for woman, but woman for man" (First Corinthians 11:7-9).

The Wife knows what she's up against, not only from popular images of Adam and Eve in cathedrals, but from the texts widely used in the church. Her fifth husband, the clerk Johnny, has read to her from his "book of wikked wives," largely based on St. Jerome's text arguing against marriage and urging young men to remain virgins and to enter the priesthood, one of the most powerful recruiting pamphlets ever penned! Jerome describes marriage as purgatory, women as destroyers of male souls. Of course Jerome repeats the standard Pauline doctrine that a husband is head of the wife as Christ is head of the church, that wives therefore are to obey their husbands.

By law and by custom women lived under male sovereignty. Those whose fathers were willing to pay a dowry to a convent had a choice of becoming a nun. Otherwise, a woman passed from the control of her father to that of her husband. The church declared girls marriageable at age 12. Both secular and religious tradition forbade divorce. In general women were considered as men's property. By canon law a husband was entitled to beat his wife. Illustrations from medieval manuscripts include image after image of wife-beating. (How much of that tradition still operates in current behavior of battering males, and of the frequent passivity of battered women?)

The church fathers failed to see that profound human love could be expressed in sexual union. The Wife's deepest conviction emerges in a countertheology; creation is good. Since God created both body and soul together, let's keep them together.

Where did the Wife come from? How did she gain the self-confidence to speak? Where did she get the freedom to leave home and go on a pilgrimage? We know that money and morals operate powerfully upon one another. The Wife is economically independent, part of a recently prosperous middle-class. She's a wealthy west-country clothier endowed with the property of her deceased spouses. Economic independence gives her social independence. She is engaged in the most lucrative trade possible at the time, the manufacture of cloth. Her legal title to property is clear. She tells us she gave freely to Johnny, her fifth husband, when she married him. "Among the burgesses married women retained the ownership and control of their property and could enter into contracts in their own names, their husband having neither legal liability nor power of consent in such matters" (Carruthers 210).

In her Prologue, the Wife offers to her fellow pilgrims a confession, but a confession with a difference. This one is public not private; not to God as a prelude to a prayer for forgiveness, but to her fellow pilgrims, unrepentant. She defends first of all her five marriages. Someone has told her that since Christ went to only one wedding, she should be wedded only once. She wonders: Jesus told the Samaritan at the well that she had five husbands, but her current man was not her husband—what did that mean? Was five the limit? No one seems to know. And what about Solomon? She wishes to God she could be refreshed half as often as he!

Another theme emerges—the exaltation of virginity. She challenges her audience to find any commandment for virginity in the *Bible.* As she reminds her audience, if no seed is sown, no virgins will be born. If Christ praised virginity, and was himself a virgin, that is for those who seek perfection, and "lords, by your leave, that am not I!"

The first three husbands were good, because they were rich, old, and subject to her control. She knows the best defense is offense. Accusing her husbands of infidelities of which they are scarcely capable, they are flattered into allowing her the freedom she wants—to visit friends, to gossip, to sing and dance, to attend theaters and religious gatherings. She is always on the look-out for another husband—well she might be, considering the ages of the first three.

Why does she marry old bacon, as she calls them? Though she doesn't say so, she would have had no choice the first time. After that, she married the next two husbands for their wealth and saw to it that they settled their estates upon her. Some careless readers have claimed the Wife is a whore; not so. She insists upon marriage, as do her first three husbands.

In her efforts to control these old men, the wife coopts the weapons anti-feminists had used against women, to her own purposes. Since women are not reasonable and patient, then the only recourse is for the husbands to be so.

The last two husbands are not "good." They are young, and she meets her match. Her fourth was jolly, playing the harp while she danced. She reminisces in an enchanted glow of memory:

> But Christ! Whenever it comes back to me,
> When I recall my youth and jollity,
> It fairly warms the cockles of my heart!
> This very day I feel a pleasure start,
> Yes, I can feel it tickling at the root.
> Lord, how it does me good! I've had my fruit,
> I've had my world and time, I've had my fling.
> (WB's Prologue 11. 469-475)

But he was unfaithful to her; she is jealous, and makes him suffer for it, fulfilling the function church fathers had declared was women's role:

> By God on earth I was his purgatory.
> For which I hope his soul may be in glory.
> (WB Prologue 11.489-490)

At the funeral of her fourth husband, the wife finds Johnny's legs irresistible. She, at forty, marries twenty-year-old Johnny for love. Forgetting her hard-earned wisdom about the role of money in independence, she gives Johnny all her land. He tries to bring her to heel, reading from his "book of wikked wives" all Jerome's denunciations of women. Says the wife

> He knew more legends of them and their lives
> Than there are good ones mentioned in the *Bible*.
> For take my word for it, there is no libel
> On women that the clergy will not paint
> Except when writing of a woman-saint.
> (WB's Prologue 11. 685-690)

When she can take it no longer, she snatches his book, his power source, from Johnny and throws it into the fire. She cuffs him so that he falls into the fire after it, and he, like a maddened lion, strikes her down, as if dead. Horrified by what he has done, Johnny pours out his love for her; up she starts,

"And have you murdered me
To get my land?" I said. "Was that the game?
Before I'm dead I'll kiss you all the same."
(WB's Prologue 11. 800-803)

On this battlefield, Johnny promises never to hit her again, giving her control of house and land and tongue and fist.

And when I'd mastered him, and out of deadlock
Secured myself the sovereignty in wedlock,
And when he said, "My own and truest wife,
Do as you please for all the rest of life,
And guard your honor and my good estate,"
From that day forward there was no debate.
(WB's Prologue 11. 818-822)

The wife has turned the marriage rules upside down. After that revolution the woman rules, and no longer needs to rule. Once having established symbolic power, she no longer wants it.

Her tale is profoundly ethical, one of the first to criticize the blindness of notions of chivalry in its implicit attitudes toward other classes and toward women. Chaucer knows and allows a woman to tell us that it is unjust to treat individual women as humanly deficient simply because they are female. Its corollary is that to talk of women unjustly is to act unjustly. One of the social corollaries of such stories may well be rape, physical or verbal (Booth 390).

In her tale of the olden days, a knight of King Arthur's court seems to be following the explicit advice of Andrew the chaplain, the author of the how-to book of courtly love, that words and long-wooing are necessary with ladies of the upper class, but a waste of time with common women. The knight, away from his own class where reputation is all, saw a maid walking alone, and in spite of everything she could do, "by very force he took her maidenhood." Chaucer is clearly criticizing a social class that reserves its respect for women to their own kind.

Is the tale immoral because a rape is included? Two lines are given to the action, with no more detail than this; certainly the way the rape is presented is not salacious. Probably some readers whose judgment of the morality of a story is based on the subject of one small part of the tale rather than the whole, and on the fact of rape rather than the way in which rape is presented, may find this story by definition immoral. Twentieth century parents and school boards are rightly dismayed at the prevalence of rape in our society. One of the most alarming elements of the Report on Pornography is that male fantasies of gang rape, appearing in such publications as *Penthouse* magazine which sells five million copies a month have led young men to believe that women enjoy it, protests to the contrary notwithstanding (Booth 393-394). There are immoral stories; they appear in "successful" American magazines.

The rest of the story is about how the knight learns his lesson and from whom. A public outcry brings the knight's case to King Arthur, who is ready to find him guilty in a court of law and, after due process, behead him. But the women of the court, including the queen, plead for the young man's life—a motif frequent in Chaucer's stories. The just men want to follow the law and the rules, ignoring their connections with the guilty; the women want to explore less absolute methods that may allow the guilty to enlarge their awareness and so, their conscience. Carol Gilligan has written a study of the difference between men and women in their responses to ethical issues, *In A Different Voice*, which makes essentially the same distinction; Chaucer understood it in the fourteenth century.

King Arthur grants the queen's request; women hand down the sentence—the knight must return in a year and a day with the answer to the question, "What is it that women most desire?" His Roper poll produces no agreement—some say wealth, some say honor, some say flattery, some say pleasure in bed, some say to do as we please, some say to be wed and widowed often (the wife is telling this tale). As the day draws near for his return, he sorrowfully turns toward the court and encounters first a fairy ring of twenty-four ladies dancing; when they vanish an old crone, known as a loathly lady in fairy tales, remains.

She offers to help him if he in turn will grant her one wish. The two go together to the court. When the queen asks the knight what he has learned women want he answers confidently that women want sovereignty over their husbands as well as over their lovers. None could contradict him; his life is saved. Whereupon the old crone reminds him of his promise; what she wants is to wed him. He has no recourse; he protests—she is too old, she is too ugly, she is too poor. A wedding is performed; the knight tosses and turns in acute self-pity. When they go to bed, the loathly lady has the most captive of audiences. She offers him as pillow talk a sermon—a sermon on gentility, courtesy, generosity—of honor and of what it means to be superior. She rebukes his class-bound ethic, citing authorities from Greek, Roman and Biblical texts—that such virtues are not genetically inherited; that poverty is no sin; that spiritual beauty far outshines physical beauty.

Having concluded her instruction, the loathly lady in turn gives the knight a choice. He may have her faithful and ugly, or unfaithful and beautiful. Now the knight has learned. Remembering his answer to the queen, he gives her the choice: she will choose which will bring most honor to them both. The ethic is now reciprocal. Whereupon, as in the fairy tale of the frog prince, she transforms herself into the bride he dreams of. Since the choice is hers, she will be both fair and good. The fairy tale ending, the wife's wish fulfillment, goes even further. She's not only, in her late years, young again, she is not only beautiful and faithful, but this woman who wanted sovereignty when it was denied her, now obeys him in all that is pleasing to him. They are happily wedded ever after.

Her tale then, a fairy tale of wish-fulfillment in one sense, in another has offered us, as Chaucer again and again stated as his purpose, both "sentence and solas," that is wisdom and delight. He has instructed us that customary morality of his day is constricted. The myth of male superiority, that men act and women are acted upon, raped if they are lower class, rescued into subordinate marriage if they are middle or upperclass, is here exploded. The knight's life depends not on his physical strength, but on a woman's wit; the class superiority implicit in the old chivalric code is exposed; the elevation of physical beauty as a supreme distinction in women is undermined; and most important, the constriction of choice in a marriage partner, experienced by women of all social classes, is here imposed upon a man (Haskell 1-13).

Rather than showing Chaucer as immoral, these two stories raise a host of moral issues for high school readers to consider. Is it moral to write stories about only one social class, denying the existence of others? Is it moral to write about women as if they are passive objects of men's desire, within or outside of marriage? Is it moral to end a story, like "The Miller's Tale," by giving each sinner a punishment fitting his sin? Is a story immoral because we laugh at the characters rather than denouncing them? Is it moral to encourage by social acceptance old men to marry young women? Is it moral to deny women access to economic independence, allowing women to choose whether to marry or whom to marry? Is a writer who tells many kinds of stories, inviting us to compare their morality, more ethical than one who writes only one kind of story? Is a reader ethical to declare a story immoral because it includes immoral speech and behavior, obscenity and adultery?

Wayne Booth, in his recent study of ethics in fiction, identifies two opposing ethics. One is an ethic of exclusion: avoid evil. This may mean avoid knowledge of disreputable behavior in the upper or lower classes, avoid knowledge of sexuality as inherently anti-spiritual. If we adopt such an ethic of purity, we may read some parables or saint's lives, but little else. Much of the *Bible* itself will be judged unsuitable. The opposite is an ethic of inclusion: we can enter into many lives, many perspectives, many definitions of the good, many mixtures of the desirable and the undesirable as a way to clarify our desiring. This vicarious experience costs us much less than learning from our own experience; those lessons we are slow to learn and pay for dearly. To read ethically may be first to enter imaginatively into life as people different from ourselves see it, to understand those perspectives, and to judge their comparable worth. Chaucer instructs us to become ethical readers, not for his sake, but for our own.

WORKS CITED

Booth, Wayne. *The Ethics of Fiction*. Berkeley: University of California Press, 1988.

Burress, Lee. *The Battle of the Books: Literary Censorship in the Public Schools.* Metuchen, NJ: Scarecrow Press, 1989.

Carruthers, Mary. "The Wife of Bath and the Painting of Lions." PMLA 94 (1979): 209-221.

Chaucer, Geoffrey. *The Canterbury Tales*. Trans. by Nevill Coghill. Baltimore, MD: Penguin Books, 1952.

Haskell, Ann S. "The Portrayal of Women by Chaucer and His Age." In *What Manner of Woman*. Ed. Marlene Springer. New York: New York University, 1977.

Hentoff, Nat. "Why Teach Us to Read and Then Say We Can't." *Washington Post* 21 Sept 1987.

Pagels, Elaine. *Adam, Eve, and the Serpent*. New York: Random House, 1988.

Reuther, Rosemary. *New Woman, New Earth*. New York: Harper & Row, 1975.

IF YOU WANT TO KNOW THE TRUTH...
THE CATCHER IN THE RYE
Norbert Blei

The Catcher in the Rye was published in 1951 when I was a student in high school ready to drop out, get a job, buy a car, and eventually marry a steady girlfriend. Which was what a number of us did then: got on with our real lives. *If you want to know the truth.*

It was a blue collar neighborhood of working class values where survival was primary, education and security secondary. Learning was encouraged. But by the time you reached high school, Auto Shop had more than a slight edge over Shakespeare.

I never heard of *The Catcher in the Rye* in high school. Most of those who got on with their real lives have little knowledge of it today. We're far removed from that place and time—the Silent Generation of the 50s.

One thing however remains: you always carry the street with you.

If you want to know the truth, I hated high school—the football crowd, the student council crowd, the honor roll crowd, the cheerleader crowd, the school paper crowd, the yearbook crowd, the after school club crowd, the audio-visual bunch who always looked sick, kids who carried *Bibles* to class, the hall monitors, the debate team, the Junior Achievers, kids who played musical instruments, those who "took" art and dramatics, the school nurse, hygiene classes, advisers who never knew your name, vapid administrators, aptitude tests, students always running around with posters for sock hops, proms, honors banquets and homecoming dances. It *was* pretty depressing.

Something about high school was *never* real—except for shop classes, smoking in the alleys, getting in trouble, having a steady girlfriend.

Teachers were both the problem and the answer. They were either good or bad and students knew this instinctively. There was no middle ground. Teachers encouraged you, destroyed you, or ignored you. But if they *loved* their subject, they often loved teaching, and some of this love, one way or another, probably spilled over to you. But you didn't always know it at the time. *If you want to know the truth.*

If you were fortunate, you might come across a teacher like old Spencer in *Catcher* who could tell you in a considerate way what you needed to hear: "I flunked you in history because you knew absolutely nothing.... Do you feel absolutely no concern for your future?... I'd like to put some sense in that head of yours, boy. I'm trying to help you, if I can" (10, 14).

And if you were very fortunate, a Mr. Antolini, who might advise:

> Among other things, you'll find that you're not the first person who was ever confused and frightened and even sickened by human behavior. You're by no means alone on that score, you'll be excited and *stimulated* to know. Many, many men have been just as troubled morally and spiritually as you are right now. Happily, some of them kept records of their troubles. You'll learn from them—if you want to. Just as someday, if you have something to offer, someone will learn something from you. It's a beautiful reciprocal arrangement. And it isn't education. It's history. It's poetry (189).

If you want to know the truth, I was very fortunate. I had both an "old Spencer" and a "Mr. Antolini"—but I didn't know it, *really* understand it, at the time. Self-knowledge doesn't come easy. Or quickly. Teachers and books are often like time capsules. It may take years to feel the effect.

I only knew that something was wrong in my world of the adolescent-coming-of-age, and I had no language for it. No way to identify the anger, confusion, concern, despair, all the rebelliousness trying to surface. No way to confirm my own suspicion that some of what I had been told and taught was untrue.

I had, instead, a "bad attitude." Lots of silence and sulking and waiting for something to happen. Truth, and all its variations, was easier sought and found on the street. There the lines were clear and the language was strong. No pretense. Early on you developed, what I would later discover Hemingway advised every good writer needed: "a built-in, shock-proof, shit detector."

Nothing Holden said came as a shock to my generation or certainly the generations to follow. It spoke to us. It came as a relief, an acknowledgement that this was the language we used outside of class. in the halls, on the street, and often heard in the home.

This was the American voice demanding to be heard as it was spoken. An update on Twain. ("What a lie it is to call this a free country, where none but the unworthy and undeserving may swear.") And if Sandburg found slang, "Language that takes off its coat, spits on its hands, and goes to work," profanity was just a little more spit. Then along came Salinger who put it all down and got it right. Put it in print. Made us smile, laugh out loud, begin to think and question life around us—what was false and what was real. And how a young person might seek his own authenticity in a world of much hypocrisy.

Even going to church, for all the good it promised (for some of us who had reached the age of Holden) did not explain what we witnessed. One seemed surrounded by the dutiful, the faithful, all the pious petitioners concerned for the welfare of one's soul, though their own lives were often in constant disarray. Which was certainly true where I came from, *if you want to know the truth.*

Nothing was what it seemed to be. What the adolescent seeks is some confirmation of his own doubts, some comparison of his experience to the stories of others. Education often begins by asking the questions that shouldn't be asked, reading the wrong or "inappropriate" books.

I had a need, perhaps, to experience chapel with Holden Caulfield when the rich undertaker, Ossenburger, who buried people "for about five bucks apiece," who "probably just shoves them in a sack and dumps them in the river," addressed the students on prayer:

> He started off with about fifty corny jokes, just to show us what a regular guy he was. Very big deal. Then he started telling us how he was never ashamed, when he was in some kind of trouble or something, to get right down on his knees and pray to God. He told us we should always pray to God—talk to Him and all—wherever we were. he told us we ought to think of Jesus as our buddy and all. He

said *he* talked to Jesus all the time. Even when he was driving his car. That killed me (16-17).

I might have related to that, *if you want to know the truth.* It killed me one time in parochial school when a priest came to class so drunk he couldn't hold an eraser. It killed me when a quiet nun sadistically beat an errant child with a yardstick. It killed me when I discovered (in high school, as I began to drift away from the church) that one of the biggest patrons of our parish was a leader in Capone's Mafia.

But I had no way to deal with my observations. No way to grasp the human comedy which might lend way to understanding or, more hopefully, compassion. Such things were not discussed among the family. Mine was not a neighborhood of readers. Ours was not a house of books.

No, I hadn't read *The Catcher in the Rye,* or even heard of it at the time, though Holden and I were about the same age, going through some of the same things, from entirely different backgrounds. Not that reading *Catcher* would have made any great difference. Not that any one book is the ticket to enlightenment and change. But one never knows. It was certainly a story I was prepared to experience.

I suspect, like most sixteen year-olds, I could have used Holden Caulfield's voice and humor to lend tenor and resonance to my own breaking voice. My own doubts. Which might have given me the perspective I lacked. The inner language to deal with all the adolescent conflicts, despair, double standards, dissatisfaction in the world as I knew it then, not to mention all the vagaries of innocence and the search for love. Which is certainly what Holden was after. *If you want to know the truth.*

What I got instead were the usual textbook-packaged authors, pasteurized, sanitized, homogenized (the hit-or-miss approach, depending on whether the teacher was ahead or behind schedule) from Washington Irving to maybe Robert Frost stopping by a woods on a snowy evening— which was all right, if you lived near a woods. Which might even begin to register as pure poetry, in the range of the beautiful and meaningful and universal—*if* you had the right teacher to guide you. *If* you had experienced enough to relate to what storytellers and poets were trying to tell you.

It seems to me "literature" is too often wasted upon the young.

Wrong books, wrong teachers, wrong time. You've got to meet individual students on their own territory, and only *then* take them back to experience all they missed, all that lies ahead. Get them to the place where they are self-generating, pursuing the only educational goal worth striving for: the freedom of self-discovery.

The problem was most students (adolescents) were accustomed to a different reality. And either they followed the program, remained tranquilized in the classroom—uninspired, untouched, as they were—or they moved out on their own, listening to the voices in the halls, on the street...some of whom may even be readers passing on the word: "Ever read *Catcher in the Rye*? Funniest goddam book! You've got to read it."

Which is how I heard of *Catcher*, the summer after I graduated from high school and decided I might go on to junior college. Thanks to my "old Spencer" (who said I was an eight cylinder engine only firing on four), my "Mr. Antolini" (who taught beyond the text, loved life, art, literature, philosophy) and to Holden who, by the end of *Catcher*, was going to give it another try himself even though he and I and most teenagers were in the same boat, in agreement entirely: "I mean how do you know what you're going to do till you *do* it?"

I had begun to read sometime in my junior/senior year, mostly on my own, mostly outside of school, beginning with *The Caine Mutiny*. There were other, required books in between (never *Huckleberry Finn*, unfortunately) none of which "stuck." Except for "Mr. Antolini" reading philosophical tidbits from a book called *Light from Many Lamps*.

Then came *Catcher*. Like a revelation. When it was all over. (High school, that is.) Only it wasn't all over. Because after *Catcher* came the deluge. After *Catcher* I discovered Thomas Wolfe. You can imagine what happened after that. You read Thomas Wolfe at a crucial stage in your life and you're never the same. And what he said about home was absolutely true.

I finished junior college, left home to attend the university, feeling and acting at times a little like Holden Caulfield in my raincoat—cynical, concerned, profane, lost, but searching for what was real, what was true.

Catcher remained with me—through college, through a short stint in graduate school, reporting, the army, construction work, foreign travel, teaching, parenting, and eventually writing books of my own as a way of life. Even fighting battles with various censorial forces seeking to deny the inalienable American rights of both writer and reader.

Students are often ahead of their teachers, ahead of their community, reading books (often the very books some communities eventually choose to censor because of language or ideas) that may take years to reach the classroom, the supplemental reading list, the approval of those who decide what's literature and what ain't.

And who's to say that any student, any reader, is ill-prepared to read/interpret any book he chooses, for whatever reason, without approval or benefit of teacher or censor?

Granted I did not "get" all of *Catcher* reading it on my own, outside the classroom, no teacher, no study guide, no class discussion, no theme papers on: "What does Holden's red hunting cap symbolize?"; "Explain the title of the book."; "What is the significance of Holden's concern for the ducks in Central Park?"; "Discuss the role of the nonconformist in society."; "Why is Phoebe's admonition, 'You don't like *any*thing that's happening' a turning point in the book?"; "Why does Holden keep saying. 'If you want to know the truth'?"

There's something to be said about discovering a book on one's own.

In the countless essays which surround any literary work, where reviewers, critics, censors, scholars, would-be scholars, literary scavengers and surgeons of all sorts, dissect a book with the intent of discovering the source of life or death, the real heart of the matter, (better yet, the soul, if the mission be mystical, excising symbols and holding them to the light, uncovering layers of fatty philosophical tissue, cutting out cancerous cells of cant run amuck) or merely celebrating/substituting their own obvious erudition in light of the author's obvious failure to "write the book he should have written," "display the language and style the form demands," "appeal to the moral standards of the community," there is always a willful shortsightedness in the pursuit of their kind of truth: the ordinary reader. The reader oblivious of critical reviews, who reads a book for the pure joy of reading.

What and when do we hear from *that* reader? Does anybody know or care? Shouldn't the experience remain personal, one-on-one? Isn't that why a writer writes: to please himself first, and *then* the general reader? One is reminded of Hemingway's response:

I suppose there are symbols since critics keep finding them.... It's hard enough to write books and stories without being asked to explain them as well. Also it deprives the explainers of work. If five or six or more good explainers can keep going why should I interfere with them? Read anything I write for the pleasure of reading it. Whatever else you find will be the measure of what you brought to the reading.

How many millions of readers, one supposes, read J.D. Salinger's, *Catcher in the Rye* without benefit of teacher, professor, community censor, or the huge volume of criticism (The Salinger industry) that has analyzed everything from why the name Caulfield?, the significance of Holden's red hunting cap, Holden as sixteen year-old existentialist, Holden as Huck reincarnate, Phoebe as evocation of the Zen Buddhist tradition: "She was sitting smack in the middle of the bed, outside the covers, with her legs folded like one of those Yogi guys," to a conscientious censor's tally of bad words in the book: "*Catcher in the Rye* takes the Lord's name in vain 295 times and uses blatant blasphemy 587 times in 187 pages of text," to the meaning of "Fuck you." *If you want to know the truth....*

Catcher's corpse seems pretty well picked clean. Still it survives, beyond criticism, and remains—real, humorous, humane, engaging, influential, very much alive more than forty years since its publication, though *still* one of the most frequently banned books in American high schools.

It is difficult at this stage in our nation's history—after Vietnam, after the 60s, after Nixon's Watergate, after Reagan's Iran-Contra affair, after televangelists on the take, MTV, docudramas, Wall Street traders, crime in the streets, drugs in the home, poverty in the schools, violence in television and movies, after the TV Mini Series: "WAR from Panama and the Gulf" (live, living color, and censored by the Pentagon to protect us from ourselves—"information management" according to Washington lipspeak), after the buying and selling of congressmen, after Jesse Helms rewrites the First Amendment to suit his artistic tastes at the expense of our liberties, after the most profane language imaginable can be heard, read, and seen graffitied on the walls all over America (with few Holden Caulfields vainly attempting to erase all the FUCK YOUs in the world to protect the innocence of children)—that The *Catcher in the Rye* or any book poses a threat to any American of any age.

Nothing is phonier in America than censorship. Or innocence.

Holden is a constant reminder that Americans must grow up, *if you want to know the truth.*

WORK CITED

Salinger, J. D. *The Catcher in the Rye.* New York: Bantam Books, 1964.

FIGHTING WORDS IN AND OVER *CATCH-22*
Marshall Toman

Literary censors assume that literature influences our political actions and social attitudes, an obvious but complicated presupposition. We know, after all, that literature's influences are unpredictable and widely varying. *Catch-22*, ostensibly about a World War in the 40s, was written in the 50s, published in the early 60s, and did only moderately well in U. S. sales until the late 60s when sales boomed. Morris Dickstein called the novel (and another by Kurt Vonnegut) "classics of the anti-Vietnam generation," "comic bibles of protest" (111), implying that those resisting the war in Asia sought guidance and inspiration from Joseph Heller's book. The correlation between the book's increasing sales and the swelling resistance to the escalating war can be pointed to as confirming the assertion: people read of the connection between war and capitalistic profiteering and read the vividly depicted horrors of an incompetent and corrupt chain of command and were confirmed in their resistance to an illegal war. But while protestors increased so did the number of recruits who went unprotestingly to Vietnam, people like Tim O'Brien, later to write his *Catch-22*-influenced novel about his Vietnam experiences. James S. Mullican has explained how readers of this comic Bible of protest could still fight. Rather than a spur to protest, the book may simply have had a cathartic effect—people frustrated with government, bureaucracy, and war have their anger and frustration against their society purged in the imagination, with the result that they continue to put up with the "system" in their real lives.

Given such antithetic explanations of *Catch-22*'s effect, we can resort to personal testimony—our own and that of our community of readers— as to the book's effect. My own experience was profound. Coming from a family whose father, uncles, and cousins had fought in Vietnam, Korea, and both World Wars, I had a very different attitude toward American soldiering after I read the novel. I would have, fairly unquestioningly, served in the armed forces before; now I am far more skeptical of the underlying motives and causes of wars, far less likely to to be willing to serve, and the novel was the beginning of my cynicism. Is my attitude good or bad? From the State's point of view, with its determination to conserve itself, my change to cynicism was unquestionably bad. But should the State determine what we need? Or shall we decide for ourselves?

Given that literary art has very different effects on different readers, what teachers of literature believe is that the reading milieu can influence readers' responses. And I submit that if teachers create the milieu in which *Catch-22* was intended to be read, the book is not only *not* detrimental but positively useful.

I use the word "milieu" rather than the more specific "classroom situation" or "pedagogical approach" because my encounter with *Catch-22* was outside of academia but was nonetheless influenced by a reading milieu. I came to the book in the 80s, after Vietnam had been exposed as a national defeat—in several senses—and after I had heard the book spoken of as a 60s protest novel. And the book, perhaps consequently, made sense to me as such.

Teachers create the reading milieu in the classroom. They influence the attitudes of students toward a book. The question then is whether any literary *work* should be censored: to the extent that society needs to control the rearing of its youth, shouldn't school boards control the reading milieu by censoring the teachers and the teaching approaches rather than the material? After all, St. Thomas Aquinas's views on women were taught to clerics in the middle ages as being a help toward understanding and ordering society and are brought up to students in Introduction to Women's Studies classes today as examples of what to react *against*— same material, vastly different uses of it. I offer this reflection as a way of standing, rather puzzledly at times, outside much of the ground on which censorship battles are fought. I could be more upset with a teacher teaching a conventionally good book (*Adam Bede?*) badly than by someone teaching a conventionally bad book (*Naked Lunch?*) well. But the ground on which censorship is usually waged examines texts, not teachers.

Often, objectors to a literary work focus on isolated aspects of content. In the late 70s a national movement toward censorship was helped by a conservative religious group founded by Norma and Mel Gabler out of Longview, Texas. Their Educational Research Analysts identified isolated passages of books considered objectionable in their categories of offenses (Negative Thinking, Promotes Humanism, Attacks on Country, Values, and so on). The organization's reviews enabled like-minded citizens to criticize books without ever reading them (Rene). *Catch-22*, for instance, was censored in Strongesville, Ohio (1974) because of its language.

Defenders of books ask that a work be considered in its totality, as the National Council of Teachers of English's Committee on the Right to Read's 1972 report evidences. Drafted by Arizona Professor Kenneth L. Donelson, the report reads, in part, that "the value and impact of any literary work must be examined as a whole and not in part—the impact of the entire work being more important than the words, phrases, or incidents out of which it is made" (8). Even if considered in the broad context, however, *Catch-22* may still pose legitimate concerns: (1) the protagonist, particularly Yossarian's attitude toward authority; (2) Heller's use of stereotypes; and (3) a reader's potential feeling that the novel presents a negative view of life.

Clearly the author is sympathetic to his protagonist to a greater degree than he is with Bob Slocum and Bruce Gold in the two novels that followed *Catch-22*. But a careful teacher, in order to demonstrate that Yossarian is a *qualified* hero, can create a reading milieu that will separate what is admirable in Yossarian from what is not. Such a separation is necessary because Heller's manipulation of plot conventions (Yossarian is a little guy against a big, dehumanizing Army bureaucracy) leaves an overwhelmingly favorable tint to the protagonist's character. Such a positive identification can then wash over into approval of some of Yossarian's other actions—lying, malingering, fornication, and mere rebellious irresponsibility. Yossarian's boredom with censoring letters, for instance, results in his blacking out their addresses instead of potentially damaging information ("annihilating entire metropolises with careless flicks of his wrist as though he were God" [8]). Such sabotage of a military procedure bears scrutiny, perhaps as a cheap authorial joke or a symbol of a common frustration. Other examples exist. Yossarian's censoring of letters leads to the chaplain's trial; his moving of the bomb line results in the loss of Major _____ de Coverley behind enemy lines.[1] A teacher can address Yossarian's qualified heroism.

A balanced perspective on the protagonist is important since one of the crucial issues the book raises is the appropriate attitude toward authority, and Yossarian is certainly anti-authoritarian. A parallel exists between Yossarian's loyalty to his "family" of buddies (rather than to the Army hierarchy, a loyalty which subverts the rule of law) and the mess officer, war profiteer Milo and his connections with Colonels Cathcart and Korn, a network which also replaces law with a crony system. Is one buddy network better than another? Such a question leads one to the novel's insights into the uses and misuses of power, and a crucial comparison must be made between Yossarian and Aarfy. The novel illustrates that the essential difference in the buddy networks is that the one Yossarian supports works to preserve life. Yossarian, for instance, unselfishly seeks out the daughter of the woman Nately was in love with in order to save this daughter from the ravages of post-liberation Rome. Aarfy, by contrast, seeks carnal pleasure in the Eternal City and then murders the prostitute he has used because she might damage his reputation. Aarfy joins the death-dealing network by being willing to lie for Cathcart and Korn; Yossarian rebels against this network by not accepting the deal Cathcart offers him, by deserting to save his life, and by thus giving an example of life–affirming defiance to the other men in the unit.

Although Yossarian's network of buddies is clearly better than Cathcart and Korn's, Yossarian's anti-authoritarian defiance of his superior officer is still misperceived as grounds for the charge that the novel is unpatriotic, that it contains "Attacks on Country" that the Gablers object to. I would argue that a close look at the novel reveals its excessive— though probably unconscious—*patriotism*. The plot resolution conforms to the American myth of rugged individualism. Instead of emphasizing cooperative group effort to change the repressive Cathcart/Korn command on Pianosa, the plot suggests that only heroic individual action leads to an individual's salvation. If I were among the ruling elite of the

United States, I could love this novel and foster its teaching in the schools. (But of course I would not foster the teaching of the book as a book that I, a member of the elite, promote because it serves my interest.) I could love the novel because the novel's conclusion encourages heroic *individual* effort to overthrow those in power. The hypothetical me (and *my* buddies) can quash any such puny attempts. The portrayal of unions, consumer organizations, or any cooperative effort that would work successfully against an elite in a novel would bother me a lot more. The novel is popular and has gained such wide currency in our capitalistic society because its structure is ultimately not threatening. Rather than the book's being un-American, I would criticize the novel's structure as being too unthinkingly, chauvinistically "American" in its mythologizing of heroic individual action.

Heller's use of stereotypes is another legitimate concern. LaVaun Daub, a critic of *Catch-22* from Snoqualmie, Washington, where an ultimately unsuccessful attempt to remove the novel from use in the school system was launched in 1979, objects to the book's language, saying that the novel "refers to women as whores" ("School Critics Attack Books"). True, the narrator as well as the characters adopts this manner of speaking, even referring to one woman only as "Nately's whore," but the deeper issue is not the language but the stereotyping of women. Women are treated superficially. Two things, however, can be brought out about the novel that reduce the force of the charge. Both considerations are a result of the novel's being written in the vein of satire, which is to say that the novel is more about ideas than characters.[2] First, as a satirical piece, the men, too, are stereotyped. Chaplain Tappman and his assistant Corporal Whitcomb, for instance, represent two divergent uses of religion: a true spiritual and life-preserving searching and an insincere, self-serving, Elmer Gantry boosterism. Second, the roles of women in this novel emphasize the life-affirming side of existence. Men like Milo and Korn who are responsible for much of the death in the novel are not interested in sex. Nurses and prostitutes fulfill Yossarian's unquenchable love of life.

It is just this unremitting valuing of *life* that makes the general objection to the novel's supposed negative and despairing view of life puzzling. The despair and the "overly descriptive passages of violence" that LaVaun Daub objected to are portrayed as results of corruption and greed and as foils to the overwhelming desire for their opposites. Many war novels are more realistic than *Catch-22*, but few have conveyed the horror of war as well as Heller's one scene of Yossarian's desperate and uncomprehending attempt to bandage what he understands is a superficial wound in the gunner Snowden. When, in an effort to help Snowden, he opens his flack jacket and views the stewed tomatoes Snowden had eaten for lunch floating in his ripped-open stomach, Yossarian is confirmed in his horror of war, an experience that up to that time had been a lark, as war is often perceived by young, Rambo-reared men. Something as shocking as this scene is needed to awaken the proto-Rambos of the world to the stakes of the game *before* they commit themselves, or (as voters) their country, to war.

Given proper handling, *Catch-22* as a whole is eminently teachable and deeply wise. But what of the isolated passages that people objected to? Finding the specific objections lodged against the novel is difficult. Objections are often based on general feelings, and when charges are specific, they rarely are reported in the newspapers. What follows, however, is one example of how to deal with a specific complaint. As all defenses must do, Nancy Skerritt's memo[1] places the objection to Cathcart's ideas of religion in context in order to evaluate them accurately.

TO: Snoqualmie Valley School District "Instructional Materials
         Committee"
FOR: Selection of *Catch-22* for inclusion in the Mount Si School Library
FROM: Nancy Skerritt, Teacher/Counselor
DATE: March 23, 1979

The Literary Tradition of Satire and *Catch-22**

The Oxford English Dictionary defines satire as "The employment in speaking or writing of sarcasm, irony, ridicule, etc. in exposing,

---

* Reprinted by permission of Nancy Skerritt.

denouncing, deriding, or ridiculing vice, folly, indecorum, abuses, or evils of any kind."

Satire, then, is a literary form of criticism. The satirist views the world as a hostile place embodying evils in a variety of forms. To correct these evils or injustices, he makes a verbal attack, though not totally in realistic terms. Rather, as pointed out in "The Elements of Prose," "He prefers to achieve his aims through ridicule, and he uses the weapons of exaggeration, understatement, incongruity, sarcasm, irony, humor, wit, burlesque, invective, parody, and any other instrument of destruction in his literary arsenal including cold, realistic detail."[1] Most of these techniques are clearly evidenced in *Catch-22*. In fact, the majority of sections presently being criticized as pornographic, sacriligious or containing negative thoughts about life are examples of Heller's excellent use of the recognized tools employed by the satirist.

The satirist's attitude can vary from mild detachment to intense anger, hatred, and bitterness. It is often marked by pessimism and distaste for certain values, customs, beliefs, and practices. The angry satirist, of which Heller is an example, will resort to denunciation and invective, the use of abusive terms, insults, profanity. Heller employs invective throughout *Catch-22*. His strong language is his tool to direct anger against that which he despises: incompetent leaders, mindless bureaucrats, exploiting capitalists, and self-centered, individuals for whom war is a game, a way to obtain selfish and often meaningless ends at the expense of death to many others.

Heller is writing in a recognized, well established literary tradition. Satire by its very nature is abusive and sacrilegious. One of the sections cited as objectionable in *Catch-22* involves Colonel Cathcart's questioning of the Chaplain in an attempt to receive divine help for the war effort so that the Colonel will gain the publicity he needs to become a general (pg. 195-202). This section is an example of a satirical attack on the weaknesses perceived in Cathcart's view of religion. His religion is one which grants wishes, in this case providing a tight bomb pattern, but makes no demands. Cathcart ultimately rejects prayer because he cannot have what he wants according to his terms. His religion is a status symbol. It excludes the enlisted man. Cathcart is amazed to learn that the enlisted men pray to the same god. He shows his prejudice, parodying a standard racial joke: "Oh, don't get me wrong, Chaplain. It isn't that I think enlisted men are dirty, common and inferior. It's that we just don't have enough room.... Some of my very best friends are enlisted men.... Honestly now, Chaplain, you wouldn't want your sister to marry an enlisted man would you?" (pg. 199) Cathcart finally rejects using prayer prior to his bombing missions because he cannot meet God on his own terms. "I'm not going to set these dammed prayer meetings up just to make things worse than they are.... Having the men pray to God probably wasn't such a hot idea anyway." (pg. 201)

At the same time that Colonel Cathcart is being satirized, the chaplain too is criticized by Heller. Chaplain Tappman is depicted as weak and ineffectual. Because he is full of doubts and fears, he cannot be a strong force in providing spiritual leadership. Consequently, we repeatedly view his feeble attempts to provide religious direction to his men. For example, he meekly expresses the men's concern to the Colonel that the number of missions has been raised again. The Colonel responds flatly: "Tell them there's a war going on" (pg. 202). With no further argument, the Chaplain merely replies: "Thank you, sir, I will" (pg. 202).

The chaplain though, like Yossarian, emerges as a spiritually power-ful character at the end of the book. It is ironic that the Concerned Parents criticize the treatment of religion in the name of their beliefs because it is the spirit ultimately that triumphs in *Catch-22*. On the contrary to asser-tions that the book projects negative thoughts on life, *Catch-22* is finally an affirmation of life, and the chaplain and Yossarian are the characters who best illustrate this theme. The chaplain is able to conquer his doubts and fears. He learns, along with Yossarian, Snowden's secret: Man is matter. Once the spirit dies, he is garbage. Seeing the injustice around him, he affirms his own spirit and stands up to those in authority, assisting in Yossarian's escape. Their inspiration can be found in the character of Orr. Orr's victory over the war, his escape to Sweden, is the miracle Yossarian and the chaplain need to affirm each's identity. Yossarian makes his choice to leave and to meet meaningful responsibilities elsewhere. "Let the bastards thrive, for all I care, since I can't do a thing to stop them but embarrass them by running away. I've got responsibilities of my own now, Danby. I've got to get to Sweden" (pg. 462). The chaplain, however, recognizes that he can now make worthy contributions to those he serves: "If Orr could row to Sweden, then I can triumph over Colonel Cathcart and Colonel Korn, if I only persevere" (pg. 461). And perseverance, finally, is what *Catch-22* is all about. Heller, the satirist, shows us, his audience, that we, too, can persevere over incompetency, exploitation, and meaninglessness by affirming our individual spirits.

SOURCES

1. Barron's *How to Prepare for the Advanced Placement Examination in English* Max Nadel and Arthur Sherrer, Jr., 1974, pg. 237.

This memo places an isolated passage, which parents found to be objectionable on religious grounds, within the context of the novel and within the context of a literary tradition in order to gain an understanding of the passage's true import.

But what of isolated passages that are objectionable *prima facie*? Although the portion of the NCTE statement quoted suggests that such passages are rare, an example from a current film is illuminating. The issue is one of information. Certain information need not be purveyed through literature. We do not need to know how a protagonist constructed a bomb from grocery store materials.[3] However integral to the plot, such information need not be spread among adolescents in a community. The Hollywood production code that the industry imposed on itself to avoid potentially more severe government censorship had the sensible stipulation that no movie could show how to commit a crime, in the sense of providing little-known information on how to pick locks, create a bomb, and so on. American films have often moved too far away from this ideal. The 1990 movie *Bad Influence*, for instance, has Rob Lowe's character turn a car into a bomb using virtually his bare hands, the tail light, and the gas tank. We can question the necessity and meaningfulness of providing millions with this simple idea. The case before authors in these instances is verisimilitude. And the case before censors is the price of such verisimilitude. As the film example suggests, a guide to such possibly legitimate censorship should be (A) the degree to which the information is potentially harmful and (B) the accessibility of the information. Few people know how to sabotage a car so effectively and the effects are potentially lethal. The details of the scene may well have been obscured.

I know of no instances in Catch-22 where the censorship of passages would apply, much less prevail to ban the book from libraries. Isolated passages objected to fall into the category of de-contextualized excerpts. The example of "overly descriptive passages of violence" vis-a-vis Snowden's death is illustrative. Or, as in the case of some of the novel's language, passages may be objectionable by community standards but the potential for harm is low and the information easily accessible elsewhere. Commenting more precisely is impossible without specific objections.

Responsible authors, presumably those taught in the schools, self-censor sensational, unnecessary material in the composition and revision process (as Owen Wister, upon Theodore Roosevelt's advice, refused to supply the details of a hideous act of cruelty in The Virginian). For other authors, the community, through its representatives on the school board, must decide. School boards must ask whether there is really, detrimental to the community, in the book, something that careful presentation in the reading milieu cannot reveal as acceptable to community standards.

In my reading of the novel the plot structure of this supposedly anti-authoritarian novel might well have the effect of being "dangerously" nurturing of complacency, fostering of the current status quo. But I would not advocate censoring it; I would advocate teaching it with some of these, truly volatile, issues in mind. Readers of Fredric Jameson will recognize parts of my analysis of Catch-22 as derived from a brief application of his Marxist, structurally analytical technique. This application suggests to me that, given a willingness to follow through with the answers' implications, the truly "dangerous" questions that the novel and its publishing history raise are

Why was Catch-22 so popular?
Should we be loyal to law?
Should we cooperate?

Should we like people like Yossarian?
Should we like people like Heller?

And, now, aren't these questions strangely like a very old-fashioned, even a biblical hermaneutics: a questioning of a text for answers to the human situation? What makes the novel "dangerous" also makes it potentially enlightening.

Catch-22, by the standards outlined here, contains nothing that should be censored and much that should be taught to students mature enough to appreciate the crucial issues.

NOTES

[1]The best exposition of Yossarian as really a rather irresponsible villain is Stephen L. Sniderman's "'It Was All Yossarian's Fault': Power and Responsibility in *Catch-22*."

[2]One of the best expositions of *Catch-22* as a novel that stresses ideas, a "rhetorical novel," is the appropriate chapter in David H. Richter's book *Fable's End: Completeness and Closure in Rhetorical Fiction*.

[3]Between drafts of this chapter, this hypothetical case was made vivid to my mind by an incident at a Minneapolis suburb's junior high. On a church weekend retreat, several of those attending shared information on how to make just such a bomb. The next week, the first bomb, wrapped in dog feces, exploded in a student's locker. Now the teachers have been alerted to confiscate those ordinary grocery store ingredients should they spy them in the halls or classrooms.

WORKS CITED

Donelson, Kenneth L. "The Students' Right to Read." Urbana: National Council of Teachers of English, 1972.

Dickstein, Morris. *Gates of Eden: American Culture in the Sixties*. New York: Basic Books, 1977.

Jameson, Fredric. *The Political Unconscious: Narrative as Socially Symbolic Act*. Ithaca: Cornell UP, 1981.

Mullican, James S. "A Burkean Approach to *Catch-22*." *College Literature*
    8 (1981): 42-52.

Richter, David H. *Fable's End: Completeness and Closure in Rhetorical Fiction*.
    Chicago: U of Chicago P, 1974. 136-65.

Rene, Gerald [Snoqualmie librarian]. Memo to the Snoqualmie Valley
    School District's Instructional Materials Committee. 23 Mar. 1979.

"School Critics Attack Books in Mount Si High Library." *The* [Snoqualmie,
    WA] *Valley Recorder*. 2 Feb. 1979: 2.

Skerritt, Nancy [Snoqualmie teacher/counselor]. Memo to the Snoqualmie
    Valley School District Instructional Materials Committee. 23 Mar.
    1979.

Sniderman, Stephen L. "'It Was All Yossarian's Fault': Power and
    Responsibility in *Catch-22*." *Twentieth-Century Literature* 19 (1973):
    251-58.

"THEY TELL YOU TO DO YOUR OWN THING, BUT THEY DON'T MEAN IT.": CENSORSHIP AND *THE CHOCOLATE WAR*

Zibby Oneal

'They murdered him.' So begins *The Chocolate War*, Robert Cormier's stunning novel about one young boy's struggle to maintain his integrity in the face of overwhelming opposition. How ironic that this novel, so deeply concerned with issues of freedom, should, itself, have encountered such opposition. How disturbing that there are schools and libraries in this country where a book of this quality has been declared unfit reading for adolescents. How ironic. How predictable. How sad.

Published in 1974, *The Chocolate War* was immediately—and understandably—controversial. It broke new ground in the world of young people's fiction, toppling dearly-held taboos, upsetting any number of conventions. Of course it was bound to be controversial, but unfit reading? I don't think so.

The characters in *The Chocolate War* are recognizably real late-Twentieth-Century American boys who sweat and pee and masturbate. They daydream fondly of girls' breasts. Their talk is explicit and laced with profanity. Certainly we had seen nothing quite like them before in fiction for the young, and adult reaction was mixed from the start. There were those of us who were captivated at once; others who were shocked. There was very little in the book to please the adult devoted to protecting some notion of youthful innocence, and the characters were only the beginning of the problem.

It is hard for me to believe that there are many people nowadays still troubled by Cormier's realism. Too much has changed since 1974. Books for the young have become outspoken and explicit in ways we would not have dreamed possible then, and we have grown accustomed to this greater latitude. It takes a lot more to shock us now.

And yet the book still shocks, or at least remains a target for criticism. Cormier's characters may seem almost old-fashioned now, innocent as they are of drugs or alcohol or anything but imagined sex. Their vices have been far out-distanced in contemporary novels for adolescents, but *The Chocolate War* has never been out-distanced in its power to disturb and provoke.

It is, above all, a novel of startling honesty. Stripped of euphemism and sentimentality, the book asks hard questions and refuses to provide the sorts of answers that, even now, we expect to find in books for the young. I think that it is in this refusal—in this deeply honest and moral refusal—that the book's value lies. But therein, also, lie its problems.

Many people who are no longer troubled by Cormier's characters, who have long accepted the disappearance of the old taboos, nonetheless have great reservations about the message they find in the book. I can understand these reservations, though I do not share them. Certainly Cormier provides hard pills to swallow.

Most of the action in *The Chocolate War* takes place in a Catholic prep school for boys. Ironically this Christian school is revealed as a breeding place for evil. Its faculty is radically corrupt. Its student body is dominated by a secret society whose ringleader is nothing if not the essence of cruelty. When the school undertakes its annual chocolate sale, corruption and cruelty merge and create a reign of terror.

Opposed to all this, almost by accident, is a young boy named Jerry Renault—a boy who doubts his own courage, who questions his ability to do anything in his life that will make a difference. In his locker he has a poster which reads, Do I Dare Disturb the Universe?

Cormier's ironic use of Eliot's line should give us some notion of the complexities we are about to encounter in this book, but in many ways it is easy to read *The Chocolate War* for much of its length as a relatively simple and familiar tale about the confrontation of Good and Evil. It is easy to recognize Jerry as the traditional hero of young people's fiction. He is an ordinary boy with ordinary capabilities who finds himself suddenly facing enormous odds with few resources but his own determination.

We are used to boys like Jerry. We have met them in book after book. Cormier gives us no reason to believe that Jerry can prevail in his struggle, and yet we readers, steeped in old traditions that extend as far back as fairy tales, are firmly convinced that he will succeed. That is how it goes and always has.

Jerry is chosen by the secret society to carry out an assignment intended to defy and disrupt the school administration's plans for the chocolate sale. He must refuse to sell chocolates for a defined period of time, making a public demonstration of his refusal. Certainly this is not an act of courage at the outset. Rather, it is a capitulation to the power of the student group. But as the story progresses, the nature of the refusal begins to alter.

Having completed his initial assignment, Jerry continues to refuse to sell chocolates, seeming, at first, hardly to know himself why he is taking this stand. Nevertheless, he persists, and his very persistence becomes a statement of identity.

Participation in the sale is, theoretically, voluntary, but there is great pressure to take part. Coercion exists on many levels, and refusal truly does seem a way to disturb the universe. Jerry's insistence on the voluntary nature of the project and, thus, on his right to choose, becomes his declaration of independence, his statement of principle, his act of courage. In all this we cheer him on.

So far this territory is familiar enough. Underlying all that seemed so new in 1974 is the age-old story of growth and self-discovery undertaken in the service of self-definition. We know this story and we know how it will end. Once the hero has endured his trials and accomplished his task of self-discovery, the future will stretch out bright and cloudless. Once again, as we have read so many times before, all will be well. But this is not the story Cormier is telling. There is nothing, finally, so simple or formulaic here. Quite the opposite. Jerry fails.

Is it this that still shocks us—this stark conclusion? Yes, of course, partly. The happy ending remains one of the unyielding conventions in fiction for the young, and with reason. Youngsters need to be told that their efforts can make a difference. Growing up is a mighty undertaking and requires large doses of optimism. We want young people to believe that bravery and honor and humane behavior can prevail in the world. But are we telling them the truth when we insist, as we always have in their books, that the right and the good and the brave will invariably triumph? That deep despair will never touch their lives?

Cormier dares to tell them something else and we gasp at his daring. Take a look at the world, he says. Failure happens. Despair ensues. This is also part of what is true. We know that, of course, we adults, but we somehow feel that young people should not have to deal with these facts. We pretend that they are not already fully aware of defeat and despair in their own lives.

Cormier abandons such pretense. He speaks to youngsters about what is real sometimes, what is sometimes unavoidable.

Jerry fails and he fails horribly. From this failure his spirit does not rise. Overwhelmed, beaten in both body and spirit, he gives in to a soul-sickening despair and the beginnings of a deep cynicism. All his trying has been for nothing, he thinks. There is no way to win against such opposition. There is no point even to try. "They tell you to do your own thing, but they don't mean it. They don't want you to do your thing, not unless it happens to be their thing, too" (187). These are very nearly Jerry's last words in the book, and they hit hard.

The conclusion of *The Chocolate War* was—and remains—powerfully disturbing. We find it hard to accept its pessimism, its refusal to provide a single gleam of hope, and harder still to accept the cynicism in Jerry's assessment of the world. But perhaps hardest of all is the glimpse that Cormier gives us into our own hearts.

Jerry's voyage of self-discovery is taken in stages, and we take it with him. Struggling with despair and disillusionment, he spirals inexorably toward a single truth. Lying beaten on the ground, he is overcome by the realization that he is no better than those who have tormented him. Pushed to the wall, he has longed for revenge. Bullied on all sides, he has agreed to participate in an act of violence. Within himself, he discovers, are the very things he has fought—the hatred and the violence—and by giving in to these things he has become Them.

But what of us, the readers? We have cheered Jerry all the way. When he longs for revenge, we approve. When he agrees to violence, we urge him on. He is right, we think. He has taken too much. As the book's final, violent episode unfolds, we are there, yelling in the stands. We have become the mob, participants in the very evil we profess to despise, strong in the belief that violence cures violence and that hate is properly met with hate. In this powerful final scene, Cormier invites us to look into the enemy's face, and Jerry's self-discovery becomes our own.

The Chocolate War is strong medicine. Cormier refuses from first to last to compromise with the truth as he sees it, and, in so doing, he shows us things about ourselves and our world that we might rather ignore. But we ignore at our peril and delude ourselves if we believe that doing away with a book will do away with the problems it addresses.

Few novels for adolescents make any attempt to take on the issues Cormier addressed in The Chocolate War. Here we are asked to contemplate freedom and how freedom comes to be abridged in a small society. We are invited to think about evil and where the roots of evil lie. We must consider courage and cowardice, effort and failure, the nature of cruelty and the nature of love.

Cormier makes us think. Perhaps, ultimately, that is his cardinal sin. He forces us to re-examine our comfortable assumptions about who we are and what we believe and what a book for young people ought to be about.

No one is required to like The Chocolate War or to agree with its conclusion or to want to take its characters home to dinner, but nobody has the right to deny it to someone else. The decision to pull a book from the shelf is dangerous business, and most dangerous of all when that decision involves the young.

We teach our young people about their First Amendment rights, then refuse them a book. We tell them that they are free to learn and question and explore in this country, then insist that we will decide the boundaries of that freedom. What can they make of this? What can they think?

Pressures to set limits abound, of course. All of us who write for the young are aware of those pressures and sympathize with the teachers and librarians who occupy the front lines in this struggle. But struggle it must be if we are to honor the promises our country makes. Otherwise, Jerry Renault is right. We tell them to do their own thing, but we don't mean it.

Is that how it is? Is that what we are really telling them? If so, how can we argue with Cormier's book? He is merely burnishing the mirror that shows us our faces.

WORK CITED

Cormier, Robert. *The Chocolate War*. New York: Dell Publishing, 1986.

ANTHONY BURGESS'S
A CLOCKWORK ORANGE
Douglas A. Pearson, Jr.

> "Oh! it is absurd to have a hard-and-fast rule about what one should
> read and what one shouldn't. More than half of modern culture
> depends on what one shouldn't read."
>   Algernon Moncrieff in Oscar Wilde's *The Importance of Being
>   Earnest*

Anthony Burgess, a writer whose talents and interests include the
history of literature, the study of linguistics, and the composition of
music, published *Language Made Plain* in 1964, the year after the publication
in the United States of *A Clockwork Orange*. The book begins with an
observation about language, about its power to disturb:

> Words (their meaning, spelling, pronunciation); the way foreigners
> talk (foreigners being everybody except us)—these frequently arouse
> strong feelings but very rarely much curiosity. Language tends to
> generate heat rather than a desire for light; the very word can be an
> accusation (Mr. Waldo, in Dylan Thomas' *Under Milk Wood*, is guilty
> of, among other crimes, 'using language.') (3)

Wilde wrote the words in the epigraph above nearly 100 years ago. It is
difficult to say exactly what Algernon means. After all, he's using language.
But, as a man of means and one likely to be in a position to know what his
culture depended upon, Algernon seems to be acknowledging, not
discovering, the idea about reading.

Is it a given, one wonders, that cultures require for their survival an
actively subversive literature? So goes, it would seem, Algernon's rather
matter-of-fact observation. In his nearly detached way, Algernon describes

the play of vital ideas in a society. For every Yin there must be a Yang, competing and colliding with its opposite. For the Dionysian, the Apollonian. For eros, agape. For the white, the black. For the underdog, the incumbent. For the young, the old. Were these oppositions exclusively rational concepts, there might be essentially reasoned discourse, an interaction likely only to advance, not retard, the development and/or improvement of a society.

But these oppositions create highly charged, emotional responses. The oppositions are essentially emotive—and they can be powerfully subversive. For example, one of my students recently wrote of his viewing of the film *The Silence of the Lambs,* a work whose portrayal of a psychotic killer has raised more than one call for censorship. My student thinks Hannibel Lector is someone you know is evil, yet someone who "ends up being a hero in your mind." More than one reader of this student's notion may be shocked, even sickened that such a claim is made for Lector. Clearly, the claim gives fuel to those who worry that the subversive influence of a Lector (notice the pun on "reader") is what leads to the destruction of values, to the decay and demise of society, to the loss of law and order.

It is with these ideas in mind that I wish to discuss Burgess' *A Clockwork Orange* (book and film version), the book a work of modern culture which has been under attack since its publication first in the United Kingdom in 1962 and elsewhere in 1963, the film scripted and directed by Stanley Kubrick and released in 1972.

To begin with, what's not to *dis*like in Burgess' novel? Its "hero," Alex, is cocky, self-indulgent, a bully, a perpetrator of sexual violence. (In the film, his attack on a female health club operator ends in her death.) He's the kind one loved to hate on the playground—smug, ready to cheat and hurt and control others. He is every parent's nightmare: a teenager (the novel says he's 15; the film pretends that he's still a schoolboy, but he appears to be nearer 21) who defies his parents, controls them really, always giving the appearance of being in some ways a part of civilized family and social life. (Perhaps Burgess has loaded the deck a bit by making the parents leading candidates for Obtuse Parents of the Year.)

Alex has established a separate life, detached himself from home and school, and has formed a surrogate family—his gang of droogs. The cycle of his lawless life is rounded nightly by robberies, beatings, fights with other gangs, indulgence in drink and drugs. Geoffrey Aggeler, in noting the many important linguistic features of the novel, points out that Alex is a name that has multiple meanings. In addition to suggesting a Russian/British context, the name *Alex* creates "The fusion of the negative prefix *a* with the word *lex* [and] suggests simultaneously an absence of law and a lack of words" (173).

In addition, the dystopian world Burgess depicts is the realization of many nightmarish views of the future. Aggeler points out that the portrayal was actually influenced by Burgess' observations of Russian gangs (stilyagi) in (then) Leningrad in 1961 and London "toughs known as the 'teddy boys'" (170). In any case, pessimists among us may feel inclined to believe that the trashiness of the city, the meanness of the teenagers, the breakdown of the social institutions and the schools, and the inability of the police to bring order out of this chaos are all results of an alien set of values that must be suppressed, wiped out.

Perhaps all society must do is rid itself of those who misbehave. Prison sentences, a conventional social and legal response to those who defy the laws of society, are the principal tool of the society in *A Clockwork Orange*. But the life within prisons is, according to Burgess' view, all the clichés we remember from all of the bad prison movies: "Now what I [Alex, the narrator of the story] want you to know is that this cell was intended for only three when it was built, but there were six of us there, all jammed together sweaty and tight" (84).

The social problem is clear: overcrowding in the jails. The malaise which has created this problem is not so easy to define. To the rescue come society's therapists, ready with a fix presumably addressed not only to the symptom (too many criminals) but more fundamentally aimed at the character traits of the individuals who engage in crime. The government chooses Alex for an experiment in behavior modification—the Ludovico Technique. (Here Burgess is responding satirically to the ideas proposed by B. F. Skinner in *Walden Two* and *Beyond Freedom and Dignity*.) Medical staff inject Alex with drugs and then expose him to films of beatings, warfare, sexual violence, and other cruelties. In just two weeks, Dr.

Brodsky produces in Alex an antipathy to violence of any kind. In fact, it makes him physically ill to watch it or to attempt any violent or indecent act.

Let's see where we are. We have a book which angers us because its principal character behaves unacceptably. He quite literally undermines our confidence that the world we live in is, or is likely to be, a safe one. We don't like knowing about that, or considering that it might be true. We would rather not have to think about it. BUT, if we do have to think about it, and it seems unavoidable (even if we don't have Burgess' book on our shelf or at our local library, the nightly news brings us the same message), then perhaps we ought to find an efficient way to deal with it. So we accept, perhaps without thinking about it very hard, the idea that we need to reduce the number of criminals and that we can do that by changing the way people behave. We can "immunize" them against crime, we think. Thus, the Ludovico Technique or its equivalent is what we call for. Using this technique, we "cure" our criminal population. In effect, this way of thinking gets us through the first two-thirds of Burgess' novel.

Not content is Burgess to leave us satisfied that a problem has been dealt with. No, he discovers a new problem in the solution to the other problem. After Alex has had the full dose of the Ludovico Technique and is displayed to a credulous audience to demonstrate how fully cured he is, a cranky prison chaplin's voice is raised in defiance—and we as readers of the novel are forced to think his query through. The chaplin puts it simply: "He [Alex, our reformed criminal] ceases to be a wrongdoer. He ceases also to be a creature capable of moral choice" (126).

It was bad enough at the start for Burgess to offer society a novel with so ill a main character and so malevolent a world. It seemed only right for him to show better judgment and provide a solution for the problems he had so vividly depicted in the early going. But to throw doubt on the solution, to raise impertinent moral questions, is to undermine totally what little confidence we had begun to sense in the middle portion of the novel. Part Three of the novel and film virtually undoes the middle, returning us to the beginning, to an Alex fully capable of good and bad choices and to a society likely to live in danger because of this unpredictable characteristic in human behavior. Ludovico's technique, seemingly a legitimate way to control the forces of evil in our society, is discredited. Those readers who would seek such a remedy are left wondering at a novelist so ready to disavow what seems eminently sensible social engineering. What, then, should the reader's response be?

We must savor this book, not censor it. We must recognize the fundamental issues it raises, the very ones we encounter, say, in Milton's *Paradise Lost*, the problem of what to do with humanity that is capable of good and evil. We must struggle with the problems it poses: the rights of the individual versus those of the society, the tensions between the old and the young, the danger we sense in moving off, as we do each day, into an unknown future from our "secure" present and past. We must allow that the presence of evil affirms the value of good works and that in the struggle between the two lies some peculiar territory valuable in its own right. It may be, in fact, that we must acknowledge the attractiveness of the evil, that through publications such as *A Clockwork Orange* we are made dramatically and emotionally aware of the importance of the issues at stake.

For readers of *A Clockwork Orange*, this willingness to suppress our censoriousness can be best obtained by reading and rereading the novel. Through this activity, we may test the ideas, examine the assumptions, and debate the issues. It is this very activity which will throw us into the arena of ideas that matter in our society, that will help us to continue to grow as human beings.

For would-be viewers of the film, there may be some difficulties. The film depicts the violence of Alex's life (the sex, the beatings, the robberies) in uncompromisingly vivid pictures. And the film shapes somewhat positive responses to Alex by showing him to be a bright, inventive young man, one who has a tremendous attraction to high art, the music of Beethoven—Ludwig Van, as Alex reminds us more than once. In some instances, the film even suggests that Alex's promiscuity is just "good fun," as when Alex takes two teeny boppers back to his room and their sexual antics are presented in speeded up motion accompanied by the William Tell Overture. But the novel arms us for dealing with the film:

This [the violent films Alex was seeing while being reprogrammed] was real, very real, though if you thought about it properly you couldn't imagine lewdies actually agreeing to having all this done to them in a film, and if these films were made by the Good or the State you couldn't imagine them being allowed to take these films without like interfering with what was going on. So it must have been very clever what they call cutting or editing or some such vesch. (103)

But society does not always look at film or literature critically, does not always understand what responsibility it has to itself in this regard. Each of us, teachers in particular, has a responsibility to understand the media, to be aware of the manipulation possible within a given medium, and to be conscious also of the powerful generator of ideas a work such as *A Clockwork Orange* is. Each of us also has the responsibility to respond to the media, aware that media can distort, exaggerate, perversely define the world we know, but aware also that the media articulate ideas and experiences which engage our deepest personal and social potential.

WORKS CITED

Aggeler, Geoffrey. *Anthony Burgess: The Artist as Novelist.* University, AL: University of Alabama Press, 1979.

Note: Aggeler introduces a special view of the dualism so evident in Burgess' work. He distinguishes between Pelagian liberals and Augustinian conservatives. Aggeler makes a very strong case for seeing Burgess' works as the embodiment of the historic philosophical and theological debate between the belief in the perfectibility of man and man's need for grace and guidance from without. Samuel Coale, too, cites the dualism in Burgess' work. Coale quotes Burgess' comments from an interview published in the *Paris Review* in 1977: "'duality is the ultimate reality'"; [life] "'is binary'" (7). Quoted in Coale, *Anthony Burgess.* New York: Ungar, 1981.

Burgess, Anthony. *A Clockwork Orange.* New York: Norton, 1963.

_____. *Language Made Plain.* New York: Crowell, 1965.

SHE'S JUST TOO WOMANISH FOR THEM: ALICE WALKER AND *THE COLOR PURPLE*

Angelene Jamison-Hall

When I was growing up in rural North Carolina, I heard mothers, including my own, tell their daughters, "Don't be so womanish." In those days, I believed, as did most little girls, that womanish was a pejorative term and that I should therefore try to rectify whatever behavior had brought on the scolding. It was not until years later—after college graduate school and several years of teaching, that I read Alice Walker's definition[1] of the term in her book, *In Search of Our Mothers' Gardens*, and realized being womanish was not such a bad thing. In fact, it was not bad at all. Walker's putting the term in the context of Black women's self-exploration and self-definition; forced me to think about how people raised their brows in disapproval when girls resisted convention, insisting on exploring and discovering new levels of themselves. Few people seemed to understand that these little girls who were daring enough to put their hands on their hips and ask questions or make audacious comments, both which challenged custom, were actually laying the groundwork for their own liberation. They were demonstrating their potential to be revolutionaries.

Alice Walker is womanish. From her first work, *The Third Life of Grange Copeland* through her most recent novel, *The Temple of My Familiar*, she has demonstrated a tendency, to be "outrageous, audacious, courageous...*willful*" in her vision (Search XI). She has dared to explore subjects and discuss issues which are generally unacceptable to many readers, and she seems to have no qualms about exposing any problems which stand in the way of people's freedom, including especially sexism and racism. Certainly, she is womanish in her creative vision and nowhere is this quality more adamantly demonstrated than in her novel, *The Color Purple*. It is perhaps Walker's womanish vision in the novel that precipitated its listing on the "most frequently challenged books of interest or appeal to young adult readers" (YASD).

The Color Purple has been the most talked about novel of the last decade. People have held forums, discussion groups, seminars, lectures and even public debates on the novel. On some of these occasions, Alice Walker was accused of everything from dividing the Black community to destroying the mind of children to being a feminist tool of white racism. More specifically, some even denounced her for writing a novel whose central focus, they believed, is the glorification of Black women and the denigration of Black men.

That Alice Walker's primary intentions in the novel are to elevate Black women to sainthood at the expense of Black men is not only a misreading of the novel, but a lack of familiarity with her development as a writer. Clearly, Alice Walker is critical of Black men and their oppression of Black women, but the substance here is not simply an attack on Black men. Rather, Walker is concerned with any oppressive behavior (even that which Black women exercise against themselves) that stands in the way of individual and collective freedom. Like many Black women writers of the last two decades, Walker is interested in examining Black women's lives, illuminating their struggles for self-definition and celebrating their unique history.

What is especially unsettling to many readers about *The Color Purple* is that it dares to tell a womanish story, a story that looks at the world from a Black woman's point of view and reflects Black women's complexity and intensity. *The Color Purple* wastes no time or talent deliberating trying to refute the myths and stereotypes that have emerged over the years; yet by emphasis, it shatters many of the illusions people have about Black women. The novel is bold enough to discuss God and sex in the same chapter, even in the same scene and during a conversation between two women, not two men. It is an audacious work which does not plead to be loved nor does it beg for acceptance. The novel simply tells a story that needed to be told.

The Color Purple brings to light the historical experiences of Black women and how their coming together as women loving themselves and each other serves as a liberating force. Innovative in form, language and theme, the novel represents "a further development in the womanish process Walker is evolving" (Christian 93). An interesting epistolary style, a series of letters from Celie, the heroine, to God and then to Nettie, and letters from Nettie to Celie, is Alice Walker's attempt to recapture one of the few early modes of expression available to women in the West (Ibid.) It is also her way of bringing the reader closer to Celie's development from a victim of mental, physical and emotional abuse to a free woman who comes to know, appreciate and love herself as a valuable member of the community.

The language of the novel, particularly in Celie's letters to God and to Nettie, is as innovative as the form. Celie's rural Black idiom is not the "acceptable" language, the language of the learned, but it is the language which provides the reader with greater insight into her character and a more intimate view of her growth. Of equal importance, Celie's letters in her own vernacular are her means of self-expression and in telling her story in her own words, she initiates the process of self-discovery.

Though form and language serve as a source of debate on *The Color Purple*, the themes have been even more controversial, specifically those that are taboo in Black literature (Christian 94). Incest in the Black family, the brutal oppression of Black women by Black men, rape and other forms of violence, and lesbianism have been the focus of much of the discussion, especially from those critical of Alice Walker. Arguing that such issues among Blacks should remain in-house, these self-proclaimed protectors of the race respond as if *The Color Purple* has exposed some hidden racial scandal which would fade away eventually if only it were kept quiet. Of course, Walker's focus on these themes also provided an excuse for book banners to challenge the book's appropriateness for young people (YASD 75).

This is not to say that these so-called "forbidden" themes completely dominate the content of *The Color Purple*. There are other subjects that broaden the range of Walker's vision: sisterhood, self-actualizing forces in a community of women, a liberating concept of God, the politics of language, the international dimensions of Black women's oppression and, of course, racism, the latter of which Alice Walker has been accused of avoiding (Forum).[2] What is particularly interesting, though, is that these themes are also questioned because Walker takes a womanish approach in her presentation (YASD 75).

Perhaps nowhere is Walker more womanish than in her treatment of love in *The Color Purple*. The novel is, after all, a story of love—self-love, women's love for each other, and God's love for all of us. It is a story of the liberating powers of love. Walker, forever challenging the reader to examine the limitations of convention, writes about situations confronting women daily and suggests that most solutions are rooted in our ability to love ourselves and others.

The most important love in *The Color Purple* is the love of self, which "energizes [the women] to the point that they break their chains of enslavement, change their own worlds, time and Black men (Parker-Smith 485). Consider for example, Shug Avery, who defies most of society's conventions and standards and elects instead to please herself. Like Ma Rainey and Bessie Smith, Shug Avery is womanish enough to challenge the notion that only men can understand the kind of life that merits the blues. Not only does she understand this life, but she lives it and is courageous and creative enough to celebrate it in her music.

As a young girl, Shug gave birth to three children fathered by Albert, not because she was forced, but because she loved sex. "...when I met Albert, and once I got in his arms," she says, "nothing could git me out. It was good, too...." (Walker 115). After the birth of the third child, her parents put her out, and she went to live with an aunt whom Shug's mother says is much like Shug. "She drink, she fight, love mens to death...cook. Feed fifty men, screw fifty-five" (116). Albert married someone else because his mother and father objected to the way Shug stepped beyond the limits of acceptability for a woman. In other words, they thought she was too wild. Now years later, Shug comes back into Albert's life with the same daring and aggressive character as when she left. The difference this time, though, is she sleeps with Albert *and* his wife.

Worldly, bold and bound by none of society's restrictions, Shug Avery is an explorer, a lover of life and all living things. She finds satisfaction in the blues and in sex, the very things women are taught to fear and shun, but which illustrate Shug's insistence on growing and experiencing life her own way. Perhaps it is Shug Avery's appetite for what some might call the *risqué* that causes Celie to think she "talk and act sometimes like a man" (82). Like most people who have not freed themselves from convention, Celie assumes any woman who dares to wander and explore, to experience life and, God forbid, love sex is bound to be "acting like a man." Shug Avery loves men, but she loves herself more, and it is this self-love which defends her against becoming the victim of male oppression. This attitude and behavior are acceptable for men, but they are simply too womanish for women.

Sofia, another one of Walker's womanish women, might not be the worldly, blues-singing, pleasure-seeking person Shug Avery is, but through her character, Walker's emphasis on self-love and the struggle to be whole are equally enlightening. Growing up in a house dominated by men and with a mother who was constantly abused, Sofia learns early that a woman must fight the male drive to control. Aware that any woman who loves herself protects herself, Sofia fights all those who seek to oppress her in any way. When her husband, Harpo, tries to "make her mind" as his father had taught him, Sofia ignores him. When he tries to beat her, she almost kills him and says to Celie, "I love Harpo...God knows I do. But I'll kill him dead before I let him beat me" (46).

Sofia is as quick to fight racism as she is sexism. When the mayor's wife asks her if she would like to be her maid, Sofia says "hell no," challenging whites' stereotype of the Black woman as servant. The mayor slaps Sofia for sassing his wife, and Sofia, bent on fighting oppression, knocks the mayor to the ground. She gets a long prison term because she is Black, female and had the audacity to defy the accepted standards of behavior for Black females.

After eleven and a half years in prison and six months probation, Sofia is nonetheless determined to challenge whites' notions about race. She shocks the mayor's daughter, Eleanor Jane, when she turns the mistress-maid relationship upside down by refusing to play the nurturing mammy whites expect of Black women. When Eleanor Jane is trying to get Sofia to say she loves her (Eleanor Jane's) son, Sofia says, "I don't feel nothing about him at all. I don't love him, I don't hate him" (233). Eleanor

Jane, stunned that Sofia would challenge yet another one of whites' sacred myths—the Black woman as loving mother, sees Sofia as an aberration and indicates as much in her comment, "All the colored women I know love children. The way you feel is something unnatural" (233).

Sofia is one of the women who helps Celie transform herself from a fearful self-hating victim of male domination and oppression to a self-assertive and self-loving woman refusing to be mistreated by any man. Sofia shows Celie that life for women need not be characterized by disrespect, abuse, neglect or any other form of persecution.

Although Sofia's self-love and her consequent determination to fight oppression and protect herself are very instrumental in Celie's growth, it is Celie's bonding with Shug Avery that is largely responsible for Celie's change. For it is Shug Avery who teaches Celie about life and love and how to raise herself from beneath the boots of men. Before Shug Avery comes into Celie's life, Celie's self-definition is based on her history as a victim of male oppression. Her stepfather, Alfonso, for example, rapes her, gives away her children and then turns her over to Albert to raise his ill-bred children. Albert, whom Celie calls *Mister*, ruthlessly abuses her and has no problems telling her exactly what he thinks of her. "You black, you pore, you ugly, you a woman...you nothing at all" (187). Interestingly, Albert's diatribe captures precisely what Celie thinks of herself.

Shug Avery teaches Celie to understand that one can be Black, female, poor and ugly *and* significant (YASD 75). This conviction is perhaps the most womanish principle in the novel, especially since society believes and acts on the opinion that the lowest thing one can be is Black, female, poor and ugly. Shug helps Celie recognize her value as a human being, a woman of worth. Although she protects Celie from Albert, she also challenges her to stand up for herself and demand respect. Shug teaches her about sexual love and her body, and explains to her the true meaning of a living and loving God. Through Shug Avery, Celie learns that a man cannot define a woman's place; the woman must define her own. It is Celie's relationship with Shug Avery that frees Celie to develop into an independent and self-sufficient woman (Christian 194).

The physical bonding between Shug Avery and Celie, one of the most talked about situations in the novel, is important to both women. Their union is not simply the fulfillment of sexual needs; it is also the coming together of two women who share a common history, and a symbol of their freedom from the restrictions society places on women. Shug's and Celie's love is stronger and more enduring than any male-female relationship in the novel, as their love survives Shug's physical need for Albert, her marriage to Grady and her fling with Germaine. It seems, in this case at least, men cannot give women what women can give each other.

Building on this womanish theme of love among women, *The Color Purple* brings the women together as helpmates, as each other's protector and as a community. In some very interesting circumstances which illustrate Alice Walker's womanish vision, the women in the novel demonstrate their love for each other. For example, Shug, Albert's lover, the woman by whom he has fathered three children, saves Celie's life. When Sofia leaves Harpo to spend some time with her sister, Harpo starts a relationship with Mary Agnes. Yet, when Sofia goes to jail, Mary Agnes takes care of Sofia's and Harpo's children. Mary Agnes gives birth to Harpo's child and later puts her life in jeopardy to get Sofia out of jail. When Sofia is free and Mary Agnes wants to go to Memphis to sing, Sofia agrees to raise Mary Agnes' and Harpo's child.

This love among women in *The Color Purple* protects them from oppression and helps them to grow into more productive people. Finding beauty in each other, the women often discover something about themselves through their relationships and are liberated from male oppression and from the problems they typically have with each other. Distrust, suspicion, jealousy and slander are eventually replaced by a physical and spiritual bonding, and these women come to understand that their quality of life often depends on their relationships with other women. The important thing is how these relationships symbolize the potential power of women to reconstruct their lives into a positive whole.

Alice Walker's womanish vision does not stop with the creation of a community of women who become each other's chief source of support. It expands to include one of the most liberating ideas of God perhaps ever discussed in American literature. In a conversation with Celie, Shug Avery articulates Walker's concept of a true God of love.

Contrary to Celie's perception of God as a judgmental and vengeful male figure thriving on our service, sacrifice, guilt and repentance, Shug's God defies gender and is in everything. This God, who recognizes us as its creation and therefore worthy, seeks our love by trying to please us and expects reciprocity *not* with sacrifice and hard work (typically part of our Western tradition in religion), but with our enjoying life and appreciating the world it has created for us. Shug says, for example, "...I think it pisses God off if you walk by the color purple in a field somewhere and don't notice it" (178). Actually, this womanish concept of God takes God out of the church and puts it in our hearts, in nature, in everything. Alice Walker's God is a real living and loving God.

A very womanish work, *The Color Purple* is one of the most significant novels of the twentieth century. It is a story that reveals several facets of the Black woman's struggle to be free and whole, and at the same time, it exposes and challenges many of the conventions which limit the intellectual and moral growth of all people.

So with the many strengths of *The Color Purple* (some I have not even discussed), what then is all the fuss about? Why are groups still meeting to challenge the novel after almost a decade? It is unthinkable that a book that argues against oppression in any form and celebrates life and love would be trashed. *The Color Purple* is a book that should be read by everyone, perhaps especially young people who often confront dilemmas in their families and among their friends similar to those in the novel. And if there are young people unfamiliar with these kinds of situations, then the novel will certainly help to rid them of some of the crippling narrowness and ignorance and perhaps encourage them to work for change.

It is ludicrous to think that removing *The Color Purple* from the library shelf or deleting it from a high school reading list is somehow going to make people less corrupt. When youth hear rap groups like Too Live Crew and NWA advocate misogyny, watch Doogie Howser lose his virginity during prime time, witness the Senate Judiciary fiasco during the Clarence Thomas confirmation hearings, and hear a man who once was and maybe still is a member of the KKK claim to be fit for governor, it is absolutely hypocritical, not to mention foolish, to talk about banning *The Color Purple* to preserve the innocence of children.

Admittedly, I have not gone through the novel counting the number of times Celie used the words, "tits" or"pussy" or variations thereof. Nor, have I concerned myself much about the number of white people who might be upset to learn that not all Black women revere the role of servant. Certainly, a few "cuss" words here and there do not warrant all the controversy, and I believe those who are somewhat frightened by Walker's upside down treatment of race relations will eventually get over it (YASD 76).[3]

There are, however, some things that do worry me. I worry that a novel which draws so much attention to the redeeming power of love poses some kind of threat to anyone, especially during these times of resurgent racism, sexism, ageism and all other forms of bigotry and discrimination. I worry that a book which argues against any form of oppression would be challenged when we can look almost anywhere—in churches, in schools, in families, on the streets, and witness the devastating signs of persecution. I worry that there is so much fear and prejudice in our world, some see The Color Purple with its focus on Black women and their struggle to claim their own lives, as a threat to moral decency. And I worry that with all the ignorance in our society, some would dare to snatch the novel from library shelves, delete it from the curriculum, erase it from the reading lists. I worry because book banning is a terrible thing.

What, then, is the real problem? Perhaps the censors find Alice Walker's womanish vision intimidating because it defies much of what too many of us hold sacred. More specifically, they fear a vision which challenges us to re-examine our thinking, to broaden our scope and to embrace real emotional, spiritual and physical freedom. The Color Purple responds to much of the craziness to which we have enslaved ourselves and Alice Walker offers us a vision of what it means to be completely free and whole.

But then, Alice Walker is womanish...very womanish.

NOTES

1. For a more detailed discussion of this concept, see Alice Walker's definition in In Search of Our Mothers' Gardens (New York: Harcourt Brace

Jovanovich, 1983), pp. xi-xii. See also Barbara Christian, "Alice Walker: The Black Woman Artist as Wayward," *Black Feminist Criticism* (New York: Pergamon Press, 1985), pp. 81-101, and Betty J. Parker-Smith, "Alice Walker's Women: In Search of Some Peace of Mind," *Black Women Writers (1950-1980)*, ed. Mari Evans (New York: Doubleday, 1984), pp. 478-493.

2. At this forum, one of the strongest arguments against *The Color Purple* was that Alice Walker chose to dramatize Black women's oppression and avoid the oppression of all Black people.

3. One of the concerns expressed by the Oakland, California Board of Education was the book's "troubling ideas about race relations...."

WORKS CITED

Christian, Barbara. *Black Feminist Criticism*. New York: Pergamon Press, 1985.

Forum. "The Responsibility of the Black Writer to the Community." African Women's Network: Cincinnati, OH, July 1984.

Parker-Smith, Betty J. "Alice Walker's Women: In Search of Some Peace of Mind." In *Black Women Writers (1950-1980)*. Ed. Mari Evans. New York: Doubleday, 1984.

Walker, Alice. *The Color Purple*. New York: Washington Square Press, 1982.

YASD Intellectual Freedom Committee. *Hit List: Frequently Challenged Young Adult Titles: References to Defend Them*. Chicago: Young Adult Services Division, American Library Association, 1989.

FUELING THE FIRE OF HELL: A REPLY TO CENSORS OF *THE CRUCIBLE*

Joan DelFattore

Throughout the 1980s and early 1990s, the American Library Association has reported a scattering of challenges to teaching Arthur Miller's play *The Crucible* in secondary school classes. The most frequent complaint is that the play promotes witchcraft and Satan worship, although protesters have also contended that it contains vulgar language and that it is disrespectful to the clergy. In view of the play's advocacy of freedom of thought, attempts to prevent *all* students—not just the sons and daughters of the protesters—from reading it are particularly ironic. This essay summarizes the content and scope of recent attacks on *The Crucible* and provides a rationale for countering them.

In the spring of 1987, the superintendent of schools in Bay County, Florida, caused a furor by banning 64 literary classics, including *The Crucible*. Shortly after taking office, Superintendent Leonard Hall announced that he considered his election a sign from God that he was to return conservative Christian values to the Bay County schools. In pursuit of that goal, he required every middle school and senior high school English department to submit detailed rationales for all of the literary works included in the curriculum or shelved in the teachers' classroom libraries.

In addition to writing a summary of each book and giving reasons for teaching it, English teachers were required to enumerate the occurrences of profanity, vulgar language, and sexual references. After receiving the teachers' reports, Hall announced that 64 of the books could no longer be taught in Bay County schools. Along with *The Crucible*, he rejected such works as Sophocles' *Oedipus Rex*; William Shakespeare's *Twelfth Night*, *The Merchant of Venice*, *King Lear*, and *Hamlet*; *The Autobiography of Benjamin*

Franklin; Stephen Crane's *The Red Badge of Courage;* and Charles Dickens' *Great Expectations.* Bay County English teachers protested that Hall was using vulgarity and obscenity as excuses for removing books with which he disagreed for other reasons; for example, he stated that one of the banned books showed the United States government in a negative light, which he considered unacceptable; and that another book was disrespectful to authority.

The superintendent's action was overturned by the school board after loud outcries from local citizens and national anti-censorship groups had embarrassed county officials. Nevertheless, the Bay County controversy is a good example of a type of incident that is occurring more and more frequently throughout the country: books containing ideas that are offensive to protesters are challenged on the grounds that they contain vulgar or obscene language. Opponents of the book- bannings argue in vain that material is being excluded for unconstitutional reasons based on the protesters' or the school officials' personal beliefs. One federal lawsuit after another has shown that if a school board claims to be removing a book because of offensive language, no amount of argument about alleged ulterior motives is likely to persuade the court to overrule the board's authority.

Bay County is not the only school district in which *The Crucible* has been challenged during the past decade, and vulgar language and sexual situations are not the only reasons given for opposing it. In Cumberland Valley High School in Harrisburg, Pennsylvania, parents tried to have the play removed from the eleventh-grade curriculum on the grounds that it contains "vulnerable, sick words from the mouths of demon-possessed people" and that public schools have "no right to give the devil equal time with God." According to one protesting parent, "There's absolutely nothing worthy in it and I'd have taken it out and burned it or erased it and rewritten it in my own words in two chapters if the school board hadn't said I would have to pay for it." She continued, "It should be wiped out of the schools or the school board should use them [copies of The Crucible] to fuel the fire of hell. The guy who wrote that book should not be able to be a writer" (American Library Association 1983, 52). Similar objections were raised in DeKalb County, Georgia, where *The Crucible* was one of 24 books listed in a 1982 survey of challenged works. Here, as in Harrisburg, the point at issue was the play's treatment of witchcraft and devil worship.

Although most school districts offer the children of protesting parents alternative readings, this arrangement does not satisfy opponents of *The Crucible*, who feel that the book should not be available to any student. This point was made most explicitly by a parent in Sinking Valley, Kentucky, who objected to four of the books used in her daughter's class: Miller's *The Crucible* and *Death of a Salesman*, William Faulkner's *As I Lay Dying* and Thomas Malory's *Morte d'Arthur*. "In my opinion," she said, "it's not just my daughter I'm fighting for—I'm fighting for the rights of others. I can't see where it [reading these books] would enrich them. They're filling their heads with this junk" (American Library Association, 1987, 90).

Incidents publicized in the national press or in the American Library Association's *Newsletter on Intellectual Freedom* represent only a fraction of local challenges to instructional materials. In the late 1980s, for example, a Delaware school board quietly eliminated *The Crucible* and Nathaniel Hawthorne's *The Scarlet Letter* from English classes in that district. The board's action came in response to parental complaints about discussions of adultery and about unfavorable portrayals of Protestant ministers. The story of the banning did not appear in any newspaper, nor did anyone report it to the American Library Association. Similarly, some classroom teachers state that they themselves have stopped teaching books that have been attacked elsewhere because they do not want to become embroiled in controversy and, in some cases, because they do not trust their school districts to back them up in the face of parental protests. The combination of publicized and unpublicized challenges to *The Crucible* and the existence of self-censorship in some schools amply justifies writing a rationale for teaching the book.

Another reason for defending *The Crucible* is that its themes not only constitute appropriate considerations for the English classroom, but also form a resounding rebuttal to the censors' overall stance on the relationship between the individual and society. The Pennsylvania protester quoted above argued that, because she disagrees with Miller's ideas, his books should be removed from the schools and he himself should not be allowed to write. Similarly, her Kentucky counterpart maintained that not only her own daughter, but also the other children in the district, should be protected from books she labelled "junk."

The ideas expressed by these anti-*Crucible* parents are representative of the attitudes of ultraconservative and ultraliberal activists throughout the country who routinely seek the elimination of educational materials that fail to promulgate their particular world view. In most censorship attempts, the protesters allege that some tangible evil, such as the triumph of atheism or Satanism, the destruction of the American family, or the promotion of juvenile delinquency, will inevitably result from the use of materials with which they disagree. Their position, in short, is that the essential rightness of their own ideas, coupled with an external threat to the common good, make it necessary and appropriate to limit the free choice and privacy of others. They also suggest that it is the business of the state, not to teach students to think critically and to respect diversity and individual conscience, but to inculcate governmentally mandated values and beliefs. This line of argument is precisely what Miller was addressing when he wrote *The Crucible*.

The play, which was first produced in 1953, was based in part on Miller's response to the activities of Senator Joseph McCarthy of Wisconsin. Although Miller himself had not yet clashed with the House Un-American Activities Committee at the time he wrote the play, he was fascinated by the extent to which the tactics of McCarthy, whom he considered a self-serving demagogue, could influence the American people. McCarthy's contention that every Communist triumph anywhere in the world showed that crypto-Communists had infiltrated the American government was never factually substantiated; nevertheless, the activities of his congressional committee damaged the careers and reputations of many of the men and women summoned to testify before it.

Some witnesses, including Miller himself, maintained that the committee had no right to inquire into the political affiliations and convictions of people who could not be shown to have engaged in any criminal activity. Their view did not, however, prevail. The heads of Warner Brothers and other large Hollywood studios, fearing economic reprisals from grass-roots Americans who agreed with McCarthy, volunteered to blacklist any writers or performers accused of harboring Communist sympathies. The resulting firings, which also extended to universities and other institutions, were based solely on the alleged beliefs of the accused, without regard for their actions. "Above all," Miller wrote, "above all horrors, I saw accepted the notion that conscience was no longer a private matter but one of state administration. I saw men handing conscience to other men and thanking other men for the opportunity of doing so" (qtd. in Weales 163).

Rather than writing about his own era, Miller chose an historical parallel—the Salem witch trials of 1692—as a vehicle for exploring the universal human qualities that make such events possible, as well as the impact of blind doctrinism on individual freedom, the social order, and the privileged status of the ruling class. In a note at the beginning of Act I, Miller states that Salem was ripe for a witch-hunt for two reasons: the reduction of external threats to the Massachusetts colony was calling into question the rigid conformity previously needed for survival; and the resulting tendency toward greater personal freedom was causing a backlash of fear. Those with a vested interest in the absolutist theocracy needed some new threat to justify suspending the rights of minority thinkers in the name of the common good.

The Salem witch-hunters described in *The Crucible* advocate an external locus of control of conscience on both theoretical and practical grounds. From a philosophical standpoint, the existence of a single absolute Truth bounded at its two extremes by quintessential good and quintessential evil eliminates all need and justification for individual thought. With regard to the practical implications of personal conscience, if violation of God-given laws results in immediate physical reprisals against the whole community, then nonconformity in thought as well as in action endangers the common good and justifies governmental invasion of individual privacy. The parallels to McCarthyism are clear: one need only substitute absolute belief in capitalism for religious faith, and the risk of a Communist takeover for the threat of demonic domination, to arrive at Miller's indictment of forced conformity and intellectual terrorism in all its forms.

The witch-hunters in *The Crucible*, like their 1950s counterparts, were not motivated solely by doctrinal considerations. On the contrary, mindless public fear of the consequences of tolerating nonconformity provided them with a convenient means of enhancing their own position and of punishing, intimidating, or eliminating their personal rivals and enemies. Reverend Parris, for example, refuses to consider the possibility that his niece and daughter are lying because he values his own reputation and position more than he respects the rights of the accused. Thomas Putnam has old scores to settle with his numerous political enemies, as well as new lands to acquire from those who are condemned. Abigail Williams sees the cry of witchcraft as a way to distract attention from her own stained character and to eliminate her rival for John Proctor's love. Judge Danforth's mind is closed to the possibility of fraud because he can see no farther than his own reputation. Throughout the play, Miller balances theological and political ideology against the concupiscence, fear, and guilt of individual characters.

Although *The Crucible* serves as a commentary on many of the implications of McCarthyism, that is not its sole reason for existence. As Miller explained in an article in *The New York Times*,

> I was drawn to write *The Crucible* not merely as a response to McCarthyism.... It is examining the questions I was absorbed with before—the conflict between a man's raw deeds and his conception of himself; the question of whether conscience is in fact an organic part of the human being, and what happens when it is handed over not merely to the state or the mores of the time but to one's friend or wife.... The vast majority of us know now—not merely as knowledge but as feeling, feeling capable of expression in art—that we are being formed, that our alternatives in life are not absolutely our own, as the romantic play inevitably must presuppose. (qtd. in Weales 170-171)

To Miller, an individual's fate depends neither on autonomous convictions nor on social forces, but on a combination of the two. He describes people as being in a continuous process of formation in which the balance of power between internal and external motivation is constantly shifting. John Proctor, for example, refuses categorically to yield to the force of the state. Most of the accused persons who proclaim their innocence concede the existence of witches—that is, they endorse the belief that justifies the government action, denying only their own involvement in it. Proctor, however, does not stop at rescinding his confession of witchcraft or at refusing to accuse others; he challenges the entire process by proclaiming, not only that he is not a witch, but that there are no witches. On the other hand, after steadfastly asserting his right to his individual conscience in the face of religious dogma, government power, and arguments that he is threatening the common good, his personal guilt impels him to give his conscience, for a time, into the hands of his wife. In the end, his decision to hang rather than confessing to witchcraft seems to result from a combination of an internal force--he will not give his name to a lie--and a social imperative--he will not shame his neighbors who choose death rather than loss of self.

Taken simply as a modern American literary work, *The Crucible* is undoubtedly appropriate and worthwhile for high school classes. It shows the connection between art and life with special clarity, helping students to understand that literature is not produced in a vacuum but is influenced by the ambient culture. It also prompts discussion of significant literary themes, such as the relationship between the individual and society and the combination of ideology and personal gain as motivating factors of human behavior. Finally, the play offers students an example of the ways in which good literature uses specific events—the Salem witch trials, McCarthyism—to illuminate universal questions about the human condition.

Apart from its overall significance as a work of literature, *The Crucible* is especially appropriate for today's students because the issues it raises are directly relevant to attacks on the students' own freedom to learn. Just as the play parallels McCarthyism, it relates to the tactics and goals of textbook censors who advocate absolutist thought on the grounds that diversity threatens the common good. Miller's horror at the idea of institutionalizing conscience, his perception that prejudice and ambition for power may underlie attempts to limit the thinking of others, and his balanced treatment of the role of individual privacy and freedom in an orderly society are among the topics that students should consider in order to take their place in the world as reflective, well-educated, responsible adults. Encouraging critical thinking and suspicion of excessive doctrinism among tomorrow's voters would be a small step toward helping them avoid the kind of trap that Miller saw during the McCarthy period. As one of his critics observed, "The real ugliness of [McCarthyism] was not the megalomanic aspirations of a cynical demagogue but the appalling ease with which his methods achieved results. A force of evil of which ordinary men and women were the unintentional agents and the unrecognizing victims, its moral damage was more serious to those who accepted it than to those who fought it or were victimized by it" (Welland 61).

WORKS CITED

American Library Association. *Newsletter on Intellectual Freedom.* (March 1983): 52.

_____. *Newsletter on Intellectual Freedom.* (May 1987): 90.

Miller, Arthur. "Brewed in *The Crucible.*" *The New York Times* 9 March 1958: II3. Weales 170-171.

_____. "Introduction." *Collected Plays.* New York: Viking Penguin, 1957. Weales 163.

Weales, Gerald, ed. *The Crucible.* New York: Viking, 1971.

Welland, Dennis. *Miller: The Playwright.* 3d ed. New York: Methuen, 1985.

DEATH OF A SALESMAN: AN AMERICAN CLASSIC

Harry Harder

Some works of art become part of the fabric of a society, and reference to those works call forth a flood of emotional and intellectual responses that can move a viewer or listener in ways that are often startling, even disturbing. For example, Moby Dick, the white whale, has unmistakable meanings for most Americans, even for those who have never read Melville's novel; and a number of recent films (See, for example, *Pennies from Heaven*, 1981) allude in their images to the powerful paintings of Edward Hopper, pictures which capture the forlorn, quiet desperation of much of American life. (And, of course, I don't have to point out to many readers the allusion to Thoreau's famous line in my previous sentence.) Great works, then, become part of our language and thought in ways that profoundly affect our lives. Such a work is Arthur Miller's *Death of a Salesman*.[1]

For over forty years audiences and readers have been drawn into the lives of the Loman family and have often found in that family their own parents and themselves. Forty-two years after first seeing *Death of a Salesman*, Mel Brooks wrote:

> ...this Arthur Miller play turned out to be the most revelatory night of my life. When Willy Loman walked on stage and put his suitcase down, I found myself becoming mesmerized. These words were breathtaking, the thoughts, the action.... This play... captured the philosophy, psychology and society of my time. It also told me that we were prisoners of our era, and of the social mores of our time, though we don't know it. Loman's story is a continuing story in America, that the dollar is more important than the person.

Brooks' understanding of the play is that it is critical of American values and our "social mores," and that criticism has led over the years to one or another kind of censorship of the play. For example, Arthur Miller, himself, recalls the problems he encountered during the production and release of the film version of *Death of a Salesman* in 1953. In the first place, the star of the film, Frederic March, was directed to play Willy as a psychotic, and the result was that "the tension between man and his society" was lost and the story focused on the fact that Willy was apparently out of his mind. As Miller says, "If he was nuts, he could hardly stand as a comment on anything." But even with this radical change in the interpretation of the main character, which Miller says, "Obliterated [the play's] very context," the film was still considered "too radical." Miller tells us that he was asked to issue a strong anti-Communist statement "to appease the American Legion," and was also asked to come to the Columbia Studios to view a short film, made on the campus of the Business School of New York City College, in which professors from the school explained that "Willy Loman was entirely atypical..." and that "...nowadays selling [is] a fine profession with limitless spiritual compensations as well as financial ones." The plan was to show this short piece of blatant propaganda before every screening of *Death of a Salesman*. Miller, of course, objected, and his strongly stated protest, including a threat of a lawsuit, probably was the reason that the film version of *Death of a Salesman* was distributed, as far as Miller knows, without the short explanatory film ever being attached (*Timebends* 315). But these events, even forty years later, are chilling ones for anyone who believes that the First Amendment is a central part of our political/social heritage.

But I want to make it clear that I am not just opposed to any restrictions on the teaching of *Death of a Salesman;* I am, rather, wholeheartedly advocating that it be taught, and taught both as a significant comment on society and human values and as an outstanding example of the art of drama.

One of the primary functions of art, I believe, is to compel us to look at things we would rather not see, but I also believe that the best art does not take us to the site of these unpleasant realities and drop us ruthlessly into the mess and let us wallow in our own agony or self-hatred; rather it guides us with compassion through that reality, enabling us to come through the experience equipped to look back with some distance at whatever epiphany has come to us from that experience. The trip through the death, or rather the slow dying, of Willy Loman along with the accompanying harsh criticism of our society and its value system is certainly not pleasant, but it is instructive and for many viewers it is an effective corrective, a universal lesson in how, finally, not to live one's life. The truly universal nature of this lesson was confirmed for Miller in 1983 when he took the play to China to be produced in Beijing. In his book *Salesman in Beijing*, Miller describes his struggle to help Ying, the Chinese actor playing Willy, understand Willy's passionate recollection of his past accomplishments as a traveling salesman (*Death* 80-81).

Ying has "understood" the speech, of course, but it still seems an entirely intellectual kind of recollection despite our previous attempts to find its emotional life. He himself was not put at risk in the way he spoke it; rather he stood safely apart from it. But Willy knows this history with his stomach, and deep down it brings anxiety and an awakened romanticism.

Miller finally asks if there isn't anything in Ying's past that resembles Willy's experience. Miller says, "Remember these men actually referred to themselves as knights of the road." This strikes a responsive chord in Ying, who tells that a hundred years ago there were armed men who escorted goods wagons across China to protect them from bandits. Then the railroads came and they were no longer needed. Many of the men took to drink or ended up performing feats of strength at local fairs for a few coins (*Beijing* 174-75).

Following this insight, the actor, Ying Ruocheng, proceeds with the speech, much more effectively internalized this time than ever before in rehearsals, and when the scene ends with Willy being fired by Howard, Ying is virtually immobilized, obviously deeply moved, and finally says to Miller, "My God—what am I going to tell Linda!" Miller explains that "The scene has entered him" (*Beijing* 175), and I would contend that this scene and the entire play will "enter" the lives of any audience if the play is presented effectively with the recognition that it is bound neither by geography nor culture.

I was further convinced of the universality of this play when I saw a 1991 production at the Guthrie Theatre in Minneapolis. In this production the entire Loman family was cast with black actors and the effect was to add yet another dimension to the play not because anything was made of the fact that the cast was African-American but exactly because nothing specifically was made of it, and it didn't matter since the experiences of the Loman family are applicable in basic ways to all of our society, and indeed to all of humanity.

Certainly I would not argue that Miller speaks for all people, or even for all Americans, but it is clear to me that when the play is presented as a drama that goes beyond mere realism or symbolism (and that is the way it is written), then it will speak *to* nearly any audience.

The powerful universal dramatic impact of this play emanates, I believe, from Miller's ability to examine the American dream with compassion and understanding, and also with a harsh objectivity. The result is a play that is neither sentimental nor satirical, but essentially realistic, and that accounts for the uncomfortable feeling audiences often have that they are not just looking inside Willy's head, but are also looking through an open window into their neighbor's house. This sense of "I know these people" derives from Miller's mastery of dramatic techniques that lie within this brilliantly crafted work of art. My love of and admiration for the play can be explained, I hope, by pointing to examples of these techniques.

First, it is important to note this is a drama about a man whose world is closing in on him, suffocating his hopes and destroying any sense of meaning life once held for him. Rather than showing that world crumbling, Miller takes us inside Willy to allow us to experience this sense of a life disintegrating from inside the man whose life is collapsing. Since Willy is a man who believes in a dream, and since he happens to be an American, this collapsing world, for some readers and viewers, has come to represent simply American values, specifically the values of capitalism. It is, therefore, not surprising that some might object to the play as left-wing propaganda and might even suggest suppressing it. While I would object to suppressing nearly any work of art, left-wing or not, it would be invalid in any terms to attack *Death of a Salesman* because it allegedly promotes one political ideology over another. What this play advocates is a close examination of our lives in terms of societal values as set against our own instinctive sense of what is worth living for, and that examination is urged upon us whether we are left, right, middle-of-the-road or off the road altogether, and whether we live in the east, west, north or south. What Willy discovers, but eventually cannot really accept, is that putting your faith in the empty rhetoric of the clichés that cover up the inadequacies of any political or economic system is dangerous unless one, like Willy's friend Charley, is able to settle for a comfortable but ultimately shallow life by taking advantage of the system without really buying into it. (At one point Charley tells Willy, "My salvation is that I never took any interest in anything" (96), and that included his son Bernard.)

The key moment of insight for both Willy and the audience comes in an office with Willy talking with his boss, Howard. All of the conflicting elements of Willy's life come together in this scene and those elements are revealed in both the verbal and literal imagery of the scene. The central imagery is seen and heard when Willy, pleading desperately with Howard to "find a spot" for him in the firm, yells at Howard: "You can't eat the orange and throw the peel away—a man is not a piece of fruit" (82). But, of course, that is exactly the way Willy and others like him are treated, and Willy's son Biff affirms this fact when he tells him during their final confrontation that Willy was "never anything but a hard-working drummer who landed in the ash can like all the rest of them" (132), that is, like peelings from a piece of fruit. This verbal imagery is effectively complemented by the minimal stage properties used in the setting of the scene with Howard. Throughout the whole play, the scenes are only sparsely furnished, although the properties that are used are essentially realistic. In the office scene with Howard these props include a wire recording machine on a typewriter table and an office chair. Although Howard listens to Willy's story and to his pleas for help, it is clear that Howard is much more interested in the machine and in the recording made by his family the previous night than he is in Willy or his problems. Not only is Willy being treated like a "piece of fruit," he is also being subordinated to a machine.

Here and elsewhere, the play abounds with images of diminishment. Note, for example, Willy's declining demands for a take home salary as he talks with Howard; first he asks for $65 a week, but as Howard shows less and less interest in having Willy do anything but travel, Willy's "needs" become, somehow, only $40 a week. And we can feel Willy's sense of weakness and helplessness increase as he drifts again into the past. At this point, as Miller, himself, has explained, the office chair comes alive, "quite as though [Willy's] old boss were in it as he addresses him: 'Frank, Frank, don't you remember what you told me?'" As Willy speaks the chair emits a strange light, illuminating the area around it rather than being illuminated itself (*Timebends* 190). Once again we are inside Willy's head and are experiencing his sense of loss and desperation, a sense expressed by his words and amplified by the stage properties and lighting.

Other images throughout the play compound Willy's sense of loss and insignificance. For example, Willy's house has been dwarfed by the huge apartment houses that have sprung up around it, and Willy laments, "There's not a breath of fresh air.... They massacred the neighborhood" (17). And even Linda, who is so careful to help keep Willy's dream alive, tells him, "Well, dear, life is a casting off" (15). This deeply detailed depiction of a human being facing the "smallness" of his life is one of the most moving characterizations in American literature. And this characterization is brought alive by the coordination of dramatic elements (like the control of color, shapes, and perspective by a painter) that work in a subtle but telling way on the emotions and thoughts of the audience.

There are few opportunities for students to experience a play that is at the same time so highly relevant to their lives and also so clearly illustrative of the mastery of dramatic techniques. To prohibit or restrict the teaching of *Death of a Salesman* would be to deprive students of a chance to experience what, I would argue, is one of the two or three greatest and most important American plays, and to deal, through that play with some of the most controversial and interesting issues in our culture. For instance, as relevant as the theme of diminishment of the human spirit was in the late 1940s, less than a decade after the depression, it is probably even more relevant to the young people of the 1990s, the first generation of Americans who cannot, with any great hope, look forward to a life of material comfort greater than or even equal to that enjoyed by their parents. Willy despairs that Biff has not "found himself," and that his failure is due to something lacking in Biff, the something that Bernard apparently has. But one might ask how many Willys today despair because society itself seems no longer able or willing to offer an opportunity for a "better" life for its children. Whatever the answer, *Death of a Salesman* serves as a valuable basis for discussion of such questions and for a serious study of the progression (or regression) of our society over the past 40 to 50 years.

And although, as I indicated earlier, it is clear to me that Miller does not espouse any specific political/economic theory (and certainly there should be no objection on a philosophical or academic basis if he did), he does, I would argue, quite clearly condemn much of what our society has done and continues to do to its citizens. A culture that throws people on the "ash can" because they have bought too fully into the phony dream peddled by that culture, and a culture that rationalizes abandoning those who have loyally served that society because they no longer can "fit them in" is a society that, I believe, needs to be examined and, yes, exposed. And at a time when there seems to be a celebratory mood afoot in this country because we have "defeated" communism, it may be time for us to reevaluate our own political/economic system and consider the possibility that capitalism did not defeat communism, but that communism, itself, simply failed, just as our system also might fail. How many Willy Lomans are there today who have slipped through our infamous "safety net," and how many Biffs wander aimlessly in our society, full of guilt and anguish because they are trying to become what they don't want to be, trying, that is, to fulfill the phony dream of their fathers? Watching Willy die, and his dream with him, may be painful, but perhaps it is time for our society to move from the self-confirming artificiality of *Dallas, Dynasty,* and the daytime soaps to a good healthy dose of the sometimes bitter-tasting medicine of truth as embodied in works like Miller's *Death of a Salesman.*

As the above comments suggest, *Death of a Salesman* is a rich mine of emotions and ideas, all of which can serve as a basis for lively, often irritating responses. But many works of art contain numerous ideas and emotions; what sets *Salesman* apart from most is that it pulls people into the lives of its characters so fully that most viewers (and readers) are prompted through that involvement to react strongly, both emotionally and intellectually, to the play. *Death of a Salesman* is no simple polemic, but it certainly can trigger one, and that, no doubt, is one of the things that has made the play subject to being restricted or even banned from the classroom. It is, of course, an important lesson for students to learn that no initial response to a work of art is to be rejected until it is carefully examined, and, one would hope, thoroughly discussed. And the exciting array of topics that tumble from *Salesman* after an attentive reading or viewing of the play should provide any class of fairly well-prepared students with opportunities to question, debate, advocate and attack; and what better response could a teacher ask for? Let me suggest a couple of subjects for such discussions, subjects that might not come immediately to mind.

First, whatever might have been Miller's original intention, it is clear that for an audience of the 1990s *Salesman* is a multiple tragedy, and in addition to Willy's tragic life, the tragedy of Linda Loman, in particular, speaks clearly to all of us, in both the older and younger generations. Certainly, I lay no claim for the play as a feminist drama, but I do contend that it has tremendous relevance to those who believe that women have suffered great limitations in their lives because of the roles society has assigned them. It is hard to imagine a more profoundly troubling ending to any American drama than Linda's cry of "We're free.... We're free...." Linda, of course, is referring to the fact that that very day she had "made the last payment on the house," and, she adds, "...there'll be nobody home." Here, then, is Miller's final comment on the theme of diminishment, and that diminishment applies directly to Linda.

Linda based her life on the underside of Willy's dream; she was the enabler who protected her husband from the truth about the shallowness of his life, and as a result, her own life was restricted to whatever Willy's was, which, of course, was not much. Linda's potential as a human being was totally absorbed by her husband's need for reassurance; put simply, she lied to both him and herself, and consequently she was unable to understand Willy's despair and was condemned, at the end, to live the rest of her life not knowing what had killed Willy and destroyed her own life.

So, where, then, does this leave us? With a play that takes us to the Slough of Despond and leaves us? No, not at all, for *Death of a Salesman*, more than any other major American play, presents us with a picture of characters who, however flawed, demonstrate a kind of dedication, conviction, and, yes, love, that leaves the audience, finally, not in despair but with hope, a hope based upon the potential that clearly exists in Willy, Linda and Biff, but which is, tragically, never achieved in their lives. And if the potential exists in them, it exists, also, then in all of us, because if those human qualities underlie the lives of the "low-mans," they certainly also exist in all of the rest of us.

For all the despair and darkness of the funeral scene (the epilogue), the end of Act II that comes immediately before that scene is marked by an affirmation of the strong bond between Willy and Biff, a relationship that stands as the dramatic focus of the play. Anyone who has seen a production of this play with either Lee J. Cobb or Dustin Hoffman in the role of Willy will no doubt have a strong and sharp memory of the moment when Willy realizes that his son loves him: "Isn't that—isn't that remarkable? Biff—he likes me?" (133). What precedes this realization is an extraordinarily convincing revelatory scene. And that revelation is achieved through a nearly perfectly realized moment, a moment in which Miller matches the action to the word and the word to the action, using a style that reaches a convincing compromise between the rather flat quality of "real" speech and the heightened quality of poetic speech.

Look, specifically, at the climactic moment of the play, the last moment involving Willy and Biff: When Biff goes into the Loman's backyard to tell Willy that he is leaving and, it seems clear, never coming back, Willy angrily refuses to accept Biff's decision and also refuses to go back into the house with him. This part of the scene is set in the pathetically small backyard of the Loman's house, a house being swallowed up by urban development. And Willy stands in the shadows of the towering buildings in a psychological state much like that of Robert Frost's hired man with "nothing to look backward to with pride,/And nothing to look forward to with hope." Willy has gone from the restaurant (where his sons have abandoned him) to a hardware store to buy seeds to plant because, he says, "I don't have a thing in the ground" (122), and now, in the dark, he is desperately planting the seeds that he hopes, irrationally but very understandably, will finally produce something tangible and meaningful in his life, a life that has been based, as Charley says at Willy's funeral, on a "smile and a shoeshine." This day, that started out with one more false hope (the hope that Biff would make it big in the sporting goods business) has ended with a final confirmation of the fact that Willy's American dream is as empty as the promises made by Howard's father those many years ago.

Finally, when Willy and Biff return to the house, the emotional climax of the play occurs, the moment at which Biff expresses, however clumsily, both his love, and, at last, absolute sympathy (or empathy if one dare use that overused word) for Willy's suffering. And, note also, how this scene ties together other key parts of the play. For instance, Willy expresses his surprise at Biff's affection for him by saying "...isn't that remarkable" (133), the same statement he used to describe the fact that Charley is "the only friend I got." The echo of these words reminds us of the irony that Willy lives with the illusion that he can make a living by being "well liked," and yet in his personal life he seems afraid of giving and receiving affection or love. These final moments, then, resonate with references to earlier parts of the play and bring the play to a coherent, emotionally powerful conclusion, and a conclusion that is, I would stress again, expressive of the hope that there is in the human makeup the potential for genuine communication, the kind of communication that is beginning to develop between Willy and Biff, albeit developing, tragically, too late.

I hope the above brief analysis of scenes from *Death of a Salesman* shows how this play can demonstrate for students the power of the theater. And I believe it is the responsibility of those of us who love drama and believe in its importance in our culture to share with students plays like *Death of a Salesman*, plays that are great art and thematically relevant to our students. That sharing should be made easier and more effective with *Death of a Salesman* than with many other plays because of the availability of the video of the 1985 Dustin Hoffman film of the play. Teaching drama, especially a play as poignant as *Death of a Salesman*, is immensely satisfying for both student and teacher when that play is brought alive off the written page, and that can be done by both a careful reading of the play and a viewing of an outstanding production of the play. To restrict that opportunity would be a tremendous loss for both students and teachers.

NOTES

[1]This play is so ingrained in the American experience that it has been used by other artists as a basis for comments on particular groups within our culture. For example, August Wilson's *Fences* quite clearly is written with *Salesman* in mind, but it is not in any sense repeating the Loman story; rather it is seeing the African-American experience, distinct and different from the majority experience, against the familiar background of a situation and setting very much like that in Miller's play. It might be an interesting teaching strategy to pair *Death of a Salesman* and *Fences* in a unit on American drama.

WORKS CITED

Brooks, Mel. "A Night to Remember." *Sunday Telegraph* (London): September 15, 1991.

Miller, Arthur. *Death of a Salesman*. New York: Penguin Books, 1980.

_____. *Salesman in Beijing*. New York: The Viking Press, 1983.

_____. *Timebends*. New York: Grove Press, 1987. All of the quoted or paraphrased material credited to Miller in these paragraphs are from this source.

THE DEBATE IN LITERARY CONSCIOUSNESS: DICKEY'S *DELIVERANCE*

Robert Beck

Deliverance was published by Houghton Mifflin Company in 1970 after James Dickey's rise to national visibility as a major poet. He had, since his first book of poetry, *Into the Stone* (1957), won every major national award of recognition for his poetry; he had been appointed to the post of Consultant of Poetry at the Library of Congress; he was being paired with Robert Lowell in the minds of several critics as a leading contemporary poet.

Understandably then, public anticipation of the novel was keen; the novel was deservedly popular, as was the movie made from it, with a bit part as a sheriff for Dickey, who was also a worker on the script. Professional book reviewers greeted it with a range of critical responses; the *Christian Science Monitor* sniffed about its machoism (7); others worried about its moral confusion and looseness. However, L.E. Sissman, a fellow poet and then a regular book reviewer for *The New Yorker* magazine, said it "...ranks high, indeed,..." among other classics of male adventure and praised its workmanlike prose style (123). It is fair to say, I think, that *Deliverance* added no more to Dickey's reputation as writer than Allen Tate's novel *The Fathers* added to his. But after its acquisition by public libraries and schools, the novel then gained notoriety as it came to the attention of the censors who in typical cases in Maryland and Virginia found it "obscene."

This obscenity charge I mean to treat as one of the central concerns of this paper, and I shall examine the alleged principal offending passage in the context of what it seems to me Dickey was trying to do. I intend not only to review the structure of the novel, but equally important, to place this book in the wider context of American literature and life.

Deliverance was written by a man with a hearty appetite for public life as a college athlete, fighter-pilot, successful businessman in advertising, woodsman, archer, and guitarist. The novel, like his poems, uses these avocations; it's about four urban, middle-aged men canoeing for three days down the wild Cahulawasee River, encountering a reality utterly different from their comfortable, middle-class lives left a world behind. However, readers of the novel and viewers of the movie ought to be cautious about accepting this view of Dickey the man as given to them on the dust jacket of his books and about accepting the surface adventures of the novel as the latest adventures of grown-up Huckleberry Finns. What is crucial to an understanding of *Deliverance* is that Dickey's vocation is that of a poet, an educated and responsive observer standing amidst humanity and nature, combining the alert passivity of the hunter with an athletic intelligence that takes outrageous chances in its wish to find reality behind appearances. Dickey seems amused but properly unapologetic about the surfaces of his life which most publishers think the reading public will find incongruous with a life devoted to poetry. But beyond his formal, excellent education in traditional literature, Dickey also reveals himself to be an imaginative and voracious reader, a student of techniques used by other men at other times, now adaptable to his own examination of reality. Melville and Conrad haunt the pages of *Deliverance*. (One remembers that Melville too received condescension from professional reviewers who were amazed to find a common sailor who wrote novels.)

What is *Deliverance* "about"? Like all good novels worth multiple readings, it's about many things, but principally it's about survival of the body through a terrible ordeal and the deliverance back into everyday society after terrible knowledge. Many of the concerns, images, and fields of interest found in Dickey's poetry continue in *Deliverance*. There is the fascination with cover of costume and nakedness, meanness and decency, sexuality, the glory and non-humanness of nature, the surprising mysteries at the heart of everyday life.

The novel has five divisions: September 14th, 15th, and 16th are each a chapter, with a "Before" and "After." The "Before" section opens with a *map*, an intellectual paper symbol of the wild territory the four men will experience; the remainder of this chapter gives us a sense of the "everydayness" of the narrator, Ed Gantry, emphasizing the comfortable, relaxed circumstances of his life. We also sense his suspicion of theorizing, his self-satisfaction, and his vague discontent with that satisfaction. The other three characters are rather flatly characterized: Lewis Medlock—outdoorsman, archer, body-builder, rash leader of the expedition; Drew Ballinger—methodical, thoughtful, guitarist; and Bobby Trippe, a social acquaintance who is inexperienced or incompetent outside a country club setting. The three days of the 14th, 15th, and 16th are spent on the wild river and are the heart of the novel.

From the city of vague discontent, the four men drive to the river, through the country, Nature. "There was a motel, then a weedfield.... " "The change was not gradual" (38). The blue mountains of southern Appalachia loom and take them in, and at last standing on a bank and looking through a "ragged, ashen window" of willows pulled aside, the four men see the river for the first time:

> It was gray-green, very clear and yet with a certain milkiness, too; it looked as though it would turn white and foam at rocks more easily than other water. It was about forty yards wide, and shallow, about two and a half or three feet deep. The bed was full of clean brown pebbles (70).

I am quoting here to show how matter of fact Dickey is about nature, and how absent the reader feels it to be of Wordsworthian or moral impulses or sermons. Here, it is energy in serene form; later we will see its amoral, irresistible destructiveness.

The beginning of the ordeal occurs on the 15th, the second day. Bobby Trippe, the pleasantly social, weakest member of the quartet is sodomized at shotgun point by one of a pair of hill people, ominous and half-sick and resembling Pap in *Huckleberry Finn*. The narrator is in danger of being sexually violated next and under threats of castration, when an arrow from Lewis' bow kills his tormentor and frightens away the other hill man. Ed's sexual honor has been saved, Bobby's lost forever, but the serious problem of murder must now be faced.

Let us freeze the frame here, in the heart of American darkness, at this moment of human horror. For the purposes of this essay, we must primarily focus on the charges of obscenity found in this scene. What does it mean in the context of what the novel is about? In the novel's careful examination of nature and the natural we have here *one* example of the influence of nature on man, since these two men from the hills have been associated with the "natural" and are deliberately seen as "other," as untouched by the artificiality of the city. This side of nature is perverse, literally, illustrating the darkest side of that freedom to follow the heart's desire that is found here in the hills outside the law, or better or more accurately, where everyone is a "deputy sheriff," a law unto himself. We are outside some imagined boundaries of ourselves, where there is a freedom where anything can happen, as on Twain's Mississippi or Joseph Conrad's Congo. The civic man also kills there, in self defense, but kills nonetheless and must come to grips with the deed, unimaginable several days ago.

Other horrible things are to follow: Drew, praised as "the best of us all," is killed by the surviving mountain man shooting from the heights of a gorge, and Lewis who has developed his magnificent body as a "mystique" has his body broken at the falls of the gorge; Ed Gantry, a man of some prideful modesty, taking charge of the expedition, must make plans for the deadliest hunt of all—the beast being the other hill man who is, in the minds of the survivors, planning to kill them all, picking them off one by one as they sit helplessly in their canoes below. And the next day, Ed, using his developed skills as an archer and hunter, kills another man and disposes of the body, before he brings Bobby's humiliated body, Lew's broken body, and his wounded body back to the law, the hospital, and civilization in the next town down river.

What began as men's play as seen on a map ended in a confused and bloody, immoral struggle for survival. Can there be any doubt that Dickey has no romantic illusions about nature or about the beneficent influences of nature on man in a state of natural freedom? One of the points the novel makes is that the reality of nature is beautiful, yes, even "glorious" as the narrator says, immortal as the gods, yes, but it is not beneficent and not of itself productive of the traditional human values of obedience to law, mutual cooperation among citizens, knowledge, or art.

I have said that Dickey for all his reputation as a man of action and his anti-academicism is a thoughtful, well-educated, well-read man. He is quite aware of the position of Nature in much of American letters and thought. To the readers of this essay, I need only remind us of optimistic assumptions about Nature and the Natural Man that run through our literature from Crevecoeur through Emerson to Ansel Adams or the newest member of the Sierra Club. There have also been rebuttals from such as Michael Wigglesworth who wrote about the forests in 1662:

> A wasted and howling wilderness
> Where none inhabited
> But hellish fiends, and brutish men....
>   (from "God's Controversy with New England")

through Hawthorne and Melville down to, say, Robert Penn Warren. The same division of opinion can be seen in the regional literature of the old Southwest and the modern South of Faulkner, Flannery O'Connor and Eudora Welty. This literary and cultural quarrel needs a clarifying discussion from any teacher of this book.

The survival of the body, however broken, is through skill, luck, and grit; the problem of the return to civility, of deliverance to "another life" is handled ambiguously. Consider what the narrator has done: secretly helped bury the body of the mountain man whom Lewis has killed, turned contemptuously on his friend, Bobby, for having submitted to sodomization at shotgun point, weighed down Drew's body with rocks before hiding it in the depths of the river, deliberately stalked and killed another hill man and sunk his body in the depths of the river, and lied repeatedly and creatively to the law, whose investigation he wishes to avoid. The "After" section shows a man who tells Drew's widow that "he's sorry" in the bluntest way, and who has a "special" "small fear" of being discovered, and whose life seems relatively unchanged. The new Lake Cahula formed from the dam slowly covers the wild river and the novel ends.

"Going back was easy and pleasant, though I was driving a dead man's car, and everything in it reminded me of him" (267). The objection to this novel on the part of the censors who found the sodomization obscene might well be shifted to this untroubled "deliverance" back into the everydayness of ordinary society. Here, the teacher ought to raise questions and ask for a careful reading and questioning on the part of the students. After a struggle for survival, when one man kills another, premeditatedly, does one just come home quietly? Is that what Dickey is saying about what survivors do? Are we to see Ed Gantry as callous? as numbed? Do we see any change in this modern descendent of Ishmael and Huckleberry Finn? It is a very strange deliverance that certainly needs careful examination.

NOTES

A useful collection of critical essays written about Dickey shortly after *Deliverance* was published is *James Dickey: The Expansive Imagination* (Everett Edwards, Inc.: Deland, FL) 1973, edited by Richard J. Calhoun.

WORKS CITED

Dickey, James. *Deliverance.* New York: Houghton Mifflin, 1970.

Marsh, Pamela. "James Dickey: Violent on Violence." Rev. of *Deliverance,* by James Dickey. *Christian Science Monitor* 2 Apr. 1970: 13.

Sissman, L. E. *"Poet into Novelist."* Rev. of *Deliverance,* by James Dickey. *The New Yorker* 46 (May 2, 1970): 123-126.

"MESSING UP THE MINDS OF THE CITIZENRY EN ROUTE": ESSENTIAL QUESTIONS OF VALUE IN *THE ELECTRIC KOOL-AID ACID TEST*

Terry Beck

The Electric Kool-Aid Acid Test is Tom Wolfe's 1968 "New Journalism" report on novelist Ken Kesey's and the Merry Pranksters' central role in the birth and development of the psychedelic scene: you know—the drug culture, man: the hippie/freak scene of the '60s.

The Electric Kool-Aid Acid Test: drugs, rock n' roll, promiscuous sex, wild irresponsible living...even the Hell's Angels glorified as heroes. Why would you ever even want to read a book like that, Bub?—much less expose innocent kids to it? Look at that title. It's all right there. You don't have to read any more than those five title words to see that it sums up all that's wrong with contemporary American society, all that's been wrong since the '60s. Look at the title word by word. "Electric"—as in the power that makes rock n' roll possible, the power that turned music (the gift of rhythm and melody and harmony) into brutal, high-velocity, eardrum-destroying, frenzy-creating immorality. "Electric"—the power source that turned this God-fearing, industrious society into a lazy nation of TV-addicted, convenience-food-munching, acid-rain-producing brownouts. Sure, electricity has its benefits, but historically electricity has to be named—along with that other gift of industrial civilization which '60s teenagers appropriated for their own immoral uses, the gasoline engine—as the primary cause for the loss of muscle and guts and hard-working industry in American society. Electricity—it leads directly to the second title word, "Kool-Aid": a prime symbol of the contemporary experience of youth and maturation in this country: empty, artificial sweetness rather than what youth always used to be, a period for learning responsibilities and skills. And "Acid Test"? Now there's a real, two-fisted, gut-wrenching irony. Not the *acid test* we used to know—the initiation into adult society, the crucial deed that determined whether you had absorbed the lessons of youth, the test of your mettle. No, sir. They're talking about *lysergic acid diethylamide:* LSD. L S D. The "test" is not whether you've learned your lessons and can apply them when the chips are down; the test is whether you can *forget* what little of the crumbling culture you have absorbed and be more flipped-out and weird than the next guy.

It's a good title, all right: sums up the whole 416-page mess. Tells it all in five words. Enough read. Enough said.

Almost.

One effect of reading Tom Wolfe's *The Electric Kool-Aid Acid Test* is that it loosens up your prose style, making you free to experiment with the language. When you've been reading Wolfe for a while, you can hardly prevent aspects of his style from seeping into yours and spreading, like a dye in water. (My first four paragraphs are evidence.) And most of my freshmen composition students need to loosen up—to become what Francis Christensen calls "acrobats of the sentence." But frequently, as a result of having had very little practice in writing or because they have been victims of the error-correction approach to teaching writing, their strategy is to write as simply as possible, thereby (as they see it) making the least number of mistakes. For *making no mistakes* is what many believe good writing to be all about. Tom Wolfe is a good antidote to that mistaken concept. He's full of exciting experiments with language. And *The Electric Kool-Aid Acid Test* can give a much more interesting approach to language study than the *Harbrace Handbook*.

But, depending upon your orientation and assignment as a teacher, Tom Wolfe's prose style may not be the most important reason for studying the *Acid Test* with your students. Though, of course, style—real, meaningful, interesting style—is never devoid of interesting, meaningful content. And full of content the book is. Without a doubt, Wolfe's 416 pages of electric prose and "kool-aid" poetry present events and ideas, characters and values that contemporary youth need to discuss and understand. In addition to offering an opportunity for studying the American language, the *Acid Test* presents the possibility for deep, searching discussions of American society and culture.

In fact, if I were asked to justify teaching the book in a single sentence, I'd say that it presents, for teenagers—through subject matter they can "relate to"—three broad and important subjects for study and discussion: 1) the American approach to the English language, complete with a wide number of literary and rhetorical devices and techniques, 2) an historical and sociological study of the birth and development of the "Counter Culture" (the drug culture, the hippie/freak phenomenon, the world of Rock, the psychedelic movement—whatever you want to call it, each name emphasizing a different aspect of the now wide-spread and diversified life style), and 3) an evaluation of the values associated with the drug culture and with the values of contemporary American culture in general—indeed, with values in the widest sense, as they exist not only in Western but also in Oriental cultures. Now that's a long sentence, my just-completed "single sentence justifying teaching the book" (147 words long, to be exact). And *you* must judge with what grace, how "acrobatically," the thought moved through it. I freely admit that I did not learn to write long sentences like that by studying Tom Wolfe. Rather, I learned how (and why) primarily from Francis Christensen, Donald Daiker, and Linda Flower—fascinating composition theorists and researchers...at least, they are fascinating and cogent to *me*. But theorists, even when they are also good teachers, are not necessarily fascinating to *students*. I know: I've tried to teach writing by using those composition researchers' excellent books (Christensen's *The New Rhetoric*; Daiker, Kerek, and Morenberg's *The Writer's Options*; Flower's *Problem-Solving Strategies for Writing*). The result? Quite mixed—some students develop varied and vigorous prose styles, but many students can be just as turned off to those fine texts as to any other instructional text. To teach writing well (to teach *anything* well?) this simple fact is primary: you must first engage the students' minds— not only their intellects but, more important, their imaginations. That means starting with subjects and modes of expression familiar and important to them.

The Electric Kool-Aid Acid Test presents exactly that. Whether or not individual students use drugs or listen to rock n' roll or experiment with unconventional behavior, those elements are never far from their lives. You can bet that some (if not many) of their peers are up to their ears in all three: for *all* youth must, somehow, come to terms with the widely varied forces and opportunities of our affluent, permissive, highly complex society. Thus the students' strong need to understand common problematic behaviors (drug use and promiscuous sex, for example) as well as their strong interest in various aspects of the popular culture which Wolfe writes about (rock music, light shows, body decoration, Kesey's novels, or, at least, the movies made from them) provide a double barb—a hook which can be strongly set, allowing the teacher to reel in...well, not so much the students, but ideas, feelings, other art forms: the cultural heritage which the Counter Culture is a branch of (however much it wishes to see itself as a substitute or alternative). What education must do, these days, is to help students see that the world is *not* as fragmented as they might think—that the music and art and life styles which they may be drawn to (or repelled by) do, indeed, have their roots in the wider culture and can best be understood by knowing the context in which they arose. Thus, Ken Kesey, the central character of the *Acid Test*—though only a few years ago a superstar/pop-culture hero—is now ancient history to contemporary teenagers. But the films made from Kesey's novels (*One Flew Over the Cuckoo's Nest* and *Sometimes a Great Notion*) represent an art form which will immediately engage students (why not show the films while reading the book?), simultaneously accomplishing two results: making the character (and the book) come alive and launching the class into the kind of discussion necessary to understand literature. For the essential concepts necessary for understanding the films—narrative structure and technique, character development, and theme—are the same concepts which will open up novels.

Wolfe himself pulls some interesting and complex narrative time shifts which will require some careful analysis to follow—the central one being the circular movement of the book. Starting with Wolfe's appearance in San Francisco just before the "Acid Test Graduation" (the trips festival at which Kesey—by then an outlaw, busted several times for possession of drugs—will supposedly announce that it is time to go beyond acid, beyond LSD), the book ends with a description of that same Graduation: that is, the Graduation is the final culmination of both the Merry Prankster experiment and *The Electric Kool-Aid Acid Test* itself ("The Graduation" is, in fact, the name of the final chapter before the two-page "Epilogue"). Through the first three chapters, we are in more-or-less straight narrative time, with Wolfe as a prominently involved, first-person narrator. Then, at the beginning of Chapter 4, the narrator slips away, and we start the story of Kesey's life, beginning when he was a graduate student in creative writing at Stanford University—just before he begins to experiment with drugs (as a paid volunteer in psychological studies). Three hundred and forty-three pages later, Wolfe (as narrator) reappears in the same Haight-Ashbury garage we left him in during Chapter 4. And the original narrative report resumes, the audience immensely richer in our understanding of the background that has led up to the Graduation. This is, of course, essentially a novelistic technique which Wolfe has brought into journalistic reporting—just one of the many sophisticated literary devices Wolfe employs...devices begging to be explored with students?

Or if you want to explore poetry with students, why not start with the poetry of the Merry Prankster's favorite band and one of the few bands of that era still active today: the Grateful Dead? You're certain to catch student interest by bringing in an album to play. And it could prove interesting to contrast the poetic technique of Robert Hunter (the Dead's main lyricist) with the technique of Tom Wolfe. Here is "Attics of My Life" from the *American Beauty* album:

In the attics of my life,
full of cloudy dreams unreal.
Full of tastes no tongue can know
and lights no eye can see.
When there was no ear to hear,
You sang to me.

I have spent my life

seeking all that's still unsung.
Bent my ear to hear the tune
and closed my eyes to see.
When there were no strings to play,
you played to me.
In the secret space of dreams
where I, dreaming, lay amazed.
When the secrets all are told
and the petals all unfold.
When there was no dream of mine,
you dreamed of me.

In the book of love's own dream
where all the print is blood,
where all the pages are my days
and all my lights grow old.
When I had no wings to fly,
you flew to me,
you flew to me.

If Hunter leans heavily on paradox and imagery and repetition, what is
Wolfe doing in these lines?

Singing Jimmy,
Hocking hoarse and phlegmy
Sticks his grizzle
In the dust-muck Brownsville drizzle,
Starts to thumbing
Up the Texas belly bumming,
Heeee! the cops and robbers game.
Lone superhero,
Superhighway Cosmo hero,
Never lies.
Honesty's the best disguise
In the cops and robbers game.
See, cop fellas?
Freaked-out head-buff Cercosporellas
Here's my Rat-tar
And my buckskin cowboy suit.

Prankster red boots
From Guadalajara.
My cowboy hat
Shows you where I'm at
In the cops and robbers game (p. 348-9).

"What is *poetry* doing in *journalism*?" might be a provocative question to ask.

But even more fun than analysis for students is imitation. You can ask them to write a general, free imitation of Wolfe's style, or you can pick out specific elements to imitate. Can they write a phrase like this one of Wolfe's: "the incredible postwar American electro-pastel surge into the suburbs"? Or like this even more extreme example of the same technique: "...the sort of outing on which the Angels did their thing, their whole freaking thing, *en* mangy raunchy head-breaking fire-pissing rough-goddamn-housing *masse*"? Such imitation exercises can lead into discussions of ideas about prose styles and syntactic structures: in these two examples Wolfe is playing with the bound modifier in contrast to the contemporary trend to let the free modifier carry the descriptive load. (Free-vs.-bound-modifier is the context for bringing in both Christensen and Daiker.) There are many other hallmarks of Wolfe's style which might be first imitated, then analyzed: the extended series, the abrupt adoption of the persona being described, the interruptive leitmotif, the repetition, the slang, the mixture of tones—it's a heady rich zingy world, this world of Tom Wolfe's prose. There is, whatever you choose to work with, much imaginative use of language associated with the *Acid Test*: Wolfe's and Kesey's, primarily, though some students may wish to pursue other writers who figure in the book (Robert Hunter, Hugh Romney, Norman Hartweg, Paul Krassner, Stewart Brand, Larry McMurtry, Hunter Thompson). Some students will already be familiar with the Grateful Dead lyrics or the Kesey books.

But few of them will know the history behind the events, or will have thought about what cultural forces made the events possible, or how the situations have developed and changed. Do they know the connection between Cassady and Kerouac? Between Stewart Brand and *The Whole*

Earth Catalog, The Co-Evolution Quarterly? Do they know who Timothy Leary is or what happened to him? Allen Ginsberg? Do they know what Kesey is doing now? What was the final result of the Prankster experiment? Do they know who the beatniks were and how they were related to hippies? What happened to the hippie scene and what its primary events were?

Following, or as part of this historical exploration, you might wish to seek, with students, the evolution of values in this country from the Puritans to the Pranksters. Or you might simply use the book as a springboard for writing and talking about values—values which most students are muddling through every day of their lives. Major questions are raised by *The Electric Kool-Aid Acid Test.* Indeed, the very *raison d'etre* of Kesey and the Pranksters seems to have been to question and experiment with the basic values which the dominant culture takes for granted. Maybe those values *should* be rejected. Maybe they should be revered. But most important, they should be *understood.* Let me just list a few of the major value problems the book raises:

* What is the purpose of existence—to work? to play?

* How important or necessary are Laws? (Why do we so admire outlaws?)

* What is a Hero and why do we need heroes? (Who are the contemporary heroes and what values do they embody?)

* How much freedom does one actually have in choosing a lifestyle?

* What are mental states? What is the value of altering them? How many ways are there to alter mental states? Has there been intelligent research into altering mental states—intelligent research as opposed to thoughtless daring-do? Who are the researchers?

* How are social relationships structured by shared assumptions about the following:

-sex?

-communal living vs. nuclear families?

-raising children?

-co-existing with neighbors?

-group decision making? (leadership? goal setting?)
-relationship to authority?

These are important questions to be asked and faced honestly. And if students at your school are experimenting with drugs, I can think of no better book for initiating a discussion of the values and problems inherent in using drugs. For while Kesey and the Pranksters advocate drugs and use them a great deal, the book neither glorifies drugs nor condemns them (which many students will find refreshing, given some of the heavy-handed anti-drug propaganda they are exposed to). Cassady uses speed to rush himself to the very limits between perception and reality. But Stark Naked, apparently freed of all societal restrictions, is unable to handle such freedom and goes—never to return—stark raving mad: a bitterly ironic result of following one of the most cherished Prankster ideals, "going with the flow." Even the Grateful Dead—the lead band of the Trips Festivals, the inventors of acid rock—do not overlook the negative side of drug use":

What in the world ever became of sweet Jane?
She lost her sparkle; you know she isn't the same.
Livin' on reds, vitamin C and cocaine,
all a friend can say is ain't it a shame.
        —Robert Hunter, "Truckin,"
        American Beauty

Though Kesey and the Pranksters thought they had the answers to many of life's burning questions, Wolfe doesn't pretend to. He merely tries to give us images of the many different aspects of the Prankster experience—the fun and the freedom...and also the failures. Wolfe doesn't pull back when the going gets rough. He doesn't clean up anyone's language, and thus distort our image. He doesn't turn his head or fail to catch the glistening details when fifty Hell's Angels have sex with an adventurous blonde who thought she was taking on only three.

More than anything else, Wolfe simply tries to give the reader *images* of the life of the drug culture—the ability to perceive it vividly in the imagination. And that ability to imagine is essential to the process of coming to grips with the complexity of ideas and feelings which sweeps over teenagers who are trying to find their way in a society that offers a mind-boggling array of choices. We cannot mold the values of the young by preaching at them or by trying to scare them away from experiences. Rock n' roll surges in and carries them off to delicious, vigorous ecstasies. "If it feels so right, you know it can't be wrong" are lyrics that appear in countless rock songs. (Are there any popular songs that advocate—as I so frequently find myself doing—careful analysis of one's situations and choices?)

It is, indeed, foolish to deny or devalue many aspects of the Counter Culture: its music is particularly vivid and alive; many of its philosophical connections are profound. And Wolfe spends some time, in addition to giving images of the Life, trying to place the ideas in historical, philosophical context, at one point linking up not only to Jung but also to "Plotinus, Lao-tse, Pico della Mirandola, Agrippa, Kepler, Leibniz" (142). In another place he points out the similarity between the LSD experience and the religious experiences of Mohammed, Zoraster, Saul of Tarsus, Christian Rosencreuz, Emmanuel Swedenborg, and Meister Eckhart (128).

In these days when there is widespread, even vehement, public argument about whether to take a few minutes out of the school day for prayer, many of us are afraid to even bring up religious or spiritual experiences as a subject in the classroom, apparently because of some vague fear of violating a student's fragile religious freedom. As a result of such areligious educations, most Americans are vastly ignorant of the great religious forces which—though they may be only minor sub-currents in our own secular culture—are major motivations for action elsewhere in the world. And the Holy Wars that threaten to topple our economy and our foreign-energy-dependent existence, go completely without understanding. Worse yet, as teachers we often find it difficult even to talk to students about the three great forces that underlie all spiritual thought: Truth, Goodness, and Beauty.

Couched in raw language and in images of unconventional living though it may be, Tom Wolfe's *The Electric Kool-Aid Acid Test* presents an opportunity to think through many essential questions of value. Nothing gets preached. The floor is merely opened for discussion. What more could a teacher want from a text?

WORKS CITED

Grateful Dead [song book for *Working Man's Dead* and *American Beauty*]. New York: Ice Nine Publishing Company, n.d.

Wolfe, Tom. *The Electric Kool-Aid Acid Test*. New York: Farrar, Strauss and Giroux, 1968.

A FAREWELL TO ARMS
James A. Michener

When I heard that school censors had banned Hemingway's *A Farewell to Arms*, I was perplexed, for I remembered the book with affection and could recall no blatant passages that would justify denunciation. So I hurried to the library and checked out a copy, and soon the famous images of the First World War came tumbling back.

It is 1916 and the young American, Frederic Henry, has volunteered to drive an ambulance for the Italian army which is fighting on the side of the Allies. It has engaged in ten straight inconclusive battles with Austrian troops along the banks of the Isonzo, a little stream that would later form the boundary between Italy and Yugoslavia. In the ugly eleventh battle Henry behaves with such quiet valor that he wins a major decoration. But his attention is focused on Catherine Barkley, a tall, slim, light-haired English nurse who serves in an Italian military hospital.

The book is a little masterpiece on two accounts: it is a powerful war narrative, but also a gripping love story, since Miss Barkley and Lieutenant Henry dominate the canvas. Because of its excellence it would be appropriate reading for today's high school students for three reasons: its honest description of war, its introduction of a masterly new writing style, and its timeless story of what happens when young men just a bit older than high school fall in love with spirited young women. As a former English teacher I would judge that high school boys especially could learn from this good book, and I'm surprised they were forbidden to read it.

I was twenty-two when the book appeared in 1929 and have vivid memories of its impact. My professor said: "You must read it! Powerful short sentences. A whole new way of telling a story. This book is going to change the novel." He was right, and soon thereafter, in 1930 I was cutting class to go into Philadelphia to attend the play made from the novel. The tragic role of Catherine Barkley was played with perfection, I thought, by the frail European actress, Elissa Landi, the American ambulance driver by Glenn Anders. Their love affair was breathtaking, a glimpse of tragedy, and for some months I thought of courtship and marriage as a search for someone like Elissa Landi. In 1932 I saw the motion picture based on the novel; this time Helen Hayes was Catherine, with Gary Cooper as her ambulance man. They too were tragic lovers, and as I look back upon those three experiences—book, play, movie—I can remember the contribution they made to my youthful life, and to think that they should now be denied to others is worrisome.

Using the standard Scribner's edition of 1957, I checked every page to determine what might have alerted the censors, and I must confess that I identified a number of scenes, situations and speeches which could have caused offense if judged by the moral standards operating in 1929. In the earliest pages a rowdy officer playfully accuses a Catholic priest he likes to tease with masturbating, but as we shall see, Hemingway used no ugly words, preferring the amusing phraseology of "five against one."

On page 47 he wants to report more rough military language but he does it in a way that sounds reticent in the free-speaking 1990s. Two Italian soldiers discuss the Austrian shelling:

"The road will be a dirty mess."
"They'll shell the ---- out of us."
"Probably."

On page 66 the men speculate about the ways they think women react to lovemaking, but the actual words are so sanitized that I probably read them in 1929 without knowing for sure what they were talking about. I can't imagine modern young people being negatively influenced by such tepid writing.

On page 92 the English nurse and her American driver finally make love, in as delicately written an account as one could wish, sixteen lines of tense, longing dialogue ending with six lines of empty space, after which Henry says:

"Catherine sat in a chair by the bed. The door was open into the hall. The wildness was gone and I felt finer than I had ever felt."

On 104 Catherine asks Frederic how many other girls he's slept with, and they tease one another amiably with evasive answers, whose lightheartedness could possibly give offense, but I don't know why.

On page 111, after Catherine has taken three nights off duty to get some sleep, the lovers come back together and the American says of her return: "Then she came back on again. It was as though we met again after each of us had been away on a long journey." Hemingway does not even say that they went back to bed.

On page 115, I ran into real trouble. The American says to himself: "I wanted us to be married really because I worried about having a child... but we pretended we were married and did not worry much." When he proposes to Catherine she says:

"Poor darling. And I know you've been with all kinds of girls and it doesn't matter to me...."

"Couldn't we be married privately some way. Then if anything happened to me or if you had a child."

"There's no way to be married except by church or by state. We are married privately. You see, darling, it would mean everything to me if I had any religion. But I haven't any religion."

On page 137 Catherine finally reveals that she is going to have a baby, and at first the lovers show no remorse, but on page 152 she suddenly appreciated the shabbiness of her situation and says that she feels like a whore, using that word. However, after brief self-recrimination she says on page 153: "I wish we could do something really sinful. Everything we do seems so simple and innocent. I can't believe we do anything wrong." I can see a censor gagging at that, except for the purity of Catherine's whole attitude.

On page 196 Hemingway offers a scene in which Italian soldiers obviously use the street word for sexual intercourse but he cannot bring himself to print it; instead he uses four conspicuous ——s which look more obscene than the word itself. And on page 284 there is a return to religion, when Henry has blistered his hands rowing them to safety in Switzerland:

> "Let me see your hands."
> I put them out. They were both blistered raw.
> "There's no hole in my side," I said.
> "Don't be sacrilegious." (It is the non-religious Catherine who reproves him.)

The obvious charges against the novel were so flimsy that I tried to visualize the kind of critic who might have lodged more serious ones:

The lady prohibitionist: "I never read a novel where there's so much drinking. In scene after scene those men are shown guzzling every kind of alcoholic drink known to Southern Europe. Most degrading for school children to see."

The southern army general, retired after gallant duty in various wars: "The hero perplexed me. In the tenth Battle of Isonzo he displayed such gallantry that the Italian government awarded him a major medal. But then in the twelfth Isonzo, the one they call The Rout of Caporetto, when the Austrians captured three hundred thousand Italians and watched even more run away, our man fled the battle disgracefully and saved his life when he was about to be shot as either a deserter or a German spy by leaping into a fast-moving river. He preferred being with his pregnant girlfriend. Bad example for young men."

Ardent but quiet spoken feminist: "I'd be hesitant about having my girl students read this book. Why? Because Catherine Barkley is such a ninny. She carries the 'wither thou goest, I will go' bit to ridiculous lengths. She actually says: 'I'll say just what you wish and do what you wish, and then I'll be a great success.' A deplorable role model."

A non-inflammatory expert: "We cannot allow children to read this book. On page 257 the heroine compares the hero to Shakespeare's Othello, and the man replies: 'Othello was a nigger,' and that disqualifies the book, permanently."

That is the totality of accusation I could bring against this book, supposing that I were a rabble-rousing crusader for censorship, and I am dismayed by the triviality and even shabbiness of such reasons. Hemingway, attentive to the niceties of opinion in his day, avoided even the sexual language which appears in family newspapers today.

Why should high school students be allowed or even encouraged to read *A Farewell to Arms*? And why do I recommend it?

First, it provides an honest picture of men at war, and since it looks as if war of one kind or another is to be with us throughout history, it is profitable for young people to acquaint themselves with its reality. There could be no better guide than Hemingway; he is honest, never overly dramatic, skilled in reporting psychological reactions of men in battle, and knowledgeable.

Second, young people with any intellectual interest whatever should be familiar with the artistic revolution Hemingway initiated when he composed his stories with short, jabbing sentences and wandering paragraphs that ended on down beats, as with the description of Henry's friend Aymo's death.

> He looked very dead. It was raining. I had liked him as well as anyone I ever knew. I had his papers in my pocket and would write to his family. Ahead across the fields was a farmhouse. There were trees around it and the farm buildings were built against the house. There was a balcony along the second floor held up by columns.

Hemingway prose swept the world, and can be considered a major American contribution.

Third, and this is the most important justification of all, young people today ought to be reminded of how rewarding relations between men and women can be. They are faced with so much casual sex, and in it women tend to be so sharply degraded, that it is refreshing to see that Frederic Henry truly loves his English nurse, that he is ready to risk his life for her, and that he is willing to save her by rowing her in a small boat from Italy to refuge in Switzerland. We see him distraught when both his newborn son and his splendid wife have died in childbirth.

Upon rereading, I find the love affair between the American ambulance driver and his English nurse to be honest and deeply moving. Young people need to see that such relationships are possible and that commitment in human affairs is more honorable than moral indifference. Furthermore, all who, as adults, are going to sponsor and protect our literature should be encouraged while young to make their acquaintance with the finest closing line of this century, Frederic Henry's farewell to Catherine and to the novel: "After a while I went out of the hospital and walked back to the hotel in the rain."

The boys and girls who were denied the right to read this book were deprived of an experience that might have served them well as they matured. Censorship has the nasty habit of killing off the big good in order to protect readers from the little wrong. Because of that fatal imbalance censorship should be condemned.

A DEFENSE OF A *FAREWELL TO ARMS*
Jim Mulvey

Ernest Hemingway realized early in his career that criticism and censorship would often dog his books. Lamenting the publication of *The Sun Also Rises*, his exasperated parents helped to establish the censorious tone. His father's aside that he preferred "healthier" forms of literature and his mother's rebuke that it is "a doubtful honor to have produced one the filthiest books of the year" embittered the thin–skinned novelist (Baker 180).

Hemingway's masterpiece, *A Farewell to Arms* (1929), was also under fire even before its publication. In a letter to Maxwell Perkins, the famous editor at Scribner's, Hemingway complained of Perkins' removing too many unsavory words from his manuscript: "There has always been first rate writing and then American writing (genteel writing). But you should not go backwards. If a word can be printed and is needed in the text it is a weakening to omit it" (Selected Letters 297). Hemingway, the prototypical "modern" writer, reacted strongly against the prudishness of the Genteel Tradition which had dominated American literature for more than 100 years and insisted that he must write truly about war and sexual love in *A Farewell to Arms*. Unfortunately, this novel continues to be condemned, having the distinction of being one of the most challenged books in America's public schools.

I see three controversial areas in the novel which appear to upset the guardians of our innocent adolescents. The first is the book's sexual content; the second, the book's violence; the third, the book's fatalism.

The novel's sexual content, fairly tame considering what adolescents are exposed to in the 1990s, receives the loudest challenge. Much of the sexual innuendo comes from the Italian officers who befriend Frederic. One of their favorite pastimes is priest baiting: "Priest every night five against one" (Hemingway 7). Although Frederic does not echo the Italians' vulgarisms, he does join them regularly at the officers' "bawdy house" (5) where he immoderately drinks and whores to escape the boredom and anxiety of war.

Discovering the beautiful and fragile Catherine to be a more suitable companion than the Italian prostitutes, he seeks to seduce her. He lies to Catherine that he loves her, and he admits that, "I knew I did not love Catherine Barkely nor had any idea of loving her. This was a game, like bridge" (26). At this stage of his relationship with Catherine, Frederic does not comprehend the stakes of game playing, and he does not understand the consequences of a commitment. Love, if it means anything at all to him at this point, means gamesmanship, seduction, and self–gratification. At this stage of Frederic's development it is difficult to accept Jackson Benson's assessment that Frederic "is a perfectly normal young man, a nice guy" (82).

Even though Frederic remains selfish and needy, it is important to emphasize that he does fall in love with Catherine while she nurses him during his convalescence in a Milan hospital. There they make love for the first time, a scene that the maturing Frederic avoids sharing with us, though he does admit that "I felt finer than I had ever felt" after the consummation (92). Reflecting on their love, we see a transformed Frederic who Philip Young says "progresses from the messiness represented by the brothel to the order that is love (16). Some might challenge the novel for its acceptance of the unmarried lovers; however, their love demonstrates commitment and order, and they constantly tell each other that they "feel" married and actually plan to be married after their baby is born.

Frederic matures in another way, for he must come to terms with Catherine's pregnancy as he prepares to return to the front. He learns the hard way that sex has consequences—consequences which the novel emphasizes in other unattractive ways. Frederic admits to Catherine that before their relationship he was treated for gonorrhea, and Rinaldi fears that he has contracted syphilis from a prostitute. Frederic also discovers a different kind of consequence; his inordinate drinking in the hospital produces a two–week bout of jaundice, preventing his taking a post–convalescent leave with Catherine.

Frederic, comprehending the consequences of his actions, returns to the front a changed man. He no longer joins the officers in their whoring, nor does he respond to their jokes. Instead, he becomes a more thoughtful, philosophical, and moderate young man, who comes to appreciate the normative voice of the priest: "When you love you wish to do things for. You wish to sacrifice for. You wish to serve (72). The ancient and wise Count Greffi, another of Frederic's tutors, explains to him later that love is a "religious feeling" (263). Although we cannot ignore the soldiers' sexual innuendoes and whoring, we discover that they disappear early in the novel, for they are replaced in Book Two by Frederic and Catherine's love story, thus beginning Frederic's moral development. Frederic, once he commits to Catherine, is no longer referred to as "boy" by her or as "baby" by Rinaldi (31, 32).

The second controversial element is the novel's violence. We dramatically witness the shelling that wounds Frederic, and observe death and atrocity during the retreat from Caparetto; however, the most singularly violent act belongs to Frederic himself. Frederic orders two Italian sergeants to help the men in his charge free the stalled ambulances mired in a muddy field. Unwilling to help push the vehicles and fearing any further delay in avoiding the advancing Austrian troops, the sergeants disregard Frederic's order to help and they desert. Hemingway describes the event this way:

> "Halt," [Frederic] said. They kept on down the muddy road, the hedge on either side. "I order you to halt," I called. They went a little faster. I opened up my holster, took the pistol, aimed at the one who had talked the most, and fired. I missed and they both started to run. I shot three times and dropped one. The other went through the hedge and was out of sight. I fired at him through the hedge as he ran across the field. The pistol clicked empty and I put in another clip. I saw it was too far to shoot at the second sergeant. (204)

Frederic then allows Bonello, who pleads to "Let me go finish him," to kill the wounded sergeant (204). What is interesting about this scene is it avoids describing the actual wounding and then killing of the sergeant. Rather, what is emphasized is the outrage of the Italian ambulance drivers against the deserters and their support for Frederic. To Bonello, the dead sergeant is a "son of a bitch." To Piani, the sergeants are "dirty scum" (204). What's also important is Frederic's silence—an important reaction in Hemingway's fiction—signifying regret, moral nausea, and guilt—and certainly contrasting the bravado of the Italian drivers. Whether Frederic's action is a necessary act of war is perhaps open to debate, yet he realizes that "It was my fault. I had led them up here" (205). Adolescents should heed Frederic's morally charged statement that "There is nothing as bad as war" (50). Later in a more thoughtful mood, Frederic says of war:

> I was always embarrassed by the words sacred, glorious and sacrifice and the expression in vain.... I had seen nothing sacred and the things that were glorious had no glory and the sacrifices were like the stockyards in Chicago if nothing was done with the meat except to bury it (184–85).

It would be a mistake to neglect the moral outrage of these words and to condemn them as being unpatriotic and cynical.

This leads us to the final controversy—the novel's fatalism, a theme which binds both love and war. Hearing that Catherine is pregnant, Frederic responds that "You always feel trapped biologically" (139). Perhaps "always" is whiny self–pity, but it nevertheless prepares for a similarly charged comment that Frederic makes about the brutality and absurdity of war:

> If people bring so much courage to this world the world has to kill them to break them, so of course it kills them. The world breaks every one and afterward many are strong at the broken places. But those that will not break it kills. It kills the very gentle and the very good and the very brave impartially. If you are none of these you can be sure it will kill you too but there will be no special hurry (249).

Frederic's fatalism finds its final and most cosmic expression at the novel's conclusion. Confronting Catherine's impending death, he articulates Hemingway's theme of an indifferent universe crushing human desire:

That was what you did. You died. You did not know what it is about. You never had time to learn. They threw you in and told you the rules and the first time they caught you off base they killed you.... Once in camp I put a log on top of the fire and it was full of ants. As it commenced to burn, the ants swarmed out and went first toward the center where the fire was; then turned back and ran toward the end. When there were enough on the end they fell off into the fire. Some got out, their bodies burnt and flattened and went off knowing where they were going. But most of them went toward the fire and then back toward the end and swarmed on the cool end and finally fell off into the fire. I remember thinking at the time that it was the end of the world and a splendid chance to be a messiah and lift the log off the fire and throw it out where the ants could get off onto the ground. But I did not do anything but throw a tin cup of water on the log, so that I would have the cup empty to put whiskey in before I added water to it. I think the cup of water on the burning log only steamed the ants (327–28).

At the end of the novel we see a new, mature, and stoical Frederic who accepts human frailty, the cruelty and inscrutability of an indifferent universe, and the finality of death. Frederic further recognizes that his tutors (the priest, Catherine, and Count Greffi) who teach him of the selflessness and commitment of love, nevertheless inconsequentially articulate a stay against death (Light 173). Thus, Frederic in his despair comes to perceive that the priest's serving God and Catherine's serving her beloved impotently falter on the steps of death and that love, though an essential and rewarding human emotion, lacks transcendence.

A Farewell to Arms is the record of Frederic's growing consciousness of what he has learned about love and war. We may disagree with the portrayal of his experience and the philosophical conclusions he draws from it, but we must accept the validity of Frederic's emotions and the artistry of Hemingway's story.

In this disturbingly repressive and jingoistic time of thought police and spin control and Schwarzkopf and Schwartzenegger, it is important to remember a passage from Hemingway's address to the 1937 Writer's Congress in New York:

A writer's problem does not change. He himself changes, but his problem remains the same. It is always how to write truly and having found what is true, to project it in such a way that it becomes part of the experience of the person who reads it...really good writers are always rewarded under almost any existing system of government that they can tolerate. There is only one form of government that cannot produce good writers, and that system is fascism. For fascism is a lie told by bullies. A writer who will not lie cannot live and work under fascism. (Baker 314)

As a writer of realistic fiction, what he calls writing truly, Hemingway understands the essential ethical construct of pragmatism: the more you learn experientially, the greater your moral vision. Frederic, in his rite of passage, epitomizes this truth. As empathetic readers of *A Farewell to Arms*, we recognize its wisdom. Those who are disturbed by the sexuality of soldiers, by the violence of war, by the despair of Frederic Henry, and by the tragic fatalism of the novel refuse the often uncomfortable challenge of literature—to think critically, to feel deeply, to live humanely.

WORKS CITED

Baker, Carlos. *Ernest Hemingway: A Life Story*. New York: Charles Scribner's Sons, 1969.

Benson, Jackson. *Hemingway: The Writer's Art of Self-Defense*. Minneapolis: University of Minnesota Press, 1973.

Hemingway, Ernest. *Farewell to Arms*. New York: Charles Scribner's Sons, 1969.

_____. *Selected Letters: 1917–1961*. ed. Carlos Baker. New York: Charles Scribner's Sons, 1981.

Light, James F. "The Religion of Death in *A Farewell to Arms*." *Modern Fiction Studies*. VII (Summer 1961), 169–173.

Young, Philip. *Ernest Hemingway: University of Minnesota Pamphlets on American Writers;* No. 1. Minneapolis: University of Minnesota Press, 1973.

FLOWERS FOR ALGERNON
BY DANIEL KEYES
Robert Small, Jr.

Daniel Keyes' *Flowers for Algernon* appeared first in the form of a long short story in 1959 in *The Magazine of Fantasy and Science Fiction*, and in 1960 received from the World Science Fiction Society the Hugo Award for the Best Novelette of that year. It seems to have been immediately recognized as a piece of literature well above the routine, for it was anthologized in the next two years in *Fifth Annual of the Year's Best Science Fiction*, *Best Articles and Stories*, and *Literary Cavalcade*. In the years that followed, it re-appeared as a television play by the Theater Guild under the title, *The Two Worlds of Charlie Gordon*, in 1966 in an expanded version as a novel, and later still in 1968 as a film with the title *Charly*. The film's star, Cliff Robertson, received an Oscar for his performance. The novel version received the Nebula Award for the Best Novel of 1966 from the Science Fiction Writers of America.

Reviews of the novel on its first appearance were generally very favorable and tended to praise its treatment of mental retardation. For example, the *Times Literary Supplement* said the following:

a good example of that kind of science fiction which uses a persuasive hypothesis to explore emotional and moral issues. By doing more justice than is common to the complexity of the central character's responses it gives body to its speculations.... In its ideas, especially in its speculations about the relationship between I.Q. and maturity, this is a far more intelligent book than the vast majority of "straight" novels. Moreover, the intelligence is displayed in a treatment of subject-matter which is bound to affect us as both important and moving (629).

It has, then, achieved literary success in an unusual variety of forms, and may well be the best known work of science fiction to the general public, that is, to non-science fiction fans. This success has come about because, as Robert Scholes puts it, "it was based on a powerful concept which worked well in all those forms" (56).

Although it originally appeared in a magazine devoted to science fiction, fictional science is used sparingly, allowing the author, with one exception to the ordinary and real, to answer the "What if?" that is the trade mark of this literary genre. Keyes raises the question, What if an operation could be discovered that allowed a retarded person to develop not only average intelligence but to become the world's most brilliant man? The author answers that question by inventing such a procedure and then allowing the reader to follow that development stage by stage as the subject of the experiment, Charlie Gordon, a slow-witted but pleasant and kind man, becomes increasingly "an impatient, aggressive, arrogant, and unlovable man as his powers increase, inspiring envy, jealousy, and even fear in others" (Scholes 57). Aware of what is happening to him, Charlie fights the negative change in his personality, but fails to overcome his contempt for the ordinary individuals around him. Here is a quotation from his journal when he is at his most arrogant:

> But there were other kinds of papers too—P. T. Zellerman's study on the difference in the length of time it took white rats to learn a maze when the corners were curved rather than angular, or Worfel's paper on the effect of intelligence level on the reaction-time of rhesus monkeys. Papers like these made me angry. Money, time, and energy squandered on the detailed analysis of the trivial. (139)

Keyes "what if" question is one that might occur to any reader, for who would not wish to become a genius? But the story is not merely a pleasant fantasy. Rather, Keyes returns the reader to reality by having the effects of the operation gradually reverse themselves. Charlie, who has been the butt of jokes by the "normal" people he works with, gradually regains their friendship as his mind returns to its retarded state and he returns mostly but not fully to his more pleasant personality, "affection grounded in pity" Scholes calls it (57). Charlie is retarded at the beginning of the story, and he is not aware that the friends he has are not real friends, that they treat him with disrespect, look down upon him, and enjoy a sense of superiority because they are not like him:

Gimpy hollered at me because I droppd a tray full of rolles I was carrying over to the oven. They got derty and he had to wipe them off before he put them in to bake. Gimpy hollers at me all the time when I do something rong, but he reely likes me because hes my frend. Boy if I get smart wont he be serprised (7).

At the end, when these former friends begin to treat him as they formerly had, he accepts them but with more understanding of who they are and why they act as they do. He comments:

Evrybody looked at me when I came downstairs and started working in the toilet sweeping it out like I use to do. I said to myself Charlie if they make fun of you dont get sore because you remember their not so smart like you once thot they were (271).

Writing in *Library Journal* shortly after the story appeared in its novel form, Keyes described his story this way:

Flowers for Algernon is the story of a man's inner journey from a world of retardation to a world of high intelligence. Charlie Gordon lives through comic, sad, and ironic experiences as he emerges from his mental darkness, through the various stages of perceiving and understanding levels of knowledge, into the light of complex awareness of the world, of people, and of himself. (*Library Journal,* 728)

A major contributor to the success of the work in novelette and novel form is the fact that the author tells the story by means of a notebook that Charlie begins to keep at the behest of the doctor involved. Thus we see both the low level of literacy and thought that marks Charlie at the start of the adventure, as well as the sweetness of his character, by means of those journal entries. And we like him and yet feel the contempt that Scholes tells us is the basis for pity (57). At the same time, the story as told through Charlie's own journal, effectively carries out one of the main qualities that proponents of literature claim for it, immediacy of experience, that is, empathetic power. In Scholes' words, "It conveys to us the deprivation involved in mental retardation as no amount of reports or exhortations could possibly do" (57). For example, Charlie writes, "If your smart you can have lots of friends to talk to and you never get lonely by yourself all the time" (16). And later, reflecting on his former state when he encounters a retarded boy, he writes,

> It infuriated me to remember that not too long ago I—like this boy—had foolishly played the clown.
> And I had almost forgotten.
> Only a short time ago, I learned that people laughed at me. Now I can see that unknowingly I joined them in laughing at myself. That hurts most of all. (177)

As the effects of the operation appear, the entries in the notebook parallel those changes. Charlie's style evolves from short, awkward sentences and partial sentences cluttered with misspellings and marked by a limited vocabulary into, first, what Scholes calls "a rich, vigorous syntax" (57). Then, as Charlie's mind begins its retreat to its former state, his style gradually reflects that change, though it can be argued at the end of the novel he has retained perhaps a bit of the grasp of language that he had at the height of his mental powers.

At first, Charlie is not aware that he is losing the intelligence that he has gained. Soon, however, his still superior mind realizes what is happening, and he struggles to keep what he has gained. As he goes over what he still knows, as he practices and practices what he has learned, each entry in the notebook showing yet further loss, Charlie takes on an heroic stature as someone who has seen the marvelous, lost it, but remains determined at least to keep its memory alive. And Charlie is not bitter. Rather, after a first bout with anger and frustration, as he works to retain what he is losing, he regains the sweetness of his temper, his kindness, tolerance, and generosity. Here he is in the midst of his struggle to keep what he is gradually losing:

I dont no why Im dumb agen or what I did rong. Mabye its because I dint try hard enuf or just some body put the evel eye on me. But if I try and practis very hard mabye Ill get a littel smarter and no what all the words are. I remembir a littel bit how nice I had a feeling with the blue book that I red with the toren cover. And when I close my eyes I think about the man who tored the book [the smart Charlie] and he looks like me only he looks different and he talks different but I dont think its me because its like I see him from the window.

Anyway thats why Im gone to keep trying to get smart so I can have that feeling agen. Its good to no things and be smart and I wish I new evrything in the hole world. I wish I could be smart agen rite now. If I could I would sit down and reed all the time (274).

The story, then, has much to offer a reader, and it seems especially well suited to a young reader. The premise is easy to understand and one that most of us, including children, can identify with—the desirability of becoming smarter. Keyes's "what if" question is, in fact, probably one that most students have wished for in the competitive world of the school. At the same time, young readers can be helped through Charlie's entries at the beginning and close of the story to see into the world of someone like Charlie and understand that it is he, not the false friends around him, who is worthy of respect. As the story progresses, they can identify with his exultation over his growing intellect; but they can also see that the arrogance and cruelty resulting from his superior intellect make him less than he could be, less in some ways than the earlier Charlie was. As the process reverses itself and Charlie becomes less smart, young readers can surely feel the terrible sense of loss that Charlie feels and realize that he faces that loss far better than they might. They can admire the determination that he displays to the very end of the story to hold on to what he can of his new found understanding.

Many teachers have recognized the fact that *Flowers for Algernon* would make an effective focus for reading and discussing in an English class, and so it has been used extensively with middle and high school classes. It appears on many recommended reading lists for these grades, including the National Council of Teachers of English *Books for You*, the American Library Association's *Outstanding Books for the College Bound*, and the H. W. Wilson company's *Senior High School Library Catalog*. The Perfection Form company has prepared a set of work sheets to accompany its study, and versions of it have appeared in school literature anthologies.

But its use has not been without censorship problems. Two of the most common points of objection to literature by would-be censors have been aimed at it: sex and religion. Charlie is, of course, a young man. As such, he would realistically have an interest in sex; and Keyes does devote a few passages to rather tame sexual encounters. As a result it has been called pornographic and sexually explicit, although it surely is neither. In addition, because the operation changes Charlie from the man that some readers feel their God meant Charlie to be, it has been accused of tampering with the will of God, of turning men—the doctors, that is—into gods, and of supernaturalism, although the story clearly dwells in the world of science fiction rather than fantasy. It is, these critics argue, only for God to give mankind intellect. It was Satan who aspired to such power; and so if a work of literature shows a human possessing such powers, that work is clearly irreligious and perhaps Satanic. The Office for Intellectual Freedom of the American Library Association and People for the American Way have documented numerous recent cases; it is listed in ALA's *Hit List* as one of the most frequent targets of censorship.

The power of *Flowers for Algernon* lies partly in the original concept, the "what if" that Keyes asks and then answers. More important, the novel gives its readers profound insights into people, retarded, average, brilliant, kind and cruel, and it does so with stylistic brilliance and control. Perhaps most important, it creates one of those rare truly round fictional characters, to use Forester's term, who surprise convincingly, who have lives before and after the story is told, who seem to possess free will. Keyes' accomplishment is all the more impressive because his character changes so drastically during the course of the novel, yet remains for the reader one human, and one we continue to care about past the end of the novel. Toward that end, Charlie writes in his last entry,

> If you ever reed this Miss Kinnian [his former teacher] dont be sorry for me. Im glad I got a second chanse in life like you said to be smart because I lerned alot of things that I never even new were in this

werld and Im grateful I saw it all even for a littel bit. And Im glad I found out about my family and me. It was like I never had a family til I remembird about them and saw them and now I know I had a family and I was a person just like evryone (273).

WORKS CITED

Intellectual Freedom Committee, Young Adult Services Division, American Library Association. *Hit List.* Young Adult Services Division, American Library Association, 1989, 31-33.

Keyes, Daniel. *Flowers for Algernon. New York:* Harcourt, Brace and World, 1966.

Library Journal. (February 1, 1966): 728.

Scholes, Robert. *Structural Tabulation.* University of Notre Dame Press, 1975.

"Making Up a Mind." *Times Literary Supplement.* (July 21, 1966): 629.

"IF WE CANNOT TRUST..." THE PERTINENCE OF JUDY BLUME'S *FOREVER*

Frank Battaglia

I had found Judy Blume's *Forever* on a drug store rack in 1981. The cover blurbs described it as a story in which young lovers fulfill physical desire for the first time and then face unsettling problems. Expecting the book to be pitched in between *Wifey* and *Are You There God? It's Me, Margaret*, I bought it as a gift for my daughter. The cashier asked if the book was for a young reader, and on hearing *sixteen* said only that the work was not for very young readers like some of Judy Blume's other stories.

My expectations for the book were about right. But it took awhile for me to be able to find out for myself. I gave the book with a request to borrow it once my daughter had read it, but I learned that the work spoke rivetingly to young readers when my daughter's stepsister had started reading the book and then passed it on to her own friend before it could be loaned back to me. Paul Zindel's appeal as a novelist had manifested itself to me earlier in the same way, so I could recognize the symptoms. I bought my own copy of *Forever*. The book surprised me in some ways, but I liked it enough to have now used it twice in a college freshman composition class. It's a valuable contemporary fiction, and I'm glad it's available for my daughter, more recently my oldest son, those of their generation, and anyone else who wants to, to read.

Forever follows Katherine Danziger, a high school senior, from a New Year's eve meeting through a love affair, summer separation and breakup with Michael Wagner, a young man her own age. The plot follows the growth of greater intimacy between them in the face of a guarded response by her parents to her getting "serious" with Michael. Her grandmother shows less reserve and encourages her to learn about birth control. Two of Katherine's peers follow contrapuntal paths. More readily than Katherine, her best friend Erica looks forward to sexual intimacy with her boyfriend, but he attempts suicide because of latent homosexuality. Meanwhile Sybil, Erica's cousin, has become pregnant, gives birth at the time of their high school graduation, and puts the baby up for adoption.

The title comes from the pledge Katherine gives to Michael after they have said "I love you" to each other. For both of them it is the first time saying the words to express romantic affection.

> [Michael:] "Remember last night when I said I loved you?"
> "Yes."
> "Well...I really meant it...."
> "I know...because I love you too." I whispered into his chest. Saying it the first time was the hardest. There's something so final about it. The second time I sat up and said it right to him.
> "I love you, Michael Wagner."
> "Forever?" he asked.
> "Forever," I said.

Michael later reciprocates the pledge in the engraving of a neckpiece he gives her for her birthday. She writes "Forever" with a birthday gift to him. The word has become the *bona fide* of a love, to express, which is to say, something *final*. When they separate for the summer they close their letters with the one word promise.

After Katherine has gotten close enough to another man, Theo, for him to ask her about the engraving, she writes a letter to Michael, telling him "I made promises to you that I'm not sure I can keep." But she can't finish the letter and tears it up.

Shortly thereafter, Michael drives hundreds of miles to visit her. When Katherine wants to talk about her uncertain feelings, Michael feels rejected, and his anger precipitates their breakup. The novel closes with Katherine believing "I will never be sorry for loving him.... Maybe if we were ten years older it would have worked out differently. Maybe. I think it's just that I'm not ready for forever."

The central theme of the novel is thus: although apt to consider itself immortal, first love is especially unlikely to be so. The simplicity of this subject does not make it unworthy of treatment. In fact Blume has built a considerable audience with her ability to treat realistically familiar kinds of growing pains. This novel, however, has stirred controversy. At least two aspects of the story share responsibility. In one, extensive physical intimacy, including intercourse, develops between high school students. Yet, secondly, Katherine does not grow to consider their love a mistake. Blume's *Forever* celebrates a teenage sexuality which does not end in marriage.

A major story form in English since Shakespeare's time has been romantic comedy--a tale ending in marriage for the protagonist as a reconciliation of aspiration and practicality. In the imaginative literature I'm loosely characterizing, the choice of a permanent sexual partner in a state-sanctioned union is pictured as the fitting vehicle for further emotional and social development. With exceptions like the Welsh *Mabinogi*, in most earlier Western Indo-European writing, if sexual love was celebrated, it took place outside of state-legitimated unions. Blume's story does not challenge the tradition of romantic comedy. She postpones the potentially "happy ever after" ending, but does not destroy it. The novel maintains a tension between this traditional frame of reference and a new kind of female protagonist who, despite, and in fact because of, the loss of her virginity becomes more self-assertive and self-respecting. As one of my students pointed out to me, the novel vindicates Katherine's parents in separating her for the summer from Michael because they were too young to be making life plans together. The parents' program for summer employment is aired after they find out that Katherine has chosen a college solely to maximize time with Michael.

The incongruity between self-discovery for the emerging female protagonist and the book's version of practical limits for social life is most acutely drawn in the relation between Katherine and her younger sister Jamie. Becoming sexually active herself, Katherine passes also into the adult view that it is desirable to control the sexual development of her younger sister. In a letter from summer camp where Jamie is a resident and Katherine a tennis instructor, she reports to her parents on a special staff meeting which discusses keeping the emphasis among the camp residents "on friendship, not sex!" She has just described a boyfriend relationship her sister has developed and so adds, "Don't worry about

Jamie, though. I'm keeping an eye on her." Her letter to Erica three days later points the contradiction even more sharply between what is right for her peers and what is right for youngsters like her sister. She asks Erica: "Remember your vow to get laid before college? Well, I've been thinking about that and I've decided it might be just what you need." Yet in the same letter she talks about Marsha, one "kid" who is not "okay." Marsha has been "hanging around the tennis court because of Theo. When I compare us at fifteen to Marsha, I can see that times are really changing...and not for the better, in my opinion. I wouldn't want to see Jamie carrying on like that in two years." Unconscious jealousy may be part of Katherine's motive, as may be resentment of Marsha's less inhibited personal style. But surely a line still exists between what is proper for adults and proper for kids. Only, Katherine now draws the line with herself and Erica on the other side of it.

Forever reflects some shifts in contemporary standards, but the novel is hardly a tract for wantonness. It gives good insight into an array of joys and pains entailed in sustaining an intimate relationship. My main problem with the book concerns the narrowness of its class perspective. Almost everyone seems obliviously affluent, with neither money worries nor ambitions. This contributes some triviality, and the characterization of Michael suffers because the "floaty" well-to-do background leaves his origins too vague. In addition, a parent troubled by the sexual ethic of the book might consider it a dangerous guide for someone less buffered by money. Life might then be more likely to include the threat of violence from a more possessive male than Michael or Katherine's father. Not every woman who might give up a baby for adoption, like Sybil, can start a new life by going off to college. And what of Michael? Why does this gently insistent, though unreflective male come up with the criterion of "forever"? The book offers no explanation, and it seems to me the focus is one that females are more likely to have been socialized to. The book gives Katherine's point of view: Michael's motives remain compulsions.

For all this, however, as much as it is possible to do so, I think the book does hope to offer wisdom to an emerging adult about becoming "completely vulnerable" to another person. Katherine's mother tells her: "It's up to you to decide what's right and wrong.... I'm not going to tell you to go ahead but I'm not going to forbid it either. It's too late for any of that.

I expect you to handle it with a sense of responsibility though...either way." Mrs. Danziger has just said she might have made different choices for herself today, and so the question of right and wrong is truly open in her statement. But even a parent with certainty needs to recognize a point when a child has to make his or her own decisions.

My title comes from a statement made in a broadcast discussion of whether we should be willing to talk with children about the possibility of nuclear war: "If we cannot trust our children, how can we ever expect them to trust us?" The words echoed enough in my head that I wrote them down and thought of their pertinence to Judy Blume's book later.

BIBLIOGRAPHY

Blume, Judy. *Forever*. New York: Gulf and Western, 1976; *Are You There God? It's Me, Margaret*. New York: Dell, 1970; *Wifey*. New York: Gulf and Western, 1979.

Zindel, Paul. *The Effect of Gamma Rays on Man-in-the-Moon Marigolds*. New York: Bantam, 1973; *The Pigman*. New York: Dell, 1968.

LeGuin, Ursula. *The Beginning Place*. New York: Bantam, 1981/A modern romance with a female dragon; *The Word for World is Forest*. New York: Berkeley, 1976.

Bryant, Dorothy. *The Kin of Ata Are Waiting for You*. New York: Random House, 1976.

Dahl, Roald. *Danny the Champion of the World*. New York: Knopf, 1976/ About a father and young boy; *Charlie and the Great Glass Elevator*. New York: Knopf, 1972.

Fleming, Karl and Anne Taylor Fleming, eds. *The First Time*. New York: Berkeley Medallion, 1975/Twenty-eight celebrities tell about their first sexual experiences.

Pollack Petchesky, Rosalind. *Abortion and Woman's Choice*. New York: Longman, 1984/A detailed demographic argument.

Ford, Patrick, ed. and trans. *The Mabinogi*. Berkeley: University of California, 1977.

"WHATSOEVER THINGS ARE PURE..."
A CASE FOR *GO ASK ALICE*

Jean P. Rumsey

I chose *Go Ask Alice* to review because I liked it, and because reading and discussing it with one student at an alternative high school had been extremely rewarding. Secondly, at that time it was one of the few books portraying the struggle to break through from adolescence to maturity from a female perspective.

Should *Go Ask Alice* be removed from high school curricula and libraries? This question in part concerns the merits and demerits of the particular book, and in part the merits and demerits of censorship itself. Because I had grown up in Arkansas, which has for years forbidden the teaching of evolution in the schools, I assumed, unreflectively, that I would be an expert on censorship. However, besides the evolution issue, I could not remember any public forum on any censorship issue in the school, community or newspaper. In Arkansas, much censorship was done privately, like Uncle Jim's handling of *The Grapes of Wrath*. He read it seated in a rocking chair by the kitchen stove, raising the stove-lid and tossing in each page as he finished it. It was not fit for his children to read, he said, and the one who had bought the book never protested.

My own parents were less autocratic: my sister acquired a list of books which could be borrowed by mail from the state library in Little Rock, and we were allowed to send for any, so long as we paid the return postage. That list was probably carefully selected to avoid offending the taxpayers, but still our mother sometimes made mild objections. She floated by, murmuring "...whatsoever things are good, whatsoever things are pure...think ye on these things." But this genteel censorship threatened to get stronger my first day at the high school. I chose from its paltry offerings a thick book entitled *Scarlet Sister Mary*, only to have the librarian refuse to check it out to me. "It's not a good book." When I protested that my sister had already read it, she let me take it. This was puzzling: was our family so upright that we could not be corrupted by "bad" books? Or (more interesting) were we so depraved that "bad" books could not make us worse? It did not occur to me then that the librarian might have been simply protecting herself—that if the book had been in our house already then my parents would not be likely to make any complaints to the school board. Later, at the University of Arkansas library, where I was a page, certain books were kept in a locked glass case. A co-worker laughed at me for thinking that the case was for rare books. She showed me sample titles—*Tropic of Cancer* is the one I remember. I purchased my own Henry Millers; his books could be checked out, but the procedure was not one I wanted to go through. You had to show that you, or your purposes, were on the level. One last instance of private censorship (though not of books) sticks in my mind. Sparked by a talented dancer brought to Fayetteville by the Ford Foundation, a group of community members began having square dances in a local barn loft. Fundamentalist neighbors considered this the devil's work so they quietly torched the barn one night after a rain. Without a good place, the dancers were unable to get together again. Those who thought they knew what was best for everyone had won again.

It took a public crusade against Shirley Jackson's "The Lottery" in our local high school to make me understand public censorship writ large. In a long evening of testimony, carefully moderated by the school district committee, students, teachers, administrators and concerned citizens spoke for or against the teaching of the book. Piecing together the statements of the opposition, an amazing picture was revealed. It was a picture of a world in which all conflict is absent. Children never question the values or customs of their parents; there is no violence (except that sanctioned by the ascending generation); in short, everyone thinks only about what the censors hold to be good and true. If there are dark pockets of evil in individuals or in the culture, these are not to be thought of or read about. It is my own position that as long as there are such, censorship is neither appropriate nor effective. However, there remains the possibility that some books should not be taught to high school students for reasons connected with those above. (I exclude here the ones that are not appropriate because they are too simple—*The Bobbsey Twins*, perhaps, or those puerile, like Harlequin Romances. I should probably also exclude some of the essays I assign my college freshmen on the grounds that they lack the vocabulary and experience to understand them.)

Go Ask Alice has been challenged by concerned citizens in many school systems across the country. What are its particular merits or demerits as a book to include in a high school library or curriculum? The pro-censorship policy is to focus on its demerits first. I will therefore reverse this policy and ask why *Go Ask Alice* is a good book to teach in high school or junior high. Why include it in the curriculum?

Perhaps the main reason has already been stated: it deals with that crucial theme, an adolescent's struggles toward maturity. Its proximate subject is the fifteen-year-old drug user on whose diary it is based, and it has the immediacy of the first person. The editors tell us that the book furnishes no answers to the problem of adolescent drug users, but that they "...hope it will provide insights into the increasingly complicated world in which we live." This theme is echoed in the diary, when the author goes with her father to see Dr.____, who is concerned about the youth of the 1960s: "1,000 college-age kids commit suicide every year and another 9,000 try to. VD has gone up 25% among kids my age and pregnancies are really growing, even with the pill. He also said that crime and mental illness among kids has skyrocketed" (104). Her own increasing drug involvement, her mental illness and institutionalization and her possible suicide will later bring this all home to the reader. Although these particular statistics are outdated, the underlying problems are still with us, and students might learn a good deal from following the author's unsuccessful efforts to deal with her complex environment. (Who was it that said that in literature we let the characters make our own mistakes, instead of ourselves?)

Peer pressure, exacerbated by her history of drug dealing, is another theme important for students. The other "freaks" won't let her go but pursue her for drugs and spike the candy that sets off her psychotic episode, despite her good resolutions. The message, for students who are tempted to use drugs (other than alcohol) is as clear as in any morality play. Actually, I was reminded of Dylan Thomas' Christmas recollection of the story of the child who was told not to skate on a particular lake, and who did, and who drowned. The message is that if you use drugs, they'll kill you or ruin your life. There is an additional message for women; the author only became a pusher to help out her boyfriend. "...since I'm Rich's chick all the way I have to do what I can to help him" (45). What happened in that relationship is surely adequate to make the traditional feminine ideal of self-sacrifice less attractive.

So far, I have been discussing the message of the book. But what's there to interest students? I have said that there is a theme as old as Daedalus and Icarus, that of a young one unsuccessfully straining to become an adult. The diarist's dreams of becoming a child psychologist, of somehow understanding the troubled young ones, are reminiscent of Holden Caulfield's dreams of becoming a catcher in the rye. As the diary opens, the writer's mood is black from some real or imagined disappointment in love, but her mother is nagging her to clean her room. Her question, "Can't I even have the privacy of my own soul?" is maudlin, but I'm certain my own children would have understood it well. Her subsequent reflections about the difficulties of being a teenager would strike a responsive chord in most students and perhaps teachers and parents also: "Adolescents have a very rocky insecure time. Grown-ups treat them like children and yet expect them to act like adults. They give them orders like little animals, they expect them to react like mature, and always rational, self-assured persons of legal stature. It is a difficult, lost, vacillating time" (66). This passage strikes a sour note after her previous note of joy. Having been allowed to help clean up after the Christmas rituals, she exclaimed "I feel grown-up. I am no longer in the category with the children, I am one of the adults! And I love it! They have accepted me as an individual, as a personality, as an identity. I belong! I am important! I am somebody!" (66)

With material like that, *Go Ask Alice* would seem to be a winner for high school students. What, then, is the matter with it? My own reading suggests the following possible grounds: 1) language; 2) drugs; and 3) sexual violence, although it is reported rather than described. Edward B. Jenkinson's book, *Censors in the Classroom* gives a brief history of the book's censorship career in which language is prominent, but other grounds are invoked. In Warsaw, Indiana, it was "found objectionable by patrons of our schools" (7); citizens testifying found "no educational value" in a book containing "these kinds of obscenities" (12). Park Rapids, Deer River, and Grand Rapids, Minnesota, thought it was pornography, mainly because of its gutter language. Adams-Friendship, Wisconsin, removed it from its library shelves because it was "filthy"; Red Cross, Pennsylvania, found the language shocking, and the Save our Children group from Trenton, New Jersey, thought it a "dirty book," or, in short, "trash."

It is clear that the primary ground for objecting to *Go Ask Alice* is its language. Persons objecting to it have gained support, and gleaned publicity, by reading, out of context, from pages 76-85. This is virtually the only section which contains objectionable language; later, in the mental institution, there are some obscenities, but they are not the writer's language. In the brief section which uses what my mother would have called "gutter language," the diarist has run away to Denver and, going farther West, is thrown among the lowest elements in society. How else could the writer get across the idea that she is absolutely at the lowest point of her life? One wonders just how those persons who favored censorship of this book found these few pages, and how they were able, in conscience, to ignore their context.

The second major, though diffuse, charge is that the book is "trash," or without educational value. I hope that my discussion of the significant themes treated in this book have convinced the reader that *Go Ask Alice* is worthwhile. But as the previous discussion was centered around its importance to the student, I should like now to emphasize its importance to all of us. The author dreams of succeeding at just what is important in a viable culture—growing up to measure up to the values of her parents. She wants to coordinate successful dinner parties for her future husband's friends, to make orange yeast rolls like her grandmother's, to go to bed with a man who loves her. Caught as she is between the raw drug world and the over-protected world of a faculty brat, she is unable to grow up. This is not perceived as a failure in those values to which she aspired but in her character and situation. In her later reflective mood she muses that "kids who aren't allowed to make any decisions for themselves never grow up, and kids who have to make all the decisions before they're ready never grow up either" (151). To my mind, as a parent and teacher, that is the real dilemma of growing up, or raising or teaching children who are struggling to grow up. How, then, can the book be trashy?

What catches us all in *Go Ask Alice* is the ideal of home, poised against the harsh realities of adolescence. It is doubtless over-idealized: "Home, Home, Home. Oh what a beautiful, divinely lovely word" (149). Indeed, since *The Wind in the Willows* I have never seen such a panegyric for home. The diarist, at rock bottom, talks to different street people about what they want from life. Most wanted to go back home "...but felt they couldn't because that would mean giving up their identity" (88). She then finds Alice, sitting stoned on the curb. "She didn't know whether she was running away from something or running to something, but she admitted that deep in her heart she wanted to go home" (88). Of course, when the diarist is home her parents love and support her but do not at all understand what she is going through.

Should *Go Ask Alice* be taught now? The white heat of the sixties is over. The problem drug in Wisconsin, for example, is alcohol, not acid. Some may find the book somewhat dated as did my friend who taught it in a small town in northeastern Wisconsin. Time that could have been spent in discussing issues of substance was spent in explaining drug jargon. Still, the struggle of the young to become adults is hardly over. "Home," considered as a nucleus of values that is supposed to sustain students as they grow older, or go elsewhere, may not suffice. How are we to prepare our students to deal with these problems? It is that problem which *Go Ask Alice* addresses, and students can learn from her mistakes.

It is perhaps appropriate to let the diarist have the last word.

> I don't think I will [keep another diary]. Diaries are great when you're young. In fact, you saved my sanity a hundred, thousand, million times. But I think when a person gets older she should be able to discuss her problems and thoughts with other people, instead of just with another part of herself as you have been to me. (158)

The author closed communication lines, and died three weeks after having decided not to keep another diary. A stronger case for continuing public discussion of the painful yet universal themes in such books as *Go Ask Alice* or *Catcher in the Rye* could hardly be made.

WORKS CITED

Anonymous. *Go Ask Alice*. New York: Avon Books, 1972.

Jenkinson, Edward B. *Censors in the Classroom*. Carbondale, IL: Southern Illinois University Press, 1979.

AN APOLOGIA FOR PEARL BUCK'S
THE GOOD EARTH
Imogene DeSmet

Pearl Sydenstricker Buck, the author of *The Good Earth*, spent her childhood and early adult years in China as the daughter of Presbyterian missionaries and as the wife of an American agricultural expert. As such, she had a thorough knowledge of China's social customs and rural folkways. The depth of her knowledge comes out in *The Good Earth* as she traces the life of Wang Lung from his marriage to his rise to wealth as a farmer and a member of the rich, leisured class to his imminent death at the end of the story and his sons' anticipatory sale of the land. Those readers with certain biases could condemn the book on a number of counts, most significantly on its exploitation of women. Embedded in the view of women, which is a strong part of the plot, are the sexual mores brought out in the story, the accepted murder or enslavement of young girls, and the dominance of men over women. What comes out in the novel is a strong statement of an overall inferiority of women under male dominance. However, anyone making a critical statement of the novel could only praise it for its honest, forthright expose of a culture and a time quite different from that of the United States today.

Alexander Pope, an eighteenth century writer whose advice to critics in his "Essay on Criticism" is as valid today as when the poem was written, tells critics that they must know thoroughly the work which they are criticizing. This does not mean the story line only but all that the story line embraces. As Alexander Pope states, the critic should know the story's "character" in all of its aspects:

His [the author's] fable, subject, scope in every page,
Religion, country, genius of his age.
(ll. 119-120)

The second of the quoted lines is most important here. The critic must know the country in which the story is placed and must know as well the country from which the author comes. The importance of this is readily apparent. In order to determine the validity of the plot and all that it entails, the critic must know thoroughly the landscape in which the plot is encased and must be certain that the authority of the writer is such as to present a credible statement overall. To fully understand and appreciate *The Good Earth*, the critic must then know something about China and the customs of China, not only about China generally, but particularly, in its agricultural nature. The critic, as is true of the writer, must know, furthermore, the age in which the plot is set. In this case the age is that in which Pearl Buck herself came to know and to love China, especially those five years after her graduation in 1914 from Randolph-Macon College when she and her husband lived in China, he as a teacher of agriculture and she as an observer of China and its people. As Alexander Pope says, the critic must weigh all elements together in reading a story, to know the "scope of every page." And Pope cautions the critic further that "Without all these at once before your eyes/ Cavil you may, but never criticize." (11. 122-123) Those, then, who condemn *The Good Earth* because they are ignorant of the story's total statement, and concentrate their criticism only on isolated aspects, are being picayune and can never be accepted as valid critics.

But to isolate some of those aspects which might cause cavillers to denounce the book and call for its removal from library shelves and classroom curricula is to highlight Pearl Buck's own sympathy for and understanding of the culture of which she writes. She does not condemn the flaws of that culture as the cavillers might wish she had. She writes the truth as she knows it, and to do less than to expose the Chinese culture of the early nineteen hundreds in all its raw humanity is to falsify an historical fact. On the other hand, to apologize for that culture is to demean a people who were living according to their time and their understanding. A dog cannot be condemned for not being a cat. The culture of one time and place cannot be condemned for not being the culture of quite another time and place. As Alexander Pope points out, a critic must judge a culture according to its own time, which forbids, then, measuring it by a supposedly more enlightened age or culture.

The exploitation of women was certainly a part of the Chinese culture of the early nineteenth century, but such exploitation was not limited to China of that time. Other cultures, even that of the United States, had yet much to learn about the equality of women to men. Pearl Buck took a universal condition of mankind and concentrated it into the culture most familiar to her. In that male-dominated world women existed only for the use of man, sexually and domestically. Outside of that, women had no reason for being; they had no entity of their own. Yet, in his own household, except for his treatment of his wife O-Lan, Wang Lung, the main character of the story, has some concern for the women in his charge—his daughters and his concubines. At the time of famine, when it would have been socially acceptable for Wang Lung to sell his oldest daughter into slavery for the few pieces of silver she would have brought to feed the family, he refused to consider the possibility. Still later, when this same daughter, probably because she did not have the nutriments necessary in her infant years, proved so mentally deficient that she had to be brought in out of the rain (184-185; 253-254), even then Wang Lung loved her, although in other Chinese households of the day such a daughter would likely have been allowed to die. Further, in Wang Lung's final years, one of his concerns was that this "poor fool," as he called her, would not, when he died, be neglected, even if it meant giving her a poisonous potion (253). While a Christian-Judaic culture would recoil at such an expedient, the reader must accept that a non-Christian-Judaic culture cannot be expected to act according to modes other than those that inform it. And in presenting the expedient acceptable in the non-Christian-Judiac culture, the author is in no way condoning it or offering it to any other culture. The author, truthful to her topic, must use what that topic presents to her. Interestingly enough, while Alexander Pope's "Essay on Criticism" is a lesson for critics, what Pope says is valid for writers as well; and a writer must know the time and the place in which the plot is set. "Follow Nature," declares Pope (1. 68). And Pearl Buck, in upholding this dictum, must truthfully portray this non-Christian-Judaic culture according to its nature. We, as readers, cannot on any grounds condemn either the author or the story for the truth which they present.

Concubinage or plural wives is a facet in a number of non-Christian cultures even today. Readers coming from a Christian culture who have a cosmopolitan rather than a parochial understanding of the world will accept this for the adherents of those cultures while recognizing that it is not part of a Christian-Judaic culture or a society formed by Christian-Judaic tenets. Although concubinage was a part of early Chinese ways, Buck's *The Good Earth* does not condone it while presenting it. When Wang Lung forsakes his wife O-Lan for Lotus, the brothel whore, Wang Lung's former attitude towards O-Lan of disinterested acceptance now turns into anger. The anger stems partly from his shame of his wife and partly from his shame of himself. When Wang Lung becomes aware of his wife as a woman, he begins to compare the workhorse O-Lan with the exotic, pampered Lotus. He speaks roughly to O-Lan and nags her for her plainness:

"Now anyone looking at you would say you were the wife of a common fellow." (121)

"...cannot you buy a little oil for your hair as other women do and make yourself a new coat of black cloth?" (121)

"I have labored and grown rich and I would have my wife look less like a hind. And those feet of yours...." (122)

But throughout his nagging Wang Lung is ashamed as he remembers how much he is indebted to O-Lan for the wealth and position which he now boasts of:

...in his heart, he was ashamed that he reproached this creature who through all these years had followed him faithfully as a dog.... (121)

...he was ashamed that he was angry at her and angry because she would not be angry in return but was only frightened (12).

His ill temper grew as he walked to the town because he remembered suddenly that all these new lands of his he could not have bought in a lifetime if O-Lan had not seized the handful of jewels from the rich man's house and if she had not given them to him when he commanded her (122).

Wang Lung watched her [O-Lan] as she went and he was glad to be alone, but still ashamed [that O-Lan had discovered Lotus in her house] and he was angry that he was ashamed....(146)

The anger, rooted in Wang Lung's shame, is an effect of guilt rising out of an injustice done to another. The offender is aware of that injustice but, refusing to accept the blame, becomes angry. Such anger, usually aimed at an innocent victim, results from an outpouring of the shame and hatred which the culprit feels toward himself at what he has done and causes the individual to act in unusual ways. This, then, and the idleness of a dry season, is what drives Wang Lung to take a concubine. He had seen the new tea house in the town, and initially, had looked upon it "filled with horror at the thought of how money was spent there in gambling and in play and in evil women" (123). Now, however, filled with shame at his treatment of O-Lan and angry with himself, or as the narrator of the story explains, "wishing to escape from the reproach of his own heart when he remembered that he had been unjust to his wife" (123), Wang Lung goes to the tea room and in time takes the petite Lotus as his mistress. While Pearl Buck does not sermonize in presenting a cultural aspect which she herself as a member of a Christian-Judaic culture could not accept, she presents it in such a way that the evils inherent in the system of concubinage are readily apparent to the reader. The injustice to the wife who has helped the husband through her work and her unselfishness comes through clearly as a condemnation of such exploitation. Of her own will O-Lan collected horse dung each day to fertilize the fields and helped Wang Lung with the hoeing and planting (20-22). When, in a time of revolution, O-Lan found a bag of jewels hidden in a deserted Great House, she gave them to Wang Lung when he demanded them; and with these he added more land to his holding (104-105). Later when Wang Lung demanded the two pearls which he had allowed O-Lan to keep from her find to give the pearls to his Lotus, the overwhelming injustice to O-Lan is readily apparent (134). Further, the problem of having a wife and a mistress in the same house condemns concubinage economically when Wang Lung discovers that he must build a second house, kitchen and all, for Lotus and her maid Cuckoo.

Finally, that concubinage was not altogether condoned by the Chinese although the practice was widespread among those who could afford it is evident in the horror of Wang Lung's father when he sees the painted Lotus for the first time standing in the court of the house which was his home. While O-Lan is sullenly rebellious at this invasion, the father calls out the truth of the situation:

> "There is a harlot in the house!" and he would not be silent...he shouted over and over, "There is a harlot here!" And he said suddenly, seeing Wang Lung near him, "And I had one woman and my father had one woman and we farmed the land." And again he cried out after a time, "I say it is a harlot!" (150)

Anyone, therefore, who would condemn *The Good Earth* on the grounds that it sanctions concubinage is grossly misreading the text. The shame that Wang Lung experiences as he becomes more involved with Lotus attests to his discomfort with the situation, and the guilt-ridden anger which he levels at O-Lan further demonstrates that Wang Lung is conscious of transgressing his marriage code. The injustice to O-Lan is strongly communicated and is, in the very narration of the multiplied incidents, a condemnation of concubinage. Finally, the horror of the father at something which had not before been a practice in his family demonstrates that even in a culture where such a practice was socially accepted, it was not accepted by everyone.

The exploitation of women sexually is again condemned by the narration of the numerous incidents in which women are shown as sex objects only. The idle life of Lotus which denies her any personhood demonstrates that she is as spiritually imprisoned by the cultural view that women are only to be beautiful for the pleasure of men as O-Lan is by the sufferings which she has undergone because she is not beautiful. The reader with any humanity of spirit must see the great misery that O-Lan has known to such an extent that her inner spirit, her person, is a dulled imprisoned entity. Her femaleness in a male-dominated world, her enslavement, her homeliness, her poverty, her marriage to an

uncommunicative husband who does not love her all contribute to a sense
of such inferiority that O-Lan is virtually dumbed by it. Again and again
as readers we are reminded through the description of her sad eyes of the
being enslaved within O-Lan's body:

> Her eyes were small and of a dull black in color, and were filled with
> some sadness that was not clearly expressed. It was a face that
> seemed habitually silent and unspeaking, as though it could not
> speak if it would (14).

> She looked quickly at Wang Lung, her eyes dumb (16).

> ...a poor silent face that lay there, having endured to the utmost (58).

> ...the face of O-Lan, inarticulate, dumb (81).

> She looked at him [Wang Lung] piteously and sadly out of her
> strange dumb eyes that were like a beast's eyes that cannot speak....
> (146)

In suffering the multipled psychological wounds from childhood on,
O-Lan had nowhere to turn for redress. Children obeyed parent: servants
obeyed employers; wives obeyed husbands, all without having anyone to
turn to for consolation and justice. Because she was not beautiful, because
she was a woman, because she was poor, O-Lan's repeated sufferings had
caused her to turn inward that she was, as it were, frozen with fear and
pain. This all began when O-Lan's parents sold her into slavery in the
house of a rich family.

In the culture of which Pearl Buck writes, daughters were of little
value because their destiny was marriage and the bearing of sons which,
in that patriarchal society, meant that the daughter would go to live in the
household of her husband where she would bear him the sons to help him
in the fields and to care for him in his old age. When O-Lan bore a daughter
to Wang Lung after the birth of two sons, he is angry and sees the daughter
as a burden. For one thing, it is a person to feed using money which will
not be repaid for, in Wang Lung's view, "daughters...do not belong to
their parents, but are born and reared for other families." If daughters

have any value, it is that they can be sold into slavery to one of the houses of the rich. This is what happened to O-Lan when she was ten (13). With a drought on the land, her family had no money from crops to sustain them; and when the rains came, no money to buy seeds for the ground. O-Lan was sold, a sacrifice so her family could live. The narrator uses the word "slave" as a synonym for "girl" repeatedly throughout the story, signifying the social attitude towards females and the common practice of selling little girls into the houses of the wealthy.

Further, in a culture that prizes beauty, O-Lan again suffered. Her lack of beauty was evidently often thrown up to her in the household of the rich family where she was a slave. When Wang Lung went to the great house to get O-Lan as his bride, the Old Mistress boldly says before her, "She is not beautiful but that you do not need. Only men of leisure have the need for beautiful women to divert them. Neither is she clever. But she does well what she is told to do and she has a good temper.... She has not beauty enough to tempt my sons and grandsons..." (13). As he looks at the woman who is to be his wife, Wang Lung is momentarily distressed that her feet are not bound, and it is this lack of an artificial beauty which later angers him further as he begins a new life in visiting his mistress Lotus whose feet "thrust into pink satin shoes no longer than a man's middle finger" (129), are so helpless that she sways on them as she stands (144). Filled with shame and anger as he nags at O-Lan, Wang Lung yells at her, "And those feet of yours...." Forgetful of the help that O-Lan had been to him in the fields when he was a struggling farmer, a help that she never could have been with feet bound, the feet now become a symbol to Wang Lung of all of his wife's ugliness.

It seemed to him that she was altogether hideous, but the most hideous of all were her big feet.... (122)

The pain that must have been a part of O-Lan's spiritual enslavement showing forth only in her dumb, inarticulate face can be heard in those words she murmurs on her deathbed as she relives the formative years of her life—the pain of parents selling her as they might an extra ox or piece of furniture; the pain of her ugliness, so that her presence was an offense to others: and the physical pain of beatings and hunger during her enslavement:

> "I will bring the meats to the door only—and well I know I am ugly and cannot appear before the great lord.... Do not beat me—I will never eat of the dish again.... My father—my mother—my father—my mother.... Well I know I am ugly and cannot be loved. (186)

And the added tragedy is that for all of the help O-Lan had been to Wang Lung, washing his clothes, preparing his meals, bearing his sons, and working in the fields beside him, he does not love her. Even though he spends days sitting beside her bed as she is dying, he does so out of shame and duty rather than love. In the culture which the story portrays, women are to be prized for beauty only; and this so blinds Wang Lung's eyes to O-Lan's goodness and concern for him in a totally unselfish love that he cannot love her in her ugliness. As he hears her murmurs, he is filled with shame but not with love:

> And he wondered and grieved at himself most of all because what she said was true, and even when he took her hand, desiring truly that she feel his tenderness towards her, he was ashamed because he could feel no tenderness, no melting of the heart such as Lotus could win from him with a pout of her lips. When he took this stiff dying hand, he did not love it, and even his pity was spoiled with repulsion towards it. (186)

In view, then, of the sufferings which sexual and domestic dominance cause, Pearl Buck's *The Good Earth* needs to be read for its humanitarian values rather than being banned from library shelves and English department curricula. The violation of women in their very humanity about which Pearl Buck writes is caught in a non-Christian-Judaic culture. Yet, what she writes about is a universal matter, as much a part of Christian-Judaic cultures as it is of non-Christian. In no way, whatever culture may be involved, does the book condone or teach the exploitation of women, either sexually in concubinage or domestically in wife-abuse. Rather, by the misery resulting from such exploitation as the novel brings out, the reader understands how demeaning it is, not only for those who are exploited but for those who do the exploiting as well. Anyone who condemns the book on the grounds that it does teach concubinage and wife-abuse is not a critic but a caviller.

WORKS CITED

Pope, Alexander, "An Essay on Criticism." In *Eighteenth Century English Literature*. Eds. Geoffrey Tillotson, et.al., Chicago: Harcourt, Brace and World, Inc., 1969: 554-564.

Buck, Pearl S. *The Good Earth*. New York: Washington Square Press 1973.

THE GRAPES OF WRATH: PRESERVING ITS PLACE IN THE CURRICULUM
Lee Burress

In February 1980 the school board of Kanawha, Iowa, a small city in the northwestern part of Iowa, voted unanimously to ban *The Grapes of Wrath* from use in a sophomore English class. The book was allowed to remain in the school library. The action was taken as a result of a complaint by a parent who was vice-president of the local bank. The bank officer complained that the book was "profane, vulgar, and obscene," according to a report in the Des Moines *Register* (Kanawha 1A).

It is an interesting coincidence that approximately at the same time the book was removed from use in the English class at Kanawha, the Sioux City Diocese of the Roman Catholic Church issued a report concerning land ownership patterns in Iowa after two years of study. The report stated that in the 14 northwestern counties of Iowa, 77% of the land was owned by absentee owners (Sioux City 6). It is probably coincidental that a banker should attack *The Grapes of Wrath* for being "profane, vulgar, and obscene" and ignore the Jeffersonian agrarianism that runs through the book. Steinbeck's charge that capital is used to buy big tractors and drive farmers off the land may not have been apparent to the banker who complained about the book. But it is ironic that a novel which has such a theme as one of its organizing principles should be forbidden in a part of the country where traditionally the family farm has seemed to be a dominant feature of life.

However, the effort to censor this book, based on a failure to understand it, or perhaps to understand it too well, began as soon as the book was published in 1939. Attacks on the hook were not confined to California, or to Oklahoma, but occurred across the entire United States. Successful efforts were made to censor the book in public libraries in

Kansas City, Buffalo, and in many other places. Several copies were burned in St. Louis. The attacks have continued, making Steinbeck one of the two or three most frequently censured and censored novelists of the twentieth century. The attacks were no doubt stimulated by the immediate popularity of the book in 1939, a popularity which has continued across the decades. By 1979 the book had had more than 40 printings in the United States and over 20 printings in England.

The Grapes of Wrath illustrates Milton's principle in the Areopagitica that "books are not absolutely dead things but contain a potency of life in them to be as active as that soul was whose progeny they are...." The potency of The Grapes of Wrath grows out of the substantial degree of success that Steinbeck arrived at in creating a significant work of fiction from a major episode of American history, the depression and drought years of the 1930s.

The continuing interest of literary critics along with general readers in The Grapes of Wrath is illustrated by the recent volume of critical essays, Twentieth Century Interpretations: The Grapes of Wrath, edited by Robert C. Davis. The essays demonstrate that, as is typical of significant literary works, critics differ with regard to the interpretation of the various aspects of the novel. But the fertility of the critical view and the continuing ability of The Grapes of Wrath to generate critical interest suggests indeed that Milton's term "potency" does apply to the novel.

Steinbeck's success in creating a potent or powerful novel may be seen in the characters of the novel, in the complete structure of the novel, in the use of symbols especially the contrast of the animal with the mechanical aspects of life, in the powerful and varying prose styles of the novel and finally in a set of themes that reflect traditional American values. Moreover, in several of these aspects of the novel, Steinbeck drew on Biblical and religious materials that add to the richness and depth of the book.

The novel's ability to catch and keep the reader's interest owes much to its characters, whom Steinbeck has endowed with vitality and thematic significance. Many reader have seen embodiments of basic Christian virtues in such characters as Ma Joad, Tom Joad, Jim Casy, and Rose of Sharon. Tom Joad's growth in insight illustrates one of the important themes in the novel. Whether Tom or Jim Casy best illustrates a Christ figure depends on the reader's interpretation of the novel; each character has seemed to some readers to be illustrative of Christ's self-sacrificial life.

The structure of the novel is based on the Joads' journey westward. The journey gives the novel a mythical quality and achieves emotional power by relating the Joads' journey to that of many previous journeys, including the exodus of the Hebrew people out of Egypt to the promised land as well as westward journeys of the American Western myth. The ironic differences between the promised land found by the Hebrews in Palestine and the tragic plight of the Joads in California is not lost on the reader.

Steinbeck's use of a series of interludes as he tells the story of the Joads is an effective method of relating the particularities of the Joad family to a more universal set of realities. There are sixteen of these interchapters; these do not refer to the Joads, Wilsons, or Wainwrights. Instead, Steinbeck uses these chapters to tell of the larger significance of the situation in which the Joads find themselves. The interchapters draw on the material which Steinbeck had found in his visits to the migrant camps and his observations of the general situation of drought and depression.

Several of the memorable features of the novel appear in these interchapters, the turtle in chapter three, the tractor episode in chapter five in which an old farmhouse is destroyed by an enormous tractor. The farmer stands helplessly by with a rifle. The observation that nature imitates art, that life is often parallel to great works of literature, is illustrated by the tragic event in Minnesota in which a farmer, dispossessed of his farm by the bank that owned the mortgage, shot and killed two officials of the bank, then later killed himself. Would that farmer have committed such a violent and useless act if he had read and thought about *The Grapes of Wrath?*

Chapter eleven describes a vacant house, symbolic of the many vacant houses left across the deserted rural landscape. In other interchapters, Steinbeck discusses land ownership in California, the development of the migratory labor situation, and the accompanying results for society. In the final interchapter Steinbeck describes the rain which sets the scene for the last chapter of the book with its poignant episode of Rose of Sharon feeding the starving old man.

While some readers have felt that scene unrealistic, others have seen in it a poetic, or mythical, or metaphorical effort to realize several themes of the book--especially the traditional Western world theme of the essential oneness of humankind. Rose of Sharon cannot save her own baby, but she can still serve as one who ameliorates suffering and demonstrates the ennobling possibilities for humanity, in even the worst of situations.

The varying prose styles add to the strength of the book. Peter Lisca has shown how the prose has a Biblical ring in several places, for example in the passage comparing horses and tractors. Lisca makes this clear by printing the passage in the style of the Psalms:

The tractor had lights shining,
For there is no day and night for a tractor
And the disks turn the earth in the darkness
And they glitter in the daylight.

And when a horse stops work and goes in the barn
There is a life and vitality left,
There is a breathing and a warmth,
And the feet shift on the straw,
And the jaws champ on the hay,
And the ears and eyes are alive.
There is a warmth of life in the barn,
And the heat and smell of life.

But when the motor of a tractor stops,
It is as dead as the ore it came from.
The heat goes out of it
Like the living heat that leaves a corpse. (175)

In a different style, Steinbeck describes a folk dance in chapter thirteen; "Look at that Texas boy. Long legs loose, taps four times for every damn step. Never see a boy swing aroun' like that. Look at him swing that Cherokee girl, red in the cheeks and her toe points out." Throughout the novel the prose style varies to fit the subject under consideration. Lisca illustrates this point further by reference to chapter seven in which there is a description of the sale of used cars: "Cadillacs, LaSalles, Buicks, Plymouths, Packards, Chevvies, Fords, Pontiacs. Row on row. Headlight glinting in the afternoon sun. Good Used Cars. Soften 'em up, Joe. Jesus

I wisht I had a thousand jalopies. Get 'em ready to deal, and I'll close 'em" (176).

Steinbeck's use of symbols in the novel is another of the ways in which the Joads' predicament is shown to extend their own limited situation. These include the turtle, the vacant houses, the enormous tractor, the worn out automobiles, Rose of Sharon nursing the old starving man, the grapes, both in the title and throughout the novel as a symbol of plenty and as ironic counterpoint of the denial of plenty to the Joads, Rose of Sharon's stillborn child, set adrift to float down the stream, again in ironic counterpoint to the child Moses in the *Bible*, who became a saviour of his people. The Joads' journey is itself an archetype of mass migration, as Lisca suggests. These symbolic objects or actions are carefully integrated into the action of the novel, contributing to the artistic success of the whole book.

Symbolic contrasts between animals and machines appear frequently in the book. Generally, the animal references stand for life and the references to machinery stand for depersonalized, inanimate ways of dealing with human problems. "I lost my land, a single tractor took my land." The phrase "tractored out" or "tractored off" appears often. Some animal references are derogatory, as when human beings behave like ants, or fight like a couple of cats. But generally, as in the contrast between horses and tractors quoted above, animal references are hopeful and positive; mechanical references suggest the destructive and negative aspects of contemporary life. The turtle, for example, symbolizes the persistence of living beings in spite of danger or hardship. As machines threaten the turtle, so machines threaten the farmer. As the turtle persists, so will the Joads.

The thematic structure of the book is a major source of its continuing power. In the decades since its publication readers have seen a number of traditional American ideas that complement each other in the texture of the book. While some critics have seen tension in the ideas of the book, on the whole most readers have seen artistic integrity in the book's thematic structure.

Frederick Ives Carpenter suggested, not long after the book's publication, that a number of the most characteristic American ideas appeared in the book--"the mystical transcendentalism of Emerson," "the earthy democracy of Walt Whitman," the "pragmatic instrumentalism of William James and John Dewey" (81). Other readers have seen in the book the agrarian philosophy of Thomas Jefferson--a faith in the small farm that has strongly influenced our society. It was agrarianism that led to the homestead laws passed by the Republican Party when Abraham Lincoln was president, and that lay back of a variety of twentieth century efforts to assist farmers and protect the family farm.

No feature of the book is better illustrative of the tendency of the American novel to protest the conflict between American ideals and American practice than the novel's agrarianism. The Joads have as a major motivation their desire to own a piece of land, where they can raise the grapes of plenty, enough so that Pa Joad can squash the grapes across his face and feel the juice run down his chin, a destiny he is not to achieve.

The essential reality of the Joads' predicament is demonstrated by the fact that between 1940 and 1980 the number of American farms declined from 6 million to 2-1/4 million. Millions of Americans in that period left their farms for life elsewhere, as the Joads left their Oklahoma home. That migration of millions of people from rural areas to the city affected the United States in many ways--increasing crime and welfare on the one hand, and providing a ready force of factory workers on the other. Few people note that, as the novel implies, we pay for our food not only at the grocery store, but also in taxes caused by crime and welfare.

It is an ironic possibility that if all the political and editorial language calling for the preservation of the family farm were printed in a single set of volumes, it might exceed the attacks on *The Grapes of Wrath*. But it is doubtful that any other American novelist has so vigorously upheld the ideal of the American family farm or so artistically protested the failure of our society to make that ideal possible in reality.

The transcendentalism in the book has led to two groundless charges by the critics, first that the book is atheistic, as expressed in the ideas of Jim Casy, and second that the book is collectivist, a code word meaning sympathetic to communism. These misreadings of the book grow out of an ignorance of transcendentalism and a misinterpretation of the call for unified action presented by the book.

The concept of the oversoul, in Emerson and in this book, is an affirmation of the universal presence of deity in all aspects of life. Emerson coined the term "oversoul" to express his understanding of the Christian tradition as he learned it from many Puritan sermons as well as from his reading of Luther, Calvin, Milton, and other theologians, as the literary historian Perry Miller has shown. Though Jim Casy probably had not read any works of theology, he does express the transcendental concept of the oversoul several times in the book in such language as this: "Maybe all men got one big soul ever'body's a part of." Transcendentalism has been criticized for its vagueness, but rightly or wrongly, it is an effort to assert that spiritual values are present in, and ultimately control, the material reality of the visible universe. It as clearly not the intent of Emerson nor of Jim Casy to deny the existence of deity. The charge of atheism is often made by those who say, "If you don't accept my definition of God, you must be an atheist." Neither Emerson nor Jim Casy would have agreed that they were atheists.

In fact the four major characters, Ma Joad, Tom, Jim Casy, and Rose of Sharon represent Steinbeck's effort to dramatize Biblical and Christian values in a realistic way among an unlikely group of poor and deprived persons. Ma Joad is one of the few saints in American literature. The qualities of saintliness--a cheerful and self-sacrificial life, and an understanding and consistent love for others--are realistically embodied in this portrait of a poverty stricken Oklahoma farm wife. Ma Joad's family disintegrates, her few possessions are lost, and she finds herself on the brink of starvation. Yet he does not fall into despair or bitterness but continues to respond in a helpful and life affirming way not only to the members of her own family but also to hungry neighbor children and a starving, unknown man. Ma Joad is a vivid dramatization of the "love that passeth understanding." It is hard to imagine what a truly saintly life would be like in the twentieth century. Steinbeck's imagination has given us a believable picture of a saint from an unlikely source--an Okie, an uneducated, migrant fruit picker, driven from her home to wander the land in search of a place to live.

Tom Joad illustrates the Biblical theme of growth, the Biblical assertion that the good life requires continued rebirth. Furthermore, Tom illustrates the Biblical notion that even the most unpromising persons have the possibility of a new life. Tom comes out of prison an unchanged person, selfishly individualistic, primarily interested in sex and drinking, though he does have a strong love for his family. But the events that follow, and the influence of his mother and of Jim Casy, greatly change him.

As the Joads experience the loss of their land, the breaking up of the family, near starvation, brutal treatment by police and landlords, and the death of Jim Casy, Tom grows in "wisdom and stature" to quote the Biblical phrase. When Ma Joad told Tom, "You're spoke for..." she contributed to his growth. When Jim Casy spoke of the Oversoul, Tom listened and grew out of his selfish concerns with his own satisfactions. He became aware, as his mother made clear to him, that he had to be concerned, not only for his own family's welfare, but for the welfare of all families, that the death of his sister's child was loss to all families, that the birth of a healthy child was cause for celebration by all families. He became quite willing to work for other families, even if it cost him his life, as it had cost the life of Jim Casy.

When Tom told his mother goodbye, as he set out to carry on the mission that he had learned from Jim Casy, she spoke with sorrow, "How'm I gonna know about you? They might kill ya an' I wouldn't know." But Tom tells her it doesn't matter. He explained in terms of the lesson he had learned from Casy of the Oversoul, of which all human beings are a part. Though we appear to be isolated individuals, still there is a transcendental unity that joins us:

> I'll be all aroun' in the dark. I'll be ever'where--wherever you look. Wherever they's a fight so hungry people can eat, I'll be there. Wherever they's a cop beatin' up a guy, I'll be there. If Casy knowed, why, I'll be in the way guys yell when they're mad an'--I'll be in the way kids laugh when they're hungry an' they know supper's ready. An' when our folks eat the stuff they raise an' live in the houses they build--why I'll be there. See? (572)

Though the dialect is lower class Okie, the ideas are derived from the Gospel of John.

Some would-be censors have mistakenly asserted that Steinbeck is sympathetic to communism. Steinbeck was in fact rather conservative; he supported the war in Vietnam, for example. His insistence in several works of fiction on the right of each person to his own piece of land can hardly be reconciled with communist tendencies toward collectivist forms of agriculture. However, Steinbeck's views outside the book are irrelevant to the implications of the symbols and actions in the book. It is clearly wrong to judge a book by the actual or assumed characteristics of the author.

The call for united action which runs through the book is not to be identified with the term "collectivist" as a synonym for communist. There is a tension between the individual and the group in the book, but its reconciliation is in the traditional Western world notion of the oneness of the humankind, as for example in the famous passage from John Donne, "Never send to know for whom the bell tolls, it tolls for thee."

The book calls for unified action that will preserve the right of farmers to their own farms, that will provide food for the hungry, that will subordinate the machine to the needs of the garden and to the needs of the human beings who toil in the garden. The book's call for unified action to meet the disasters of the 1930s is no more collectivist than was the action of the colonists who dumped the tea in Boston Harbor or who took up arms at Concord to fight the redcoats. There are many illustrations in the book of the need and ability of ordinary citizens to work together in solving problems, as for example when the migrants helped each other on the journey, or maintained order in the camp. This aspect of the novel is typical of American pragmatism--not of Marxist ideas.

In the original meaning of the word, a classic is a book taught in the classroom. Steinbeck's book is certainly a classic in this sense of the word. As with a number of other classics, it is likely that many people read this book in high school. This use is appropriate because the book lends itself well to studying many aspects of American literature and life. *The Grapes of Wrath* won a Pulitzer prize in 1940 and is one of the major works of an American novelist who won the Nobel prize in 1962. It is difficult to understand how any American high school or college could forbid the teaching or use of the book while maintaining a claim to act as a proper agency for the education of the young in this democratic republic.

WORKS CITED

Carpenter, Frederick Ives. "The Philosophical Joads." In *A Case Book on The Grapes of Wrath*. ed. A. M. Donohue. New York: Thomas Y. Crowell Company, 1968.

"Kanawha Bans Classic Book from Classes." [Des Moines] *Register* 12 Feb 1980: 1A.

Lisca, Peter. "The Grapes of Wrath as Fiction." In *A Case Book on The Grapes of Wrath*. ed. A. M. Donohue. New York: Thomas Y. Crowell Company, 1968.

Sioux City Diocesan Coalition to Preserve the Family Farm. *Fourteen County Study* (Unpublished report). Sioux City, IA: 1980.

Steinbeck, John. *The Grapes of Wrath*. New York: Viking Press, 1939.

BIBLIOGRAPHY

Readers who wish to explore further the rich body of commentary that the novel has stimulated might find some of the following books in their library.

Davis, Robert C., ed. Twentieth Century Interpretations of *The Grapes of Wrath: A Collection of Critical Essays*. Englewood Cliffs, NJ: Prentice Hall, Inc., 1982.

Davis, Robert Murray, ed. *Steinbeck, A Collection of Critical Essays*. Englewood Cliffs, NJ: Prentice-Hall, Inc., 1972.

Donohue, Agnes McNeill. *A Casebook on The Grapes of Wrath*. New York: Thomas Y. Crowell Company, Inc., 1968.

French, Warren, ed. *A Companion to The Grapes of Wrath*. New York: Viking Press, 1963.

French, Warren. *John Steinbeck*. Boston: Twayne Publishers, 1975.

Lisca, Peter. *The Wide World of John Steinbeck*. New Brunswick, NJ: Rutgers University Press, 1958.

A HERO AIN'T NOTHIN' BUT A SANDWICH: A RATIONALE FOR CLASSROOM USE

Frank Zidonis

Why does Benjie Johnson use dope? His immediate family is distressed by it, and so are the two best teachers he's encountered as well as his closest friend, Jimmy-Lee. In contrast to the conviction of everyone who knows him, Benjie himself does not admit that he has a drug habit. He further thinks of himself as basically honest, stealing only on occasion from his relatives (and that with the optimistic intention of repaying them even before they notice that anything is missing).

Life has turned sour for Benjie at age thirteen. When he was six, seven, and eight, he and his mother had really good times--going out for ice cream, reading the funnies, watching TV. Even his grandmother, with whom they lived, was easy to get along with. But then Butler Craig moved in with them, replacing Benjie in his mother's affections and ending the enjoyable twosome they had been. Benjie blames himself for the missing father he has never seen: "Musta gone cause he didn't dig me." He is bored at home and especially so at school, where he comes to believe that teachers are actually phonies, whether white or black. He feels particularly betrayed by Nigeria Greene, a fellow black, who together with another teacher, Bernard Cohen, gets the principal to sign the papers hospitalizing him for detoxification. After this treatment, he is released to home care where all try to be, and indeed are, supportive. Benjie, however, decides to get one more fix (to remember what it is he's giving up!), searches the rooms fruitlessly for money and finally makes off with Butler's best suit and overcoat.

Shortly thereafter, the climactic episode of the novel takes place. Butler surprises Benjie stealing a toaster from a neighboring apartment into which he moved, and, infuriated with Benjie, chases him to the icy roof top of their building. Benjie slips near the ledge and almost plummets to the pavement below before Butler manages to grab him with one hand. "Let me die," Benjie yells, and Butler--their eyes locked on each other-- realizes a fundamental truth about himself in their relationship: "I was runnin' from him...cause he wasn't mine." The rescue enables Benjie finally to see Butler in a new light: He even calls him *Dad*. In the closing scene, open-ended, Butler is anxiously waiting for Benjie to show up for continued treatment at the drug rehabilitation center.

Young readers can learn much about the literary form of fiction--and about life--from the masterful crafting of this novel. Four areas are particularly suitable for further exploration: point of view, characterization, language, and themes.

Point of view: The twenty-three relatively short chapters are each told from the point of view of the different characters that inhabit this realistic inner city setting painted by Childress, in effect a mosaic that gradually presents a sharp portrait of how the problems of one young man affect the intricate relationships of those who care about him. A simple count of chapter headings shows who the main protagonists are: Benjie has seven chapters, Butler has four, and all of the others have either one or two. As the characters share their perspectives on the events in the unfolding story, and on one another, readers find themselves engaged in two kinds of responses: the more immediate one involves the constant need to reappraise each character, but especially that of Benjie, as new information is provided; the other response, cumulatively building up, is to be drawn more deeply into the structure of this remarkable family.

Characterization--There are no stereotypes in the characters Childress has created here. The emotions are real, their economic and social situations are depicted convincingly, and their previous backgrounds (in a then still strongly racist South) are briefly but tellingly capsuled. Even a very minor character, Walter the pusher, can rail against the very junkies whom he supplies but actually despises, seeing himself as no worse than a salesman who has a business to operate. With the main character Benjie it becomes clear quite soon how ambivalent his feelings toward Butler are. He admires Butler, who's cool and self-assured, most notably with the social workers that have to be dealt with. At the same time Benjie resents him, blaming him for the lessened role he now perceives to be his with his mother.

Rose Johnson, his mother, also experiences conflicting emotions: the three people she loves—her mother, her common-law husband, and her son—create demands on her that are becoming oppressive. Eventually she explodes at Butler, critical of her for taking Benjie to a fortune teller:

> Dammit,...Kill me! Why don't you and Benjie buy guns and shoot me through the heart! His father could run, you can run, he can run, even my mother can slam her door; but I got to hold my ground and keep a roof over our heads, clean house, put food on the table, and also hit it on out here to work each and every day. Dammit, get offa me! (119-120)

But she does not succumb to despair; her love for them is too strong. After a brief retreat to her room, she returns to offer them a piece of pie and milk. As Benjie's narration concludes: "She smilin' like nothin' happen" (121).

Butler—steady, compassionate, strong—provides the salvaging link that binds this family together. He has finally won the admiration of Benjie, who now calls him *Dad* purposely and with pride. He has earned the respect of Benjie's grandmother, whose dancing of the shimmy is the final sign of approbation for Butler and what he has meant to them. What he has provided them is stability and protection—and in heroic measure. One of the social workers involved in rehabilitating Benjie had told Butler that he needed to identify with some male figures, proceeding then to list books on Black history as well as urging him to take Benjie to see movie stars and sports figures. Butler's common-sense understanding of the real world leads him to put things straight for the social worker:

> Some these big-time, celebrity-high-lifers can't take care-a themselves, they in as much trouble as you and Benjie. Yall gotta learn to identify with *me*, who gotta get up to face the world every damn mornin' with a clear head and a heavy heart. Benjie once told me a hero ain't nothin' but a sandwich--and you say a hero is a celebrity! Listen to my credentials; then maybe yall can pin me on a hero button. I'm supportin' three adults, one chile, and the United States government on my salary...and can't claim any of em for tax exemptions. So,

explain me no heroes. Yeah, and some-a our neighborhood success stories are livin' offa Benjie's veins, while they ridin' round in limousines and grandstandin' to win everybody's admiration! (126)

Language--As the excerpts reveal, the language used in the novel is a variety of Black English, certainly not the language by which the general commerce of our society is conducted. But it is vital, forceful, and essential: it has the bite that stimulates other characters to action or important self discovery. Shortly after Benjie stole Butler's best suit and overcoat, Butler moved out of the apartment to a neighboring one. Mrs. Ransom Bell, the grandmother, castigates Butler for this move:

"You ran out on Rose. Men are good for nothin' but runnin'. Some these colored men ain't nothin' but breath, britches, and shoe leather! When trouble comes, you run! I told Rosey to keep a sharp eye on the kinda man who runs when trouble comes." (105)

Memorable in its style and impact, this message comes back to gnaw at Butler in the roof-top scene where he realizes that indeed he has been running from Benjie.

Many street terms for drugs are used throughout the book and there are occasional instances of profanity woven into the dialogue. Both these instances are well motivated for depicting the ugly side of the real life that confronts modern urban youth. Sanitized language would in fact detract from the realistic, but not overly grim, setting created by Childress. Benjie has drifted into a drug mess and dragged his family in with him: there's no "pretty" way to describe this ugly situation. Nor are most of the vivid metaphors used in the novel objectionable. Examples abound that are forceful, inventive, and memorable: "walkin' with short bread" for short of cash; "bespoke suit" for tailor made; "It's nation time!" Nigeria Greene's rallying cry for his students; and Benjie's description of the boring way his geography class taught: "If I was to pick out middle C on the piano and keep hittin' it...."

A useful exercise for readers to undertake would be to explore the language styles as they vary from character to character. They would come to appreciate in general the edited American English form in the presentations by Nigeria Greene, Bernard Cohen, and the principal contrasted with the variety of the Black dialect styles used by the other characters. Within the Black dialect varieties--none of which poses any real problems of intelligibility--it would be instructive for students to search out the differences in style between adult and youth and between male and female. This kind of inquiry would enable students to more fully assess the novelistic techniques of Alice Childress, and it might further serve to alert them to such possibilities in their own writing.

Themes--There are two major themes in this novel. Focusing on Benjie, one theme deals with his drug problem and raises this question: Can family love and support overcome the perceived alienation of a troubled teenager? An optimistic answer would be a positive one--and there are grounds for it in the novel--but the question remains an open one at the very end: in the book, as in life. The other theme focuses on Butler's role and deals with the theme foreshadowed in the very title. Whereas the title is a pun on the definition of a hero, the novel itself explores in rich detail the substantive attributes of what constitutes a real-life hero. A hero is not the sandwich, as in Benjie's taunt, nor the celebrity figure that the social worker wants Benjie exposed to: it is the person who regularly meets the daily responsibilities thrust upon him or her, regardless of the difficulties they impose, and even when no credit is granted for doing so. Individual responsibility is a highly prized value in Butler's view of reality. At one point, for example, Benjie says he can drop the habit if somebody believed in him. Butler's response is sharp and to the point:

> "Dammit, Benjie,...you gotta do it even if *nobody* believe in you, gotta be your own man, the supervisor of your veins, the night watchman and day shift foreman in charge-a your own affairs." (120)

Childress has surrounded Benjie with three important environments in order to deal with these two major themes in her novel: the home, the school, and "the society," the latter term assuming ironic proportions when it depicts Nigeria Greene's gradual disillusionment with the Black movement. To the extent that each of us is what others perceive us to be, the interaction in each of these settings helps to determine for us what kind of person Benjie is. These environments are also important in permitting Childress to deal with a rich array of sub-themes and topics, ones that young readers will find stimulating. In the home environment, in addition to individual responsibility and the nature of the hero, students can explore communication as a sub-theme. How would students explain this dilemma of Benjie's mother, for example:

> One day I almost said it...after goin' over the words in my mind, "Benjie, the greatest thing in the world is to love someone and they love you too." But when I opened by mouth, I said, "Benjie, brush the crumbs off your jacket." (54)

Or how would they contrast Butler's advice to Benjie that he be his own man with Nigeria's father's suggestion that he give back the lie? The family values in Benjie's household, which consists of three generations, are also worth discussing and writing about. The grandmother's views on the process of aging might be revealing to young readers.

The school environment takes up topics of immediate concern to most students: fair teachers, boring classes, vandalism, school cafeteria food, unfair teachers. In the society at large, the poverty cycle, the role of social agencies, racism, drug addiction--all are legitimate and provocative topics for exploration in the reading of this novel.

Why should students read this novel, finally, given that it is about drug addiction and that the language is not standard English and is occasionally vulgar? The reasons for doing so are compelling. It is an optimistic, even humorous, book. It is skillfully crafted. It is realistic without being grim. But, more important, it presents a Black family with a strong commitment to individual responsibility, a family that is warm and caring. It's a novel that depicts a striking array of Blacks--from the mean and radical to the professional and saintly. And the drugs (and their users) are depicted as offensive and trouble-causing; they are not made to appear attractive.

WORK CITED

Childress. Alice. *A Hero Ain't Nothin' But a Sandwich*. New York: Avon, 1974.

IF BEALE STREET COULD TALK:
A RATIONALE FOR CLASSROOM USE
William G. McBride

If Beale Street Could Talk, it would tell, moving successfully backward and forward in time, an age old story of love that survives adversity, of enduring personal relationships that defeat cruelty and indifference, of human values that transcend both race and culture.

Nineteen-year-old Tish, the novel's principal voice, begins her story by telling the readers that she had, that day, visited her twenty-two-year-old fiance, Fonny, in prison, partly to tell him that she was pregnant. During the next several months, as the novel unfolds, Tish shares current happenings and introspective feelings about herself, the people she loves, and the cruelty of a social system that demeans minorities. Throughout, she interweaves enough of her childhood and young adulthood that the picture is complete.

Fonny and Tish have been friends since childhood. Although their families lived across the street in those days, the children had relatively little to do with each other until they became involved in a fight. When Tish hits Fonny with a stick that has a nail in it and draws blood, the fight ends abruptly. Sure that he'll die of lockjaw and that she'll spend the rest of her life in jail, Tish spends several miserable days. Then, Fonny appears on her stoop with a doughnut and an apology, and friendship begins.

As Tish illustrates her childhood, she establishes the characteristics of members of both her family and Fonny's. Readers learn that Fonny and his father, Frank, have a warm, loving relationship but that the relationships between Frank and his wife and daughters and between Fonny and his sisters are much less cordial. On the other hand, the love in Tish's home is strongly visible, made apparent to readers by Tish's telling of the way her parents met and then shifting to the present and the announcement of her pregnancy.

Tish's parents and sister assure Tish of their love and support. They know that Tish and Fonny's plans to marry ended abruptly when Fonny was falsely accused of raping a Puerto Rican woman and sent to prison. And from having watched the youngsters grow up together, they accept a union of faith if not of fact. Their concern now is for Tish and her unborn child—and for Fonny who must somehow be rescued from confinement. Their approach is to invite Fonny's family over for a drink so that the two families might plan their strategy together.

But the best laid plans.... Fonny's family, never on the best of terms, quarrel openly and insult Tish. Tish's announcement causes Fonny's mother to curse the mother and her unborn child yet cry that her son would be forgiven for this "lustful action." Fonny's father strikes his wife with the back of his hand, knocking her to the floor. Then, the two men leave. The women become more and more verbally abusive; and when Fonny's mother and sisters leave, any hope of two-family solidarity has been shattered.

The attempts to gain Fonny's release seem doomed. The white lawyer wants more money. The policeman who arrested Fonny is a white racist. The only witness for Fonny—besides Tish, whose testimony will be disregarded—has been arrested and is being held incommunicado. The victim has disappeared.

Yet, there is hope. Angered by the injustice and the callousness of the system and driven by his own pride, the lawyer becomes more interested and more involved. He finally locates the victim in Puerto Rico, but someone will have to go there to see her. The lawyer can't go because he needs to stay on top of the local situation and because he must avoid being accused of intimidating a witness . Tish can't go because, without her, Fonny will panic. Tish's sister, Ernestine, can't go because she has to keep applying pressure on the lawyer. Neither father can go for obvious reasons. That leaves Tish's mother, Sharon, who fears planes and dreads leaving New York but who will go because she must.

Sharon meets the victim but runs into a blank wall. The fathers' attempts to make additional money for bail have been only partly successful. Fonny's mother and sisters aid the prosecution's case by saying that Fonny has always been incorrigible.

And the novel ends with the suicide of Fonny's father, the birth of Tish's baby, and the hope that bail money has been raised. In the unending cycle of life, there is birth as well as death; in the midst of despair, there is light and hope. The will to survive triumphs, and love and caring create the bond that transcends race or culture or creed.

Objections to Baldwin's novel may arise from several sources. The language is straightforward, often profane, and the tone is frequently bitter. Sexual scenes, while neither frequent nor titillating, are specific. Orthodox religion is treated lightly. The social system, dominated by the white man, is decried by Hispanics, Puerto Ricans and blacks—even by the poor Italians who also find themselves at the mercy of the establishment.

Overall, though, the values should outweigh the objections. However profane, the language is realistic. Tish and Fonny are children of the streets; the families, their friends, and their enemies are all caught in a ghetto environment. Tish, as narrator, uses common four-letter words for bodily functions and sexual parts and activities. When she relates a story from a different perspective, she retains the vernacular. Although the words may not please the readers, such words are commonly used and understood, even by the naive. And to divest the characters of their natural speech patterns would destroy the story because it would destroy the character's credibility. Unless the characters are allowed to tell their story in their own way, the novel is neither realistic nor meaningful.

Baldwin's tone is bitter. He speaks of those who prey on the poor: "The poor are always crossing the Sahara. And the lawyers and bondsmen and all that crowd circle around the poor, exactly like vultures..., scavengers, indecent garbage men..." (7). He says of the environment: "...New York must be the ugliest and the dirtiest city in the world. It must have the ugliest buildings and the nastiest people. It's got to have the worst cops. If any place is worse, it's got to be so close to hell that you can smell the people frying. And, come to think of it, that's exactly the smell of New York in the summertime" (10). He speaks of the attitude of the poor: The Italian lady says, "I have been in America a long time. I hope I do not die here" (151). Through Fonny he describes the system: "They got us in a trick bag, baby. It's hard, but I just want for you to bear in mind that they can make us lose each other by putting me in the shit—or, they can try to make us lose each other by making you try to protect me from it. You see what I mean?" (153)

Readers might anticipate that minority spokespersons would be cynically outspoken about a system that had, historically, done them few favors. And reviewer Arthur Curley comments: "...as a social document, this moving novel is a powerful assault upon the cynicism which seems today to drain our determination to confront deep social problems." And further: "The balance of bitterness and love which we associate with Baldwin's writings appears to have shifted in favor of the latter. Some may see this as a symptom of weariness; more likely, it signifies the evolution of anger into a deeper passion" (1056).

Tish's initial sexual experience is quite detailed; at the same time, the experience is encompassed by an emotional closeness and a gentleness between Tish and Fonny that creates an openness and cements a bond that they have shared since they were children. Passion exists, but so does love—and love endures. Other sexual scenes are heightened by understatement when Tish identifies the night the baby was conceived, by a kind of wry humor when Fonny describes for Tish his parents' lovemaking ritual, and by a sense of isolation and loneliness that leads Fonny to masturbate in his prison cell. In no case are the readers seduced into any kind of sexual gratification.

On the other hand, to deny the sexual implications would be to deny the novel's base. After all, Tish is pregnant and Fonny has been imprisoned because a woman has accused him of raping her. One of the primary urgencies of the novel is to gain a father's release from prison so that he might care for his family. The relationship between the cops and the blacks often carries sexual connotations, but generations of stories have established a precedent for depicting that kind of relationship. There is comment about rape and attempted rape in prison, but again, to include such statements is to include reality.

And, finally, there may be an objection to the way religion is treated. Fonny's mother is Sanctified, but all of the characters—except, perhaps, her daughters—believe that her soul is never truly touched, that her devotion is superficial and hypocritical. The sexual scene between Fonny's parents, as Fonny describes it, is irreverent. Tish comments that her family is Baptist, but orthodox religion has little to do with their lives. Still, the novel is deeply religious. Part One is entitled, "Troubled About My Soul"; Part Two, "Zion." The love and loyalty and willingness to sacrifice for each other reach to the very depths of religion. In true Biblical fashion Tish assures Fonny that where he goes, she will follow. And Joseph, as the father figure, cares for his family and provides for them.

Those who would condemn the novel can undoubtedly find sufficient grounds. But the novel deserves a place on library shelves and it deserves reading. *If Beale Street Could Talk* portrays a strong family balanced not only by love but by equality. Each member of Tish's family—father, mother, older sister—has equal voice in family council and an equal role in solving the problems. There is no matriarchy here, nor is there a male dominated household. There is, instead a united family. And that family fights for survival against incredible odds—and succeeds!

Neither is it a one-sided novel. The white lawyer becomes increasingly an advocate for—and perhaps even a friend of the family. The relationship between Fonny and Tish and their Spanish friends is sensitively drawn. When Sharon goes to Puerto Rico to confront the victim, she is befriended by a young native taxi driver who recognizes both the legion of motherhood and the fact that Sharon is a lady. Sharon and her family realize and appreciate the plight of the Puerto Rican victim; and while the readers might wish that she would change her story, they, too, can appreciate the trauma the victim has undergone and understand why she will not—cannot—change her testimony.

All of us can only grow from reading about and trying to understand cultures beyond our own. And we can profit by learning that beneath the surface, all human beings are compelled by the same needs and desires, are driven by the same passions and fears, and are comforted by love—the final answer.

If Beale Street Could Talk, it would tell a compelling story. And, through James Baldwin, it does.

WORKS CITED

Baldwin, James. *If Beale Street Could Talk*. New York: Dial, 1974.

Curley, Arthur. "Book Reviews—*If Beale Street Could Talk*." *Library Journal* 99 (April 1, 1974): 1057.

MAYA ANGELOU IS THREE WRITERS: *I KNOW WHY THE CAGED BIRD SINGS*

James Bertolino

After reading Maya Angelou's autobiographical volume *I Know Why the Caged Bird Sings*, I find myself thinking of her as three different writers. The first is a writer of extraordinary imagination and verbal originality, well worth reading for her artistic effects, her style. The second writer is one who bears honest witness to her own development as a sensitive, highly intelligent human being, probing deeply into powerful childhood experiences, examining how wounds can bring the gift of awareness. The third is a socially conscious writer whose portrayal of the pain, frustration and waste caused by racial prejudice is stunning and persuasive. Reading any of these three "writers" can be a rewarding experience, but do they together create something that is greater than the sum of its parts? The answer is, of course, yes, but before discussing how these identifiable elements enhance each other, let's look at them separately.

When Angelou was a child in the town of Stamps, Arkansas she fell in love with William Shakespeare. It's remarkable for any child under the age of ten to be seriously involved with Shakespeare, but for a black child in a small, southern community, it was a phenomenon. While her ears were full of the rich inventiveness of black colloquial speech, her mind was engaged by the fine-tuned lines of Shakespeare, W.E.B. DuBois and Paul Lawrence Dunbar.

Her own writing, no matter how masterfully controlled, seems ever ready to embrace unexpected bursts of imagery and sound that seem encrusted with life—language that stretches syntax and breaks free: "The sounds of tag beat through the trees while the top branches waved in contrapuntal rhythms. I lay on a moment of green grass and telescoped the children's game to my vision. The girls ran about wild, now here, now there, never here, never was, they seemed to have no more direction than a splattered egg" (115).

What is perhaps most distinctive about Maya Angelou's writing is its consummate felicity. She not only writes with unflinching honesty about her most painful moments, she crafts language that will enact the reality: you feel the textures, smell the odors, shiver with the chill of stunned awareness.

While she was recognized early as a gifted child, she was physically different from her peers as well. Tall and skinny, by age sixteen she was six feet with a body "shaped like a cucumber." Her parents were both beautiful and, at least in her father's case, quite vain. Her only brother, Bailey (a year older), whom she treasured above all else, was also a beautiful child. "Where I was big, elbowy and grating, he was small, graceful and smooth.... His hair fell down in black curls, and my head was covered with black steel wool" (17).

As a young child Maya, or Marguerite, was so unhappy about her appearance she fantasized a personal myth: "...a cruel fairy stepmother, who was understandably jealous of my beauty, had turned me into a too-big Negro girl, with nappy black hair, broad feet and a space between her teeth that would hold a number-two pencil" (2). As she approached her teens, her Uncle Tommy often told her, "...don't worry 'cause you ain't pretty. Plenty pretty women I seen digging ditches or worse. You smart. I swear to God, I rather you have a good mind than a cute behind" (56).

Her personal development did become focussed on her mental abilities, and her creative talents. She apparently was wise enough to take her uncle's advice, though as she matured she also managed to turn her physical limitations to her advantage. She trained her deep, theatrical voice, took dance lessons, and became well-known for her commanding presence on the stage and, later, television.

A key event in her development was being taken in as a protege by a Mrs. Flowers, the only black woman in Stamps with aristocratic bearing. She encouraged Maya to memorize and recite poetry, insisting that "...words mean more than what is set down on paper. It takes a human voice to infuse them with the shades of deeper meaning" (82). Maya was about nine years old at the time, and had already suffered through an intense emotional period when she would not, or could not, speak—a reaction to having been molested and raped when she was eight.

From the age of three Maya and her brother had been raised by her grandmother ("Momma") and her crippled Uncle Willie in Stamps. Her mother and father were separated and pursuing their respective lives free of the children. Maya, Bailey and Uncle Willie helped Momma run the only black-owned general store in the region. Maya learned to be responsible, and while she was a superior student in school, at home she was learning many practical lessons, and how to understand and deal with different kinds of people. She also respected her elders. Her grandmother's world "was bordered on all sides with work, duty, religion and 'her place.' I don't think she ever knew that a deep-brooding love hung over everything she touched" (47).

When she was eight, she and her brother were taken to their mother in St. Louis, where they entered a world peopled by gamblers, numbers runners and men named Hard-hitting Jimmy, Two Gun, Sweet Man and Poker Pete. When Maya saw her mother for the first time in five years, she "knew immediately" why her mother had sent them away. "She was too beautiful to have children" (50).

A man named Mr. Freeman lived with her mother, and supported the family, while mother brought in a little extra by "cutting poker games in gambling parlors" (58). Maya felt Mr. Freeman was a little pathetic when he sat up late waiting for her mother. He, like the men on the streets and in the saloons, was "hypnotized by the beautiful lady who talked with her whole body" (54). Maya felt as sorry for him as for "a litter of pigs born in our backyard sty in Arkansas. We fattened the pigs all year long for the slaughter on the first good frost, and even as I suffered for the cute little wiggly things, I knew how much I was going to enjoy the fresh sausage and headcheese they could give only with their deaths" (60).

Maya had never had a father around, and when Mr. Freeman held and stroked her in a gentle way, she felt that for the first time she had a real father. Even when he became sexually aroused, her combination of innocence and hunger for loving attention kept her from becoming alarmed. One morning, after Mr. Freeman had been up most of the night waiting for her mother, and neither mother nor her brother were home, he turned up the radio to drown-out her cries and raped her. He threatened to kill her precious Bailey if she told anyone.

Angelou's description of her molestation and rape is probably the most valuable part of her remarkable book. We live in a time when the issue of child abuse has almost become an obsession in our society, and it's important that such a story be told honestly, without sensationalism, yet with enough palpable detail and enough insight so we, the readers, might begin to understand. Her language resonates with the New Testament at the same time it strikes us with its psychological insight and stark details: "A breaking and entering when even the senses are torn apart. The act of rape on an eight-year-old body is a matter of the needle giving because the camel can't. The child gives, because the body can, and the mind of the violator cannot" (65).

Mr. Freeman was convicted of his crime; however, his lawyer got him released on some technicality, and before the day was over Mr. Freeman was dead. The policeman who delivered the news said it looked like he'd been kicked to death (probably by Maya's uncles, though the responsible parties were never found). For many years Maya felt guilt and remorse over Mr. Freeman's death, for the fact that her words had convinced the court. For though he'd ravaged her horribly, he'd nonetheless been the closest thing she'd had to a real father. And though Mr. Freeman "had surely done something very wrong...I was convinced that I had helped him do it" (70).

While the Negro section of St. Louis in the 1930s "had all the finesse of a gold-rush town" (51) it still was a place where black people had power and often led the kind of lives they preferred. When Maya and Bailey were sent back to Arkansas, after less than a year with their mother in St. Louis, they were again faced with the depressing reality of overt racial oppression. "The idea came to me that my people may be a race of masochists and that not only was it our fate to live the poorest, roughest life but that we liked it like that" (102).

When Maya was very young—her first years in Stamps—people thought it odd that she spoke without a southern accent. She had her own ideas about that: "Wouldn't they be surprised when one day I woke out of my black ugly dream, and my real hair, which was long and blond, would take the place of the kinky mass that Momma wouldn't let me straighten? My light blue eyes were going to hypnotize them" (2).

It wasn't long, however, before she began to be critical of white people rather than envious: "I couldn't understand whites and where they got the right to spend money so lavishly. Of course, I knew God was white too, but no one could have made me believe he was prejudiced" (40). One "terrible Christmas," when she was about seven, her vain father sent her his photograph, and her mother sent "a doll with blue eyes and rosy cheeks and yellow hair painted on her head" (43). Maya went outside into the cold Winter air, sat down and cried. She and her brother tore the stuffing out of the white doll the day after Christmas.

A few months later their father came to Stamps to take the children to St. Louis to live with their mother. At this point Maya was eight and Bailey nine. Being black had already become a source of pride for them, and Maya was critical of her father. "He sounded more like a white man than a Negro. Maybe he was the only brown-skinned white man in the world. It would be just my luck that the only one would turn out to be my father" (48).

The irony is that one of the reasons Maya did so well as a student, and loved to read from so young an age, was because her parents had taught her to speak perfect English and to respect the great works of literature and all things associated with high white culture.

A pivotal moment for Maya Angelou came at her grade school graduation. A local white politician had been invited to give the commencement address and, after he'd detailed his plans for improving the educational opportunities for the white schools, he described how his second most important priority was to develop the athletic facilities in the black schools. "The white kids were going to have a chance to become Galileos and Madame Curies and Edisons and Gauguins, and our boys (the girls weren't even in on it) would try to be Jesse Owenses and Joe Louises" (151).

When the class valedictorian (he being the only student with higher grades than Maya) gave his address from Shakespeare, Maya couldn't believe her ears. "Hadn't he got the message? There was no 'nobler in the mind' for Negroes because the world didn't think we had minds, and they let us know it" (154). She determined that day to always have control over her life, despite her race (within a few years she would become the first black woman employee on the San Francisco trolley car system). When the program concluded with the Negro national anthem ("Lift Ev'ry Voice and Sing" by James Weldon Johnson and J. Rosamond Johnson) Maya again felt "a proud member of the wonderful, beautiful Negro race."

An experience that would set the tone for her adult life happened when she was fifteen, on vacation with her father in Los Angeles. After her father's girlfriend attacked her, cut her with a knife for coming between them, Maya ran away for a month, then rejoined her mother in San Francisco. After wandering aimlessly with no money, having no friends or family she could call, as night approached she found an automobile junkyard where she slipped into a fairly clean car and spent the night. When she awoke the next morning, the car windows framed Negro, Mexican and white faces, all staring in at her.

She had happened on a small society of homeless children and teenagers, one that had a system of rules for "citizenship." People of opposite sex could not share the same automobile for the night; no criminal activity was allowed, for fear of drawing the police. To provide the essentials for survival, the boys mowed lawns, ran errands for merchants and swept out pool halls. The girls collected bottles for the deposit, and worked weekends in diners. All the money was held communally. "After a month my thinking process had so changed that I was hardly recognizable to myself. The unquestioning acceptance by my peers had dislodged the familiar insecurity.... The lack of criticism evidenced by our ad hoc community influenced me, and set a tone for my life" (216).

The non-judgmental atmosphere of the junkyard community also became an effective model for her writing. All of her experiences became valid as markers on the path to self-awareness, no matter how troubling or apparently insignificant. Her powerful feelings about racial prejudice and her criticisms of white people were resolved in that social gathering where all the races, ages and both genders worked together for the good of the community. Finally, the brilliant glue that made it all cohere as literature, was her extraordinary writing style. That atmosphere of permission helped give her the courage to write the way that felt best, the way that excited her, and brought forward for comprehension the deep information that lay behind the formation of her personality.

I believe *I Know Why the Caged Bird Sings* is one of the essential books produced by our culture, and we should all read it, especially our children. Maya Angelou's generosity is beyond compare.

WORK CITED

Angelou, Maya. *I Know Why the Caged Bird Sings.* New York: Bantam, 1969.

LEARNING TO LIVE: WHEN THE BIRD BREAKS FROM THE CAGE

Opal Moore

> I bring the dreaded disease. I encourage their children to open their hearts to the "dark" side. To know the fear in them. To know the rage. To know the repression that has lopped off their brains—
> Toi Derricotte *"From The Black Notebooks"*

There is, it seems, a widespread movement afoot to assert the innocence of children even as we deny or sabotage that innocence. There is what appears to be a head-in-the-sand impulse to insist upon this innocence by simply refusing to acknowledge its non-existence. Never mind the "mean streets," never mind the high teen pregnancy rates and drug use, or the phenomenal school dropout rates, or spiraling teen suicide statistics—never mind these real dangers to childhood. There are agencies at work to shield these unprotected children from books that might reveal to them the workings of their own minds and hearts, books that engender the agony of thought and the fearfulness of hope. If we cannot protect children from experience, should we protect them from knowing?

I Know Why the Caged Bird Sings, the autobiography of Maya Angelou, is the story of one girl's growing up. But, like any literary masterpiece, the story of this one black girl declaring "I can" to a color-coded society that in innumerable ways had told her "you can't, you won't" transcends its author. It is an affirmation; it promises that life, if we have the courage to live it, will be worth the struggle. A book of this description might seem good reading for junior high and high school students. According to People for the American Way, however, *Caged Bird* was the ninth "most frequently challenged book" in American schools (Graham 26, 1). *Caged Bird* elicits criticism for its honest depiction of rape, its exploration of the ugly spectre of racism in America, its recounting of the circumstances of Angelou's own out-of-wedlock teen pregnancy, and its humorous poking at the foibles of the institutional church. Arguments advocating that *Caged Bird* be banned from school reading lists reveal that the complainants, often parents, tend to regard any treatment of these kinds of subject matter in school as inappropriate—despite the fact that the realities and issues of sexuality and violence, in particular, are commonplace in contemporary teenage intercourse and discourse. The children, they imply, are too innocent for such depictions; they might be harmed by the truth.

This is a curious notion—that seriousness should be banned from the classroom while beyond the classroom, the irresponsible and sensational exploitation of sexual, violent, and profane materials is as routine as the daily dose of soap opera. The degradation of feeling caused by slurs directed against persons for their race/class/sex/ sexual preference is one of the more difficult hurdles of youthful rites of passage. But it's not just bad TV or the meanness of children. More and more, society is serving an unappetizing fare on a child-sized plate—television screens, t-shirt sloganeers, and weak politicians admonish children to "say 'no' to drugs and drugpushers"; to be wary of strangers; to have safe sex; to report their own or other abusing parents, relatives or neighbors; to be wary of friends; to recognize the signs of alcoholism; to exercise self control in the absence of parental or societal controls; even to take their Halloween candy to the hospital to be x-rayed before consumption. In response to these complications in the landscape of childhood, parent groups, religious groups, and media have called for educators to "bring morality back into the classroom" while we "get back to basics" in a pristine atmosphere of moral non-complexity, outside of the context of the very real world that is squeezing in on that highly touted childhood innocence every single day.

Our teenagers are inundated with the discouragements of life. Ensconced in a literal world, they are shaping their life choices within the dichotomies of TV ads: Bud Light vs. "A mind is a terrible thing to waste." Life becomes a set of skewed and cynical oppositions: "good" vs. easy; yes vs. "catch me"; "right" vs. expediency.

In truth, what young readers seem most innocent of these days is not sex, murder, or profanity, but concepts of self empowerment, faith, struggle as quest, the nobility of intellectual inquiry, survival, and the nature and complexity of moral choice. *Caged Bird* offers these seemingly abstract (adult) concepts to a younger audience that needs to know that their lives are not inherited or predestined, that they can be participants in an exuberant struggle to subjugate traditions of ignorance and fear. Critics of this book might tend to overlook or devalue the necessity of such insights for the young.

Caged Bird's critics imply an immorality in the work based on the book's images. However, it is through Angelou's vivid depictions of human spiritual triumph *set against a backdrop* of human weakness and failing that the autobiography speaks dramatically about moral choice. Angelou paints a picture of some of the negative choices: white America choosing to oppress groups of people; choosing lynch law over justice; choosing intimidation over honor. She offers, however, "deep talk" on the possibility of positive choices: choosing life over death (despite the difficulty of that life); choosing courage over safety; choosing discipline over chaos; choosing voice over silence; choosing compassion over pity, over hatred, over habit; choosing work and planning and hope over useless recrimination and slovenly despair. The book's detractors seem unwilling to admit that morality is not edict (or an innate property of innocence), but the learned capacity for judgement, and that the necessity of moral choice arises only in the presence of the soul's imperfection.

Self empowerment, faith, struggle as quest, survival, intellectual curiosity, complexity of choice—these ideas are the underpinning of Maya Angelou's story. To explore these themes, the autobiography poses its own set of oppositions: Traditional society and values vs. contemporary society and its values; silence vs. self expression; literacy vs. the forces of oppression; the nature of generosity vs. the nature of cruelty; spirituality vs. ritual. Every episode of *Caged Bird*, engages these and other ideas in Maya Angelou's portrait of a young girl's struggle against adversity—a struggle against rape: rape of the body, the soul, the mind, the future, of expectation, of tenderness—towards identity and self affirmation. If we cannot delete rape from our lives, should we delete it from a book about life?

Caged Bird opens with the poignant, halting voice of Marguerite Johnson, the young Maya Angelou, struggling for her own voice beneath the vapid doggerel of the yearly Easter pageant:

"What you lookin at me for?"
"I didn't come to stay...."

These two lines prefigure the entire work. "What you lookin at me for..." is the painful question of every black girl made selfconscious and self doubting by a white world critical of her very existence. The claim that she "didn't come to stay" increases in irony as the entire work ultimately affirms the determination of Marguerite Johnson and, symbolically, all of the unsung survivors of the Middle Passage, to do that very thing—to stay. To stay is to affirm life and the possibility of redemption. To stay— despite the circumstance of our coming (slavery), despite the efforts to remove us (lynching) or make us invisible (segregation).

Angelou, in disarmingly picturesque and humorous scenes like this opening glimpse of her girl-self forgetting her lines and wetting her pants in her earliest effort at public speech, continually reminds us that we survive the painfulness of life by the tender stabilities of family and community. As she hurries from the church trying to beat the wetness coursing down her thighs, she hears the benedictory murmurs of the old church ladies saying, "Lord bless the child," and "Praise God."

This opening recitation lays a metaphorical foundation for the autobiography, and for our understanding of the trauma of rape that causes Marguerite to stifle her voice for seven years. In some ways, the rape of Marguerite provides the center and the bottom of this autobiographical statement.

Critics of the work charge that the scenes of seduction and rape are too graphically rendered:

He (Mr. Freeman] took my hand and said, "Feel it." It was mushy and squirmy like the inside of a freshly killed chicken. Then he dragged me on top of his chest with his left arm, and his right hand was moving so fast and his heart was beating so hard that I was afraid that he would die.... Finally he was quiet, and then came the nice part. He held me so softly that I wished he wouldn't ever let me go. (61)

The seeming ambivalence of this portrait of the dynamics of interfamilial rape elicits distaste among those who prefer, if rape must be portrayed at all, for it to be painted with the hard edges of guilt and innocence. Yet, this portrait reflects the sensibilities of eight year old Marguerite Johnson— full of her barely understood longings and the vulnerability of ignorance:

> ...Mama had drilled into my head: "Keep your legs closed, and don't let nobody see your pocketbook." (61)

Mrs. Baxter has given her daughter that oblique homespun wisdom designed to delay the inevitable. Such advice may forewarn, but does not forearm and, characteristic of the period, does not even entertain the unthinkable improbability of the rape of a child. Aside from this vague caution, and the knowledge that "lots of people did 'it' and they used their 'things' to accomplish the deed...," Marguerite does not know how to understand or respond to the gentle, seemingly harmless Mr. Freeman because he is "family," he is an adult (not to be questioned), and he offers her what appears to be the tenderness she craves that had not been characteristic of her strict southern upbringing.

When asked why she included the rape in her autobiography, Angelou has said, "I wanted people to see that the man was not totally an ogre (*Conversations*, 156). And it is this fact that poses one of the difficulties of rape and the inability of children, intellectually unprepared, to protect themselves. If the rapists were all terrible ogres and strangers in dark alleys, it would be easier to know when to run, when to scream, when to "say no." But the devastation of rape is subtle in its horror and betrayal which creates in Marguerite feelings of complicity in her own assault. When queried by Mr. Freeman's defense attorney about whether Mr. Freeman had ever touched her on occasions before the rape, Marguerite, recalling that first encounter, realizes immediately something about the nature of language, its inflexibility, its inability to render the whole truth, and the palpable danger of being misunderstood:

> I couldn't...tell them how he had loved me once for a few minutes and how he had held me close before he thought I had peed in my bed. My uncles would kill me and Grandmother Baxter would stop speaking,

as she often did when she was angry. And all those people in the court would stone me as they had stoned the harlot in the Bible. And Mother, who thought I was such a good girl, would be so disappointed. But most important, there was Bailey. I had kept a big secret from him (70-71).

To protect herself, Marguerite lies: "Everyone in the court knew that the answer had to be No. Everyone except Mr. Freeman and me" (71).

Some schools that have chosen not to ban *Caged Bird* completely have compromised by deleting "those rape chapters." It should be clear, however, that this portrayal of rape is hardly titillating or "pornographic." It raises issues of trust, truth and lie, love, the naturalness of a child's craving for human contact, language and understanding, and the confusion engendered by the power disparities that necessarily exist between children and adults. High school students should be given the opportunity to gain insight into these subtleties of human relationships and entertain the "moral" questions raised by the work: should Mr. Freeman have been forgiven for his crime? (After all, he appears to be very sorry. When Marguerite awakens from the daze of trauma, Mr. Freeman is tenderly bathing her: "His hands shook" (66). Which is the greater crime, Mr. Freeman's rape of Marguerite, or Marguerite's lying about the nature of their relationship (which might be seen as having resulted in Mr. Freeman's death)? What should be the penalty for rape? Is the community's murderous action against Mr. Freeman's unthinkable crime merely a more expedient form of the state's statutes on capital punishment? Might we say he was "judged by a jury of his peers"? Which is the greater crime—if Marguerite had told the truth and Mr. Freeman had been acquitted, or Marguerite's lie, and Mr. Freeman's judgement by an outraged community? What *is* the truth? Didn't Marguerite actually tell the basic truth, based on her innocence, based on her inability to understand Mr. Freeman's motives? As Maya Angelou might say, "Those are questions, frightful questions, too intimate and obscenely probing" (*Black Women Writers*, 3)[2] Yet, how can we deny young readers, expected to soon embark upon their own life-altering decision-making, the opportunity to engage in questions so relevant as these. How can we continue to forearm them solely with t-shirt slogans?

Caged Bird, in this scene so often deleted from classroom study, opens the door for discussion about the prevalent confusion between a young person's desire for affection and sexual invitation. Certainly, this is a valuable distinction to make, and one that young men and women are often unable to perceive or articulate. Angelou also reveals the manner by which an adult manipulates a child's desire for love as a thin camouflage for his own crude motives. A further complication to the neat assignment of blame is that Marguerite's lie is not prompted by a desire to harm Mr. Freeman, but out of her feelings of helplessness and dread. Yet, she perceives that the effect of that lie is profound—so profound that she decides to stop her own voice, both as penance for the death of Mr. Freeman and out of fear of the power of her words: "...a man was dead because I had lied" (72).

This dramatization of the ambiguity of truth and the fearfulness of an Old Testament justice raises questions of justice and the desirability of truth in a world strapped in fear, misunderstanding, and the inadequacy of language. The story reveals how violence can emerge out of the innocent routines of life; how betrayal can be camouflaged with blame; that adults are individual and multi-dimensional and flawed; but readers also see how Marguerite overcomes this difficult and alienating episode of her life.

However, the work's complexity is a gradual revelation. The rape must be read within the context of the entire work from the stammer of the opening scene, to the elegant Mrs. Flowers who restores Marguerite's confidence in her own voice (77-87) to the book's closing affirmation of the forgiving power of love and faith. Conversely, all of these moments should be understood against the ravaging of rape.

Marguerite's story is emblematic of the historic struggle of an entire people and, by extension, any person or group of people. The autobiography moves from survival to celebration of life and students who are permitted to witness Marguerite's suffering and ascendancy might gain in the nurturing of their own potential for compassion, optimism and courage.

This extended look at the scene most often censored by high school administrators and most often criticized by parents should reveal that

Angelou's *Caged Bird*, though easily read, is no "easy" read. This is, perhaps, part of the reason for the objections of parents who may feel that the materials are "too sophisticated" for their children. We should be careful, as teachers, designers of curriculum, and concerned parents, not to fall into the false opposition of good vs. easy. What is easier for a student (or for a teacher) is not necessarily good. In this vein, those parents who are satisfied to have this work removed from required lists but offered on "suggested" lists should ask themselves whether they are giving their kids the kind of advice that was so useless to Maya Angelou: "keep your legs closed and don't let nobody see your pocketbook." Without the engagement of discussion, *Caged Bird* might do what parents fear most— raise important issues while leaving the young reader no avenue to discover his or her relationship to these ideas. Perhaps the parents are satisfied to have controversial works removed to the "suggested" list because they are convinced that their children will never read anything that is not required. If that is their hope, we have more to worry about than booklists.

If parents are concerned about anything, it should be the paucity of assigned readings in the junior high and high school classrooms, and the quality of the classroom teaching approach for this (and any other) worthwhile book.[3] Educators have begun to address the importance of the preparation of teachers for the presentation of literature of the caliber of *Caged Bird* which is a challenge to students, but also to teachers who choose to bring this work into the classroom.[4] *Caged Bird* establishes oppositions of place and time: Stamps, Arkansas vs. St. Louis and San Francisco; the 1930s of the book's opening vs. the slave origins of Jim Crow, which complicate images related to certain cultural aspects of African-American life including oral story traditions, traditional religious beliefs and practices, ideas regarding discipline and displays of affection, and other materials which bring richness and complexity to the book, but that, without clarification, can invite misapprehension. For example, when Marguerite smashes Mrs. Cullinan's best pieces of "china from Virginia" by "accident," the scene is informative when supported by its parallels in traditional African-American folklore, by information regarding the significance of naming in traditional society, and the cultural significance of the slave state practice of depriving Africans of their true names and cultural past. The scene, though funny, should not be treated as mere comic relief, or as a meaningless act of revenge. Mrs. Cullinan, in insisting upon "re-naming" Marguerite Mary, is carrying forward that enslaving technique designed to subvert identity; she is testing what she believes is her prerogative as a white person—to establish *who* a black person will be, to call a black person by any name she chooses. She is "shock[ed] into recognition of [Marguerite's] personhood" (*Black Women Writers,* 9). She learns that her name game is a very dangerous power play that carries with it a serious risk.

With sufficient grounding, *I Know Why the Caged Bird Sings* can provide the kinds of insights into American history and culture, its values, practices, beliefs, lifestyles, and its seeming contradictions that inspired James Baldwin to describe the work, on its cover, as one that "liberates the reader into life simply because Maya Angelou confronts her own life with such a moving wonder, such a luminous dignity," and as "...a Biblical study of life in the midst of death." A book that has the potential to liberate the reader into life is one that deserves our intelligent consideration, not rash judgements made from narrow fearfulness. Such a work will not "teach students a lesson." It will demand an energetic, participatory reading. It will demand their seriousness. With the appropriate effort, this literary experience can assist readers of any racial or economic group in meeting their own, often unarticulated doubts, questions, fears, and perhaps assist in their own search for dignity.

NOTES

1. Joyce Graham, in her dissertation "The Freeing of Maya Angelou's *Caged Bird,*" offers a comprehensive overview of the history of censorship efforts directed specifically against *Caged Bird:* the issues and arguments raised in connection with the teaching of the work, a look at the National Council of Teachers of English's efforts to provide guidelines for the improvement of teacher preparation in the teaching of literature, and a case study of one well documented censorship challenge. Dr. Graham also includes an interview with Dr. Angelou discussing the nature and motive of censorship. This timely examination of the rising fear of literature in

schools provides an invaluable look at the parents and administrators behind the news reports on censorship challenges.

2. Dr. Angelou makes this comment in response to her own questions: Why and how frequently does a writer write? What shimmering goals dance before the writer's eyes, desirable, seductive, but maddeningly out of reach? What happens to the ego when one dreams of training Russian bears to dance the Watusi and is barely able to teach a friendly dog to shake hands?

3. In "The Other Crisis in American Education," college professor Daniel J. Singal discusses the decline of competency among the "highest cohort of achievers," those students who eventually apply to America's most prestigious colleges and universities. This general failing in the achievement levels of juniors and seniors is attributed to the assigning of "easier," less challenging reading materials, and the failure of teachers to design written and oral activities that demand higher levels of comprehension. As a result, students entering college are unable to function adequately in their coursework. Singal quotes a college professor: "No one reads for nuance. They [students] pay no attention to detail." Says Singal, "I have been amazed at how little students have managed to glean from a book I know they have read.... Twelve to fifteen books over a fifteen-week semester used to be the rule of thumb at selective colleges. Today it is six to eight books, and they had better be short texts, written in relatively simple English." In other words, college professors are simply unable to assign traditional work loads given the skill levels of their students.

4. Donnarae MacCann and Gloria Woodard have collected a number of essays on the images of African-Americans in literature, and discussions related to children's responses to the literature. Some of the essays address the matter of censorship as it relates to racist depictions in literature. Paul Deane provides a look at the seldom acknowledged racist images to be found in the traditional serial novels which are typically considered to be wholesome, completely unobjectionable adolescent fare.

WORKS CITED

Angelou, Maya. *I Know Why the Caged Bird Sings.* New York: Bantam, 1969.

_____. "Shades and Slashes of Light." In *Black Women Writers (1950-1980): A Critical Evaluation.* Ed. Mari Evans. Jackson, MS: University Press of Mississippi, 1984. 1-3.

Cudloe, Selwyn R. "Maya Angelou and the Autobiographical Statement." *Black Women Writers.* 6-24.

Deane, Paul Ç. "The Persistence of Uncle Tom: An Examination of the Image of the Negro in Children's Fiction Series." *The Black American in Books for Children: Readings in Racism,* 2nd ed. Eds. Donnarae MacCann and Gloria Woodard. Metuchen, NJ: Scarecrow Press, 1985. 162-168.

Derricote, Toi. "From the Black Notebook." *Kenyon Review* 13.4 (Fall 1991): 27-31.

Graham, Joyce L. "Freeing Maya Angelou's *Caged Bird.*" (Ph.D. Dissertation, Newman Library, Virginia Polytechnic Institute, Blacksburg, VA, 1991).

Singal, Daniel J. "The Other Crisis in American Education." *The Atlantic Monthly,* (Nov. 1991): 59-74.

Tate, Claudia. "Maya Angelou." *Black Women Writers at Work.* (New York: Continuum, 1983): 1-11. rpt. in *Conversations with Maya Angelou.* Ed. Jeffrey M. Elliot. Jackson, MS: University Press of Mississippi, 1989. 146-156.

THE STOP OF TRUTH:
IN THE NIGHT KITCHEN
Paula Fox

On June 14, 1643, the English parliament ordered licensing of the press. All licensing authority was to be wielded by two archbishops who had the power to stop publication of any book "contrary to the Doctrine and Discipline of the Church of England."

John Milton, protesting the parliamentary order in his essay, *Areopagitica*, wrote, "(it) will be primely to the discouragement of all learning and the stop of truth, not only by exercising our abilities in what we know already, but by hindering and cropping the discovery that might be yet further made."

In Camden, New York, in the early 1970s, a mother was reading a book, *In the Night Kitchen*, by Maurice Sendak, to her 7-year old son. In the first few pages, she came upon a drawing that made her shut the book and put it aside. Subsequently she asked school officials to remove *In the Night Kitchen*, from elementary school libraries. Children, she said, were already exposed to enough profanity in the media. The school superintendent, Richard McClements, agreed with her. He did not see that the book had "sufficient merit" to be kept in libraries. Schools, he said, have "a real obligation to represent what is moral, what is honest, what is decent."

Wanda Gray, the director of elementary education in Springfield, Missouri, devised a way to mask the offense in Sendak's story. Several of the drawings in the forty copies sent to forty Springfield kindergarten classes were then altered with a black felt pen. "I think *it* should be covered," said she. (my italics)

The *it* that the Camden mother and Mr. McClements appeared to have found immoral, dishonest and indecent, the *it* which Wanda Gray thought best to cover with what the director of curriculum development in Springfield called "shorts," was the discreetly drawn penis of a small, occasionally naked boy named Mickey.

The Springfield solution brings to mind certain religious orders which obliged their members to bathe themselves only when their bodies were entirely covered in order to avoid sexual arousal, thus, one surmises, dramatically emphasizing that which the coverings sought to conceal.

In the Night Kitchen is a dream adventure. Mickey flies through a starry night in an airplane made of bread dough to the night kitchen where three bakers—all of whom resemble Oliver Hardy, lack only milk to make morning cake. Mickey finds the milk, the cake is made, and he slides back into his bed and into dreamless sleep. As Mickey falls out of darkness into the light of the night kitchen, he loses his pajamas.

Mr. Sendak's work is always distinguished by imaginative power, wit and tenderness, and it is tenderness that is especially marked in this book, in his drawings of Mickey's infant nakedness.

Yet in the eyes of some beholders one must conclude that Mickey appears primarily as a disembodied sexual organ, and that for them, any nakedness is implicitly pornographic and immoral *ab ovo*. Most young listeners, and readers, discover their corporeality when they discover their fingers and toes, and Mickey's penis is unlikely to seem a revelation. To this writer, the intensity of the response of so many communities throughout this country, reflects that strange stew of prudery and prurience which so characterizes certain aspects of American cultural life.

In Lansing, Michigan, two mothers said the book was pornographic, and opposed the use of school funds to buy books "incorporating such nudity or immorality." One of them asked, "if nudity is acceptable in a kindergarten children's story, how can I teach my children that *Playboy* is not acceptable?"

One is inclined to suggest—by *teaching* your children that *Playboy* is not acceptable.

John Milton writes: "Impunity and remissness, for certain, are the bane of a commonwealth; but here the great art lies, to discern in what the law is to bid restraint and punishment, and what things persuasion only is to work."

What I have said about Mr. Sendak's work reflects my own response to it, and the opinion of it I have arrived at. I am permitted to express this opinion by virtue of the First Amendment to the Constitution of the United States. The Amendment does not allow me to coerce others into sharing my judgment any more than it allows me to insist that all children be made to read *In the Night Kitchen.*

Wanda Gray, Mr. McClements, and the other indignant parents who found the book offensive are also permitted expression of their opinions. The First Amendment does not allow them to enact their opinions as censorship.

"Why should we then affect a rigor contrary to the manner of God and nature," writes Milton, "by abridging or scanting those means by which books freely permitted are, both to the trial of virtue and the exercise of truth?"

In Beloit, Wisconsin, a mother of three children said, "It's our responsibility as parents to protect our children. We have all sorts of laws to protect our children, but why aren't books restricted?"

As reported in the Beloit *Daily News*, this mother promised to become more active in book selections for the schools, and to keep on looking for what she called "bad books."

From the *Areopagitica:* "...how shall the licensers themselves be confided in unless we confer upon them, or they assume themselves to be above all others in the land, the grace of infallibility and uncorruptedness?"

The Beloit mother also asked a question: "What right does a degree give anyone to make unchangeable rules? You don't have to have a degree to know that teaching low morals and disrespect is wrong."

In these two sentences, she manages to imply the elitism of the educated, the value of instinctive response as opposed to the hard work of informed reflection, and to reveal her own ignorance when she speaks of unchangeable rules. Rules are laws, and the most cursory knowledge of law, to the interested student, shows that it alters constantly as it reflects the contesting and changing views of the people whom it serves.

Roger Baldwin, one of the founders of the American Civil Liberties Union in 1920, was a vociferous opponent of capital punishment. A journalist asked him, "What would you feel about capital punishment if your wife was raped and murdered?"

Mr. Baldwin was quoted as replying, "In that circumstance, I would be the last person to ask."

In crises of grief and outrage, we are all the "last person to ask." It is then that we most need the principles of law to protect ourselves, and others, against our own impulses. In a less savage situation than that envisioned by the journalist who questioned Mr. Baldwin, we need the same protection against our vagaries and caprices which, when justified by ideology or by the conviction that our interpretation of religious dogma excludes all other interpretations, can lead us to level cities as well as to burn books.

Milton says, "He who destroys a good book kills reason itself, kills the image of God...."

That some people regarded Mickey's nakedness in *In the Night Kitchen* as "pornographic," and "incorporating...immorality," and that some others even detected a subtext in Mickey's discovery of milk (i.e. nocturnal emission) did not lead to very edifying argument about the meaning of good and bad, or aesthetics. On the one side, there was rigid opposition to the book; on the other, expressions, often disdainful, of outraged democratic sensibilities.

In the best of all possible worlds, we should show respect for beliefs contrary to our own, an awareness that they are inevitable. In this democracy, we have agreed to differ.

Of course, it is a problem. Democracy is full of problems. E. M. Forster articulated its deficiency in the title of his book, *Two Cheers for Democracy*, and I believe it was Winston Churchill who declared it to be a terrible system of government but the best we have.

Books must not be censored no matter how appalling we find their content. Censorship metastasizes, moving ineluctably, often invisibly, from a part to the whole.

In *Democracy in America*, Alexis de Tocqueville wrote: "I can conceive of nothing better prepared for subjection in case of defeat than a democratic people without free institutions."

It is my belief that Mr. Sendak's book, in the long run, will continue to exist as itself, merry and intransigently human, long after the din of argument concerning Mickey's nakedness has faded away.

In any event, Mr. Sendak is in good company.

Paul the IV, at a moment during his 4-year papacy (1555-1559), ordered that the genitals of naked figures be covered in Michelangelo's fresco of *The Last Judgment*, in the Sistine Chapel of the Vatican. Daniele da Volterra, a contemporary painter, was given the task of covering the offending areas of the figures with underwear, or breeches. In Italian, *bragha* meant breeches. Thenceforth, da Volterra was nicknamed "Il Braghettone" (the breeches maker).

Michelangelo, in a retort to the Pope concerning the nudity of the figures he had painted, said: "Tell the Pope that this is a trivial matter, and can easily be arranged. Let him straighten out the world, for pictures are quickly straightened out."

IT'S OK IF YOU DON'T LOVE ME: EVALUATING ANTICIPATED EXPERIENCES OF READERS

Nicholas J. Karolides

Despite its seemingly contradictory title, *It's OK If You Don't Love Me* is a novel of first love. Given the title, however, you won't be surprised to discover that it isn't the stereotyped girl-meets-boy, girl-gets-boy romance. It does provide elements of the familiar format, initiated in the standard way. Jody Epstein, a seventeen-year-old New Yorker, meets Lyle Alexander during a summer job working at the laboratory of the Sloan-Kettering Hospital. He has recently moved to New York from small-town Ohio to live with his married sister; his parents have been killed in an automobile accident. The meeting is fortuitous for Jody; she has broken up with her boyfriend who has graduated from high school and gone away to college. It is equally a boon for Lyle who is friendless in the big city.

There are some of the usual trappings--dates, family dinners--that establish the novel's game plan and move the plot. The substance of the novel, however, is dramatically different from the standard romance genre. Projecting this average situation and introducing seemingly average teenagers, Norma Klein recognizes their inherent sexuality. Thus, in playing out the events and feelings of their relationship, this sexuality takes on a significant role. Through them and other characters we understand that adolescents ask questions about sex--what it's like, whether to do it, when to do it--and are concerned about sex--how effective a partner they'll be, how they'll be affected. They talk about it, anticipate it and experience it. In a transactional sense, the novel for the reader becomes a "discussion" of this anticipated experience.

Another qualification of what the novel is not: it isn't about out-of-wedlock pregnancy, neither the situation when a young woman is forced to confront her predicament in the face of probable family or social rejection (as in Patricia Dizengo's *Phoebe* or Jeanette Eyerly's *Bonnie Jo, Go Home*) nor that in which the young couple is catapulted into premature marriage (as in Ann Head's *Mr. and Mrs. Bo Jo Jones*). These novels project a quite different set of problems and developments.

The concerns that surround Jody and Lyle are not limited to questions of sex. They care about how they relate to others, adults as well as peers. Indeed, the nature of relationships, especially that of love, is the thematic core of the novel.

> "Is it that you don't want to do it! I (Jody) said. "Because we don't have to. It doesn't matter."
> (Lyle) frowned. "Well, the thing is, I'm just not sure I'm in love with you."
> I felt relieved. "That's okay. I'm not sure I'm in love with you."
> "That's what I mean."
> "I don't care if you love me or not."
> "You should."
> "Why?"
> "That's your birthright, Jody, to be loved."
> "It is?"
> "Sure. And I think maybe it will happen with us. We just have to get to know each other better." (98)

This conversation, a line of which recalls the title, occurring not quite midway through the book, brings into focus this theme and the interrelatedness of love and sex.

Lyle presumes the relationship, stating it unhesitantly. It is he who hesitates in this situation, who curbs the desire he feels to which he later admits. But there's more to it than that, for feelings and behavior are shown to be multi-faceted. Part of his reluctance is his lack of experience; part is his basic kindness and his regard for Jody--he rejects premature advances. Despite these feelings, however, his understanding that you have to know a girl well, that there needs to be love between them before experiencing sex, expresses a significant principle upon which the subsequent actions pivot.

Love does develop between Jody and Lyle as does their sexual relationship. But this emotional-physical rite of passage, while providing valuable learning, also serves as the catalyst by which Jody experiences a values-forming rite of passage. She must come to grips with her behavior in relation to her feelings; she must develop the thought and codes—the values that generate those behaviors and feelings. And since she recognizes she isn't an island unto herself, she must understand how she relates to others, how *they* relate to each other. The book, charged with the emotions of her first-person perspective, explores how she is affected by her own acts and those of others so that her passage reveals a light at the end of the tunnel.

To comprehend Jody's development, it is useful to reveal first some of the elements of the text used by the author as counterpoints for the action and ideas, as instructional devices to illuminate the issues. The past is used as an alternative model; the experiences of the parents, particularly Jody's mother, are conveyed to contrast and clarify Jody's choices. Classroom discussions, contemplated in retrospect for insights, highlight the issues.

Conversational flashbacks reveal that Jody's mother grew up in another social milieu, one that promoted inadequacies and interpersonal failures.

"You don't have to live through that hideous, repressed thing we did.... When I was in college and started having sexual feelings, you wouldn't *believe* how guilty and scared I felt! No one your age would even believe it! I was too ashamed to talk about it to anyone. I thought I was some sort of freak, just for having feelings that were the most normal, natural thing in the world. So I went leaping into marriage with the first guy I slept with, and, well you know the rest." (118)

And what is "the rest?" A loveless marriage, a marriage initiated in response to appearances, a marriage hurried into and endured. There was little communication and less understanding. It ended in a less-than-amicable divorce. Besides the bitterness, there is a continuing sense of inadequacy.

The assessment is that Mrs. Epstein got herself into this because of her innocence-ignorance. The social practices and contraints of her youth fostered behaviors that were pressured and superficial. The social norms also created ignorance, if not repression, of normal sexual feelings which could not be adequately dealt with and understood. Beyond this was social ostracism:

> "...and she's always regaling me with these horror stories about girls who admitted they had slept with someone and then were shunned and never had dates and married awful people as soon as they got to college just because their self-image was wrecked forever." (65)

These pressures affected the men as well. We don't find out specific effects upon Jody's father, though we come to see him as a sexist, self-centered, status-seeking bore, but we do get an inside view of Jody's ex-stepfather. An amiable man, he admits to having been "scared out of my wits" (111), as a young man, to having been made insecure by the expectations of male knowledge and performance in a love-sexual situation. Actually, he informs us, men are uneasy, even terrified. These responses are evidenced in the younger generation both by Lyle's tentative behavior and in Jody's younger brother's uncertainty, masked by quipping bravado.

It is clear that both adults have struggled--are still struggling--to come out from under the handicaps of the past. Unlike her first husband, Mrs. Epstein has attempted to face the problem. To forestall the recurrence of such ignorance and negation, she has created an "open" home. This openness is manifested in the willingness to converse about love and relationships and to respond to questions about sex. These conversations range from dinner table interaction about pregnancy, child rearing and population control to mother-daughter intimacies about men. The presumed impact of this openness is to diminish responses of mystery and fear, to build the ability to develop honest and fulfilling relationships. Clearly, it is offered as a recommended model.

The author introduces two interrelated and provocative issues in three classroom discussions, helping to focus them for Jody (and the reader) while she is in the throes of change. Student comments portray "typical" adolescent views and expectations; the teachers, speaking apparently for the author, offer advice and interpretation. The first of these issues is sex by opportunity; the second is "romance or some ideal version of true love" (107). Many of the students (boys and girls) in the sex education class admit to being virgins because of the "lack of opportunity" (74) and in an English class when responding to a composition, "most of the boys couldn't believe that there was a boy who wouldn't sleep with a girl who was willing to sleep with him" (107). These reactions suggest both misplaced values and a non-realistic conception of relationships. A valid relationship, sexual and otherwise, needs more than mere opportunity. As the teacher remarks:

> "Listen, don't get the wrong idea, kids. Don't come away with the idea that I'm advocating you all jump in bed together. Frankly I think there's too much of that already, not too much in that it's bad in and of itself, but too much sex for the wrong reasons. But it puzzles me that for a generation that's supposed to be so realistic about things, there was this kind of pseudoromantic image of: One day I'll see her across a crowded room. I mean, fine. But you can get just so much mileage out of that kind of thing, the mystery thing, and then what?" (75)

This and the later comments of the English teacher suggest that the students need to reconsider the reasons for their behavior, in this instance, their sexual behavior, that they need to reformulate their view of reality.

These forewarnings are solidified by the sex education teacher's "The Right to Say No" lecture toward the novel's end which Jody relates in retrospect:

> He claimed that women and girls, especially today, feel they somehow have to agree to sex, now that they can no longer claim they're afraid of getting pregnant, and that's bad. He said no one, even if they're married, should agree to sex if they don't like it. I thought that was a good point....(223)

Jody's favorable response helps her to crystallize her developing value structure. And these passages, along with the plot's developments, establish a major point of the book: casual sex, opportunistic sex, is ill advised. In addition to the need for a deeper relationship, girls (and women) need to value--and have ownership of--their own bodies and to value themselves.

These concerns are not academic for Jody; her situation is a test tube example. Her initial responses seem opportunistic, superficial, both those with her previous boyfriend and the first stage with Lyle. In the first instance she's flattered to be chosen by this popular senior and does what seems to be expected; the factor of desire complicates the situation with Lyle, but it is otherwise parallel. Lyle's introduction of the concept of love--"That's your birthright, Jody, to be loved"--initiates a process of evaluation. This process is founded on honesty. She tells him of her previous experience; he tells her of his inexperience and uncertainty--no false bravado here. Mutual trust and love develop: she feels secure in having Lyle meet her father's family with her; during that tense weekend Lyle offers her emotional and verbal support. Jody's acceptance of this is conscious, and yet unconscious as evidenced by her indiscretion with her former boyfriend. Belatedly, she does have feelings of guilt. She struggles with her behavior codes and her deeper values. Lyle's anger at her betrayal of trust and love bring her through, eventually, defensive feelings, then remorse and loneliness to apology. And Lyle forgives. She has recognized not only the fragility of love but its importance, beyond mere physical satisfactions, and that trust and loyalty are critical ingredients of a love relationship. At the end of the novel when Jody rejects the "invitation" of a young man at a party, it is clear she has developed a voice in the choices she makes; she has gained some control.

It is easy to imagine what the objections to this book are. The book contains language--three and four letter words--that raises censors' hackles. It contains sexual asides and innuendoes, nudity and references to the body--at one point Jody contemplates her own, at another she fleetingly admires Lyle's towel-wrapped physique. There also are references to body parts, using anatomical language. Frank comments and questions about sexual feelings and activities coincide with the developing love relationship of the two central characters. And it is apparent that they enjoy the sexual side of that relationship which does not lead to pregnancy or disease or societal condemnation.

While these are the major potential objections, certain features of characterization might come under attack as well. Jody could be perceived as too socially-sexually aggressive; she is not the demure heroine of romance who waits by the telephone. The parents, too, might be criticized for their seeming permissiveness. As an example, aside from the "open" home aspect, Mrs. Epstein is cited by Jody in believing that "people should live together before they get married for a year at least, to see if they're going to get along or not" (154).

This perspective, however, ignores the author's method, purpose and ultimate statement. The method is based in effect on a principle of honesty comparable to a code manifested by Jody in the book. Klein's premise of young adult sexuality, their concerns, imaginings, and experimentation, has validity in our late twentieth century reality. Portraying them thus, depicting their insecurities, their innocence under the veneer, their searchings, has comparable validity. In this context her book becomes an effort to inform, to develop insights and values. She does not promote insensitivity or license--to the contrary. Also, there is no voyeurism in the sex situations. Her characters grope towards valuing each other, valuing their emotions and bodies. But it's not exactly groping in the dark. The trials and errors include stumbling, but the moves grow out of open discussion and increasing knowledge. The characters model this standard for the readers. As the readers experience vicariously the chameleon emotions, as they consider the viewpoints which Jody contemplates, as they respond to her choices and understand her betrayal and its repercussions, they can begin to establish appropriate behavior built from preconsidered values.

There are additional informing comments and presentations which support these directions in the text. Klein restructures the role of women in our society, attempting to reduce their victimization, by establishing an assertive heroine, a thinking, processing heroine who doesn't just let things happen to her. (In contrast to typical romance heroines, Jody has professional goals, a career in the sciences, after attending college.) The anti-sexist stance is reiterated in discussions about male predominance and insecurities when faced with strong women, in the rejection of the social-sexual double standard which promotes a women-as-object response in men. It is heightened by the overt sexist behavior of Jody's father who ignores his daughter's abilities and goals while exaggerating those of her brother. This reduction of second-class citizenry for women is furthered by the knowledge base-of-operations for young women promoted by the text.

Klein chides the "know-it-all-generation" of young adults who think they can do everything and anything. They clearly don't know it all. A specific rejection of ignorance and irresponsibility is the commentary about contraception. For example, the sex education teacher identifies the "bridge-crossing school of contraception":

> ..."We'll cross that bridge when we come to it" which, as you ought to know, is simply a time-honored means of passing the buck..."I won't be prepared, I won't take responsibility for my actions." (76)

This, of course, parallels the statements for action based on knowledge.

A minor but important element of this novel is the presence of the parents. Many romance novels, perhaps as a matter of adolescent focus on independence and apron-string cutting, operate in a world spectrum essentially devoid of adults. Realistically, parents are included in this one both as interactive members of a family unit and also as representatives of a life continuum. That the parents are shown to have problems and needs in their relationships, past and present, that their relationships too are flawed and changing and growing adds another continuum: the reality--not the romance--of human relationships.

These applaudatory remarks are not to say that It's Ok If You Don't Love Me is without flaws. Overall there seems to be an overindulgence in sexual asides and innuendoes, a sense of too much pressed into one book. Some statements seem extraordinary, thus unnecessary, as when Jody's ten-year-old half-cousin asks a provocative, personal question about sex. It is possible that this and all other remarks and incidents could naturally take place in the time frame of the novel. Because many intervening incidents are omitted, the compressed composite creates an unfortunate sense of overstatement. Some balance, I believe, is needed to validate the total impression.

Another concern is the datedness of the text. Published in 1977, it precedes the AIDS epidemic, the dramatic rise of other sexually transmitted diseases and, also, teenage pregnancies. Thus, it is not informed by the recognition of the need of the condom for health protection, as well as contraception, nor the increased valuation of abstinence.

Despite this flaw and this concern, this book is well worth its reading. It could serve as a fine source of discussion between adults and teenagers who face comparable concerns.

WORK CITED

Klein, Norma. *It's OK If You Don't Love Me*. New York: Ballantine Books, 1984.

JOHNNY GOT HIS GUN:
A DEPRESSION ERA CLASSIC

James DeMuth

For the life of me I can't understand why *Johnny Got His Gun* is on a list of frequently censored books. I was surprised, though, to discover that Dalton Trumbo himself had conspired in the suppression of his novel during the early years of World War II. In his introduction to the 1959 Ace Paperback edition of the book, Trumbo explained that as World War II deepened certain unnamed, right-wing, presumably pro-Fascist groups "proposed a national rally for peace-now, with me as cheer leader; they promised (and delivered) a letter campaign to pressure the publisher for a fresh edition" (np). Distressed by this political campaign for a negotiated, conditional peace with Hitler, Trumbo worked quickly to forestall any new edition of his novel during the war (149). Sixteen years later, in 1959, he adamantly maintained the sense and necessity of his wartime decision: "Nothing," he insisted, "could have convinced me so quickly that *Johnny* was exactly the sort of book that shouldn't be reprinted until the war was at an end. The publishers agreed" (np).

The suppression or frustration of artistic expression in the interests of an overriding national cause as significant and perilous as the Allied war effort against Axis fascism is understandable. I do not agree with this rationale for censorship and would argue against it in whatever forum was open to me, but it is understandable. Now, however, I can recognize no understandable reason for suppressing *Johnny Got His Gun* and I can imagine few capricious reasons. Instead, it seems more plausible to me, though the evidence apparently doesn't bear me out, that parents, school board members, teachers, librarians, professors and publishers would be encouraging the teaching of the novel as a classic of American literary and moral expression.

My only hesitation in deciding to teach the book would be my discomfort with the awkward and strident political rhetoric of its concluding two chapters and with the sentimentality tainting some characters, stylistic traits that diminish the book's literary quality but which it clearly shares with other American novels of the 1930s (*Johnny Got His Gun* was published on September 3, 1939, two days after the start of World War II). Particularly in the final chapters, Trumbo succumbs to the hackneyed Depression era dichotomy between bosses and victims and, considering the book's reputation as a pacifist fable, he expresses his political rage in an ironically militaristic rhetoric:

> We will use the guns you force upon us we will use them to defend our very lives and the menace to our lives does not lie on the other side of a nomansland that was set apart without our consent it lies within our own boundaries here and now we have seen it and we know it.

> Put the guns into our hands and we will use them.... You plan the wars you masters of men plan the wars and point the way and we will point the gun. (242-243)

However, the reservations I have about the style of *Johnny Got His Gun* are minor. The novel's concluding words do limit it to a historical period and conventional style, but, preceding this outburst, Trumbo achieves an art that spans the years; his diction is usually understated and his characters sensibly rendered. The novel is a 1930s classic and should, I believe, be taught as such. One teaching strategy that occurs to me would be to pair as companion novels *Johnny Got His Gun* and *Grapes of Wrath*. Each book dramatizes the exploitation of "little people," one in an international environment and the other within a native region, and each seeks to portray convincingly the human dignity of simple characters.

The characters of *Johnny Got His Gun* are especially memorable: Joe Bonham, of course, but also Jose and the other energetic, irrepressible workers in the Los Angeles bakery; Corporal Timeon, the Scotchman and others in the mixed English and American regiment who struggle to maintain their sanity and humor, as when the Scot refused to fight his Bavarian Prince, the last Stuart heir to the English throne; the "unafraid and gentle" nurse who opens communication with Joe by playfully tracing with her finger the greeting "Merry Christmas" on his chest. Uniting all these simple, appealing characters and epitomizing their qualities of decency, self-reliance and good humor is Joe's father, a portrait Trumbo based closely on the character of his own father.

The autobiographical power of Trumbo's novel is considerable. Joe Bonham's Shale City, Colorado, is Trumbo's Grand Junction, Colorado, and the county fair, birthday party, camping trip, and bakery night-shift, among others, are keenly remembered episodes of Trumbo's life. Repeatedly the novel impresses us with its quality of authentic experience: we are moved by such endearing details as Joe's mother playing sentimental songs on the piano for his father listening at the end of an eight-party telephone line from Cole Creek to Shale City, or of the young Joe carrying home the Saturday night treat of hamburgers in a bag pressed close to his chest under his shirt to keep them warm. These sharply detailed memories of Joe Bonham's family resemble John Steinbeck's attentiveness to the ordinary speech, mannerisms and values of the Joad family in the Oklahoma, New Mexico and Arizona chapters of *Grapes of Wrath*. Both novelists express well the sensitivity of literary and visual artists of the 1930s to the authentic culture of laborers, tenants and migrants. This sensitivity was inspired by the idea, dramatically realized in these two novels, that in simple people of stable traditions we can understand our humanity and then witness our resilience to degradation in their efforts to survive the traumas and dislocations of unemployment, injury and war.

Both Trumbo's bias in favor of simple people and his technique, well maintained in Book I, of understated, calm rendition are essential to the success of *Johnny Got His Gun* because Joe Bonham would otherwise be incredible. We need to be convinced of his sanity, emotional stability and secure values all the quintessential products of his small town culture and affectionate family-in order to hear and accept as plausible his calm recital of his grotesque injuries:

> It was funny how calm he was. He was quiet just like a storekeeper taking spring inventory and saying to himself I see I have no eyes better put that down in the order book. He had no legs and no arms

and no eyes and no ears and no nose and no mouth and no tongue.... But he couldn't die because he couldn't kill himself. If he could only breathe he could die. That was funny but it was true. He could hold his breath and kill himself. That was the only way left. Except that he wasn't breathing. His lungs were pumping air but he couldn't stop them from doing it. He couldn't live and he couldn't die. (62-63)

Incredible though he seems, Joe's character is based on a real person; Trumbo told his biographer, Bruce Cook, of a newspaper account he had read in the early 1930s of the Prince of Wales' tour of a Canadian veterans hospital to decorate a totally disabled veteran who, like Joe Bonham, had lost all limbs and senses except touch. The Prince could only communicate his admiration and gratitude by kissing the soldier on the forehead (125); this incident is the framework for the decoration and kiss of Joe Bonham in Chapter 13.

It is a measure of Trumbo's artistry that he did not allude to outside sources to corroborate Joe's condition. Instead, Trumbo established Joe entirely within the novel's reference. The means by which he does this, though potentially confusing to high school and college age readers, are, I believe, well carried through. First, he divides the novel into two books, "The Dead" and "The Living." Book I, "The Dead," concerns Joe's emergence into sustained consciousness and his deliberate mastery over the possibility and temptation of insanity, nowhere more powerfully represented than in Joe's hallucination of a rat nibbling at the open, draining wound in his side, an hallucination triggered by his horrifying memory of trench rats feeding on corpses:

> The rat came crawling over him stealthily. It came with its sharp little claws up his left leg. It was a great brown trench rat like the ones they used to throw shovels at. It came crawling and sniffing and smelling and tearing away at the bandage over his side. He could feel its whiskers as they tickled the edges of the draining wound. He could feel its long whiskers as they trailed in the pus from the hole. And there was nothing he could do about it. (90)

He thought Jesus Joe there must be some other way. He thought it's asking very little for a man just to want to be able to prove that he's awake. He thought come on Joe this is the only way you can lick the

rat and you've got to do that so you'd better figure out some way
quick to prove whether you're awake or asleep. (96)

We are convinced of Joe's capacity for the deliberate, rational mastery
of his horrors because throughout Book I we have observed him recover
his sane identity in increasingly detailed and coherent memories. And of
all these memories in Book I there is only one extended memory of the
war, which doesn't occur until Chapter 7. By emphasizing memories of
peace rather than war, Trumbo quite subtly unfolds the revelation of Joe
Bonham's physical incapacity and appalling experience within an
environment of sanity and health; he reveals the essential Joe Bonham as
a restrained, calm voice, as a man whose sanity and identity are secure in
his living memory of family and community.

Whereas Book I works to establish Joe Bonham's strength of character,
Book II, "The Living," tests that strength, just as the California chapters of
Grapes of Wrath test the rural independence and virtue of the Joads.
Depression era literature is noteworthy for its conviction that ordinary
people would necessarily face severe tests of their values, traditions and
dignity. The most frustrating tests Joe faces in his five-year hospitalization
are not the horrors of the past war, though these memories become more
frequent and sustained in Book II, but the indifference of his present
guardians. Within the intensely charged environment of increasingly
long and detailed memories of the trench war, leaves in Paris, troop train
departures and the final bomb explosion that disabled Joe, Book II
describes Joe's persistent, sane effort to break from his past and
communicate with his nurses and doctors. He methodically, obsessively
thumps his head against his pillow in the Morse code of SOS.

It is Trumbo's intention in Book II, I believe, to connect the war and
the peace, to expose the same conditions of exploitation in each
environment. That is why Joe's effort to communicate is set within
chapters of war memories and, just as in the war, what Joe discovers in
peace is that he is treated as a conscript, one without authority or rights.
When his efforts at communication are first dimly recognized in Chapter
15, not as sensible communication but as a disturbance that must be
quieted, Joe is drugged into unconsciousness. As he fights the drug's
effect, he dreams for the first time his vivid nightmare of Jesus Christ

astraddle the locomotive of a troop train hurtling to its ruin. Then, in the tender scenes of Chapters 18 and 19, when the nurse initiates communication and he responds, he is again rejected; this time more devastating because those rejecting him have understood his message. In response to the doctor's question, "What do you want?", Joe had tapped his request to be let out. The doctor responds that such a request is against regulations and drugs him. He again dreams the troop train nightmare and this time hears the wail of the mother at his train departure "crying my son my little boy my son" (238).

I am convinced that *Johnny Got His Gun* has endured because of its literary qualities; in Joe's memories and in his conscious efforts to retain and assert his human identity, we are impressed by Trumbo's restrained diction, memorable characterizations and subtle construction. The novel did not endure because it was a convenient political sermon; in fact, the pacifism of *Johnny Got His Gun* is neither simple nor dogmatic.

Trumbo's biography reveals his own unsettled notion of pacifism; he firmly supported the Allied war effort against fascism, considering unconditional surrender the only acceptable resolution. In his novel, his pacifism is limited and retrograde; it looks back to World War I and applies only to wars that resemble that one. What distinguished World War I was its outrageous butchery in service of absurd, shamefully hypocritical slogans. It was neither a war of ideology nor a war that impinged on American interests:

> He lay and thought oh Joe Joe this is no place for you. This was no war for you. This thing wasn't any of your business. What do you care about making the world safe for democracy? All you wanted to do Joe was to live. You were born and raised in the good healthy country of Colorado and you had no more to do with Germany or England or France or even with Washington, D.C. than you had to do with the man in the moon. (24)

To Trumbo's mind, World War II was an ideological war directly threatening United States security. Vietnam, however, reminded him of World War I and he promoted a new edition of his novel during that war. In the introduction to that 1970 edition, he echoes the World War I realities and post World War I attitudes of *Johnny Got His Gun* in detailing

Vietnam's slaughter, its distance from any real concern of the United States, and its moral vacuity:

Over breakfast coffee we read of 40,000 American dead in Vietnam. Instead of vomiting, we reach for the toast.... Vietnam has given us eight times as many paralytics as World War II, three times as many totally disabled, 35% more amputees.... But exactly how many hundreds or thousands of the dead-while-living does that give us? We don't know. We don't ask. We turn away from them. (introduction, n.p.)

Dalton Trumbo's anti-war novel is not pacifism but the selective pacifism of the Great Depression. Students of American history and literature will be enriched by reading this vivid expression of the emotions and ideas that sustained the isolationist conviction of that era. Angered with phony wars fought for hypocritical ideals, Joe Bonham asserts that the only concrete value is life:

The most important thing is your life little guys. You're worth nothing dead except for speeches. Don't let them kid you any more. Pay no attention when they tap you on the shoulder and say come along we've got to fight for liberty or whatever their word is there's always a word.

Just say mister I'm sorry I got no time to die. I'm too busy and then turn and run like hell. (118)

It took the aggression of Nazi Germany, the attack on Pearl Harbor and the invasion of Soviet Russia to convince Dalton Trumbo that war could be the necessary means of defending ideas, values and life. Joe Bonham lacked such experience. He speaks to us from within the limits of World War I, a victim sacrificed for hollow words.

WORKS CITED

Cook, Bruce. *Dalton Trumbo*. New York: Charles Scribner's Sons, 1977.

Trumbo, Dalton. *Johnny Got His Gun*. New York: Bantam Books, 1983.

JULIE OF THE WOLVES
BY JEAN CRAIGHEAD GEORGE
Geneva T. Van Horne

Challenging the right to teach Jean Craighead George's *Julie of the Wolves* to upper sixth to eighth grade students is a travesty. Its plot is engaging; its themes are noble; its literary quality and expression, artful; its factual information, accurate; its main character, inspiring; and its content, eminently appropriate and appealing to middle school students.

This compelling realistic fiction story has three distinct sections, The first has to do with the experience in the Arctic; the second, a flashback of the main character's life; and the third, the protagonist's resolution of conflicts. In essence, it concerns Miyax (Julie in English) and her experiences in Alaska. Until nine, she lived with her widowed father, Kapugen, in the true Eskimo fashion. She absorbed the culture of her people and an appreciation, understanding, and respect for nature and wildlife. When she became nine, she was forced to live with her Aunt Martha so she could attend school. Prior to leaving, her father arranged for her to be married later at age thirteen, to David, the son of his hunting partner.

Life with Aunt Martha was dreary though Julie did make some schoolmate friends. She became acculturated gradually, becoming more Julie than the Eskimo Miyax. She also commenced a pen pal relationship with Amy Pollack of San Francisco. Amy invited Julie to visit her.

At thirteen she married retarded David though the marriage was not consummated. Life was harsh and miserable for she was required to spend most of each day sewing parkas and boots for the tourist trade. A turning point occurred the day David attacked her sexually. She escaped and with her friend Pearl's help, packed to leave Barrow for Point Hope where she planned to work on a ship bound for San Francisco. She began her travels over the tundra during the Arctic summer. About five days from Barrow, lost and without food, she encountered a pack of wolves. Recalling her father's advice, she attempted to communicate with them. She built a sod house near the wolves' den where she observed them intently. By imitating their sounds and body language she became accepted, a "member" of the pack. Amaroq, the leader, became her wolf-father. There were five pups, one of whom she named Kapu. There was a second male, Nail, and another adult whom she named Jello, a misfit.

The wolves made frequent kills. They supplied her with food by regurgitating, as they do for their young. Miyax, thus, survived. She began to cure and store meat for she knew that when summer ended, the wolves would leave. Unfortunately, upon returning to her sod home after a period of several days she discovered that Jello had destroyed her sleeping gear and equipment and eaten most of her food. Amaroq turned on Jello and killed him.

By constructing a sled, Miyax found she could keep up with the wolves. All went well for some time. She marveled at and appreciated the beauty and serenity of the tundra. Besides the companionship of the wolves, she nursed a golden plover back to health. She named it Tornait, bird spirit.

One dreadful day, a plane carrying bounty hunters shot Amaroq and wounded Kapu but as a result of Miyax's gentle ministrations, Kapu became well and the leader of the pack. Miyax insisted that he lead the pack back to the wilderness to ensure their safety.

For some time Miyax lived successfully off the land and only killed enough game to sustain herself. On one expedition, she learned from a caribou hunting family that a mighty hunter, Kapugen, lived in the village of Kangik. She joyously set out for a reunion. Upon her arrival she learned that he had adopted "gussak" ways and was married to a white woman. Disillusioned and heartbroken, she returned to her winter ice house on the tundra. She was faced with another disappointment. Tornait died. She began to realize that "the hour of the wolf and the Eskimo is over." And, "Julie pointed her boots toward Kapugen."

Not only does the plot captivate young readers, but any one of a number of themes are relevant to contemporary youth especially, projecting a truthful self-image, investigating personal and family relationships, struggling for identity, meeting expectations, and affirming environmental stewardship. Perhaps students would respond in literature reading logs or during class discussions to affective questions which aid them in gaining insight into how Julie coped with and adapted to change by courageously persevering against great odds to come to terms with her personal challenges. Miyax/Julie is a character with whom they can identify and empathize.

Besides worthy themes, this work has subject content that provokes a range of "whole language" explorations and research possibilities. What choices! A student might select two or three activities such as suggested among the following. The choices should appeal to varied interest and ability levels and integrate naturally with other subject disciplines. For example, in science, students might research wolves or any of the numerous birds and animals introduced in the book, explain the cause of the northern lights, or describe the environmental problems civilization has brought to the Arctic. In social studies, they might make a time line of events, study the geography and make a map locating the settings in the story, compare snowmobile and dog sled transportation, build an igloo, or create a tundra. In creative drama, students might dramatize a scene that was action-filled such as the caribou or bear scenes or pantomime Miyax's initial encounters with the wolves. In art, they might make "Eskimo" carvings from balsa wood or Ivory soap or create a diorama of a favorite tundra scene. In music, students could listen to Eskimo music or create music to accompany Miyax's songs. And in composition, they could summarize each day's reading in their literature reading logs, or write a short sequel or a different ending to the book, correspond with a pen pal, investigate the Eskimo language, write a positive or a negative review of the book, or produce a news documentary on living on the tundra. The students themselves would have other related activities to recommend for the book invites inquiry and response.

One of the pleasures of reading good literature is the savoring and sharing of beautifully written passages. Sensory images, similes, metaphors, personification, and vivid descriptions abound. Picture these: "Her face was pearl-round...." "The wind was screaming wild high notes and hurling ice-filled waves against the beach." "She leaped with grace, her fur gleaming like metal." "...every wind-tossed sedge was a sliver thread." "...colored memories...lemon-yellow...fire-red...rose-gray...flickering yellow..." "The bear snarled, lunged forward and galloped toward..." "The great wolves eyes...hardened into brittle yellow jewels..." and "...blood spread like fish ripples on the snow." Undoubtedly students would discover the many symbols and wish to share them, too. Would they include the wolf pack, the oil drums, Tornait, the hunter's planes, Amoraq, and Jello? What would they say each represents? George's style is intellectually stimulating and unique.

A particular focus should be character delineation. Though there are minor characters, the fully-developed, round character is Miyax/Julie. Constructing a character map to point out three or four textual references each of her many acts of courage, of perseverance, of loyalty, of astute reasoning, and of appreciation of nature, wild life, and the environment could result in a lively and cooperative class venture. Students might even be challenged to identify and "prove" one or two flaws the protagonist possesses. The heroine might also be compared to other heroines such as Karana in *Island of the Blue Dolphin* using a Venn compare/contrast diagram to do so.

Another component of fiction, that of setting, is particularly significant in this work. It impacts upon the main character, and in fact, illuminates her character. Students might wish to ponder whether it is a symbol, whether it is an antagonist, or whether it accomplishes multiple purposes.

Though this is a realistic fiction work in which the literary components of theme, style, characterization, plot, and setting are significant facets, it also contains information about wolves, other fauna, the flora, and the Arctic tundra that is factually accurate. The author, Jean Craighead George, has a degree in English and a Master of Science degree from Pennsylvania State University. She has collaborated in writing a series of nature stories, served as a publisher's consultant in the natural sciences, and writes both fiction and well-researched nonfiction. Her works reflect original research, scientific observation, and personal experience. Before writing *Julie of the Wolves*, for example, she studied the behavior of wild wolves in the Mt. McKinley National Park; she observed the ecology of the Alaskan tundra on site and at the Arctic Research Laboratory in addition to doing much library research while writing the book. It is unusual for a writer to excel in both fiction and nonfiction as this author clearly does.

When the book is so outstanding, why are there reports that some teachers are reluctant to use it? There are two reasons, neither of which is justifiable. The first has to do with the so-called "rape" scene. It is not graphic. It is sensitively recorded. It is not sensationalized. It is central to the credibility of the plot. Only a horrifying personal experience of great gravity could induce a young, sensible girl to commence a three hundred mile trek across the frozen Arctic tundra.

The second objection concerns the description of a human eating regurgitated food from wolves. It has been labeled "gross" and "unlikely." Quite the contrary. If Miyax had not known the true, intelligent nature and habits of wolves, and that they respond precisely the way the author describes, she would have starved. All information regarding wolves is factual and can be documented.

Overshadowing these minor objections are the merits of a wellcrafted 1973 Newbery Medal winner for literary quality. The book will forever be timely and appropriate for upper elementary grade students. Not sentimental nor didactic, it emphasizes significant themes, develops a distinctive main character, offers an engaging plot, portrays an historically accurate environment, and employs language that has descriptive power and elegant beauty.

WORK CITED

George, Jean Craighead. *Julie of the Wolves.* New York: Harper and Row, 1977.

GORDON PARKS' *THE LEARNING TREE:* AUTOBIOGRAPHY AND EDUCATION

Gilbert Powell Findlay

Who speaks for Gordon Parks? Who should have to? Such a "Horatio Alger" life speaks for itself. Parks was born in 1912 in Fort Scott, Kansas, youngest of fifteen children in a poor, black farm family. When he was sixteen, his mother died, and Gordon moved to St. Paul, Minnesota, to live with a married sister. He dropped out of high school, held low-skill jobs, and spent six months seriously ill. Though he tried painting, sculpture, and song writing, he was, at twenty-one, still a railroad porter and bar-car waiter, but in 1937 he decided to become a professional photographer, so he spent $12.50 for a Voightlander Brilliant at a pawnshop. Remarkably, he soon had a lucrative business doing portraits of society women in Chicago. During World War II he was a photographer for the Office of War Information and afterward a staff photographer for Standard Oil of New Jersey, then for twenty years, for *Life*. In 1968 he became the first black to direct a major Hollywood studio film when he adapted and composed the score for his own book, *The Learning Tree*, which he followed with *Shaft, Shaft's Big Score, The Super Cops,* and *Leadbelly*. He has composed concertos and sonatas performed by symphony orchestras in the United States and Europe. Among his thirteen books are *Flash Photography* (1947), *The Poet and His Camera* (1968), *Gordon Parks: Whispers of Intimate Things* (1971, poems), Born Black (1971, illustrated essays and interviews), and most significant, four autobiographical works, *The Learning Tree* (1963, an autobiographical novel), *A Choice of Weapons* (1966), *To Smile in Autumn* (1979), and *Voice in the Mirror* (1990). Though he did not graduate from high school, he has at least seven honorary degrees, including a Litt. D. from Kansas State University.

Gordon Parks speaks for Gordon Parks. Autobiographers, self-life-writers, transform the remembered history of a life into literary form, thus sharing their experiences while, unlike a Horatio Alger hero, exploring identity and probing motivations behind their actions. Autobiography is the most powerful genre available to us in this time when identity itself is in jeopardy, a period characterized by alienation, the absurd, and dehumanization. In *The Learning Tree*, a slightly fictionalized story of his youth, Parks offers, especially to the adolescent reader, such an account of education and the formation of character from the end of childhood to his premature independence precipitated by his mother's death. Gordon Parks lived this. He shares it.

It is difficult to describe the plot of autobiography beyond a series of "this happened's," but in *The Learning Tree*, Newt Winger, Parks' alter ego, confronts love, death, play, school, sex, hate, race, religion, law, nature, friendship, loneliness, and the truism that only fiction, not life, can end happily ever after. Newt's mother, Sarah, provides as much outline as one needs when she tells her son

> If you learn to profit from the good and bad these people [of Cherokee Flats, *The Learning Tree's* Fort Scott] do to each other, you'll learn a lot 'bout life. And you'll be a better man for learnin' someday.... No matter if you go or stay, think of Cherokee Flats like that till the day you die—let it be your learnin' tree. (35-36)

The Learning Tree describes a boy growing up. It begins so fast that the pace is sometimes exhausting, risking melodrama and cliche, but there is a steady development of the boy's character. Newt is twelve as he begins his progress toward maturity. It opens

> Newt Winger lay belly-flat at the edge of the cornfield, his brown chin close to the ground, his eyes glued to a hill of busy ants. He singled out one struggling with tree bark twice its size, tugging it forward then sideways then backward up the incline.... For five of his twelve years he had watched these creatures, remembering that his father often spoke of their energy and work habits in contrast to those of the listless blacks and whites in Cherokee Flats. (7)

Newt, at twelve, is still a child, trained in observation but without experience, or the ability to analyze or generalize. He is unaware that to succeed in the life ahead of him he will need to "pull a tree trunk up a mountainside," with energy and work habits and direction. "As the ant reached the top, the glitter suddenly dimmed and bits of mound blew into Newt's eye" (7). Thus, the story itself starts with a cyclone, a violent natural act that catapults Newt out of his passive childhood into the road to maturity. This cyclone does not land Newt in Oz, however, but on the borderline of Kansas, borderline for the black man, where "freedom loosed one hand while custom restrained the other," where "the law books stood for equal rights, but the law never bothered to enforce such laws in the books" (26). Within the next few hours he experiences violence—the storm itself, a slashed leg, a blow to the head; sex—his rescuer, Big Mabel, goes beyond the limits of Florence Nightingale to warm the wet, cold, injured boy; death—as the storm abates, a good neighbor is discovered under his tornado-crushed roof. The primal life forces, sex and death, start Newt on the path to maturity. The observer of ants becomes an initiate or participant in life. But the path is not easy. There is as much bad (racial injustice, poverty, doors closed, hate, the siren song of quitting the "work" of becoming mature) as there is good.

He begins to observe others' behavior—in response to the storm, his father gives skin for a graft to a girl burned in a storm-related fire, while his brother-in-law, Clint, just retreats from the chaos into drunken irresponsibility. He begins to question—he startles his mother during a conversation about "people and things" by questioning the ways of God relative to who was lost and who was saved during the storm and expressing fear of death as the mysterious limit of life. He begins to act— he is caught in a boy's crime, stealing peaches with his little band of merry friends, a caper which turns ugly when an outcast acquaintance, Marcus Savage, beats the orchard owner; Newt confesses, not out of self-service, but in respect for the truth. He begins to learn—at a house where his mother is a domestic servant, he is inspired by "a whole new world of knowledge," misfocused at first on words such as *papilionidae* and *zygomorphic*, but still a vision of a future that possibly could include college and music and art. And he begins, just begins, to mature—despite his sexual initiation during the cyclone, he still is innocent enough to be bowled over by "boy-she's-pretty" first love for Arcella Jefferson.

The observation intensifies as the book catalogues a spectrum of social mores and character types: a comic minister who "preaches it" and eats Sister Winger's fried chicken, a redneck sheriff, a spoiled rich kid, an ambitious politician, and a good country doctor. Newt's questions do not have simple answers. The book, which begins with death, also ends with it. The acts, the learning, and the maturation join together in what emerges as the central theme: the lessons of experience.

Meanwhile, Newt has a counterpoint in Marcus Savage. Newt is poor and black, but he is provided with strength, love, and faith of his parents. Marcus is black; and poorer and is emotionally starved by his abusive, drunken, widowed father, Booker. Newt strays from right behavior: stealing peaches, fighting, or romantically lusting for Arcella, but he is guided toward choices that build responsibility, sensitivity, and decency. Marcus is also an outlaw, but he responds to his social confrontations with anger, violence, and inarticulate bitterness. Newt vows growth, Marcus revenge. They clash after the peach episode, and Marcus is sent to reform school. They fight in a staged "Mississippi free-for-all" (reminiscent of Ellison's battle royal in *Invisible Man)* at a circus, the boys unified, ironically, by the animal cruelty of the white audience. And they fight again, finally, when Marcus seeks to kill Newt, whom he sees as a symbol of all the oppression and degradation that has crushed him. Thus, as Newt responds to the good and bad of his racial status, his economic limitations, and his social interactions, all source material for formation of his identity, Marcus furiously submits to all its negative force. *The Learning Tree* is a powerful book: about growing up, not merely black, but human.

So who would speak against Gordon Parks? Why, "they" do, of course. On Lee Burress's 1982 list of the 600 books challenged since 1965, prepared for the National Council of Teachers of English, *The Learning Tree* ranks seventeenth in frequency of citation (15-16). Denigrating racial epithets toward blacks and whites, "vulgar language," "cheap, explicit passages on sex," and objectionable words are among the charges (*Newsletter* 88). Though one hates to do Gabler work, I tallied possibly "objectionable" words (forgive any inaccuracy; I really can find more ennobling uses for my time than counting "dirty" words). There are seventy-three curses, mainly from the mouths of drunks, mobs, or redneck jailers and sheriffs. Jack Winger never curses; Marcus Savage seldom does not. The vicious Sheriff Kirky swears in every sentence, though when he says "damn" in the Winger house. Sarah Winger corrects him, "You watch your tongue in this house, Kirky. We don't use cuss words here!" (50) The *damns, hells,* and *bastards* appear in clusters to show inarticulate ignorance, self-degrading character, and violent situations. Add twenty-three obscenities, including the f-word once, during Marcus's crazed death struggle; thirteen blasphemies, all *goddamns* except for a ludicrous scene where the drunken brother-in-law, Clint, is standing on a hen house, firing a shotgun at "Christ" (the strong, devout Sarah stops the foolishness and models the way for sensible behavior); seventeen sexual descriptions including one sex act, but mostly boyish giggles about breasts and underpants; and twelve potential indecencies such as *rump* (Beansie burned his, you will be shocked to know, stuffing stolen hot sausages in his hip pocket). Parks is not very subtle. The mob scenes at the free-for-all, the lynching of Booker Savage, and the Spit Reform School probably all go on too long or repeat too much. But autobiographer Parks describes his characters and illustrates their bigotry and ignorance by drawing from life. An adolescent reader may be distracted by the indecencies, but the drama and character conflict should emerge powerfully enough so the cussin' would sink into background atmosphere.

As to racial epithets, blacks are called "niggers," whites "pecker-woods." However, the two times Newt is called "nigger," he is shocked into more intense awareness of pervasive racism; his consciousness is raised, in modern parlance. Each time the scene is followed by something offering perspective: first, a discussion with his blind and wise Uncle Rob; second, by an ironic ignorant use of "nigger" by a white schoolfriend of Newt's. I suspect from the number of books about minorities on Lee Burress's list that it is not racial opprobrium but the existence of racial minorities *per se* that makes the censors nervous.

One could find other elements to challenge. The comic Pastor Broadnap might be considered anticlerical, and there is some serious skepticism in Newt's maturing consideration of religion. There is a scene depicting a hypocritical school board, and more than one teacher, black and white, is displayed as foolish, so perhaps authority is shown in less than perfect light. Arcella and Newt's sister, Prissy, are sometimes sketched as mere female stereotypes. Except for Sarah [Parks] Winger, Parks does not recreate women (or the rich) with much skill. If *The Learning Tree* is considered for young readers, one might even challenge the grammar of the characters' speech. Last, and this is called 'criticism' rather than censorship, the book is not great literature, not the equal of *Huck Finn*, *Black Boy*, or Angelou's *Caged Bird*. It is often melodramatic, sometimes cliché-ridden, and as repetitive and as disjointed as life itself. A teacher, recommending this book for public school, might have to spend more than one evening speaking for Gordon Parks.

However, I will speak for Gordon Parks' *The Learning Tree*. It's a d—d good book. In an address at Kansas University in 1973, Gordon Parks said "the trick has been to try and tell the entire story—to interlock in some reasonable way, the good experience with the bad" (A Look 8). Such an exploration of human experience, charting a real human progress, cannot be dismissed because the reality described is sometimes indecorous. Sarah Winger sets Newt's course in the "learning tree" analogy—only if you profit from the good *and* the bad, can you possibly achieve the better mature life, though it is not guaranteed. Milton, in *Areopagitica*, rejects censorship because cloistered virtue is not virtue at all, but ignorance. The profit, says Sarah, is a

> matter of givin' more to this world than you take away from it.... It's bein' able to love when you want'a hate—to forgive them that work against you—to tell the truth even when it hurts—to share your bread, no matter how hungry you are yourself. Dyin' comes easy when you know you've done all these things right. (36)

She gives this advice to Newt at the beginning of his adolescence, and the rest of the book demonstrates how he must convert this advice slowly into his own identity, a new generation finding a new voice. His counterpart, Marcus Savage, to whom the world gives almost nothing, nevertheless gives even less back to it and fails to survive. Newt, on the contrary, is able to stand at his mother's deathbed, strong enough to receive her last directions: "believe in somethin' and live up to it."(227)

We, in education, believe the only path to maturity is lifelong learning. Readers of the autobiographical *Learning Tree* have the opportunity to experience this theory. First comes the advice from blind Uncle Rob Winger: "Learn all you can, so when bigger things come you'll be ready for them" (69) and from his mother, who contradicts his father's defeated resignation: "the white man's got the money and guts—that spells power," with "schoolin's more powerful than guns or money in the end" (72). Newt realizes this advice in a variety of contexts. He learns to box from his brother, Pete, before he finds he must fight Marcus in the ring. He maintains his curiosity about science and dictionaries before he is confronted with the unexpected obstacle of a guidance counselor's prejudice (he is told blacks "aren't college material"); he does not submit to reduced self-esteem because he already has an "educated" perspective on education itself (his principal supports his ideals). He "schools" his character, with help from his family; in a murder trial (the dramatic center of the plot) in which he, only, knows the truth which, if told, would save an innocent man but probably provoke racial violence, he nevertheless has matured enough to put truth above consequences. The result is full maturity: "he was free now, free to meet violence if need be, as he had met the truth" (205). A reader can recall Sarah's earlier promise, "dyin' comes easy when you know you've done all these things right." The human storm rages, bigotry, sex, violence, greed, hate, death—there are nine deaths in this book—but Newt Winger weathers through to faith, belief, love, and understanding.

After Sarah's death, when Newt is once again at a transition, this time from adolescence to independence, he must confront Marcus, who in his savage anger, hunts Newt in order to kill him. Marcus reviews his stunted life. "'Ain't got nobody now....' He plucked a small ant crawling over his knee, held it for a moment, watching it wiggle helplessly; then his powerful black fingers rubbed it into nothingness" (219). But when Newt, the ant-watcher, meets Savage, the ant-killer, the four years of schooling in love, work, dignity, education, pride, freedom, and truth give him superiority. Though wounded, Newt gains physical superiority. "For a split second their eyes burned into each other" (238). Newt is tempted to kill. But he then gains something greater, moral superiority, and he lets

Marcus escape (though Kirky chases Marcus to his death). "Able to love when you want to hate," his mother had said. I hope the censors have not been closed to the Christian teaching in this book.

Thus, *The Learning Tree* is a compelling history of growing up, available to anyone who can identify with a universal exploration of human experience. No matter if a reader's time, race, religion, gender, or social environments are different. Any honest book about growing up is a story of learning, the hard choices, here guided by the love and faith of family, in search of the sources of identity and even more realistic and mature understanding (Burger 55). This book allows the reader to share insight into how a Gordon Parks is "miraculously" transformed from a cipher on the plains of Kansas to a man prepared for his success in such a variety of creative expressions. The autobiographical *The Learning Tree* is also a moral fable. Gordon Parks said "look at me and know that to destroy me is to destroy yourself...*I too am America*" (A Look 10). I, your critic, am white, affluent, chaste of language and behavior, even grammatically above reproach. But I need not speak for Gordon Parks. He speaks for me.

WORKS CITED

Burress, Lee and Edward B. Jenkinson. *The Students' Right to Know.* Urbana, IL: National Council of Teachers of English, 1982.

Burger, Mary. "I, Too, Sing America: The Black Autobiographer's Response to Life in the Midwest and Mid-Plains." *Kansas Quarterly* 7, No. 3 (1975).

Newsletter on Intellectual Freedom (July 1978): 88.

Parks, Gordon. *The Learning Tree.* Greenwich, CT: A Fawcett Crest Book, 1963.

Parks, Gordon. "A Look Back." *Kansas Quarterly* 7, No. 3 (1975).

TEACHING RATIONALE FOR WILLIAM GOLDING'S *LORD OF THE FLIES*

Paul Slayton

Lord of the Flies is William Golding's parable of life in the latter half of the twentieth century, the nuclear age, when society seems to have reached technological maturity while human morality is still pre-pubescent. Whether or not one agrees with the pessimistic philosophy, the idiocentric psychology or the fundamentalist theology espoused by Golding in the novel, if one is to use literature as a "window on the world," this work is one of the panes through which one should look.

The setting for *Lord of the Flies* is in the literary tradition of Daniel Defoe's *Robinson Crusoe* and Johann Wyss's *The Swiss Family Robinson,* and like these earlier works provides the necessary ingredients for an idyllic utopian interlude. A plane loaded with English school boys, aged five through twelve, is being evacuated to a safe haven in, perhaps, Australia to escape the "Reds," with whom the English are engaged in an atomic war. Somewhere in the tropics the plane is forced to crash land during a violent storm. All the adults on board are lost when the forward section of the plane is carried out to sea by tidal waves. The passenger compartment, fortuitously, skids to a halt on the island, and the young passengers escape uninjured.

The boys find themselves in a tropical paradise: bananas, coconuts and other fruits are profusely available. The sea proffers crabs and occasional fish in tidal pools, all for the taking. The climate is benign. Thus, the stage is set for an idyllic interlude during which British fortitude will enable the boys to master any possible adversity. In fact, Golding relates that just such a nineteenth century novel, R.M. Ballantyne's *Coral Island,* was the inspiration for *Lord of the Flies.* In that utopian story the boy castaways overcame every obstacle they encountered with the ready explanation, "We are British. you know!"

Golding's tropical sojourners, however, do not "live happily ever after." Although they attempt to organize themselves for survival and rescue, conflicts arise as the boys first neglect, then refuse, their assigned tasks. As their "society" fails to build shelters or to keep the signal fire going, fears emanating from within—for their environment is totally non-threatening—take on a larger than life reality. Vines hanging from trees become "snake things" in the imaginings of the "little'uns." A nightmare amidst fretful sleep, causing one of the boys to cry out in the night, conjures up fearful "beasties" for the others. Their fears become more real than existence on the tropical paradise itself when the twins, Sam 'n Eric, report their enervating experience with the wind-tossed body of the dead parachutist. Despite Simon's declaration that "there is no beast, it's only us," and Piggy's disavowal of "ghosts and things," the fear of the unknown overcomes their British reserve and under Jack's all-too-willing chieftainship the boys' retreat from civilization begins.

In the initial encounter with a pig, Jack is unable to overcome his trained aversion to violence to even strike a blow at the animal. Soon, however, he and his choirboys-turned-hunters make their first kill. They rationalize that they must kill the animals for meat. The next step back from civilization occurs and the meat pretext is dropped; the real objective is to work their will on other living things.

Then, killing begins to take on an even more sinister aspect. The first fire the boys build to attract rescuers roars out of control and one of the younger boys is accidentally burned to death. The next death, that of Simon, is not an accident. He is beaten to death when he rushes into the midst of the ritual dance of the young savages. Ironically, he has come to tell the boys that he has discovered that the beast they fear is not real. Then Piggy, the last intellectual link with civilization, is killed on impulse by the sadistic Roger. Last, all semblance of civilized restraint is cast-off as the now-savage tribe of boys organizes itself to hunt down and kill their erstwhile leader, Ralph, who had tried desperately to prepare them to carry on in the fashion expected of upper middle-class British youth.

That Golding intended *Lord of the Flies* as a paradigm for modern civilization is concretely evident at the conclusion of the work. During the final confrontation at the rock fort between Ralph and Piggy and Jack and his tribe, the reader readily forgets that these individuals in conflict are not adults. The manhunt for Ralph, too, seems relative only to the world of adults. The reader is so inclined to lose sight of the age of his characters that Golding must remind that these participants are pre-adolescents: The naval officer who interrupts the deadly manhunt sees "A semicircle of little boys, their bodies streaked with colored clay, sharp sticks in hand...." Unlike that officer, the reader knows that it was not "fun and games" of the boys that the naval officer interrupted. The officer does not realize—as the reader knows—that he has just saved Ralph from a sacrificial death and the other boys from becoming premeditated murderers. Neither is the irony of the situation very subtle: The boys have been "rescued" by an officer from a British man-of-war, which will very shortly resume its official activities as either hunter or hunted in the deadly adult game of war.

Golding, then, in *Lord of the Flies* is asking the question which continues as the major question haunting the world today: How shall denizens of the earth be rescued from our fears and our own pursuers—ourselves? While Golding offers no ready solutions to our dilemma, an understanding of his parable yields other questions which may enable readers to become seekers in the quest for a moral world. Even if one disagrees with Golding's judgment of the nature of human beings and of human society, one profits from his analysis of the problems confronting people today.

There are reasons for teachers of English to select literary works for study other than the specific content of the literature. It is the task of the English teacher to prepare students to become lifelong readers of many and varied works of literature. Consequently, a literary work is often chosen for in-class study in spite of rather than because of the story line. That is, the objective of the selecting teacher may well be to choose a piece of literature which demonstrates the techniques and the artistry with which the work is written rather than because of the issue or purpose espoused by the author. The teacher does not choose the work nor teach the content of the piece as if it were a textbook in some discipline, but, instead, uses the work because it is exemplary of the writing process and to enable the students to learn the keys to reading and understanding other pieces of literature, not just the specific work in question. *Lord of the Flies* is one work which might well be chosen for just such a reason.

Golding is a master at his trade and *Lord of the Flies* has achieved critical acclaim as the best of his works. Indeed, a dictionary of literary terminology might well be illustrated with specific examples from this piece of prose. The development of the several focal characters in this work is brilliantly and concretely done. In addition, the omniscient narrative technique, plotting, relating story to setting and the use of irony, foreshadowing, and certainly, symbolism are so carefully and concretely accomplished that the work can serve as an invaluable teaching aid to prepare students to read other literature with a degree of understanding far beyond a simplistic knowledge of the surface events of the story. Golding's characterizations will be used in this rationale to illustrate these technical qualities of the novel.

A strength of *Lord of the Flies* lies in techniques of characterization. There are five major characters who are developed as wholly-rounded individuals whose actions and intensity show complex human motivation: Ralph, Jack, Roger, Simon and Piggy. A study of these characterizations shows the wide range of techniques for developing persona utilized by Golding and by other authors:

Ralph, the protagonist, is a rather befuddled everyman. He is chosen for leadership by the group for all the wrong reasons. Ralph does not seek the leadership role; he is elected because he is older (12 plus), somewhat larger, is attractive in personal appearance and, most strikingly, he possesses the conch shell which reminds the boys of the megaphone with which their late adult supervisors directed and instructed them. In the unsought leadership role Ralph demonstrates courage, intelligence and some diplomatic skill. On the negative side he quickly becomes disillusioned with the democratic process and without Piggy's constant urgings would have cast aside the chief's role even before Jack's *coup d'etat.* Ralph also demonstrates other weaknesses as he unthinkingly gives away Piggy's hated nickname and, more significantly, he gets caught up in the mob psychology of the savage dance and takes part in the ritualistic murder of Simon. Thus, by relating causes and effects, Golding reveals Ralph's change from a proper British lad to group leader to his disenchantment and finally to his becoming the object of the murderous hunt by the boys who once chose him as their leader.

Jack, the antagonist, is developed as the forceful villain. Outgoing, cocky and confident, Jack marches his choir boys in military formation up the beach to answer the call of the conch. Jack is a natural leader who, except for his exploitative nature, might have been a congealing force for good. Instead, his lust for power precipitates the conflict with Ralph and Piggy's long-range planning for rescue. To attain leadership, Jack caters to boyish desires for ready delights and after he is assured that his choir boys will follow in this new direction, he resorts to intimidation to increase his following. In Jack, Golding has developed a prototype of the charismatic leader who gains adherents by highlighting the fears and fulfilling the ephemeral needs and desires of followers.

Roger, "the hangman's horror," is a stereotyped character who does not change. He readily sheds a thin veneer of civilization which has been imposed upon him by the authority of the policeman and the law. So easily his arm loses the restraints which had once prohibited him from hitting the littl'uns with tossed rocks to a point where he can kill Piggy on impulse. It is but one more small step for him to proclaim the ritual dance must end in killing and to premeditate the murder of Ralph.

Simon is the quintessential Christ-figure. A thin, frail little boy, subject to fainting spells, he alone has the mental acumen and the courage to go onto the mountain and disprove the existence of the "beast." He is martyred for his efforts by the group which no longer wishes to hear his "good news."

Piggy, the pragmatic intellectual, is of necessity the most steadfast in motivation. He is tied to civilization by his physical weaknesses. Overweight, asthmatic, and completely dependent for sight upon his spectacles, the life of the happy savage has no allure for him. Without the aids of civilization, such as eye glasses and allergy shots, he cannot long survive. Consequently, he must reject the ephemeral allures offered by Jack and steadfastly hold, and seek to hold Ralph, to maintaining the smoke signal, his only hope for the aid and succor of rescue. His steadfastness in this aim enables him to call up the uncharacteristic courage to make the last appeal to Jack and his tribe before the rock fort because "right is right." His plea is to no avail; the sadistic Roger releases the boulder which throws Piggy from the cliff to his death.

Another minor character, Percival Weems Botts, is developed as a stereotype to demonstrate the fragility of rote learning. This "little'un" who can only recite his name and address as a response soon forgets even that as all trappings of civilization are lost by the boys.

Thus, Golding's techniques of characterization afford superior examples of the writer's craft and apt material to use to help students learn to interpret authorial voice and to respond to a piece of literature as a level beyond the denotative.

Lord of the Flies has earned for itself and its author great critical acclaim. It has also been extolled by teachers for the excitement it can engender in readers and as a work in which the motivation of characters is readily understood by adolescent readers. Despite these accolades for the novel as a work of literary art and as a teaching tool, *Lord of the Flies* has on occasion aroused the ire of would-be censors.

Some have opposed the use of the novel in the classroom because of the use of "vulgar" language. Certain words, notably "sucks," "ass," and the British slang word "bloody," are used. It is patently obvious that there is no prurient motivation behind the author's choice of these words. Not one of these words is ever used outside of a context in which the word appears to be quite naturally the word the character would use. The choir boys may well sing like "angels," as is stated; nevertheless, these are perfectly normal pre-adolescent boys. Given the proclivities of such youth the world over, verisimilitude would be lost had they, amongst themselves, always spoken like angels.

The sexual symbolism of the killing of the sow has also raised some puritanical brows. This violent scene is described in terms which might well be used to describe a rape. Such symbolism is fully justified, however, if the author is to be allowed to make his point that the motivation of the boys, casting away the cloak of civilization, is no longer merely securing food. Rather, they have moved front serving practical needs to an insane lust for working their will upon other creatures. The next step is the slaughter of their own kind.

Objection, too, has come upon that very point: children killing children. One must remind those who object to this violence that this piece of literature is a parable. Children are specifically used to show that even the innocence of childhood can be corrupted by fears from within. Those who would deny Golding this mode of establishing his theme would deny to all authors the right to make their point in an explicit fashion.

The most vociferous denunciation of *Lord of the Flies* has been vocalized by those who have misread the book to the point that they believe it deals with Satanism. The symbolism of the title, which is the English translation of the Greek word "Beelzebub," is surely being misinterpreted by such folk. In fact, theologian Davis Anderson states unequivocally that "Golding is a Christian writer." Anderson defines the central theme of *Lord of the Flies* as a statement of what it is like to experience the fall from innocence into sin and to experience damnation. Thus, a theologian sees the novel as one dealing with the Christian doctrine of original sin and of the rupture of man's relationship with God! Consequently, one who would attack this novel as an exercise in Satanism assuredly holds an indefensible premise.

Thus, *Lord of the Flies* meets all criteria for use in the classroom. It has demonstrated its appeal and delight to adolescent readers. It has met with critical acclaim and is generally accorded a place among the modern classics of literature. It deals with a significant universal theme with obvious contemporary ramifications. Moreover, it is rendered with artistry and in an exemplary style and manner. And, last, the accusations of those censors who would deny its use in the classroom are demonstrably false. In the final analysis *Lord of the Flies* is a novel which has been highly recommended by critics and teachers for more than three decades for study by mature, senior high school students of literature.

SHIRLEY JACKSON'S "THE LOTTERY"
Jack Stark

Many literary critics think that Shirley Jackson's "The Lottery" is one of the classic short stories in the English language. Although it is approachable, even by teenage readers, it subtly develops a number of profound themes. That unusual combination of attributes has made it a staple of high school English courses. However, it is among the targets of censors. Their attacks are disturbing because they are groundless and because if they succeed students will lose an invaluable learning experience.

Most of the story's attackers are probably disturbed by its "violence." At the outset it is important to note that, although a single incident of violence is about to occur when the story ends, Jackson does not describe any violence. She foreshadows the impending violence with a few references to the gathering of stones, but virtually throughout the story she concentrates on violence's social and psychological roots. That emphasis, along with the understated prose style and the profusion of homey details, distances the impending violence. The story is anything but the kind of lurid and sensational pandering to base urges by depicting violence that is standard fare an television. Jackson also clearly implies that she disapproves of the kind of behavior she describes. For example, the story is replete with irony, such as a reference to the proceedings as one of the village's "civic activities." Moreover, the last direct discourse in the story, which appears in the final, brief paragraph is "it isn't right," a judgment that no doubt is Jackson's.

If Jackson is not engaged in purveying in violence in the story, what are her interests? One of them is examining the role of tradition in human behavior. The villagers have maintained the tradition of the lottery even though they have altered some details. That tradition has persisted for so long that it has acquired a momentum of its own, which encourages its adherents to maintain it for itself, quite aside from its consequences. One reason for that phenomenon is the village's isolation; the villagers know little about developments elsewhere, and that little bit is mainly vague rumors. For whatever reasons, this tradition has foreclosed thought, in particular thought about itself, just as tradition has had that effect often in history, sometimes with disastrous consequences.

The tradition, rather than being merely an intellectual phenomenon, is embodied in a ritual that supports it. The villagers perform that ritual publicly, on the same day each year and in much the same way as they have performed it for decades. They automatically disapprove of most attempts to vary the ritual. Like the topic of tradition, the topic of ritual is one that teenagers can comprehend and have experienced. Because of their lack of sophistication they will probably recognize only obvious rituals, such as religious ones. Pointing out some less obvious rituals, including ones that are specific to them, such as high school homecomings and dating rituals, will help them understand the world in which they live and the ways that it shapes them.

"The Lottery" is also a useful means for enlightening students about the law. Many of them probably think of the law as mainly a way to define and prevent or punish deviant behavior. Jackson shows that it exists also in informal modes in unsophisticated societies. One of her story's major ironies is that an activity leading to a triumph of antisocial forces over civilized restraint is carried out very meticulously according to "laws." That is, the methods used to choose the victim are codified, although not in writing, and have the force of the society behind them. That irony emphatically makes the point that law not only does not guarantee safety but also can be used to threaten safety. After those insights are derived from this story, it is easy to lead readers into a consideration of law's function and its relation to human behavior.

Veneration of tradition, ritual and law causes the villagers to feel that their actions are inevitable. That feeling in turn results in a denial of responsibility. One character has a cosmic view of the lottery, believing that performing it punctiliously will cause a bountiful harvest. His view, too, offers an escape from responsibility. Discussion in a high school class of these themes can easily lead to a more general discussion of factors that make it difficult to assert responsibility and even to realize that one is abdicating responsibility. Students will be able to identify some of those factors and can be helped to identify others. That is, this story can be used to help them mature into responsible adults.

"The Lottery" will also aid maturation because another of its themes is the interaction between generations. In one sense the children lead the community in the lottery ritual; they are the first to gather the stones. Not being very reflective, they are easily caught up in the mob psychology. In another sense, however, they are, as their age indicates, only junior members of the community and junior performers of the ritual. For example, some of the adults, showing "their protectiveness, hope that no child will draw the deadly slip of paper, and occasionally adults gently guide the children into performing their roles correctly. This generational theme will, of course, both interest and be very helpful to youthful readers, who will probably be adept at discerning the ways in which the adults influence the children.

Readers, such as high school students, who are trying to "find themselves" and establish an identity to take into adulthood will be interested in the story's theme of the individual who is opposed to the community. At first glance, Jackson seems to be pessimistic about the possibility of dissent in communities that are tightly restricted by the methods of social control she describes. Mrs. Hutchinson, the unlucky loser of the lottery, does not object to the lottery until it identifies her family as the one that will supply the victim. She objects more strenuously when she is identified as the member of her family who will be sacrificed. Before the lottery's results are known a reader waits in vain for a villager to declare that the lottery is madness. However, Jackson's analysis is a bit more incisive. Mrs. Hutchinson is late arriving at the lottery and when she does arrive she makes an inappropriate remark that causes nervous laughter. That is, even before she knows she will be the victim she indicates that she is incompletely socialized and thus does not fully accept the lottery ritual's legitimacy. Unfortunately for the village, the lottery destroys its only apparent opponent, albeit a very minor one.

Jackson adds another dimension to these themes by developing them in the context of a lottery, to which she draws attention in her title. In other words, she raises the issue of chance's influence over human affairs. Throughout history individuals have taken three basic positions on this issue. One can be called the Augustinian view, under which chance plays little or no role and humans have very little room in which to maneuver, their fates having been worked out long ago. In his view they were worked out to a large extent by Adam and Eve. Machiavelli takes a moderate position on this issue, in *The Prince*, using the metaphor of the flood of fortune, which cannot be controlled but which can to a minimal extent be directed by building dikes. The third position is that chance is rampant. In a superficial view this story illustrates the third of those positions because of the lottery's centrality. However, the villagers have to go through the ritual and at any point they could abandon it. Also, by conclusively demonstrating her understanding of her themes, Jackson indicates that humans can make sense of their lives. Where there is understanding there can also be some control.

Perhaps even more important, beliefs about the power of chance have moral dimensions. In an utterly determined world, moral choices have no consequences, so morality is attenuated. In a totally random world choices have effects but it is impossible to predict those effects and thus difficult to assign blame. In a world like the one that Machiavelli describes, choices matter and their consequences can be predicted but only to a certain extent, so life is frustrating but moral questions are meaningful. Jackson's fictional world, despite its central metaphor, the lottery, is not totally determined, so in it meaningful moral decisions are possible. However, in that world the status of moral judgment and in particular of its relation to chance are far from clear and thus are fruitful subjects for discussion. In other wards, far from being immoral because it broaches the topic of violence, "The Lottery" encourages speculation on the most basic moral issues.

Finally, "The Lottery" has an implicit historical dimension, which becomes clear if one realizes that it was published during 1948. By that year World War II had ended; Its horrors were widely known and persons had had some time to reflect on its meaning. Persons who had reflected on it had encountered many of the issues that Jackson raises, such as the power of mass psychology, the possibility that blind adherence to tradition will forestall judgment, and the ease with which responsibility can be denied. Reading this story naturally leads into consideration of the rise of Nazism, and some students can be encouraged to read such relevant historical analyses as George Mosse's work on Nazi ideology. Other students will be interested in identifying more recent historical analogues to "The Lottery." In any case, this story is well suited to a multidisciplinary approach.

In sum, Shirley Jackson's "The Lottery" is an important work. It is particularly important for young readers because it encourages reflection on some of the issues they need to understand if they are to become admirable human beings and citizens. For that reason alone its inclusion in high school English classes is fortunate. Its removal from those courses would be a serious misfortune. Ironically, if that removal occurs it may very well be the result of some of the dangerous human traits that the story depicts.

Editor's note: The censorship of Shirley Jackson's "The Lottery" has a very unusual history. Originally published in 1948 in *The New Yorker*, it became a regular feature in many high school anthologies during the 1950s and 1960s. The story began to draw fire in the early 1970s after *Encyclopaedia Britannica* released a film version and a filmed commentary. The film used the townspeople of two small California communities in presenting the realistic and trenchant story. First the films were attacked and then the story. By the mid 1980s, the story had disappeared from all anthologies.

MANCHILD IN A WORLD WHERE YOU JUST MIGHT MAKE IT: CLAUDE BROWN'S *MANCHILD IN THE PROMISED LAND*

Sue Bridwell Beckham

It was Harlem in 1954. Claude Brown had just run into his friend Danny recently back from Kentucky where he had been treated for heroin addiction. Although this was the third time Danny had tried the cure, he convinced Claude that this time he was off the stuff and he was going to stay off. There was something different in Danny's determination to make a success of his life without the drug and the social climate of which it was a part. Danny was in his early twenties and Claude was a very mature and very experienced seventeen. In anguish, the friends spoke of the waste the drug was making of Harlem's youth and the odds against a recovery such as Danny's. Finally Brown wailed, "Damn, man, if you could write something about this or talk to the younger cats comin' up, it might stop somebody, turn 'em around" (250).

Danny convinced his young friend, temporarily at least, that writing about it wouldn't cause anybody to reject the drug culture if all the real life examples on the streets of Harlem couldn't. Within a decade, however, Brown was indeed writing not only about the disastrous effects of heroin—smack, dugi, shit, stuff—on young city blacks, but about the disastrous effects of coming up in a complex city culture cut off from race memory and deprived of any conclusive identity within that culture. In *Manchild in the Promised Land* Brown did not tell of hopelessness alone but of hope as well, of ways city blacks create identity for themselves and escape the self-fulfilling prophesy that growing up black in a city ghetto is a hopeless cycle of poverty, deprivation and alienation.

It is this tale of a vital, sometimes dangerous, sometimes wasted, segment of American life that well-meaning parents have from time to time since its 1965 publication sought to remove from high school library shelves, sought to expunge from high school curricula. And glancing through the pages or reading only the first hundred pages or so, one can see why parents might think the book unfit for teenage consumption. The pages are filled with language the dominant culture finds objectionable. They are also replete with stories of young prostitutes and younger professional thieves, of hungry children forced to steal their food while their mother spends her welfare money on liquor, of a favored character named Pimp because an independent prostitute provided taxi fare for his mother to deliver him in a hospital. The infant Pimp was, after all, the first man to take her hard earned money.

The book, an autobiography, recounts the childhood and youth of Claude Brown who before he was seven had mastered successful hookey playing and shoplifting, before he had passed thirteen was a successful thief and knew the safest fences, had been chain whipped and had almost died from a gun shot wound sustained while stealing bedsheets to pawn. By fifteen Brown was a veteran of several years as a drug dealer, and he had learned the ropes of living successfully in reform school—each term being like a vacation for him because, in the company of his similarly sentenced friends, he was, for a time, relieved of having to prove himself on the streets. To Brown, mastery of crime was the way to the top. He wasn't forced into this type of life; he *chose* it because it got him the recognition he wanted, the identity he needed: Claude Brown set out to be a "bad nigger."

On the surface young Claude had no reason to turn to street life. His family was intact, both his parents were regularly employed, and his was not a family wracked by alcohol abuse or serial mates. So it was for many of his street-wise friends. Though Brown does present the picture of the broken homes and dire poverty often associated with American black culture, he and many of his associates did not have such excuses for their decision to turn to the streets. Even so, by the end of Brown's autobiography when he was only twenty-one, most of his childhood associates were dead—of knifings, of overdoses, of suicide—or hopelessly "strung out" on heroin.

Why then would anyone want to teach this book in a high school?

To begin with, it introduces most students to a culture they could not possibly understand in any other way. A culture capable of wreaking violence on itself and on the society, a culture that induces hatred, bewilderment and rabid prejudice in those who cannot understand. Reading the book, we not only learn the story of Claude Brown's bizarre boyhood as a child adult; if we pursue it to the end and if we read carefully, we learn why young Harlemites seek the form of recognition, of belonging, Claude sought. We become thoroughly familiar with an isolated group of American people in but not of the American culture. And the nearly thirty-year old volume remains vital. Near the end of the book Brown explains, "There are so many things about Harlem that have changed, and they don't seem possible for Harlem. I suppose no one who has ever lived in a Harlem of the world could ever imagine that it could change so drastically and yet maintain so much of its old misery" (402). Brown could still make that statement today. The changes in Harlem since the mid-sixties remain only superficial, and black youngsters are still choosing crime and drug abuse as alternatives to seeking out the promise of the American dream.

But Brown does not show us only the negative side of Harlem existence. Though most of his friends do succumb to the pressures of cultural alienation, though the possibilities are bleak, some do endure, some even prevail. There was "Tony" (Brown used fictitious names for the street people he wrote about) who successfully avoided the drug culture, the crime, who successfully worked and lived outside of Harlem and its temptations, but who did finally commit suicide because outside his own culture he had no identity. Danny is a better success story. He kicked the habit, and several years after his triumphant cure he continued to work and live the middle-class life with family, religion and house in Harlem. There was Turk who made it big in boxing. There were Claude's sisters and his childhood sweetheart, Jackie, who married and set up stable homes for their children. And there was Claude's brother Pimp who was, when the book was published, fighting the same battle Danny had won. Pimp was likely to succeed because like Danny and Claude, he had found who he wanted to be—or at least the determination not to be what he didn't want to be. He had found an identity.

Brown himself learned early—and he teaches his readers—that the satisfaction he received from being a leader in street crime was hollow, that, for him at least, there had to be something else. He was aided in his rejection of the street life by a fortunate accident. His first and only experiment with heroin turned out to be a "bad trip" fraught with painful vomiting and violent pain, and he did not soon want to experience that again. More important, however, than his rejection of heroin was his recognition at fifteen that, unless he changed his ways before he reached sixteen, he would have great difficulty finding that something else. He knew—and he makes very clear to his readers—that as long as he was being sent to reform schools, his future was fairly safe, but that once he reached sixteen, reform school days were over. He knew that once he was sent to jail, he would have a "sheet on him," and that a jail record would deprive him of those limited opportunities available to ghetto blacks. And so he quit. He stopped stealing, he refused to carry a weapon and he abjured drugs—first only heroin, and later he gave up cocaine as well and finally marijuana—as crutches a true citizen of our culture does not need.

Even having rejected drugs and having given up the street scene, life would not be easy for Claude. Through the book we are given insight into the difficulties Harlem people (and people from ethnic ghettos all over America) face when they venture out. To hold a job in the white world, to work out in a non-segregated but nevertheless white gym, Claude, for whom an innate affinity for language provided an advantage denied to most people, had to mask his natural behavior and speech patterns:

> Everyplace I looked I wasn't understood. I felt like a misfit on just about every job I went to.... I always had to find out where I was and what things were like. I always wanted to run. It was so difficult.... There was still the language problem. The Harlem dialect was something that I was a little afraid to use.... I knew these were gray boys [white men], and I felt I had to be careful around them or else I might frighten them.... I was careful to pronounce my r's and say "you are" and "you're not." I'd say, "Hello. How are you?" very properly. Occasionally somebody would say, "Hi, How you doin'?" and I'd feel ridiculous. There was always this uncertainty, this thing

of feeling your way through. I became aware that I was a new thing. The average cat who ventured out of Harlem would be afraid and run back. It was safer dealing drugs or doing something like that (288).

And there were difficulties with so-called liberal whites. Quite by happenstance, Claude's first love was a white student at the night school where he completed high school after he had dropped out in Harlem. She was the daughter of liberal, tolerant Jews—at least so she thought and taught Claude to believe. Even so, he was wary enough always to meet her away from home, never to be introduced to her parents. As it turned out, his instincts were correct. Once her parents stumbled onto the racial identity of their daughter's friend, they shipped her away to live with distant relatives. Again white middle-class readers are invited to contemplate restrictions faced by American blacks which most of them will never have the opportunity to experience first hand.

Not only could high school students learn from this book about a culture most of them will never experience, about the evils of drugs, the hollowness of the street life and the difficulties members of America's minority groups experience when they venture out of their own little world; they learn of the institutions America's alienated devise to deal with their alienation. Claude was tempted to cast his lot with the Coptic religion, with the Black Muslims, with black Christianity all of which are baffling and sometimes threatening to American whites and probably to non-urban blacks as well. And with each of Claude's experiences, we gain a little bit of inside insight into these mysterious forms of expression which can go a long way toward creating understanding between America's two largest ethnic groups. Perhaps more important, we pick up a few more tools with which to seek understanding of Hispanic and Asian minorities as well. Any reading young white and non-urban Americans can do that helps to demystify these "strange" groups for them is a step toward American unity—a step away from prejudice, suspicion and discrimination.

High school students can find everything Claude Brown offers in sociology textbooks, drug education programs and linguistic training, but no lesson is so well taught as it is with concrete examples, and no textbook is so vivid as Claude Brown's prose. In 1965, *Manchild in the Promised Land* was greeted with almost universal critical acclaim, but there were exceptions. One reviewer charged that this book was written with a vocabulary of a couple of hundred words and phrases—not a language at all but an impoverished patois...an argot [that] makes for a literary disaster" (Miller 49). A limited vocabulary, maybe, but certainly not a literary disaster. Brown has written in the language of the streets, the language he was afraid to use in white society precisely because he feared such responses as the one above. In so doing, he has made his message accessible both to the young blacks he so wants to help and to young whites. The very plain words and phrases he uses make for fast and enjoyable reading, and they make the material so very immediate. Parental objections have been raised to the book's language itself. That is because, in the dialogue, Brown has accurately recorded street language with all its propensity for the so-called "four letter words." Only by so doing can he tell his story with all its vivid detail, and he certainly has not introduced American middle-class youth to any words they haven't already learned from their friends and the walls of public restrooms. He doesn't condone such language, and he seldom uses it himself in the narrative. He merely represents his culture as he lived it.

The fiction of James Baldwin and Ralph Ellison is often taught in high schools and colleges to introduce black culture and black anger, and it is a wonderful introduction. Baldwin and Ellison have written classics of American literature, and they deserve recognition in the literature course. But, because they are creating fictional worlds and because they demand the interpretive skill required for reading literature, they have not the immediacy of Brown's simple account of his young life. Ellison's *Invisible Man*, one of our great novels, is so filled with the figurative, with a stream of consciousness and with fantasy that it is accessible only to the top high school students. *Another Country*, by Baldwin, is so full of resentment and hatred that it could do more to alienate white readers than to win their understanding. *Manchild in the Promised Land* is neither of these. Brown's prose is clear and accessible to the average reader, and his anger is youthful anger at circumstances, not resentment toward the whites. The book is dedicated to Eleanor Roosevelt who founded accepting and encouraging schools for black kids in trouble, and alongside the black heroes of Brown's conversion from gang member to useful society member, stands one white adviser who had perhaps as much influence as anybody. Brown is not prejudiced. He prefers black company where he can be comfortable with his own language, his own culture. But he recognizes that whites also are individuals and that race prejudice is not a foregone conclusion.

The message in the book is subtle. Brown does not often spell out his judgments. Both the negative effects of the culture in which street crime is the highest form of attainment and the hope that exists even when a young addict seems to be so lost that his friends speak of him in the past tense are implicit. The message is certainly clear enough that no teenagers are going to read it and rush out to try hookey playing, shoplifting and drugs for themselves, but it's much more complex than most young people will recognize on a first cursory reading. They will certainly learn that heroin is destructive and that Claude Brown saved himself from cultural burial. But to get all of the myriad sociological lessons in the book requires more careful and structured reading. For that reason *Manchild in the Promised Land* belongs in the classroom where a wiser head can lead young minds to see all of the implications of Brown's youth for young blacks and for themselves in a pluralistic culture.

WORKS CITED

Brown, Claude. *Manchild in the Promised Land*. New York: Macmillan Publishers, 1965.

Miller, Warren. "One Score in Harlem." Rev. of *Manchild in the Promised Land*, by Claude Brown. *Saturday Review* 48 (Aug. 28, 1965): 49.

REFLECTIONS ON "THE SHYLOCK PROBLEM"

Gladys V. Veidemanis

"He's a Shylock," I would hear now and then when I was a child, but didn't realize the implications of the charge until I was much older. Like such words as "Judas," "Jezebel," "McCarthy," "Quisling," and "Benedict Arnold," "Shylock" is today a commonplace pejorative term, and, sad to say, equated with "Jew." Who's to blame? For many parents and teachers the culprit is Shakespeare and the source of poison *The Merchant of Venice*.

When I was a student at the University of Wisconsin in the early '50s taking Shakespeare for English majors, my textbook was *The Art and Life of William Shakespeare* by Hazelton Spencer, who, in his discussion of *The Merchant of Venice*, baldly asserts: "The bond story has an anti-Semitic edge, and in recent years many secondary schools have wisely removed the play from the curriculum..." (239). He goes on to say: "I do not see how a Jew can read *The Merchant of Venice* without pain and indignation. It is a tribute to the comprehensiveness of a great race that some of Shakespeare's warmest admirers and most learned students have been Jews" (240).

Spencer has not been alone in applauding the suppression of the play because of its alleged anti-Semitic overtones. In 1911, for example, a citizens' committee in Meriden, Connecticut, won its fight to "'eliminate the study of Shakespeare's *Merchant of Venice* from the curricula of Meriden schools,'" claiming that "the play and its chief character—the Jewish usurer Shylock—fanned hatred against the Jewish people" (Nelson and Roberts 4). In the case of *Rosenberg v. Board of Education of City of New York*, petitioners sought an order directing the removal of *The Merchant of Venice* as well as *Oliver Twist* from New York public schools "because they tend to engender hatred of the Jew as a person and as a race." Whereas *Merchant* was once the most commonly taught "first" Shakespearean play (generally in Grade 9), in recent years it has been supplanted by *Romeo and Juliet* and largely eliminated from the secondary curriculum. Many theatre companies have also chosen to abstain from mounting productions of the play for fear of boycott or hostile reviews.

Recently I attempted to engage my Jewish friend Adele, an English curriculum coordinator, in a discussion of the suitability of *The Merchant of Venice* in the high school curriculum. Pained and obviously embarrassed, she conceded that, as much as she abhors censorship, she prefers that *Merchant* be sidelined because, in her belief, even with the best of teaching, immature students are not likely to see past the negative Jewish stereotype and prejudices the play can imprint. Friends Bert and Susan, also Jewish, reacted far more casually when I asked their opinion, recalling that both had studied the play as high school freshmen and found the character of Shylock intriguing. Bert further added, "If there are problems, let them be debated and discussed."

I'm with Bert, though I also understand where my friend Adele is coming from. Unquestionably Jews take a verbal beating in the play, one that has special reverberations in the second half of this century. In the trial scene alone, twenty-two times Shylock is referred to as "the Jew," only six times by his proper name. He is castigated for his "hard...Jewish heart," repeatedly mocked and taunted by Gratiano and his friends, and finally compelled to undergo a forced conversion to Christianity—surely the most offensive incident of the play for modern audiences. And immediately after the "Jewish dog" has been "unfanged," the scene abruptly shifts to happy lovers idyllically reveling in the moonlight at Belmont, one of them Jessica, the "dog's" unrepentant renegade daughter.

Interestingly enough, as John Barton points out in his discussion of Shylock in *Playing Shakespeare*, "...in Israel they don't seem to have many scruples about the supposed anti-Semitism. There have been quite a number of productions of the play there since the war" (170). But the fact remains that many Americans continue to feel very strongly about the anti-Semitic question, and teachers introducing the play into the curriculum need to be sensitive to their concerns and prepared to deal with them.

Apart from "the Shylock Problem," as a work of proven dramatic, literary, and ethical merit *The Merchant of Venice* needs no defense.

Though really too difficult and subtle for most high school freshmen, for older students the play can be dramatically riveting and socially relevant with its three intertwined plots, a suspenseful trial scene, and rich infusions of humor and romance. Characters are complex and multi-faceted: What is the true source of Antonio's melancholy? Is Jessica "wise, fair, and true," as Lorenzo portrays her, or, as Morris Carnovsky proclaimed, "an apostate, really a little bitch, who willingly changes her religion to have a good time" (cited in Barber 8)? Is Bassanio a profligate fortune-hunter or the shining knight Portia and Nerissa perceive him to be? And what about Portia, the seemingly angelic heroine of the play, who dismisses the luckless Morocco from her thoughts with a racist remark: "A gentle riddance...Let all of his complexion choose me so"? Layered in irony and ambiguities, the play raises more questions than it resolves while also yielding a treasure trove of themes for class discussion and contemplation.

If "moral edification" is a desired curricular objective, *Merchant* delivers "in spades." As Sylvan Barnet writes, *Merchant* "...is largely about giving"—of material goods, friendship, love, oneself (3). Antonio stakes all his wealth, and, finally, his very being for his friend Bassanio, thereby exemplifying the most supreme form of Christian love—the readiness to lay down one's life for another. To win the hand of Portia, Bassanio picks the leaden casket, despite its ominous inscription—"Who chooseth me must give and hazard all he hath"; and, later, during Antonio's trial, tells his friend: "I would lose all, ay, sacrifice them all / Here to this devil, to deliver you." The play is additionally concerned with such lofty themes as mercy versus retribution, love as opposed to hate, spirituality in contrast to materialism, forgiveness in place of vindictiveness. Of special significance, *Merchant* is a landmark work in its advocacy of responsiveness to the "spirit" rather than the "letter" of the law in the administration of humane justice. Ironically, Shylock, the defender of the Old Law in all its rigid exactitude, is crushed by the same intractable standards he has sought to apply to Antonio, then reprieved, in part, by the New Law of mercy, charity, and love.

Given, then, that no one is likely to dispute the play's literary and aesthetic excellence, obviously the primary challenge for teachers and directors of *The Merchant of Venice* is resolution of "the Shylock Problem"—

that is, determination of a defensible interpretation of this character that is true to the text, informed by the criticism, and framed in the context of Elizabethan as well as contemporary times. Teachers need to be prepared to answer such questions by the would-be censors as: Is the play anti-Semitic? Are the characterization and treatment of Shylock likely to poison student attitudes towards Jews as a people? Is the portrayal of Shylock, as the Meriden citizens' committee charged, simply an offensive stereotype, a "grossly exaggerated caricature of anything human" (Nelson and Roberts, 4)? Did Shakespeare hate Jews?

A survey of the criticism and reviews of notable productions of the play—a necessary starting point for teachers and students of the play—illuminates three principal views of Shylock that merit careful consideration and debate:

(1) **Shylock as unadulterated villain.** In the words of E. F. C. Ludowyk, Shylock is "a detestable ogre," a "'dog,' wild beast and devil," evil incarnate in a Christian fable of good and evil (124-125). In the five scenes in which he appears, critics of this school of thought remind us, we learn that Shylock has starved his servant Launcelot so severely his ribs can be counted; has kept his daughter Jessica isolated and miserable (she tells Launcelot "Our house is hell"); and has personally become consumed by cupidity, hatred, and vindictiveness. Of Antonio he says, in a bitter aside:

I hate him for he is a Christian;
But more for that, in low simplicity,
He lends out money gratis and brings down
The rate of usance here with us in Venice.
If I can catch him once upon the hip,
I will feed fat the ancient grudge I bear him.

While initially he declines Bassanio's invitation to supper, declaring he will not go "to smell pork" of Christians, after the sealing of the bond he consents to "go in hate, to feed upon/The prodigal Christian," dialogue that supports the image of a "shark" poised to devour its victim. As many critics have pointed out, never in the play does Shylock express open affection for his daughter nor, after her departure, long for her recovery for any reason other than the reclamation of his lost jewels and ducats. For that matter, he callously tells his friend Tubal he would rather see her dead at his feet, "the jewels in her ear...and the ducats in the coffin." In the trial scene, driven by long-seething malice and an insatiable desire for revenge, Shylock refuses triple recompense in exchange for Antonio's life, declines to send for a physician ("Is it so nominated in the bond?"), and coldly resists Portia's eloquent appeal for mercy, all the while whetting his knife on the sole of his shoe in expectation of carving open Antonio's bared breast.

Like many other critics, Warren D. Smith, in his discussion of "Shakespeare's Shylock," locates the specific source of Shylock's villainy in his practice of usury ("...condemned by the Middle Ages and the Renaissance as both unnatural and irreligious. The Inquisition declared it to be a heresy") and as an "unbeliever," that is, in the eyes of Elizabethans, "the slayer of Jesus Christ" (194-195). Smith further charges that Shylock "attempts to excuse his own villainy by emphasizing what the Christians in the play do not emphasize, the fact that he is a Jew" (196). As have other critics, Smith refutes "The common assumption that Shakespeare's Shylock was created to compete with Marlowe's play, *The Jew of Malta,* in pandering to a wave of anti-Semitism greeting the arraignment and execution for treason in 1594 of Elizabeth's Jewish physician, Roderigo Lopez...," concluding that, "to the dramatist, surely, he was above all a hypocrite who concealed his innate evil behind the mask of a religion he himself did not believe in" (199). In the opinion of critics portraying Shylock as villain, the words of Lorenzo to Jessica in Act V—

> The man that hath no music in himself,
> Nor is not mov'd with concord of sweet sounds,
> Is fit for treasons, stratagems, and spoils—

are obviously intended to refer retrospectively to Shylock, who, as his parting commands to Jessica in Act II betray, has elected to bar all music, and thereby harmony, from his home and life.

(2) **Shylock as tragic victim**. "A terrible old man," in the words of

John Dover Wilson, but one who is the inevitable product of centuries of racial persecution" (114). Wilson concludes: "The dramatist seems to have excited our interest in and our sympathy for this Jew to such a degree that we find the levity after his exit intolerable and the happiness of the last Act heartless" (106). Harold Goddard, in *The Meaning of Shakespeare*, is especially impassioned in his defense of Shylock, stating:

> Though he was rendered coldhearted by his vocation, made cruel by the insults that had been heaped upon him by everybody from the respectable Antonio to the very children in the streets, driven to desperation by his daughter, there is nothing to indicate that Shylock was congenitally cold-hearted, cruel or desperate. On the contrary, it is clear that he had it in him, however deep down, to be humane, kindly, and patient, and his offer to Antonio of a loan without interest seems to have been a supreme effort of this submerged Shylock to come to the surface. (100)

For many modern readers the text seems to support not only a case for Shylock-as-victim, but also of Christians as hypocrites, bigots, and oppressors. Shylock tells us Antonio has "spat" upon him in public, and Antonio replies he would do so again on a person so unconscionably usurious. Indifferent to Portia's sermon on "the quality of mercy," Gratiano openly gloats over Shylock's downfall, sarcastically reiterating his demand that Shylock be given a "halter gratis" to use on himself or be brought to the gallows by the state. Sympathetic critics also make much of the scene in which Shylock, when told by Tubal that Jessica has given away one of his stolen jewels in exchange for a monkey, poignantly responds: "Out upon her! Thou torturest me, Tubal: it was my turquoise; I had it of Leah when I was a bachelor: I would not have given it for a wilderness of monkeys." Here is proof, they contend, of a Shylock once capable of love and sensitive feeling, hardened only by the abuse he has been made to endure. *The Merchant of Venice*, then, in the words of A. D. Moody, is an "ironic comedy," one that "does not celebrate the Christian virtues so much as expose their absence" (101).

(3) **Shylock as "flawed, contradictory, human"** (Barton 170). As John Barton states, Shakespeare

...shows us a bad Jew and some bad Christians and yet he doesn't directly articulate his view of these characters. He lets them betray themselves *by* their words and actions. That is Shakespeare's way. He rarely makes his characters all black any more than he makes them all white.... If we are to read Shakespeare truly, we must look for the deliberate ambiguities and inconsistencies that he delights in" (173).

Critics of Barton's persuasion argue that, through the genius of Shakespeare, Shylock transcends his stereotype—a villain, yes, but one who reminds us repeatedly of his humanity, wasted potential, and pitiable isolation. Even though he appears in only five scenes, his is clearly the stand-out role in the play, and, not surprisingly, as C. L. Barber notes, "...already in 1598 the comedy was entered in the stationer's register as 'a book of the Merchant of Venice, or otherwise called the Jew of Venice,'" indicative of the importance in the public mind the character of Shylock was assuming (12). Not surprising, too, is the practice of most contemporary directors to isolate a troubled and pensive Jessica on the stage at the conclusion of the play to convey a sense of inner disquietude not expressed in the text and to provide a telling visual reminder of Shylock's wounded humanity. John Dover Wilson states that the greatness of Shylock's character lies in the fact that "he is one of ourselves. And, as he goes out, what we ought to exclaim is not..'The man is wronged,' but 'There, but for the grace of God, go I...' "(108).

From a legal standpoint the case for Shylock in the classroom is solid. In denying the plaintiffs' bid to censor *The Merchant of Venice* and *Oliver Twist* in New York's public schools, the judge in the earlier cited *Rosenberg* case wisely stated:

Except where a book has been maliciously written for the apparent purpose of promoting and fomenting a bigoted and intolerant hatred against a particular racial or religious group, public interest in a free and democratic society does not warrant or encourage the suppression of any book at the whim of any unduly sensitive person or group of persons, merely because a character described in such book as belonging to a particular race or religion is portrayed in a derogatory or offensive manner. The necessity for the suppression of such a book must clearly depend upon the intent and motive which has actuated the author in making such a portrayal (346).

The decision goes on to assert: "Removal from schools of these books will contribute nothing toward the diminution of anti-religious feeling; as a matter of fact, removal may lead to misguided reading and unwarranted inferences by the unguided pupil" (346). Clearly, where there is a "Shylock Problem," the place to deal with it is precisely in the classrooms of our public schools.

In teaching *The Merchant of Venice* I would want students first to talk and write about their personal responses to and perceptions of Shylock, then explore and discuss the various schools of thought represented in the criticism and production reviews, perhaps through reading of selected essays. I would further want them to be informed about the harsh treatment of Jews in the Middle Ages and Elizabethan times, specifically the expulsion of Jews from England by Edward I in 1290, an edict not lifted until 1655 by Oliver Cromwell. In addition, I would want them to know Elizabethan attitudes towards usury, which, in part, explain Shakespeare's characterization of Shylock as a Jew. To provide a polar opposite to the noble Antonio he obviously needed an "outsider" as well as an object of hate, and, as W. D. Smith attests, "...the usurer was by definition a villain in the public mind and the term *Jew* was frequently made equivalent to *usurer*" (195).

Most important, I would remind students that *The Merchant of Venice* is not, as Sylvan Barnet reminds us, a "treatise on 'the Jewish problem'" since, "for the Elizabethans there was no 'Jewish problem,' no mass of unassimilated Jews" (1). It is, instead, a work portraying a multi-faceted character who happens to be a Jew and whose behavior and treatment have evoked passionately divergent response. The fact that critics, directors, and actors have brought such a wide range of interpretations to the role— e. g., Shylock as comic buffoon, sinister villain, tragic victim—gives proof that Shylock is no simple stereotypical character or "caricature" but, rather, a triumph of Shakespeare's creative genius.

Oft-quoted is the story told by the great German poet Heine, himself a Jew, of the time he saw *The Merchant of Venice* at Drury Lane and found behind him "a pale, fair Briton, who at the end of the Fourth Act, fell to weeping passionately, several times exclaiming, 'The poor man is wronged!'" Deeply affected, Heine wrote: "I have never been able to forget those large black eyes that wept for Shylock" (cited in Wilson 105). Nor should we. As this anecdote confirms, the miracle of *The Merchant of Venice* is that Shakespeare has given us a villain for whom one can weep.

WORKS CITED

Barber, C. L. "The Merchants and the Jew of Venice: Wealth's Communion and an Intruder." In *Twentieth Century Interpretations of The Merchant of Venice*. Ed. Sylvan Barnet. Englewood Cliffs, NJ: Prentice-Hall, Inc., 1970. 11-32.

Barnet, Sylvan. "Introduction" to *Twentieth Century Interpretations of The Merchant of Venice*. Englewood Cliffs, NJ: Prentice-Hall, Inc., 1970. 1-10.

Barton, John. *Playing Shakespeare*. London: Methuen Paperback, 1984.

Goddard, Harold. *The Meaning of Shakespeare*. Chicago: University of Chicago Press, 1951.

Ludowyk, E. F. C. *Understanding Shakespeare*. Cambridge University Press: 1962. 118-144.

Moody, A. D. "An Ironic Comedy." In *Twentieth Century Interpretations of The Merchant of Venice*. Ed. by Sylvan Barnet. Englewood Cliffs, NJ: Prentice-Hall, Inc., 1970. 100-107.

Nelson, Jack and Gene Roberts, Jr. *The Censors and the Schools*. Boston: Little, Brown and Company, 1963.

Rosenberg v. New York City, 92 N.Y.S. 2d 344, 345 (Sup. Ct. Kings Co. 1949).

Smith, Warren D. "Shakespeare's Shylock." *Shakespeare Quarterly* 15.3 (Summer 1964): 193-199.

Spencer, Hazelton. *The Art and Life of William Shakespeare*. New York: Harcourt, Brace and Company, 1940.

Wilson, John Dover. *"The Merchant of Venice* in 1937." In *Shakespeare's Happy Comedies*. Evanston: Northwestern University Press, 1962: 94-119.

SUPPORTING TRADITIONAL VALUES: *MY DARLING, MY HAMBURGER*

Lee Burress

My Darling, My Hamburger went through twenty-one printings between 1969 and 1977, the date of the edition used for this review. It is pleasing that a book which so gracefully illustrates the traditional values of our society should be so popular among young people. This book makes clear that wise family support is all important if young people are to have a good life, and that wealthy family life is not necessarily advantageous. It emphasizes that outer beauty is not nearly so important as inner good sense. It makes clear the judgment of the writer that sex before marriage is likely to lead to great trouble. The book also raises the issue of abortion; different readers will draw different conclusions from the discussion of abortion in this book.

The book illustrates a number of traditional, moral values by the author's use of various characters and events. The main characters include four young people whose families in various ways demonstrate how important good family life is. Maggie illustrates several of the major themes. Her family is a wisely loving family though not greatly affluent. Her mother makes clear that cosmetic attractiveness is unimportant for genuine love by saying that her bald-headed husband is no fashion plate, but he loves her. That is why she will do such dirty jobs as cleaning the kitchen oven. Maggie herself has plain brown hair and doesn't have the most fashionable clothing. But Maggie sails through the last year of high school successfully in spite of her inner qualms. She resists the sexual pressures of boys; she realizes how much her mother loves her, that baggy green sweaters tell nothing about the wearer. In short, she achieves a high degree of maturity and serves as an attractive role model to the many readers of this book.

Liz, who is the most beautiful girl in the class, a blond with beautiful hair and good clothing, comes from a family that does not offer her wisely supporting love. Her stepfather probably does not love her at all. Her mother loves her, but not wisely. Liz goes with the most attractive young man in the class, who comes from a wealthy family, but who in the end lets her down terribly.

Liz's boyfriend Sean makes her pregnant. He promises to marry her but then gives her money for an abortion. But he believes that abortion is wrong and writes a theme in an English class in which it is made clear that abortion is murder and that he has participated in murdering a baby.

Liz believed that her only realistic choice was an abortion. She used the money that Sean gave her for an illegal abortion. (Roe v Wade was decided by the Supreme Court in 1973). The result of an illegal abortion was very unpleasant for Liz; she hemorrhaged badly. She had to drop out of school and didn't graduate with her class.

The book shows how important is the role that Sean's father plays in Sean's cruel treatment of Liz. He attempts to talk to his father about Liz being pregnant. His father suggests an abortion, thinking that Sean is asking for another boy, a friend.

Sean says, "Suppose he loves her?" His father replies that marriage for a high school graduate would cancel any chance for college and success in life. He says, "Christ, if it was you and...that little blond you are running around with, I would slap you right across the face...tell your friend to give that girl of his a kick in the behind and get it over with. A man's got to protect himself (124)." It would be difficult to imagine a stronger protest against the mistreatment of women.

Sean's father then says to him, "Why doesn't he ask his own father?" Ironically, Sean replied, "He can't talk to him" (125).

Maggie has the last word about Sean. During the graduation ceremony she sees Sean: "He'd have his punishment, she thought. For the rest of his life he'd remember Liz. He could go on to college and date dozens of other girls. He could get married and have children--but from time to time he'd remember. Just before going to sleep, perhaps, in a dream. He'd have to remember Liz and something he couldn't be very proud of. The past wasn't that easy to get away from" (165).

Dennis, who dates Maggie, also has a father to whom he cannot talk. Dennis' father is more concerned about carrying out the garbage and protecting the lawn than the inner life of his son.

The wisdom with which Maggie's mother talked to Maggie is in sharp contrast to the other parents and teachers in the book. The title refers to the useless advice a teacher gives in a class when a girl asks her how to "stop a guy on the make." The reply: "Suggest going to get a hamburger" (6).

Thus by contrasting the two girls and their families, the author of this book has written a morality lesson for our time, showing that family life is all important for supporting young people in their transition from childhood to adulthood. The book also contradicts the notion so prevalent in our culture that outer beauty or appearance is all important and that wealthy families are advantageous for young people. The book is powerfully supportive to girls in urging them to resist the sexual pressures that are so vigorous in our society by making clear how tragic is the situation of the teenage pregnant girl.

The book has no explicit sex scenes; it has no four-letter words. The most suggestive scene (in which a boy attempts to open the back of a girl's dress) ends with the girl pressing a thumb tack into the boy's neck, a new weapon for self-defense for girls.

A library that removed this book would, if consistent, have to remove hundreds of other books that have the same traditional themes and realistic manner of presentation.

WORK CITED

Zindel, Paul. *My Darling, My Hamburger*. New York: Harper & Row, Publishers, 1977.

WHY *NINETEEN EIGHTY-FOUR* SHOULD BE READ AND TAUGHT

James E. Davis

George Orwell's *Nineteen Eighty-four* has been challenged on such grounds as profanity, immorality, and obscenity. It has been charged with being Communistic, containing sex references, and being depressing. Some of these charges are absurd, and though some have a grain of truth when items are taken out of context, on the whole the book stands up well and though frequently challenged has a history of rarely being removed from classrooms and libraries. Critics, as well as readers in general, have recognized the book as significant and valuable since its appearance at the end of the 1940s. Some examples: On the dust jacket of the first American edition of *Nineteen Eighty-four* Bertrand Russell and Alfred Kazin are quoted. Russell states, "*Nineteen Eighty-four* depicts...the horrors of a well-established totalitarian regime of whatever type...with great power and skill and force of imagination." He adds that it is important that we should be aware of these dangers. Alfred Kazin characterizes the book as "an extraordinary experience...overwhelming in its keenness and prophetic power." He further comments: "I hardly know which to praise more— Orwell's insight into the fate of man under totalitarianism, or his compassion for him." Reasons for reading and teaching *Nineteen Eighty-four* continue today to be much the same as these critics gave four decades ago.

The book does express a mood of near but not complete despair. The mood is despair only if readers do not heed the warning of what will happen if we continue on some of our present courses. But we do not have to become soulless automatons. It is not foreordained. The scenario of *Nineteen Eighty-four* is that atomic wars had started in the 1940s, accelerated ten years later in Russia, Western Europe, and North America. This atomic war led the governments (Eurasia, Oceania, and Eastasia) to conclude that unless atomic wars stopped, organized society would be doomed. Of course, this would also mean the end of governmental power. Thus atomic war stopped, but bombs continued to be stockpiled awaiting the right time to kill a large segment of the world's population without warning in a few seconds. Orwell portrays this continued military preparedness as essential also for the continuation of the economic system and shows the consequences of a society in a constant state of war readiness, always afraid of being attacked.

As Erich Fromm says in the Afterword to the 1961 New American Library paperback, "Orwell's picture is so pertinent because it offers a telling argument against the popular idea that we can save freedom and democracy by continuing the arms race and finding a 'stable' deterrent" (262). With technical progress geometrically progressing, the caves will never be deep enough to protect us.

The novel begins on a bright cold day in April, "and the clocks were striking thirteen." From there on a world is presented that is permeated by fear and hate with such slogans as HATE WEEK, WAR IS PEACE, FREEDOM IS SLAVERY, IGNORANCE IS STRENGTH. The society has nothing like our first amendment. Everything is censored by the MINISTRY OF TRUTH. It is even a crime to keep a diary and Winston Smith's life is endangered by doing so. Ironically Winston is employed by the MINISTRY OF TRUTH, and his job is to constantly rewrite history. Government predictions which do not come true (and they never do) are made to disappear. And, of course, people have to be made to disappear too (to become nonpersons) if they commit THOUGHT CRIME, which the THOUGHT POLICE are to control. BIG BROTHER affirms that: "Who controls the past controls the future: Who controls the present controls the past." The following extended quotation from the book demonstrates in some detail how this control of the past was accomplished:

As soon as all the corrections which happened to be necessary in any particular number of the *Times* had been assembled and collated, that number would be reprinted, the original copy destroyed, and the corrected copy placed in the files in its stead. This process of continuous alteration was applied not only to newspapers, but to books, periodicals, pamphlets, posters, leaflets, films, sound tracks, cartoons, photographs—to every kind of literature or documentation which might conceivably hold any political or ideological significance. Day by day and almost minute by minute the past was brought up to date. In this way every prediction made by the Party could be shown by documentary evidence to have been correct; nor was any item of news, or any expression of opinion, which conflicted with the needs of the moment, ever allowed to remain on record. All history was a palimpsest, scraped clean and reinscribed exactly as often as was necessary. In no case would it have been possible, once the deed was done, to prove that any falsification had taken place. The largest section of the Records Department, far larger than the one in which Winston worked, consisted simply of persons whose duty it was to track down and collect all copies of books, newspapers, and other documents which had been superseded and were due for destruction. (36-37)

A few cubicles away from Winston is Ampleforth, who juggles rhymes and meters, producing garbled versions of poems which have become ideologically offensive but for one reason or another are to be retained in anthologies. There is also a whole army of reference clerks who spend all of their time preparing lists of books and magazines to be recalled. There are also huge warehouses where corrected documents are stored and furnaces where original copies are burned.

By controlling all information BIG BROTHER controls responses of citizens, primarily through the giant two-way TV screens in every living space. These permit THOUGHT POLICE to observe all citizens to see that they are responding in a desirable manner—hating enemies and loving BIG BROTHER. Reality control, DOUBLETHINK in NEWSPEAK, means an "unending series of victories over our memory."

In *Nineteen Eighty-four* orthodoxy means not thinking or even needing to think. It is unconsciousness. Orthodoxy is to close the book. One of the U.S. Supreme Court justices in the Island Trees case talks about censorship resulting in a "pall of orthodoxy." One of the functions of literature in a free society is to help protect us from this "pall of orthodoxy." This book is one of the best examples of a work of considerable literary merit worth reading and studying in the classroom as part of a protection program against the orthodoxy pall. It is also a very interesting study of the effects of an orthodoxy that finally convinces Winston Smith, a party member who opposes the system, that four is five. It takes brain-washing and torture by the MINISTRY OF LOVE to accomplish this convincing. Winston's final orthodoxy is: "Whatever the Party holds to be true is truth. It is impossible to see reality except by looking through the eyes of the Party" (205).

In answer to the question of why this particular novel to study the relationship between totalitarianism, technology, psychology, and language instead of a social studies, science, or language text, Roy Orgren, writing in the Fall 1983 *Connecticut English Journal,* says:

> Simply because, set forth in a work of fiction, the ideas are more accessible, more interrelated, and more engaging; the sheer horror of totalitarianism is more real. We flinch when the truncheon-wielding guards in the MINISTRY OF LOVE crack Winston's fingers and shatter his elbow; we writhe in our armchairs as O'Brien virtually disembodies Winston with electric shocks; we shudder as moist pads are applied to Winston's temples; and we, like Winston, are dazed by the "devastating explosion," "the blinding flash of light" which so numbs his mind that he consents to seeing—no, actually sees—five fingers when only four are held to him. (41)

We are jolted out of our complacency so that it is likely that we will never slacken our vigil against oppression and human rights violations.

Orwell, with his presiding interest in language, shows how BIG BROTHER manipulates society and controls reality by corrupting language. NEWSPEAK is calculated to get rid of individuality by limiting the range of thought through cutting the choice of words to a minimum. As Syme, the NEWSPEAK expert, says, "You think, I dare say, that our chief job is inventing new words. But not a bit of it! We're destroying words—scores of them, hundreds of them, every day. We're cutting the language down to the bone. The Eleventh Edition won't contain a single word that will become obsolete before the year 2050" (45).

Studying the effects of NEWSPEAK can only help us in cherishing our language with all of its rich diversity and ambiguities. Valuable, exciting classroom discussion and writing projects can grow from this, and surely the lesson of the importance of using language that is not vague and misleading but clear and precise can be learned.

Another major emphasis of the novel is the use of technology combined with advertising techniques (especially by the government) that are deeply psychological to eliminate individuality and privacy. Many of the same techniques used in *Nineteen Eighty-four* are in use today in our world, and many of them have become much more sophisticated. We surely have full-wall TV screens and the two-way television. Closed circuit security systems are not just for banks anymore. In fact, they are practically everywhere. Heartbeat, respiration, surface tension of the skin, stiffness of hair, and temperatures can be measured remotely by voltage sensors and ultrasensitive microphones. Our government puts out a glut of newspeak. It is significant that National Council of Teachers of English Doublespeak Award has twice been awarded to Ronald Reagan. The number of records, many kept without our knowledge, on each of us stored in computers, retrievable in seconds by almost any person or organization with the knowhow, is frightening. Behavior modification and drug therapy are widely used. Studying about these technologies and techniques, discussing them, exposing them, can make students aware in a way that may serve to make them less vulnerable to these techniques.

Perhaps the most interesting and discussable feature of Orwell's novel is its description of the nature of truth. Is there an objective truth, or is "reality" not external? Does it exist only subjectively and internally? Is it reality that what the Party holds to be truth *is* truth? The Party believes that truth is only in the mind and that by controlling the mind truth is controlled. Controlling minds and truth is ultimate power. Truth is subordinated to the Party. As Erich Fromm says, "It is one of the most characteristic and destructive developments of our own society that man, becoming more and more of an instrument, transforms reality more and more into something relative to his own interests and functions. Truth is proven by the consensus of millions; to the slogan 'how can millions be wrong' is added 'and how can a minority of one be right'" (Afterword 264). The "one" must be insane. The "consensus truth" concept can serve as the basis for much valuable discussion about many things such as individuality, minority rights, majority rule, and, of course, values.

It is hard to imagine a modern novel that has more reasons to be read and taught. In addition to its literary merit, it has special implications for our times and the society toward which we may be heading. Its depiction of a well-established totalitarian regime, a nuclear stand-off with a world in constant fear, total censorship, NEWSPEAK, DOUBLETHINK, orthodoxy, and consensus truth offer almost sure-fire topics for discussion and writing in classes—discussions that can serve to foster sincere thinking and maturity. Yes, the book is depressing, but readers can react to that by trying to do positive things to influence the future rather than becoming more depressed and pessimistic. *Nineteen Eighty-four* teaches us, as Erich Fromm says at the end of his essay, "the danger with which all men are confronted today, the danger of a society of automatons who will have lost every trace of individuality, of love, of critical thought, and yet who will not be aware of it because of 'doublethink'. Books like Orwell's are powerful warnings" (267).

Critical language involving reading, thought, and discussion of books like *Nineteen Eighty-four* may help us to avoid Winston's fate of total loss of self, of humanity, as presented in the last paragraph of the novel:

> He gazed up at the enormous face. Forty years it had taken him to learn what kind of smile was hidden beneath the dark mustache. O cruel, needless misunderstanding! O stubborn, self-willed exile from the loving breast! Two gin-scented tears trickled down the sides of his nose. But it was all right, everything was all right, the struggle was finished. He had won the victory over himself. He loved Big Brother. (300)

WORKS CITED

Orgren, Roy. "Nineteen Eighty-four by George Orwell." *Connecticut English Journal* 15 (Fall 1983): 41-44.

Orwell, George. *Nineteen Eighty-four*. New York: New American Library, 1961.

A TEACHABLE GOOD BOOK:
OF MICE AND MEN

Thomas Scarseth

There is one good reason for reading John Steinbeck's short novel *Of Mice and Men*—it is a very good book.

There is one good reason for teaching it—it is a teachable good book: simple and clear, yet profound and beautiful.

Of Mice and Men is a book to use to show beginning readers the paths to greater books which might at first be too difficult for them. This short book is easy—in the accessible sense. But it is not "easy" in the moral sense: it raises large issues of the sort raised in and by the greatest and often more difficult literature.

For *Of Mice and Men* is a Tragedy, a tragedy not in the narrow modern sense of a mere 'sad story' (though it certainly is that), but a tragedy in the classic Aristotelian/Shakespearean sense of showing humanity's achievement of greatness through and in spite of defeat.

Some people seem to believe that the function of literature is to provide vicarious "happy endings," to provide in words a sugary sweetness we would like to have but cannot always get in real life. To such people, true literary tragedy is distasteful. But the greatest writers and the best readers know that literature is not always only mere sugar candy; it can sometimes be a strong medicine: sour perhaps—at least to the untrained taste—but necessary for continued health:

> And Take it; if the smack is sour,
> The better for the embittered hour.
> (A. E. Housman)

Some readers may object to the book's presentation of low class characters, vulgar language, scenes suggestive of improper sexual conduct, and an implied criticism of the social system. But none of this is presented indecently, or beyond the ordinary norms of contemporary literature. Compared to many modern works, (or to movies and TV) this book is tame indeed. Furthermore, these features are necessary in this book in two ways.

First, they are part of the accurate precise reporting of the reality of a particular time and place and environment. Part of Steinbeck's literary point is that this is *true to life*. As such, the dirty details are part of Steinbeck's enlargement of the realm of Tragedy, the democratization of the tragic world. Traditionally, the subjects of Tragedies have been Kings and other Great Ones: Job, Oedipus, Lear. But Steinbeck's point—a truly American point—is that all men are created equal: Tragedy exists even among the lowly of the earth; even the least of us—even a Lennie or a George—has the human potential for tragic nobility. *Of Mice and Men* is a tragedy in the modern tradition of *The Hairy Ape* and *Death of a Salesman*.

Second, the grossness is a way of presenting briefly the complex turmoil of life. This book is not stereotype melodrama. It is not a simple-minded book. There are no purely bad people in it. Conversely, there are no purely good people in it either. All the characters are complex mixtures of good and bad, or rather of bad results from good intentions. They are all—in their ability and in their outlook—limited. And they live in a gross and dirty world. Given their position in that world, they are not able to achieve much. But they are trying to do the best they can; they are trying to be good people and to have good lives. They have good intentions. They have noble aims.

The tragedy is that, limited as the characters are, the world they live in is even *more* limited; it is a world in which the simplest dream of the simplest man—poor dumb big Lennie—cannot come true. "The best laid plans of mice and men gang oft a-glae [go oft a-stray]," wrote Robert Burns in the poem which provides the book's title and its theme. And Steinbeck's story shows why: The best laid plans go oft astray because they come in conflict with one another. The simplest good intention—simply to stay alive—of a simple mouse, a simple pup, a simple young woman, is thwarted by Lennie's urge to pet something soft and beautiful.

Lennie's drive to touch beauty kills the things he loves.

But his problem is the same problem that bothers Curley, the Boss's son, the closest thing to a villain in the book. Like Lennie, Curley doesn't know how to hold on to what he finds important: his young wife, his status as the Boss's son, his reputation as a man. He loses each by trying to hold on too tightly. Curley's aim to be a respected husband/boss/man is foiled by his own limited abilities.

The similar but simpler aim of Lennie and George to have a small place of their own where they can "live offa the fatta the lan'" is doomed to frustration also by their own limitations and the tragic chain of circumstance and coincidence that ends with Lennie dead by George's hand.

The point, of course, is that they all—*we* all—live in a too limited world, a world in which not all our dreams can come true, a world in which we—all of us some of the time and some of us all the time—are doomed to disappointment. The tragic dilemma is that for our basic humanity, for the goodness of our aims, we all deserve better than we get. But because of our human limitations, by our weaknesses of character, none of us is ever good enough to *earn* what we deserve. Some philosophers, seeing this dilemma, pronounce profound pessimism for humanity. Some religions promise for this world's disappointments supernatural intercession and other-worldly compensations. The tragic viewpoint (the view of Shakespeare, the Greek tragedians, the Old Testament Job, and John Steinbeck) finds in it the chance for nobility of soul: even in the blackest of disappointments, a human can achieve individual greatness. One may be defeated physically—but one need not be crushed spiritually. One can remain true to one's dream and true to one's friend. We humans may die, but we can love one another.

Friendship. Love. That too is what *Of Mice and Men* is all about. Lennie and George, disparate types, are, against all good reason, friends. They share a good dream. They love one another. They are too limited, too inarticulate, to know how to say it, but they do show it—or rather Steinbeck shows it to us readers.

So the book treats the great themes of Dreams and Death and Love with simple powerful clarity. It does so with a classically elegant structure—

another reason for using the book as a teaching tool: it allows a reader—especially an untrained or beginning reader of literature—to see (or be shown) how structure supports and presents content. *Of Mice and Men* has the classic situation/complication/ twist/and/resolution plot structure uncluttered by diversions, distractions, or subplots. There is an inevitableness, a starkness that makes the point of the story unavoidable.

The story has the classic unities of time and place and action. It begins in a small spot of beautiful nature, a secluded camp in the woods by a stream; it moves to the buildings of a California ranch, and ends back in the woods by the stream.

The style is simple: clear, direct sentences of description and action, direct quotation of the speech of simple people. Few long words, no hard words.

The action is simple: two poor and vagrant workers, big, dumb Lennie and small, clever George, take jobs at a large ranch. Lennie has trouble with the Boss's son, Curley. Lennie accidentally—more or less—kills Curley's wife. George kills Lennie to save him from the horrors of a lynch mob led by Curley, bent on revenge.

The settings are simple in detail, and simply powerfully symbolic. The secluded spot in the woods by the stream is the uncomplicated world of Nature; the bunkhouse is the bleak home of hired working men trying to make sense of their lives and gain comfort in a limited environment; the barn is the place of working life, of seed and harvest, birth and death; the harness room with Crook's bunk symbolizes social constraints; the "little place of our own" about which George and Lennie dream and all too vaguely plan is the Paradise on earth we all hope for.

The characters, too, are simple yet significant. "Begin with an individual, and before you know it you find you have created a type," wrote F. Scott Fitzgerald; "begin with a type, and you find that you have created—nothing." Steinbeck begins with individuals: clearly and sharply crafted characters, a whole set of individuals who are so clearly realized that *each*—without surrendering individuality—becomes a *type*, an archetype, a universal character: There is Candy, the old, one-armed worker with no place to go, as useless as his toothless dog; there is Carlson, gruffly and deliberately "unfeeling," who can coolly kill old Candy's ancient dog simply because "he stinks" and "he ain't no good to you"; and there is Crooks, the dignified "proud and aloof" but helpless and lonely victim of racial discrimination. There is Slim, calm, reasonable, compassionate, the real leader of men. And there is Curley, the arrogant but inept Boss's son. The man who could lead well does not have the position; the one who has the position and the authority is not a true leader.

Curley hides his insecurities behind a mask of macho toughness. His competitive bravado makes him push too far and Lennie, after enduring much, is given permission by George to "get him." Lennie in self-protection crushes Curley's fist in his own big hand, crippling Curley somewhat as Candy and Crooks have been crippled by the punitive harshness of life.

Curley is also the one man who has a woman. But clearly he does not—does not know how to—relate to her as a person. She is to him a thing, a possession, a sex-object and a status symbol. For the men, in braggadocio, he flaunts the sexuality of the relationship; and yet, out of his own self-doubts he is intensely jealous of the men's awareness of her.

The young woman has no name—she is merely "Curley's wife." She knows she wants—and somehow deserves-something better than this. "I don't *like* Curley" (97), she says of her husband. She has grandiose ambitions of being a Hollywood star "in the pitchers." She is a lost little girl in a world of men whose knowledge of women is largely limited to memories of kind old ladies and rumors of casual prostitution. All these men are afraid of Curley's wife, afraid and aware that her innocent animal appeal may lead them into temptation and trouble. In self-protection they avoid her. Only Lennie, in naive goodness, actually relates to her as a person to a person. She talks to him. For a little time they share in their aesthetic sense; they both admire beauty. Unfortunately, she is too naive, and Lennie is too strong and clumsy. In trying—at her invitation—to pet her lovely hair he is panicked by her quick resistance, and ends by killing her. Just as he had earlier killed a puppy and a mouse. Curley's wife, a naive Romantic, wants love and tenderness in a harsh crude Naturalistic world; Lennie, big and ignorant, tries to give love. But he is too weak in the mind, too strong in the body. His tenderness is too powerful for weaker, unsuspecting creatures .

We readers can identify with Lennie. We sympathize; we empathize. We care. We have—most of us—been in his position; not quite able to cope with the complexities of the world around us, wanting only security, peace, comfort, and something soft and beautiful to pet and love.

Perhaps one reason that this book has evoked controversy and censorious action is that it is so simple and clear and easy to understand— and so painful! It *hurts* to read this book. And some people don't like their books to hurt them; they want soothing. But great Tragedy is *meant* to hurt. One needn't subscribe wholly to the Aristotelian doctrine of 'catharsis' by Art to see that one function of literature is to help us deal with the pain of real life by practicing with the vicarious pains of tragic art.

Of course *Of Mice and Men* contains unpleasant attitudes; there is brutality, racism, sexism, economic exploitation. But the book does not advocate them; rather it shows that these too-narrow conceptions of human life are part of the cause of human tragedy. They are forces which frustrate human aspiration.

Lennie and George have a noble dream. They are personally too limited to make it come true, but they do try. They try to help each other, and they even enlarge their dream to include old one-handed Candy and crippled black Crooks. Theirs is the American Dream: that there is somehow, somewhere, sometime, the possibility that we can make our Paradise on earth, that we can have our own self-sufficient little place where we can live off the fat of the land as peaceful friends.

What is sad, what is tragic, what is horrible, is that the Dream may not come true because we are—each and all of us—too limited, too selfish, too much in conflict with one another. "Maybe ever'body in the whole damn world is scared of each other," says Slim (38). And George expresses the effects of loneliness, "Guys that go around...alone...don't have no fun. After a long time they get mean. They get wantin' to fight all the time" (45).

What is *ennobling* in this tragedy of mice and men is the Revelation of a way beyond that loneliness and meanness and fighting, a way to rise above our human limitations: Two men—Lennie and George—who have nothing else, do have each other. "We kinda look after each other." says George. And they do have their Dream. And the Dream is there even in the final defeat. For in the end the one thing George can do for Lennie is to make sure he's happy as he dies. He has Lennie "look acrost the river...you can almost see [the place]" (115). And as Lennie says, "Let's get that place now" (117), George kills him mercifully. It's a horrible thing to do, and George knows that. And *we* know that. But in this limited world in this limited way it is all that George can do for his friend. And he does it. That is the horror and the nobility which together make up Tragedy. The Tragic pattern closes. There is a sense of completeness, of both defeat and satisfaction.

In *Of Mice and Men*, Steinbeck has shown us something about the pain of living in a complex human world and created something beautiful from it. In true great literature the pain of Life is transmuted into the beauty of Art. The book is worth reading for a glimpse of that beauty—and worth teaching as a way to show others how such beauty works.

WORKS CITED

Houseman, A. E. "Terence, This Is Stupid Stuff." In *A Pocket Book of Modern Verse* (Revised). Ed. Oscar Williams. New York: Washington Square Press, 1954.

Steinbeck, John. *Of Mice and Men.* New York: Bantam, 1954.

ONE DAY IN THE LIFE OF IVAN DENISOVICH
BY ALEKSANDR SOLZHENITSYN
Frederik Pohl

One Day in the Life of Ivan Denisovich is the first and most famous novel written by Aleksandr Solzhenitsyn, who is not only a Nobel laureate but very possibly—there are no more than a handful who could challenge him—the 20th Century's greatest and most courageous writer.

It is the business of literature to tell us truths about ourselves and the world we live in, and in that way to give us understanding about what life is really like. This is an accomplishment of great value, because without it we can never really mature as human beings.

That is what *Ivan Denisovich* does for us. It tells us the story of one man—a single human being, whose story nevertheless is the story of many millions of other human beings—who has committed no fault, but through the evil caprice of a tyrant has been condemned to the terrible ordeal of life in a Soviet prison camp. Ivan Denisovich Shukhov has been stripped of everything. He has lost his wife, his children and his freedom. He owns nothing but the ragged clothes he wears and the crust of bread he has hidden in his mattress, and he is condemned to labor long hours in the deadly cold of a Russian winter, at the mercy of sadistic guards and "trusties" among his fellow prisoners...and yet he still remains human, and even decent. The novel is not a cheerful story, because the truth is not always cheerful. But it is a noble one.

And yet *One Day in the Life of Ivan Denisovich* has an unexpected distinction, for it is also one of the thirty-three books that those who would sanitize America's school libraries are most avid to suppress.

To learn that fact is to look into the naked face of madness.

What can the censors be thinking of? What child could be harmed, in what improbable way, by reading this splendid novel? Is it, for example, obscene?

But of course it is not; there is not a salacious passage, or even the hint of one, anywhere in the book. It does, to be sure, contain a few individual words—I have been able to count less than a dozen of them in the whole novel—which most of us would prefer not to hear from the lips of our children. Most of us also realize, though, however much we may regret it, that none of our children will grow up without having encountered those words many times, in many places, perhaps even starting with the casual conversation of their littlest schoolmates. I do not believe that there is even one child, anywhere in the world, who will have learned any of those words through the reading of Solzhenitsyn's novel—but what a child may well learn from this book is the extent to which even decent people may be driven to crudeness in both speech and actions when they are being systematically dehumanized by brutes, and that is a lesson well worth having.

There are those, too, who do not wish to "spoil childhood" by acquainting the young with the more distasteful facts of human life. That's understandable. We would like to see our children happy and untroubled, because we love them. But children must grow, and to grow they must learn the bad things as well as the good: If we don't allow that, if in some unimaginable way we were possibly able to *prevent* that, all we could achieve would be to keep them childish forever. It is, I think, far better for children to learn what evil is from books than to put them in the position of learning it in some far more damaging way from real life later on.

When Solzhenitsyn wrote *One Day in the Life of Ivan Denisovich* the very process of writing it was an act of conscience. His reason for writing the novel was simply that he could not live with himself if he didn't. Solzhenitsyn could not have seen any real possibility of getting the book published before the world, so that others could know the truth he had to tell; books containing far less hurtful truths had been suppressed in his country for forty years. More than that, he certainly knew that the mere act of writing it, if discovered, would mean his immediate arrest. That would at least send him back to those same degrading prison camps, if indeed it didn't cost him his life.

That *Ivan Denisovich* was published at all was almost an accident. It happened because Nikita Khrushchev, then the ruler of the Soviet Union, had his own political reasons for wanting at least some of the truths about the Stalin regime made public at last. It took courage for Solzhenitsyn to write it. It took courage for his first editor, Alexander Tvardovsky, to attempt to get it past the censors so that he could publish it in his magazine. It even took courage for Nikita Khrushchev to order that it be permitted, since Khrushchev himself had been a part of Stalin's bureaucracy and thus was not without guilt of his own for some of its evils.

It does not take nearly as much courage for any of us to allow the book to be read by our children—and I hope that we will find at least that much courage, all over this country of ours that has made dedication to freedom of speech and writing a part of its most sacred and fundamental law.

MOBY DICK VS. BIG NURSE: A FEMINIST DEFENSE OF A MISOGYNIST TEXT: *ONE FLEW OVER THE CUCKOO'S NEST*

Laura Quinn

One Flew Over the Cuckoo's Nest, Ken Kesey's 1962 novel of life in a hospital for the mentally ill, is a document of the sixties. Its anti-institutionalism, its celebration of boisterous rebellion against a seemingly rational (but actually unnecessarily repressive) establishment spoke to a generation of long-haired beaded and bearded anti-war activists. That the novel records something important to that era is not enough (perhaps) to justify its inclusion in a public school curriculum; we generally seek a universal and timeless quality in the works we teach to students. *One Flew Over the Cuckoo's Nest* possesses this broader vision, however, and transcends its own timeliness by addressing a social problem that is both ever and omnipresent—that of the relationship between institutional authority and individual and/or subjected group desire for autonomy and self-determination. Kesey's novel raises crucial questions about power and control, about how groups establish and maintain the particular kind of order that they deem necessary to their survival, about ways in which the "controlled" resist that order. This book belongs in the high school curriculum for the following reasons:

a) It "opens" the issue of social control in the truest sense. The novel offers no simple answers to the question of what to do with the "dysfunctional"—with those whose behavior disrupts the social order. While some of the ward's inmates are there for socio-cultural reasons (Chief Bromden, the narrator, most notably), others are "voluntary," that is, self-committed and clearly hiding from a threatening and hostile outside world; still others are Chronics, the radically dysfunctional psychically and physically, in need of total institutional care—though the question is repeatedly raised in the novel of whether the institution itself is not the agent of much of the dysfunction of its wards.

b) It treats a problem that is particularly relevant to teenaged readers, whose chafing under institutional rules and constraints and whose ambivalence toward authority is often acute.

c) It is a readable book, dramatic, immediate, accessible to young readers.

d) It is a work of substantial literary merit that features an interesting narrative situation—Chief Bromden, the towering Indian who has posed as a deaf-mute on the ward for many years, narrates the novel, creating a complex, ironic, and privileged perspective on events and personalities in the hospital, privileged by virtue of his deaf-mute disguise which tricks authority figures into speaking freely in his presence.

e) Finally, it is a work that is seriously problematic in its treatment of gender and race. While this might seem a spurious asset in our age of multicultural and gender-balanced curricular imperatives, I believe that the particular nature of its race and gender problems as a text makes these issues accessible at the high school level in illuminating ways. Far from justifying any censorship in the interests of political correctness, the novel's lapses afford teaching opportunities (to be elaborated later in this chapter).

The novel's structure is that of a contest between Nurse Ratched and Randle McMurphy, the new guy on the block/ward. The contest is waged and staged in the mind of Chief Bromden, whose narrative goes back in time (when prompted to do so by disturbing events on the ward) to recall his father's degradation at the hands of white government agents who coerced him into selling the tribal lands. In shame his father descended into drunken oblivion while the young son lapsed into silence as a means of self-protection and as a reaction to the discovery that he was a voiceless nonentity anyway in the white community. In addition to his silenced persona, the Chief (this ward nickname) has developed the theory of the "Combine," his reification of the ubiquitous social control machine which subdues all autonomous human behavior by means of wires, fogs, implants, recording devices, and robotics; only, he muses, moving targets like McMurphy, those who stay outside of and on the edges of institutions, can evade the Combine, and their evasions are precarious. The notion of the Combine is important, because it connects the abuses of authority within the hospital to the larger society outside; as one patient, Harding, says, (referring to the submissiveness of the ward's population) "we are—the *rabbits*, one might say, of the rabbit world!" (65). Clearly the inmates/ rabbits have been waiting for a savior, for a newcomer with "a very wolfy roar" (65) to model resistance to the form that the Combine takes on the hospital ward, to the "Big Nurse."

When the novel opens, the Chief has been in the ward longer than any of the other patients and has spent most of that time pushing a broom from room to room. Like most of the others on the ward he has no sense of himself, and despite his six foot eight frame the Chief believes that he has grown small and weak. He sees Big Nurse, the ward supervisor, as much larger than she is and, further, capable of growing before his eyes when the need to exert control arises. Indeed, our narrator (whose reliability is a complex issue) hallucinates much of the time, believing firmly that Big Nurse and the forces she represents have the ward wired and rigged with a dizzying number of control devices—objective correlatives of the very effective kind of control exerted over the ward's residents by sheer power of suggestion, by exploitation of patient fears, and by the medications that atrophy, distort, and deaden responses. (For instance, when Chief believes that Big Nurse has activated the fog machine to flood the ward with a blinding fog, he is probably reacting to his latest dose of little red pills; the reader is forced to read his narrative as that of a pharmaceutically controlled subject.)

The Chief functions as central reflector on the activities of the new resident, McMurphy, who's been doing time at a work farm for assault and who finagles his way into the hospital as an easy way of doing time. Mac bursts intrusively upon the ward, bringing energy, lust, and levity into the drugged, robot-like lives of its inhabitants. He is instantly at odds with Nurse Ratched/Mother Ratched/Big Nurse, a buxom, middle-aged tyrant who is proud of her well-regulated ward: "...I've watched her get more and more skillful over the years. Practice has steadied and strengthened her until now she wields a sure power that extends in all directions on hairlike wires..." (26). McMurphy attempts to subvert all this control, urging the men on to defiance and self-assertion and setting them an example. His sustained power struggle (a true battle for the souls of the men) with Big Nurse is like an elaborate chess game between formidable opponents and is often comic, as when Mac confronts Big Nurse at the door of the latrine wearing only a towel. When she informs him, calmly and therapeutically, that a towel is inappropriate attire on the ward, he dismays her by pulling it off; she is relieved to find that he has shorts on underneath, only to discover that they are outrageous black shorts with huge white whales leaping around on them (a present from an Oregon State coed, a literature major, who gave them to McMurphy because he was a symbol):

> "And you, Mr. McMurphy," she says, smiling, sweet as sugar, "if you are finished showing off your manly physique and your gaudy underpants, I think you had better go back in the dorm and put on your greens.
>
> He tips his cap to her and to the patients ogling and poking fun at his white-whale shorts, and goes to the dorm without a word. (97)

Big Nurse's controlled, parental response, McMurphy's feigned gallantry, and the sexual over and undertones of the exchange are part of the elaborate dance they do. The light tone of their struggle darkens as the novel moves on, however, and the narrator begins to feel afraid for McMurphy who realizes himself that his activities on behalf of the men on the ward may cost him dearly. This realization comes with the knowledge that he is a "commitment," not a "voluntary," as are most of the men— thus, Big Nurse can determine the duration of his stay. The play here on the word "commitment" is rich; because he is a state "commitment," Mac needs to lay back, to protect his future, to cooperate with ward policy so as to be released. Of course, because of his growing, unwilled, communal commitment to the men on the ward, he will sacrifice himself in the effort to empower them, to teach them to resist.

This second commitment leads, climactically, to a violent outburst in which Mac attacks Big Nurse in retaliation for her brutal and destructive treatment of the vulnerable "son" of McMurphy, Billy Bibbit. Mat is decisively defeated in the violent physical encounter via a frontal lobotomy, all other means of control having failed Big Nurse and her careful and enlightened system. Acting out of love and gratitude, Chief Bromden, who believes that McMurphy is responsible for the restoration of his size and strength, smothers his diminished comrade and hurls a huge control panel (significantly) through a window to escape. The novel, thus, ends in both tragedy and triumph; McMurphy's momentous sacrifice has liberated the Chief, physically, verbally, emotionally.

Since it achieved popularity in the sixties, *One Flew Over the Cuckoo's Nest* has been subject to censorship in the public school system in the United States. In Greeley, Colorado in 1971, parents objected to three books with "obscene, filthy language" which appeared on a non-required reading list in a course on American culture. These three titles were *I Never Promised You a Rose Garden, Love Story*, and Kesey's novel (*Newsletter* 1971, 59). In Strongsville, Ohio in 1974, five residents sued the Board of Education to keep two books—*One Flew Over the Cuckoo's Nest* and *Manchild in the Promised Land*—out of the classroom. Their suit alleged that both books "allow[ed] minors access to pornographic materials," and stated that the books "tend to glorify criminal activity, have a tendency to corrupt juveniles, and contain descriptions of bestiality, bizarre violence, and torture, dismemberment, death, and human elimination" (*Newsletter* 1974, 152). The *Newsletter on Intellectual Freedom* reports that the book was removed from public school libraries in both Alton, Oklahoma and Randolph, New York in 1975 (May 1975, 41; July 1975, 108). A drama teacher at a high school in Glen Burnie, Maryland was forbidden in 1980 to stage a version of the novel on the grounds that its use of sexual innuendo was objectionable (*Newsletter* 1980, 52). In 1972 an English teacher from Bellevue, Washington felt compelled to defend the novel in an article in *English Journal* when she was attacked by parents for teaching an indecent, obscene, racist, immoral book (Sutherland 28-31). All of these charges are, from a surface standpoint, understandable; the novel contains four-letter words in abundance, and McMurphy expresses his sexuality blatantly, constantly, and in a sexist manner. Moreover, the four-letter words and the sexual language are uttered by characters with whom we sympathize and identify, often in reaction to characters with far more propriety and institutional legitimacy whom we, as readers, loathe. The book, thus, seems to advocate or at least sanction profanity and male sexual braggadocio. Further, it seems to encourage and support disruptive, anti-authoritarian behavior. The reader experiences exhilaration when McMurphy puts his fist through the nurses' station window to grab a forbidden pack of cigarettes; we applaud the weekend furlough fishing expedition in which the group from the ward, led by Mac, steals a fishing boat. Disregard for rules, property, and the rights of others on the part of protagonist/heroes may (somewhat understandably) not be what parents and teachers beset with disciplinary problems want their children to celebrate in their reading.

Those who don't find raw language, sexual remarks or mutinous behavior necessarily offensive in reading material for young people may still take issue with *One Flew Over the Cuckoo's Nest* for two other reasons: first, it contains disturbing material that some may find too distressing for young readers. Kesey depicts electro-shock therapy and lobotomy graphically. The patients who die in the text die gruesomely—Cheswick, Mac's first disciple, drowns in the therapeutic swimming pool when his fingers get stuck in the grate at the bottom; Billy Bibbit, the over-aged, underdeveloped stutterer, cuts his own throat when Big Nurse threatens to tell his overpowering mother of his sexual escapade with a prostitute, sneaked onto the ward by McMurphy; the lobotomized Irish hero himself is smothered, flailing in his bed, by the Chief:

> The big hard body had a tough grip on life. It fought a long time against having it taken away, flailing and thrashing around so much I finally had to lie full length on top of it and scissor the kicking legs with mine while I mashed the pillow into the face. I lay there on top of the body for what seemed like days. Until the thrashing stopped. Until it was still a while, and had shuddered once and was still again. Then I rolled off. I lifted the pillow, and in the moonlight I saw the expression hadn't changed from the blank, dead-end look the least bit, even under suffocation. I took my thumbs and pushed the lids down and held them until they stayed. Then I lay back on my bed. (309)

This is a difficult moment for a reader. The resistance of McMurphy's body to death is consistent with his character, the euthanasia decision taken by the Chief may be controversial, the homoerotic overtones of the passage are unmistakable. Even though the novel ends on a positive note with the empowering and the escape of the Chief, much of what facilitates his liberation is brutal.

The second "liberal" objection to the novel as a high school text is to its stereotyped treatment of blacks and women. Big Nurse's hatchet men are three black orderlies who are despised and feared by patients, are referred to as boys, coons, and niggers at various moments in the text, and who are presented as being lazy and sneaky. The Chief first presents the trio to us in this way:

> They're out there. Black boys in white suits up before me to commit sex acts in the hall and get mopped up before I can catch them. (3)

The black orderlies are "them," the enemy, or, at least, agents of the enemy Big Nurse. They are sneaky, perverted, and sadistic (in the eyes of the inmate/narrator), but they are also powerless, like the patients, in the face of Big Nurse's authority and powerful manipulative skills. She is herself, of course, a stereotyped castrating female of mythic proportions. Chief Bromden alludes to her size and sees her grow larger at times—this from a man who is 6'8," whom Mac calls the biggest Indian he's ever seen. Big Nurse is also known as Mother Ratched by the male patients. The Chief gives us McMurphy assessing her power in these terms:

> There's something strange about a place where the men won't let themselves loose and laugh, something strange about the way they all knuckle under to that smiling flour-faced old mother there with the too red lipstick and the too big boobs. (46)

That "something strange" is what Mac, newcomer on the ward, is so incredulous about—the fact that grown men tremble in the formidable woman's presence. She fuels the Chief's imagination in a variety of interesting ways; he, whose white mother tricked his Indian father into selling tribal land, whose father took the white mother's name upon their marriage, believes that a gust of cold follows Big Nurse as she walks through the ward, believes that, as she gets angry, "she blows up bigger and bigger, big as a tractor, so big I can smell the machinery inside the way you smell a motor pulling too big a load" (5). Images of cold steel, machinery, wires, porcelain, hard glitter, and whiteness are what he repeatedly associates with her. She is the nexus of all of his fears, and the main reason the Chief grows to love and admire McMurphy is that the latter refuses to fear her.

Authority, then, in the novel is female—a large-breasted mother figure, "a bitch and a buzzard and a ballcutter" (58). Strong women are evil and emasculating. The women viewed positively in the novel are the kind-hearted whores whom Mac introduces to the men and the sympathetic—and very tiny—Japanese nurse who works on the Disturbed ward. Once authority is constituted in this gendered manner—and once the clichéd mother/whore dichotomy is established in the novel—the form that resistance "naturally" takes is that of machismo, of the restoration and re-emergence of phallic power. The intellectual and articulate patient, Harding, explains to McMurphy that "we are victims of a matriarchy here, my friend," (61) and a bit later refers to big Nurse as being "impregnable" (70). All of the challenges that McMurphy organizes against institutional authority are reassertions of maleness—poker games, fishing trips, watching the World Series on television, smuggling in prostitutes, drinking, locker-room jokes, insistently asking Big Nurse if she wears C or D cups. A teacher or parent may well hesitate to recommend or teach a text in which the center of authority is a large, white mother figure, the subordinate authority figures are black males, and the endorsed protagonists are all subjugated white males (with the exception of Chief Bromden, whose treatment as a Native American figure in the text also partakes of cliché and stereotype, even if he is given the subject position of narrator) who are exuberantly acting out adolescent male fantasies of competition and sexual aggression. *One Flew Over the Cuckoo's Nest* is a text which violates a whole spectrum of contemporary versions of "political correctness."

I wish to argue that it is the proliferation of "problems with the book that combines with its anti-authoritarian appeal to render this novel a profitably teachable text for high school students. Indeed, each of the objections presented above (and there may well be more I've missed)—to the book's language, its sexuality, its anti-institutionalism, its particularly disturbing violence, its racism, sexism, celebration of machismo—can open stimulating, illuminating, and, indeed, vital classroom discussions. In her 1972 defense of her own use of this book in her Bellevue, Washington high school English class, Janet R. Sutherland says that "to charge that the book is obscene, racist, or immoral because it gives a realistic picture of the world of the insane is to demonstrate lack of the minimum competency in understanding literature we expect of high school students" (30). While I concur with her implication that we often underestimate the ability of students to come to terms with difficulty in literature, I take issue with the notion that the "problems" in the novel, whether those of racism, sexism, obscenity, immorality, are the function of a "realistic" representation of the world of the insane. The definition of insanity as well as the power to define insanity are questioned in the book; McMurphy does not engage, for instance in racist invective against the orderlies out of insanity. What the book affords is the opportunity for questioning almost everything in it. Once the issue of power and who wields it and what that means is pried open by the novel, classroom discussion is authorized, if you will, by the text itself to pry open all instances of the use of power represented, including McMurphy's phallic campaign, Chief Bromden's mercy-killing, the position of the black orderlies as coerced workers in undesirable jobs, the author's choice of Big Nurse as center of authority in an institution in which, historically, male doctors have held sway over female nurses—all of these opportunities to question and resist even the text and the author's authority come about precisely because the "world of the insane" is not by any means confined to the hospital in this novel. If institutions can exhibit their own particular forms of insanity—electro-shock treatment, drugs, unnecessary regimentation of daily activities—then we, as readers, are invited to raise questions about *all* of the institutions represented in the novel—including those of culturally constructed gender and racial roles and stereotypes. High school students are capable of coming to these questions, particularly if confronted with a pedagogy that facilitates such questioning.

A pedagogical approach to the novel that is designed to take full advantage of the issue-opening opportunities it affords would, I believe, begin with presenting the novel to a class as a text with a history of censorship; this history establishes the categories of objections which the novel has given rise to and enables the teacher to use those categories to structure critical discussion of it. As the language/profanity issue is one of the most immediately apparent "violations" of which the text is guilty, one might begin with it. Inasmuch as profanity exceeds the boundaries of acceptable social behavior, it becomes (often) the language of the powerless, the expression of their anger. When the small apoplectic Cheswick rants and curses Big Nurse, having gained courage from McMurphy's example (116-117), he moves a step away from the servile, rabbit-like acquiescence of the others and acquires some dignity.

Linguistically, the four-letter words, the slang, Mac's irreverent, hyperbolic, hillbilly idiom—"'I been a bull goose catskinner for every gyppo loggin operation in the Northwest and bull goose gambler all the way from Korea, was even bull goose pea weeder on the pea farm in Pendleton—so I figure if I'm bound to be a loony, then I'm bound to be a stompdown dadgum good one'" (19)—are a response to the mechanistic jargon of Big Nurse with its constant refrain of control, order, calm, and propriety. Careful consideration of the different characters' speech idioms in this text is revealing and can lead to student insights into their own use of language (and that of others—parents, teachers) in contexts in which power, powerlessness, anger and intimidation are operating. Harding's formal academic speech (he precedes Mac as ward leader, albeit a weak and cynical one), which masks his pain and feelings of emasculation, Mac's street language, the doctor's abstractions, Big Nurse's language of control are all recorded, ironically, by the Chief who has had no spoken idiom for all the years he's posed as a deaf mute—who can barely bring to utterance the "thank you" that he offers McMurphy, breaking years of silence (205). Why people speak or fail to speak as they do and how this is related to who they are and how much power they have in an institutional context are questions that the book invites and that can shed much needed light on the use of profanity as rhetorical.

Similarly, the sexuality in the novel—probably the main reason for its presence on lists of frequently censored texts—needs to be seen as an affront to order, a breaking loose, a bringing to bear of the force of chaos and disorder upon the anesthetizing regimentation of the ward. McMurphy, of course, introduces this force to his drugged, sexually dysfunctional fellow patients. Billy Bibbit cannot speak to women without stuttering, so Mac supplies a "whore" for his first sexual experience. Harding is afflicted with an attractive, promiscuous wife in whose presence he is impotent and cowed. The Big Chief has a voyeuristic and prudish fear of the black orderlies' sexuality and doubts his own manhood when he is tempted to touch the sleeping McMurphy (210). Into this den of repression explodes Mac and his incorrigible, swaggering heterosexuality: "'My psychopathic tendencies? Is it my fightin' tendencies or my fuckin' tendencies? Must be the fuckin', mustn't it? All that wham-bam-thank-you-ma'am...'" (64). To the other ward residents Mac is the symbol of male potency, the last hope against that larger-than-life repository of male fears of castration, Nurse Ratched. When he goads the other patients about their sexuality—"'Are you the renowned Billy Club Bibbit? Of the famous fourteen inches?'" (99) he is trying to empower them in the only way he knows how. Important insights into the intimate relationship of power and sexuality can be gleaned from this aspect of the novel. Issues such as rape as a political crime, the relationship between racism/sexism and sexual fear, and sexual stereotypes are all played out richly in the book, and discussion of these may help students learn much about the complexities of their own sexuality.

When the Strongsville, Ohio litigants claimed that *One Flew Over the Cuckoo's Nest* glorified criminal activity and tended to corrupt juveniles, they expressed deep-seated and universal fear of disruptive behavior, rule-breaking, the transgressing of boundaries. Societies need rules and limits to survive. When Mac attends his first group meeting on the ward, the doctor explains the theory of the Therapeutic Community to him: "...how a guy has to learn to get along in a group before he'll be able to function in a normal society; how the group can help a guy by showing him where he's out of place; how society is what decides who's sane and who isn't, so you got to measure up" (47). Student readers can discuss the novel's world as both a mental hospital ward in which various kinds of abuses and outrages take place and as a representative social institution which must exercise control over and establish limits for its members. Trying to access the points in the novel in which excessive or unnecessary control is exerted is a useful discussion activity. Imaginative identification with the hospital staff—their fear of losing control, the threat that McMurphy poses to them—can help to complicate readerly perspective. By *opening* the issue of the institution versus the institutionalized, by examining it under different lights, a teacher can make clear that, far from advocating a scoff-law attitude, vandalism, or disruptive behavior, the book sheds light on the nature and causes of these breaches. Since, as educators, we must be committed to the belief that seeing clearly results in acting wisely, the illumination of the complexities of power and powerlessness in Kesey's novel makes it a must read rather than a don't read.

Another crucial category of discussion for students is that of the violence in the novel. Here, the literary question of whether the novel's redemptive structure contains and neutralizes its violence can be raised. What many young readers tend to remember most sharply about *Cuckoo's Nest* is Chief Bromden's heroic (and unrealistic) escape at the end. Having smothered his beloved McMurphy, the Chief is reminded by another patient in the dark of the night that Mac showed him how to escape in Mac's first week on the ward. What he's referring to is McMurphy's plan to throw a huge, heavy control panel through a barred and screened window, something Mac himself attempts at one point, to no avail. But since his dead friend and mentor had gradually convinced the Chief of the latter's own strength, the Chief finds himself able to do what Mac could not. Just before the attempt, the Chief had grabbed the cap that his now dead friend always wore and tried it on, only to find it too small. McMurphy has created a frankenstein, has awakened a giant, has sacrificed himself for and transformed himself into this big Indian. The transformation of Mac's tragedy into the Chief's triumph helps to allay the disturbing aspects of this narrative. The novel is often brutal, but it is also merry, and the good guys do win, after a fashion. Nurse Ratched does destroy McMurphy, but many of the voluntary commitments sign themselves out or transfer to another ward after Billy Bibbit's suicide, and she is diminished in size. What McMurphy's Christ-like (is lobotomy the mental health version of crucifixion?) sacrifice accomplished and how he succeeds in empowering the underclass he joins on the ward provides good discussion material and also a very positive reading of the text. The novel is disturbing, but it is far from hopeless.

In getting at its redemptive features, a teacher can seize the chance to raise further questions about the "realism" of the narrative; in order for the Chief to escape, for the book to be transformed into the triumph of the weak over the strong, elements of wish-fulfillment, of faith, need to be invoked. The Chief is an exceptional physical specimen, but the heaving of a 400 plus pound control panel through a window is the stuff of a Hollywood ending. We are prepared for such goings-on early in the text when Chief tells us that we will have trouble with his narrative reliability:

> I been silent so long now it's gonna roar out of me like floodwaters and you think the guy telling this is ranting and raving my God; you think this is too horrible to have really happened, this is too awful to be the truth! But please. It's still hard for me to have a clear mind thinking on it. But it's the truth even if it didn't happen. (8)

The relationship of this statement to events in the novel can lead students to a deeper understanding of the ways in which art represents reality; it also provides an escape valve or some distance from the more disturbing moments of the narrative.

Any teacher of this text must address the problems of racial and sexual stereotypes directly. At one point early in the novel Chief chronicles the history of black "boys" who have come and gone as ward workers:

> The first one she gets five years after I been on the ward, a twisted sinewy dwarf the color of cold asphalt. His mother was raped in Georgia while his papa stood by tied to the hot iron stove with plow-traces, blood streaming into his shoes. The boy watched from a closet, five years old and squinting his eyes to peep out the crack between the door and the jamb, and he never grew an inch after. (28)

The Chief has contempt for this black dwarf as he has for all of the orderlies, but he does supply us with this mitigating narrative, one that calls attention to and makes connection with the experience of people of color in the United States. The Chief also lets us know that Big Nurse treats her black orderlies (wonderful job title in this institutional context) in a degrading, dehumanizing manner; they, in turn, "kick ass below," by mistreating the patients. The fact that their jobs are demeaning, low-level, no doubt poorly paid, dangerous, and unlikely to lead anywhere needs to be brought to light in a discussion of the treatment of race in the novel. When Chief Bromden awakes one night (he is tied to his bed) to discover one of the orderlies scraping his carefully hoarded and rechewed gum from the underside of his bunk, we see all the pathos and degradation of the orderlies' work life, of the Chief's poverty (he is a ward indigent) and of the antagonism that this institution generates in two characters who may have a connection to one another as men of color in white America. Discussions of race and racism in the novel must attend to such narrative moments, to the position of the black orderlies within the institution, and to the class and ethnic background that helps to account for McMurphy's bantering racist remarks.

It is not, alas, so easy to mitigate the castrating female stereotype that Big Nurse embodies nor the way in which institutional power and authority are so aggressively gendered in the novel. Here, it is crucial to bring students to an understanding of the limitations of first person narrative. Big Nurse is far more a creation of the Chief's and other residents' imaginations than she is a representative reality. Deep archetypal male fear of a dominant mother figure finds expression in her narrative treatment. The Chief's own experience of his traitorous white mother is projected onto Big Nurse. Student readers must learn to step back from the narrative perspective to see that the Chief's unreliability—to a degree— lies in his overblown sense of this woman—a distortion in which all of the residents participate. Because so much of the Chief's experience is perceived metaphorically—the wires, gadgets, buttons, fog machine, that he sees Big Nurse manipulating are metaphors for her manipulative skills, institutional power, and pharmaceutical regime—her representation in his narrative can, by extension, be seen as metaphoric; indeed, the way in which she grows larger and then reverts to size for him, regularly, places her in the metaphoric field. Careful readerly attention to those moments in which she expands in the Chief's eyes will help students to see her as an allegorized force rather than a realistic character in the novel. Still, we must eventually confront the distressing artistic choice that Kesey made when he chose to present his conflict in gendered terms. I find myself resisting angrily the *unfairness* of such a portrait of power, of locating what is vile and repressive in the novel in a female figure that is granted no mitigating story of her own, no redemptive moments, no context that will at least reveal her power to be exceptional, unusual, un-nurse-like. Nonetheless, I would teach this book to high school students. In teaching it, as a feminist teacher, I would engage in the following interventions:

a) I would acknowledge to students—at an advanced rather than an early stage of the discussion, so as not to establish mine as the "original" position on gender in the novel—my resistance to the use to which Big Nurse is put in the text.

b) I would encourage full discussion of gender and power, of male fears of emasculation, or the mother as a site of power, of the way in which Big Nurse's body—her breasts in particular—becomes the target of male anger.

c) I would pair *One Flew Over the Cuckoo's Nest* with a parallel text that represents institutional power as male; Charlotte Perkins Gilman's "The Yellow Wallpaper" or Margaret Atwood's *The Handmaid's Tale* could each engage Kesey's novel in a dialectic that would preclude reductive reader acceptance of Big Nurse as quintessential female power principle.

Finally, the novel opens one way out of the gendered deadlock that it creates, and that is the particular form that male bonding ultimately takes in the narrative; there is identifiable tenderness in this bond that transcends the locker room talk, the poker games, the fishing trip, the "rape" of Big Nurse as projected solution to the ward's problems. The group develops a solidarity, sensitivity, and protectiveness that permits McMurphy to subside for a while as their leader/savior when he begins to realize the price he will pay for assuming that role. When he does pay this price—the lobotomy—for having resumed leadership to avenge the death of Billy Bibbit, the love which prompts Chief to murder him is much like that which moves George to shoot Lenny in *Of Mice and Men*. After Chief breaks his silence and he and Mac have their first conversation from their neighboring bunks, the Indian experiences a strong urge to touch McMurphy. He fears for his masculinity at first, then realizes that he just wants to touch him because of who he is and what he means to all of the men on the ward. McMurphy's gift to him includes more than the power to speak, more than the restoration of his mammoth strength—it includes the power to love and, thereby, goes some distance toward subverting the machismo that provides so much of the text's momentum.

One Flew Over the Cuckoo's Nest is rich in teaching possibilities; it stimulates literary, cultural, historical, and psychological questions. It is alas, for many of us, a problematic text. Because the classroom is a space in which teachers and students can and should grapple with difficult problems, this book should be taught.

WORKS CITED

Kesey, Ken. *One Flew Over the Cuckoo's Nest*. 1962. rpt. New York: Penguin, 1976.

Newsletter on Intellectual Freedom. Vol. XX, No. 3 (May 20, 1971).

_____. Vol. XXIII, No. 5 (November, 1974).

_____. Vol. XXIV, No. 2 (May 1975).

_____. Vol. XXIV, No. 4 (July, 1975).

_____. Vol. XXIX, No. 3 (May, 1980).

Sutherland, Janet R. "A Defense of Ken Kesey's *One Flew Over the Cuckoo's Nest*." *English Journal*. 61, 1 (January, 1972): 28-31.

THRESHOLD LITERATURE: A DISCUSSION OF *ORDINARY PEOPLE*

Ron Neuhaus

Booger--a word which T.V.'s urbane Tony Randall once characterized as the worst in the language, including slang, vulgarities and obscenities. And one that some people find so objectionable that were they members of any book selection or evaluation committee, they would blackball all works containing it, regardless of whatever socially redeeming value the books might hold. Paradoxically, no one imputes latent harm in the word; no one considers its use or users immoral. Yet its disputants would eagerly applaud any surgery or gene-splicing of the language that would render it incapable of ever again linking its letters to form that word.

Ordinary People has a few sparks of vernacular obscenity to create atmosphere and intensity, but it does not employ "booger." If it did, people of this persuasion would probably try to nail it and ally themselves with any compatriot protestors to petition for its removal. However, no book has ever been banned because of that "booger," and no author has ever had an editor pluck it out. Yet I wonder how much opposition to certain works of literature has a similar booger-hunting whimsy under it, concealed behind an intricate tapestry of righteousness or moralizing.

Still, no matter what the motivation, people have a right to do their best to help create what they consider to be a wholesome educational ambience. Nor are books and schools singled out for scrutiny by this concern for what goes on in the ecology of a community. When parents or school boards apply pressure to put material outside student access, they exercise the same type of environmental determination that leads people to keep bars and X-level adult bookstores out of residential areas. Such efforts reflect a scenario which hopes to have a gardening effect; and to implement their goals, most communities establish codes of decorum, some of which carry legal clout: prohibitions against such things as open air nudity, public urination, and obscenity.

Oddly enough, people usually do not regard these matters as categorically immoral in themselves; they only wish to control the context in which they occur. The same person who inveighs against flashers may fondly recall some youthful skinny-dipping, and no camper would undertake a return trip to a service station in order to heed a call of nature.

Keeping certain books out of school libraries and classrooms is first cousin to these decorum efforts. It simply shows that parents wish to exercise discretion regarding two things: 1) the conditions under which children experience sensitive matters; 2) the nature of the experiences themselves. I doubt that anyone opposed to *Ordinary People* would say that the book should have been suppressed through censorship--they only want to determine the conditions under which it enters their community or schools. If such an attitude exists, whether or not a book is to be in the school library or classroom may then become a matter of negotiation, not of fiat from governmental agencies, book-banners, or the open door policy of *Hustler* magazine.

Censorship itself is one of those red-flag words that gets all sorts of hormonal activity going. Spectres of Gulags loom in the mind; the spirits of Milton and Tom Paine are invoked. Unfortunately, discretionary access and censorship are often used to describe the same action, even though they differ markedly. Censorship prevents material from entering the public domain; "book-banning" regulates access once it has entered. Censorship prohibits choice: discretionary access allows the full range of choice from writer to consumer. If the process and attitude described above surround whether a book is to be involved in education, censorship, as such, is not involved.

A citizen or organization has the right to expression, but the market has no responsibility to publish that material. Nor are consumers constitutionally compelled to purchase, read it, or acquire it for their schools once it has been published. As individuals, we decide for ourselves; as parents and community members, we exercise similar choices for our children and students. We avidly guard that ability to choose; although we may on our own petition to have a book taken from the shelves, we would resent any governmental or legislative agency usurping that prerogative.

So when a book like *Ordinary People* creates a fuss, we need to make a case for it, to show that it will enrich its readers and enhance the educational environment instead of detracting from it. Can such a case be made? Of course, and a strong one. Once made, will it prevail? Well—it might or it might not. One would like to assume that the right to discretionary access carries with it the responsibility to make judgments based on a reasonably thorough consideration of a book merits, not simply whimsy or bias. However, no one seems to relish being reminded of responsibilities, although humanists do what they can to restore that equilibrium between right and responsibility. The efforts may be fruitless, but we might remember the story of a sage who saved a scorpion from drowning in a stream. The scorpion instinctively stung the hand that had helped it and scurried back into the stream. The sage saved him again and again, and was stung each time for his efforts. A passerby, his curiosity piqued, asked the sage why he persisted in saving the scorpion. Didn't he realize the insect would keep stinging him? Replied the sage, "The scorpion stings because it is his nature." "But then why do you help him?" asked the observer." I help him because that is *my* nature," answered the sage.

First, instead of praising this book, let's look at the worst in it. Let's lean on it hard and inventory its controversial points in a ruthless biased summary.

Ordinary People, Judith Guest. The trauma as a suicidal teenager struggles for normalcy, while his parents move toward divorce. Uses obscene language, sexual scenes, nudity and violence. Includes grim representations of adolescent depression, suicide and psychosis. Contains unresolved pessimism and disillusionment.

Obviously this book would serve no purpose in the primary classrooms. But where do we go from here? What would particular groups object to? A short taxonomy of objectors may outline the problems the book presents. The five groups here identified do not encompass all objections. They represent the most salient:

Fetishists	Dominoes
Monkey Sees	Catchers-of-the-Raw
Ostriches	

The first three groups tend to be the most whimsical and adamant: they need to be outvoted. The last two groups are receptive to argument and will enter into dialogue. But the substantial rationale behind their convictions makes them formidable discussants.

First of all, the Fetishists, the "booger-hunters." They will object categorically to one thing or another and let that objection harpoon the whole book. They will not compromise; all they need to know is that the word, situation, action, or relationship occurs, and the book is out—unless the objectionable parts are excised. From a censorship perspective, they're easily pleased: omit this word or that scene, bowdlerize the script, and all is well.

Ordinary People, it must be admitted, does provide grist for the fetishists. It does use a few four-letter words. Although it lacks the blase tour-de-force *a la* Henry Miller, it does not have the antiseptic diction of a Tom Swift novel. Nor would it suffer greatly if the objectionable language were removed. The question is, why do so? What harm could be done? The language would be titillating only to a grade school child delighted to see the forbidden words in print. Older readers would respond to the language in terms of its intention: to highlight the emotional state of the person using them. A similar rationale could be made for the scenes, but fetishists don't respond to rationales, so the effort is purely for the eavesdropping allies on both sides, the principle involved, and to evoke a sense of righteousness that humanists delight in as much as Fetishists.

Next, the Monkey Sees. These assume that children will imitate selectively what they read and invariably model undesirable over virtuous behavior. There may be a germ of truth here. Huck Finn's penchant for corncob pipes inspired my own experience with smoking. But *Ordinary People* offers very little to imitate. Suicide? 24-hour-a-day depression? Guest presents these with no glamour, no allure, no factor of temptation. The harshness with which she presents her study argues for the book as a warning against the moods it explores.

The Ostriches. An endangered species who exclude certain moods and themes from any kind of consideration. These might well react to the depression and stress throughout the book by wishing their portrayal to disappear. This helps them ignore what they do not want to admit exists. They haven't experienced similar situations, nor do they see any point in contemplating them. To their extent of receptivity, this group can be answered in the same way as the next.

In these next two groups, the nature of the objections shifts. The arguments are more articulated and broader in perspective. The logic is often sound, but the assumptions create the controversy.

The Dominoes. They will admit all the merits of the book, they have no objection to it, and may even agree that it should be in the library or school. However, they fear the precedent the presence of the book will establish. They assume, and with some cause, that when a door opens for one, it's difficult to close it for others. The difficulty in responding to this is that a historical continuum exists from *Ulysses* to *Hustler*, from *Lolita* to child pornography. Here is where the negotiation and discussion play their strongest role. Apologists for a given book should make clear that acceptance of one book does not guarantee admission of another. A separate rationale must be put forward on the merits of each document; we need to be ready with an apologia when the need arises.

Last of all, the Catchers-of-the-Raw, or Holden Caulfields. These people understand and acknowledge the reality of the sensitive material portrayed in a given work but wish to guard their children from such matters as depressing experiences and sordid reality. It's a losing battle, of course, but theirs is a delaying action, not a decisive one. Yet given the inevitability of actual encounters with the sharp edges of experience, a work like *Ordinary People* can serve as a buffer that informs and actually protects—a quality of threshold literature, which prepares the sensibility through imagination for what it will soon encounter in experience.

And granted that the book does deal with depression and the more visceral moments in life, it redeems itself from being a depressing book in several ways. It makes severe depression less intimidating by examining it and revealing it as a normal reaction to abnormally stressful situations.

There is even a triumph over depression, an affirmation of the reservoir of human strength. During an unexpected acceleration of his despondency, Conrad makes contact with this sense of affirmation after his analyst clarifies emotional impotence with this observation.

> Geez, if I could get through to you, kiddo, that depression is not sobbing and crying and giving vent, it is plain and simple reduction of feeling. Reduction, see? Of all feeling. People who keep stiff upper lips find that it's damn hard to smile. (225)

Simple, straightforward advice--enough to turn the tide in Conrad's favor.

In this book people survive, endure, and mature--despite the death of the elder son, the attempted suicide of Conrad, the atrophy of Calvin and Beth's marriage. Its theme conveys the positive implication that we can survive problems, even though we may not be able to solve them. There is even a qualified "happy" ending in this endurance, an ending which ironically constitutes the major fault of the novel in that the depression gets resolved too easily. The guilt that has prompted Conrad's suicide attempt and plagued him through the novel gets neutralized in that fairly easy scene with the analyst. The answer is a bit too pat, and although the alchemical transformation of Conrad's attitude doesn't quite approach Dumbo's realization that he can fly without the feather, it's from the same school of thought--one the "catchers" always commend.

It's always gratifying to respond to objectors such as those above. There is the sense of battle for a virtuous cause against a dangerous and substantial opposition. But one cannot rely on the defensive strategy of an apologia to make the best case: better to affirm the strong points first. And *Ordinary People* has plenty, but one stands out as particularly relevant.

Some works function as thresholds. They can lead a reader into an awareness and understanding of wider dimension of the human spirit, either by expressing a situation shared by the reader or by allowing insight into the kaleidoscopic variations of the human condition. There has been little threshold literature for young adults, even though the increasing stress and diversity of living almost demands it. We can see documentaries on such problems as teenage alcoholism and pregnancy and gain only surface knowledge of the problem. Where technology provides us with a window to the externals of the world, art must keep pace by its investigation of the inner domain. Books such as the Hardy Boys and Nancy Drew novels illustrate what threshold literature is not--adventures of young adults, yet with no significant attention to how sensibilities change or mature with experience. Such stories could easily feature talking horses or bipedal Great Danes; cartoons can easily be made of them.

On the other hand, books such as those contributed by Judy Blume address the inner world, the world of emotions instead of events. Her work illustrates what threshold literature can do: create a controlled situation where the readers can encounter in fiction what they may soon experience in real situations, either as observers or participants.

Ordinary People also belongs in this category. It divides its focus between the subjective experiences of the son, Conrad, and the father, Calvin, and initiates the reader into the complementary perspectives of adolescence and maturity. Both perspectives give insight into the deserts that open up between people when they most need contact.

Teachers could well focus on Conrad as an entry-level persona. Although we would hope no reader shares his particular situation, his emotions are typical ones with which a reader could easily identify, and the motifs of his encounters are those that begin intruding into the hyperborean climate of most adolescent minds. We see the drawbacks to emotional independence--how it can lead to isolation and separation from the very forces that can heal its injuries. We also see how his awakened sense of history grows from guilt over the past to confidence in the future. The problems and tangles of evolving maturity receive insightful attention here, as do several others quite recognizable to the teenage reader: peer-pressure, school harassment, the struggle with emotions that emerge with ferocious intensity.

Although Conrad's material may be initially appealing to younger readers, Calvin's perspective may prove most enlightening. It allows them to experience the vulnerability of the adult mind, to enter a world they usually know only through a taciturn exterior. The veil of parental inaccessibility is lifted, and they can observe a correlation between the frustration and anxiety they experience and that which occurs in matured minds. While Conrad has his nest of hooks to sort out, Calvin has a similar batch. Their emotional odysseys follow roughly parallel courses. Conrad is involved with sports; Cal has his career.

Both feel the powerful influence of the past on present events.

Conrad must come to terms with the death of his brother; Calvin must deal with the breakup of his marriage. Calvin shows the adult mind charted: the relationship with a youth that Conrad has yet to encounter, the constant worry about family and career, the tragic sense of restriction in reaching out toward loved ones. The portrayal of these complementary sensibilities could well yield compassion for the younger, sympathy for the older.

The book abounds with similar entrances, and several general themes come to mind: that ordinary people often find themselves in unusually taxing situations which distort and amplify their emotions; that people in such struggles must not be seen as deviant types but representative types reacting to abnormal situations; that there is a certain haphazard nature in the universe of the human spirit, matters beyond the pat rational assumptions of post-Freudian analysis.

This all may be quite commendable stuff, but what about the questionable material exposed in the synopsis? At the risk of making an apologia for the book too simple, let me say that books of a certain style contain a built-in safety factor: they turn away any reader not mature enough to handle them. *Ordinary People* has this quality. There is nothing in it to gratify the thrill seeker. For one thing, the heavy emphasis on introspection and interior monologue generates a fairly static physical environment in order to highlight emotional dialectics. Conversation and reflection slow things down more. Most of the attention falls on the "housekeeping" aspects of life: the stress of school on Conrad, the complications of a career for Calvin.

And all of the episodes of sex and violence referred to in my synopsis are presented in a fairly discursive style, with little graphic focus. In fact, for a sexual scene between Calvin and Beth, the author ushers in language so oblique it could double as vocabulary suitable to describe a checkers match. And when Conrad and Jeannine have an intimate scene (very near the end of the book), the dialogue receives the emphasis. The entire scene serves to confirm the emerging optimism in Conrad and to strengthen him even after the news of a friend's suicide. So, if someone is looking for a book to appeal to or encourage prurient interest, *Ordinary People* holds only disappointment.

Each questionable scene has a similar explanation, and there are few such scenes, at that. In fact, if we cut out all the particular passages dealing with "sensitive" areas, they would lay out to a little over one of the books 263 pages. So yes, the situations are there, but this book derives from a different genus than *The Valley of the Dolls*.

However, this statistical approach is not quite fair to those who would object to elements of theme and mood. The book does explore some raw wounds in the human psyche, and some people may object to such a focus in reading material even for a secondary school audience. But objections of this sort often do a great injustice to the potential literature offers. The unacknowledged premise in such a criticism is that literature functions essentially as entertainment or escapism--emotionally safe stuff that can aid reading skills. This ignores literature's potential to create a threshold by which the reader can enter a wider expanse of the human topography and develop a more mature perspective through that vision.

Threshold books reveal one of good literature's finest characteristics. Some such books even attain the status of "classic." But strangely enough, their very utility as tools of insight subjects them to attack, such as has happened with *Huckleberry Finn* and *The Scarlet Letter*. On the other hand, some books are never challenged: those that are infused with an irrelevance to a reader's personal situation and relationships. Many of the popular "classics" provide examples of this. They employ baroque, superbowl passions that engage us as awestruck observers, not emotionally involved participants. They're safe. Parents don't get into bitter debate with their children over the issues in *Crime and Punishment* or *Moby Dick*. Nor can anyone acquire credible insight into children's ingratitude from *King Lear*. We can appreciate occasional doses of inflated sentiments, however, because such experiences transport us away from the bothersome concerns of our lives. But we also need art that enters us as we are, that presents us with parameters of feeling we might actually have, with situations that we see as possible around us. As "ordinary people" we need words that can reveal insight into how we are, and where we are. *Ordinary People* assays out to do that; it lacks the lofty level of intellectual melodrama possessed by the "safe" book, classic or otherwise, and that's the quality that justifies making it accessible to any heart it speaks to.

WORK CITED

Guest, Judith. *Ordinary People.* New York: Viking, 1976.

IN DEFENSE OF *OUR BODIES, OURSELVES*
Alleen Pace Nilsen

Our Bodies, Ourselves: A Book by and for Women is a health book, but not a health book like you studied in seventh grade, nor in high school biology class, nor even in college. It differs in that it gives as much attention to mental and emotional health as to physical health. It's heavy on sex-related issues, and it puts the responsibility for one's health on the individual instead of the medical profession. The assumption is that women can become so knowledgeable about health issues that they will be able to talk to the all-knowing "gods" who rule a vast and mysterious kingdom of hospitals, clinics, and labs.

Defending such a book is different from defending a piece of fiction. Its history as well as its future must be taken into account. The book, written by the Boston Women's Health Book Collective, disproves the notion that a committee can't possibly write a good book. On the opening pages of the first edition one hundred individuals and four institutions are thanked for providing information, advice, and support, and on the authorship list nearly fifty individuals are listed as writers.

The Boston Women's Health Book Collective had its beginning at a local women's conference held in the spring of 1969. Members of a discussion session on "women and their bodies" decided to keep meeting. They were brought together by their common frustration with the medical profession. At first they called themselves "The Doctor's Group." Then, as they decided to explore the various things they wanted to know about and to share their new-found information with each other, as well as with newcomers, their discussion meetings turned into a course called "Women and Their Bodies." They did research on different subjects and wrote papers which were mimeographed as course-discussion material.

In 1971 the papers were printed and bound in an inexpensive edition by the New England Free Press. Reprinting followed reprinting and it soon became obvious that there was a national market for the book. Simon and Schuster published a 276-page edition in 1973, and then a 383-page expanded and revised version in 1976. Extra attention was focused on this edition when the American Library Association Young Adult Services Division chose to put it on their 1976 list of outstanding books for young adults. A related book, *Ourselves and Our Children: A Book by and for Parents* authored by the Boston Women's Health Book Collective, was published in 1978 by Random House. In 1980 Random House also published *Changing Bodies, Changing Lives: A Book for Teens on Sex and Relations* by "Ruth Bell and other co-authors of *Our Bodies, Ourselves* and *Ourselves and Our Children* together with members of the Teen-book Project." *Talking with Your Teenager: A Book for Parents* by Ruth Bell and Leni Zeiger Wildflower published by Random House in 1983 was also tied in with *Our Bodies, Ourselves*. None of these books was meant as a sequel or a replacement for the first book. (Note that they were published by different companies.) However, the authors and publishers apparently wished to capitalize on the reputation of the earlier book or they would not have acknowledged the authors' previous writing experiences in bold face print on the covers.

In January of 1985, Simon and Schuster published a third edition of *Our Bodies, Ourselves*. In a telephone interview (August 27, 1984) with Ann Godoff, the Simon and Schuster editor, I asked if she expected the new edition to be equally controversial. "I certainly hope so," she responded and then quickly added that the company knew from the very beginning that it would be a controversial book, but that they are, nevertheless, very proud of it. "It is unprecedented as a self-help book." Two-and-a-half million copies have been sold. It is impossible to know whether, or to what degree, the notoriety of the book contributed or detracted from the sales. Certainly, the controversy brought it to people's attention. Ms. Godoff noted that, as we were talking, almost fifteen years after publication, the book with related news clippings and correspondence was the featured attraction at a Newark library display calling attention to Banned Books Week.

I asked Ms. Godoff about changes from the first to the second edition.

For example, in the second edition an apologetic footnote was added to the chapter on abortion:

> Because this is a chapter on abortion, it inevitably seems that we are advocating abortion as the "right" or the "best" or "most liberated" thing to do. We do not believe that everyone with an unplanned pregnancy "should" have an abortion. We give so much space to abortion information here because it has been so unavailable in the past and because it is an issue that so many are confronted with. (216)

And early in the first book a woman is shown doing carpentry work, apparently remodeling a bathroom. The toilet looks dirty and there is no seat on it. In the second edition the photo has been cropped so the toilet doesn't show.

I asked editor Godoff if such changes had been made in hopes of appeasing the censors. She responded in the negative, explaining, however, that she and the authors had made a conscious effort to keep readers from different socio-economic levels and different ethnic groups from feeling excluded.

Photographs are especially revealing of such matters. They go a long way toward establishing tone. I wish that someone could figure out a kind of research that would tell us how much of the negative reaction to *Our Bodies, Ourselves* came because of the factual information that was presented, how much because of underlying feminist philosophies, and how much because of a negative "gut" reaction to the photographs—sort of an I-don't-want-these-people-to-be-role-models-for-my-children reaction—and how much because the book is a "downer." The "downer" aspect of the book relates to the way it strips away some of our favorite security blankets. In American culture medical doctors hold a place of respect that borders on worship. *Our Bodies, Ourselves* questions this reverence and makes a strong case for the necessity of people taking responsibility for their own physical and mental well-being. Another security blanket that the book yanks away is the idea that for each of us a knight in shining armor will appear out of nowhere, sweep us off our feet, and then walk with us into the sunset where we will live happily ever after. That's such a pleasant dream that it's painful to relinquish.

Another "downer" is the way *Our Body, Ourselves* reminds us that there are a lot of scary things out there. Within the last few months at my university someone has installed at eye level on the inside of the door of each cubicle in the women's bathrooms an 8-1/2" x 11" placard which gives a miniature lesson on how to examine one's breasts for cancer—"the leading cause of death in American women." This information is accurate and valuable and it may save my life. Nevertheless I resent being reminded several times a day of how vulnerable I am. As I sit down and begin to read over the chart—I can't avoid it unless I close my eyes—I feel as if I belong to some "primitive" tribe whose members must offer daily prayers for protection to their gods. The only difference is that in our efficient, mass-media society where time is at a premium, I read my prayer from a printed card while I go to the bathroom, and the god I pray to is the great god of science and technology.

The feeling of malaise that this gives me is similar, I think, to the feeling that people get when they read *Our Bodies, Ourselves.* And the new topics added, to the 1985 edition include growing old, non-medical approaches to health care, addiction to alcohol and drugs, violence toward women, environmental health issues, body image and reproductive technology. Except for the information on reproductive technology and perhaps the non-medical approaches to health care, these topics do not qualify as good news and will therefore do little to endear the book to people who have an if-you-don't-like-the-message-kill-the-messenger reaction.

Now as to my advice for people who want to have this book in their libraries or use it in classes with students, I offer the following very personal and admittedly biased thoughts.

1. *Do not force the book on anyone.* Have it available along with several other books that treat similar topics, but respect the wishes of those parents who do not want their children reading or looking at this book.

Remember that it is a book written by and for grown women. The authors' ages ranged from twenty-five to forty-one. They were writing to their contemporaries and so parts of the book treat topics far removed from many teenager's experiences. I have a new empathy for parents ever since one of my neighbors—a gun buff—decided to take my two teenage sons out to the desert and teach them marksmanship. I didn't like what I considered interference in the raising of my boys. I felt an implied criticism of my own absent-minded-professor-type husband, who in my neighbor's eyes, was not helping his boys develop their "masculinity." I also resented this neighbor offering himself as a role model to my boys. I didn't want them to aspire to drive a pick-up truck with a gun rack in the back window.

The next summer this neighbor's eight-year-old son used one of his father's guns to shoot his twelve-year-old brother in the stomach. The injured brother lived but will have to have a kidney transplant before he is twenty. In the midst of this tragedy, what came forcefully home to me was the realization that my neighbor never changed his mind about the wisdom of having guns in his home. He simply regretted that he hadn't taught his children carefully enough. It occurred to me how similar the situation would be if one of my children were to have a sex-related misfortune. I wouldn't think it was because I had taught my children about sex or because I had such books as *Our Bodies, Ourselves; Changing Bodies, Changing Lives; What's Happening to Me; The Joy of Sex;* and *Growing into Love* on the family bookshelves. Like my neighbor I would simply regret that I hadn't taught my children carefully enough.

2. *Help people realize that no one book can be all things to all people.* The women who put this book together made more of an effort than do most authors to include diverse opinions, but such an effort goes unappreciated by readers who skim the book looking only for opinions or ideas with which they either strongly agree or disagree. On page two of the preface is one of the most important statements in the book

> Many women have spoken for themselves in this book, though we in the collective do not agree with all that has been written. Some of us are even uncomfortable with part of the material. We have included it anyway, because we give more weight to accepting that we differ than to our uneasiness.

Bring this statement to the attention of readers and be ready to discuss its implications.

3. Help people realize the complexity of the issues that are being discussed. Whether we are looking at the Greek myths, Shakespeare's plays, the *Holy Bible*, the writings of Sigmund Freud, Robert Havighurst's developmental tasks of the adolescent, Gail Sheehy's *Passages*, or the dozens of tabloid newspapers that line the racks of grocery store checkout stands, the conclusion to be drawn is that human sexuality is exceedingly complicated. The matter is so individualistic that in trying to restate Havighurst's adolescent developmental task of "achieving a _____ relationship with the opposite sex," I can't remember what word should go in the blank. Is it *proper, comfortable, beneficial, exhilarating,* or *satisfactory?* I think the latter is what Havighurst used, but then the question must be asked, satisfactory to whom? To the individual? To the individual's partner or partners? To the family? To society? Also, today many people are outspoken enough to question the latter half of the statement. Does the relationship have to be with the "opposite" sex? And is it accurate to think about sexuality only in terms of a "relationship"? A further complication is that the authors of *Our Bodies, Ourselves* do not treat sexual activities and attitudes in isolation. They show how, in a broad sense, such things are tied in with political as well as religious ideologies.

4. *At the same time that you recognize the value of the information in Our Bodies, Ourselves and that you ensure its availability to those who want to read it, listen sympathetically to parents and others who protest the book.* Such protests are in many cases emotional releases for heartfelt frustration.

Sexuality is an area where most of us feel uneasy. Advertisers, popular writers, our best friends, and television and radio talk-show hosts all know that most of us occasionally wonder if our sex lives are all that they could or should be. The doubts and uneasiness that we feel for ourselves, we feel much more strongly for our children. We worry because they are physically mature and yet have had so little time to accumulate the intellectual and emotional experience that we hope can protect them from making harmful sex-related decisions. We also worry because traditional restraints and patterns of behavior are being questioned so that today's young adults have no clear-cut models to follow. Marketing techniques, television, movies, books, magazines, newspapers, and radio keep the matter of sex in the public eye.

This constant display of sexual material forces people to consider and take stands on such controversial issues as homosexuality, masturbation, premarital sex, violence in relation to sex, the effects of pornography, the role of sex in love and family relationships, child abuse, teen pregnancies, sexually transmitted diseases and "open" marriages. The makers of sexy advertisements, movies, song lyrics, etc. cannot be blamed for creating an interest in sex. Instead, there is a circular effect. The messages grow out of people's natural interest in sex, but in turn such messages also feed this interest. It would be naive, indeed, for us to say that our grandparents knew nothing of the sex-related controversies listed above. However, it was certainly easier for those of our ancestors who chose not to think about such matters to remain in a state of relative innocence.

I am convinced that many of the people who want to censor sex education books are simply filing a protest against the overwhelming bombardment of sexual material which all of us meet in our daily lives. The sex education book in the school or public library is the closest thing at hand. It is the only part of the matter which parents have hopes of controlling. Looked at in this way, we can see that when a parent demands that a book be taken from library shelves the action is more emotional than intellectual. It's taking a stand, a kind of twist on the old hymn "Brighten the corner where you are." In response, we need to empathize with the parents' feelings and their desire to "do something." But at the same time we also need to remember our professional obligation to protect people's access to information and ideas. New ways of looking at old ideas have always frightened people. As educators our job is to listen to those who are frightened or angered and to conduct discussions in such a way that people with opposing opinions are brought closer together rather than driven further apart.

This is the challenge we face. I hope we're up to it.

WORK CITED

The Boston Women's Health Book Collective. *Our Bodies, Ourselves: A Book by and for Women*. 2nd ed. New York: Simon and Schuster, 1976.

A LOOK INSIDE A LANDMARK: *THE OUTSIDERS*

John S. Simmons

A glance at the young adult section of almost any mall bookstore these days will reveal a generous number of novels by the widely heralded writers of the moment: Robert Cormier, Judy Blume, Norma Fox Mazer, Lois Duncan, and Richard Peck, to name but a few. Standing right there beside them, almost assuredly, will be S. E. Hinton's *The Outsiders*—which is quite remarkable when one stops to consider the fact that the life spans of most young adult novels, even the initially popular ones are brief indeed. Most of the highly popular works of the mid to late 60s—*The Outsiders*, appeared in 1967—are now long forgotten. But *The Outsiders*, written when its author was 17 years old and making her maiden voyage on the publication waters, continues to hold the attention of the teenage reading audience as well as the English Education gentry. It would be hard to imagine a college or university instructor of a Literature for Adolescents course not calling attention to this novel somewhere along the line.

The question, then, is *why* this relatively short, rather simply written novel about a fourteen year old boy from the other side of the tracks in a moderately large, unnamed town has remained on the high interest list for so long—25 years. What follows is an attempt to answer that question and also to deal with some of the reasons it has been challenged from time to time by the would-be book banners so currently vocal all across the U. S. A.

AS PART OF THE YOUNG ADULT NOVEL'S MATURATION

Briefly stated, the American young adult long fiction genre has gone through three discernible evolutionary stages during this century. For the first 40 or so years, it provided little more than escape and recreational reading matter for the children and teenagers of that period. The Hardy Boys novels, along with the adventurous, picaresque, contrived, melodramatic works of Zane Grey, Edgar Rice Burroughs, and William Heyliger held the interest of boys, especially those who fantasized about their exploits on the gridiron, the diamond, the jungle, or the battlefield. For girls, the career and love sagas (although not necessarily in that order) of Emily Loring, (Sue Barton, girl nurse), Daphne du Maurier, Grace Livingston Hill, and Carolyn Keene (the Nancy Drew series) provided a wealth of entertaining books. In that pre-television era, such "light" reading preoccupied millions of young people in their search for escape from the world of homework and tedium. Escape yes, literary study no, in the eyes of classroom teachers, librarians, and teacher educators alike. For just about all of those professionals, a loosely defined set of "classics," largely written by Victorian era novelists and poets, served as objects of serious classroom study.

During the next three decades, however, a "new" kind of young adult novel began to emerge. Writers such as John R. Tunis, Paul Annixter, Fred Gipson, Esther Forbes, and Maureen Daly continued to include substantial doses of action, suspense, and adventure in their novels, but they also attempted to portray the world of the adolescent in a more realistic, self conscious manner. As Stephen Dunning said of *this* young adult novel, "It pretends to treat life truthfully." As the more credible young adult novel appeared on bookshelves everywhere, teachers, especially those in the junior high schools, began to consider their *teachable* aspects, as did the growing number of university faculty members who called themselves English Educators.

Along with this tentative, critical acceptance, came a wave of criticism, much of it from the academic and intellectually elite communities. In 1956, Frank Jennings denounced the genre, in scathing tones, in his *English Journal* article, "Literature for Adolescents—Pap or Protein," a piece on which readers took sides for months in their Letters to the Editor. At about the same time, the newly formed, intellectually reactionary group, the Council for Basic Education (James Bryant Conant, Clifton Fadiman, John

Ciardi, Jacques Barzun, and Admiral Hyman Rickover were among its more prominent members) took swipes at the young adult novel at frequent intervals. Council members saw it as one more element of Progressive Education, that insidious Deweyan movement whose ultimate effect would be the destruction of all academic integrity in the public schools. A decade later, in 1965, the exalted Commission on English of the College Entrance Examination Board leveled the following blast in their widely read text.

FREEDOM AND DISCIPLINE IN ENGLISH

Claims are frequently advanced for the use of so-called "junior books," a "literature of adolescence," on the ground that they ease the young reader into a frame of mind in which he will be ready to tackle something stronger, harder, more adult. The Commission has serious doubts that it does anything of the sort. For classes in remedial reading a resort to such books may be necessary, but to make them a considerable part of the curriculum for most students is to subvert the purposes for which literature is included in the first place. In the high school years, the aim should be not to find the students' level so much as to raise it, and such books rarely elevate. For college-bound students, particularly, no such concessions as they imply are justified. Maturity of thought, vocabulary, syntax, and construction is the criterion of excellence in literature, and that criterion must not be abandoned for apparent expediency. The competent teacher can bridge the distances between good books and the immaturity of his students; that is, in fact, his primary duty as a teacher of literature. (49-50)

Thus the 1940s, 50s, and 60s were turbulent years for both the authors and defenders of this evolving literary form. Unquestionably, however, the young adult novel had become a force to be reckoned with by the time that *Freedom and Discipline...*was published. Before moving on to describe its third period of growth, however, it is useful to note another statement from Dunning's study, a 1958 doctoral dissertation on the nature of the currently popular young adult (then the junior) novel. Although most of these novels "pretended to treat life truthfully," they were also "rigidly wholesome and insistently didactic." In other words, there were certain aspects of adolescents' life experiences which were either omitted entirely, judiciously undescribed or blatantly distorted in the novels he analyzed.

With the publication of three novels in the academic year 1967-68, the Dunning judgment cited above could no longer be legitimately applied. Robert Lipsyte's *The Contender* (1967) dealt with the plight of the young ghetto black. It included police brutality, other forms of racism, anti-semitism, violence, sex, and alcohol abuse among its elements. Paul Zindel's *The Pigman* (1968) portrayed its teenage protagonists as cruel, insensitive, willful, self-absorbed and, to a degree, criminal. It, too, treated sexual activity and substance abuse. The third novel, currently the most popular of the three, Hinton's *The Outsiders* (1967), has *remained* absorbing despite its indifference to the taboos noted by Dunning. The appearance of these three novels opened the door for a veritable avalanche of young adult works some of which focus on heretofore taboo topics: teenage pregnancy, homosexual relationships, brutality and sadism, divorce, abusive parents, corrupt public officials, gang violence, murder, substance abuse, and on and on. The "new realism" ushered in by Lipsyte, Zindel, and Hinton has been broadly characteristic of the young adult fiction ever since, now spanning a quarter century. And with this thematic direction has come a wave of criticisms and censorship challenges mounted by individuals and (more frequently) groups who oppose the inclusion in school curricula of virtually *any* literature which genuinely seeks "to treat life truthfully."

AS REFLECTING LITERARY MERIT

In 1869, Thomas Bailey Aldrich, a man of letters who was generally regarded as a Boston Brahmin, published *The Story of a Bad Boy*, a novel which seemed to most of his friends and colleagues to be out of character. Writing in *The Atlantic Monthly*, however, William Dean Howells claimed that Aldrich "had done a new thing" in creating a juvenile character who was not in the Little Lord Fauntleroy tradition of past works. The Aldrich protagonist was angry, devious, erratic, spiteful, and generally redolent of the traits most people have attributed to real teenagers for centuries (124-125). Not long after Aldrich's work, Mark Twain published *Tom Sawyer* (1876) and then *Huckleberry Finn* (1884), and the novel of adolescent initiation into adulthood, also sometimes labelled the "loss of innocence" and the "rites of passage," came into being. This theme has developed into one of the dominant literary considerations among the American novelists of this century, as celebrated in a number of scholarly appraisals, principally Ihab Hassan's *Radical Innocence*. As the twentieth century nears its end, the exploitation of the initiation theme has come to represent one of the trademarks of significant American literary artists.

Since the young adult novel has developed more recently as a *serious* literary endeavor, it comes as no surprise that the representation of ostensibly unsavory characters and settings should emerge only after other types had been featured. Main and supporting characters in the novels of Tunis, Annixter, Daly, *et. al.* were from suburban, rural, or historical backgrounds. Thus one of Susan Hinton's significant achievements in *The Outsiders* is to hold up for scrutiny young people from economically, culturally, and socially deprived circumstances. In Ponyboy Curtis, his brothers Sodapop and Darry, and his "Greaser" companions, Hinton has introduced readers, most of whom have probably been from white, middle class origins, to the desires, the priorities, the frustrations, the preoccupations, and above all, the *anger* of those young people who may live in the seedier parts of town but who have established a code of behavior which reflects (to the dismay of some) their sense of dignity and self-worth. As developed by their author, there is little which has been considered contemptible, callous, or even objectionable about the Curtis brothers and most of their friends. Faced with poverty and limited opportunity, they maintain a certain determined optimism and aspiration for a better life. Most important, they believe in, trust, and support each other, all sentiments which can be universally admired despite the circumstances in which they are displayed. Hinton's novel is not "rigidly wholesome" nor "insistently didactic" as were many young adult works of preceding decades. It offers a number of *complex* human beings whose strengths and limitations are left to the readers themselves to infer and judge.

Breaking from the pattern of third person omniscient narrators which characterized the majority of earlier young adult novels, Hinton has presented her story from her protagonist's angle of vision. As with Salinger's *Catcher in the Rye* (1951), wherein we view the world from the perspective of the disturbed, vulnerable teenage Holden Caulfield. Hinton establishes the 14-year-old Ponyboy as both protagonist and narrator. It is through *his* eyes that readers view the events and analyze the individuals who make up this novel. His naivete, lack of sophistication and commitment to an established lifestyle give the novel its tone. Amazingly, the author, a teenage female, has created a credible teenage male protagonist/narrator. In doing so, she has contributed significantly to the new realism of the contemporary young adult novel mentioned earlier.

In his 1958 study, Dunning pointed out that one of the major weaknesses of the young adult novels of that era was the authors' unrealistic depiction of adults and their relationships with adolescents, especially their sons and daughters. Hinton has dealt with this problem quite decisively; she virtually excluded adults from the narrative. This is truly a novel of the teenager, by the teenager, and for the teenager. It is devoid of significant adult characters, and the few that are included serve the most perfunctory of purposes. Thus the focus here is on the young people, particularly the two rival gangs: the Greasers (Ponyboy's) and the Socs (a group of upper middle class individuals whose main goals in life seems to be to embrace hedonism and to wreak havoc on the Greasers, although not necessarily in *that* order. In *The Outsiders*, adults would only serve as a nuisance, and the author does not allow that to happen.

Hinton does provide an element of mature influence, however, in the person of Ponyboy's older brother, Darry. A reluctant school dropout, Darry has assumed the responsibility of parenting his two younger brothers in the face of the untimely, accidental death of their mother and father. At age 20, Darry has taken on an adult role and, given his limited education and financial resources, does the best he can. It is through his character that readers perceive the fight for survival in an underclass situation. But Darry, perhaps more than the other Greasers, accepts his lot stoically and with dignity. He asks for neither material aid nor sympathy. To provide what is needed for family survival, he works longer hours and enforces house rules. In Darry, Hinton has added a note of prophecy to her story. As have countless young single parents of America's 1990s, he has become an adult before his time.

The theme of human fragility is given eloquent voice in *The Outsiders*. Violent confrontations with their rivals place the well-being of both gangs in constant jeopardy. The absence and indifference of parents lead most of the Greasers to the conclusion that they must pretty well fend for themselves. Death and serious, sometimes disabling, injury are possibilities which the latter group faces as a matter of course. During an interlude in which Ponyboy is hiding out with his friend Johnny, a fugitive from the recent murder of a Soc, he recites Frost's poem "Nothing Gold Can Stay" to his distracted friend. The poem has a profound impact on Johnny, who relates it to his own imperiled youth. Later, as he is on *his* deathbed, Johnny's last words are, "Stay gold, Ponyboy. Stay gold...." In an environment, where the concern with survival is omnipresent, the joy and promise of youth are both perceived with irony by Ponyboy and his Greaser cohorts, a far cry from the idyllic teenage days described in so many novels written in the decades before Susan Hinton's first literary effort. As teachers attempt to introduce their classes to a meaningful example of the ironic in literature, they may well look to *The Outsiders*.

The dour tone of *The Outsiders* prevails throughout although the novel is punctuated with examples of humor, selflessness, courage, and humanitarian acts. Despite their heroic quest for dignity and self-determination, both Darry and Ponyboy reflect an alienation from conventional middle class values largely through no fault or their own. Their contempt for the Socs and their lives of luxury, as well as their distrust of public institutions, particularly the law, may stamp them as undesirables in the eyes of some witnesses. It is an aspect of Susan Hinton's creative acumen that most thoughtful readers, both secondary school students and contributors to *ALAN Review*, do not demean these two young people for their attitudes toward middle class mores nor their stubborn adherence to the Greaser code of street-wise self reliance. Their alienation does not result in anti-social, self- destructive behavior and their restrained optimism/hope for better days is made believable by the author's subtle portraiture. While there seems to be little hope for a privileged but emotionally disoriented Holden Caulfield at the end of *Catcher in the Rye*, Ponyboy and Darry exit the book with their heads held high and their eyes on the future. In establishing, most convincingly, her characters' ability to cope, Hinton has led her readers to accept that positive outlook.

In one further stratagem Hinton has assisted the opening of new doors to her young adult novelist successors. The "life goes on" spirit reflected in the ending of *The Outsiders* stands in sharp contrast with the young adult novels of earlier decades. All of the Horatio Alger-style books of the era before the 1940s included the Hollywood boy-gets-girl endings, which remain with us through endless TV dramatic offerings. Many of the well-written novels of the second phase described earlier were mixed, with the protagonist suffering some losses, usually minor, and some gains, usually crucial. As he leaves his readers, Ponyboy gives a few hints that he'll be okay, but there is no evidence that the quality of life, for either him or those around him, will improve to any degree, any time soon. "That's life" is what Susan Hinton seems to be saying in providing this ending to her book. Clearly, this perspective is consistent with the rest of the tale.

Undoubtedly, *The Outsiders* is, to a degree, a period piece, as indeed are the overwhelming majority of today's young adult novels. Paul Newman is probably a sex symbol only to the over-50 theater patrons. Other cigarette brands have replaced Kools among those widely smoked and advertised in this country. Affluent youngsters stopped wearing madras shirts long ago, and few, if any, 1990s teenagers are impressed by the Beatles or their hair style. Moreover, such words as "rumble," "chicken," "punkout," and "greasers" are terms long absent from teenage patois. The themes described above, however, are with us now and probably forever, and Susan Hinton has treated them with sensitivity. Thus, at least in this precinct, *The Outsiders* possesses a considerable dollop of literary merit. Yes, the book is still being read, taught, and discussed a quarter century after its publication. This is a solid reflection of its merit.

AS A TARGET FOR BOOK CENSORS

In the late 60s, young adult novelists began to produce texts that were *not* rigidly wholesome nor were they insistently didactic, and *The Outsiders* was in the forefront of such books. As junior high and middle school teachers of the 70s and 80s were soon to learn, the once "safe" young adult novel, now imbued with a spirit of honesty and thematic comprehensiveness, began to draw fire from those parents and "interested citizens" who demanded that only sanitized reading materials be served up to the young people in English classrooms.

Concurrent with the broadening of thematic investigation among young adult novelists came a wave of challenges by organized right-wing groups, largely fundamentalist in religious orientation, on texts and related materials used by teachers in public schools. Few subject matter areas were safe from such intrusion, and elementary courses of study were attacked as often as those at the secondary level. Spurred on by the passage of the Hatch amendment, which was part of the Omnibus Education Bill (1979) and the election of the Reagan-Bush ticket (1980), these groups increased the tempo of their challenges throughout the 80s. Such groups as The Eagle Forum, Concerned Women of America, Focus on the Family, and Citizens for Excellence in Education have launched attack after attack on any materials which reflects anything of the "secular humanist," to use their argot. As this statement is written, no abatement of their activities is in sight.

As the challenges to materials used in public school curricula have increased, the focus of these challenges has changed markedly. In earlier years, the appearance of language deemed to be vulgar, profane, or obscene was most often found unacceptable as well as the inclusion of explicit descriptions of sexual activity. In the past 15 years, that focus has been replaced by a preoccupation with any attack (in text materials) on those institutions held dear by the attackers. Any explicit or perceived degrading of organized religion, capitalistic philosophy, parental authority, patriotic zeal, or other elements of the orthodox social order was likely to receive the single minded targeting of these zealots.

Given that shift in emphasis, it is little wonder that *The Outsiders* has been challenged on several occasions in recent years. High on the list of objectionable elements in the novel is the implicit criticism the censors perceive of parental authority and overall behavior. The parents of the

Socs seem too involved with their own social activities to pay much attention to the anti-social, destructive and often criminal behavior of their offspring. More glaring are the indifference and physical abusiveness displayed by the mothers and fathers of several Greasers. Johnny's cruel treatment at the hands of both parents leads him to abandon his home and find shelter, as well as emotional support, wherever he can. While no parents are treated intensively by Hinton, there is plenty of evidence in the novel to indicate that they as a group have figured prominently in the difficulties encountered by their children. To the fanatical and persistent members of such ultra-conservative groups as Focus on the Family, this will never do.

Left to their own devices, both the Socs and the Greasers engage in such pastimes as their spirits move them. Smoking, to Ponyboy, Johnny and their fellow Greasers has become a way of life. Several imbibe heavily in alcohol as do the great majority of Socs. Skillful womanizing is a badge worn prominently by several Greasers, especially Dally Winston whose sexual conquests have become legendary before the story even begins. Late hours, indifference to school, and contempt for the police are also part of Greaser sensibility. (Interestingly, they use little profanity, and when bad words are used, Hinton employs the "expletive deleted" approach.) To the smug, self-righteous, would-be book banners of the times, however, their most objectionable trait is the constant reliance on violence to deal with problems.

To the Socs and the Greasers, fighting is a matter of course. Generally, the "rumbles" take place under one strict rule: no weapons. When groups of a gang descend on individual prey, however, guns, knives, broken bottles, and brass knuckles are often brought into play. The result: two deaths in the novel and a number of serious injuries. The deaths have been the object of numerous challenges over the years. One of the continuing objections to Hinton's novel is that it glorifies violence as a means of coping. Although most teenage readers perceive the underlying distaste for such behavior as they find it in the text, a considerable number of their parents have not.

Finally, the whole treatment of class conflict in *The Outsiders* has been the subject of frequent reactionary criticism. The story, after all, is told by a member of the underclass. Only the more obtuse readers would not infer the sympathetic treatment of the struggle being waged by the Greasers for survival, self-understanding and esteem. To the large numbers of apostles of orthodoxy who roam abroad today on their divinely inspired witch hunts, it is the *Socs* who should emerge as the heroic ones: those impeccably dressed, clean cut, well-mannered youngsters who live in pretty homes in the nice part of town. If those kids have any warts, they should be overlooked. Conversely, the laziness, vulgarity, socially uncouth behavior of the Greasers should be the object of indignation, not sympathy. That Susan Hinton has refrained from such a show of repugnance toward these low lifes has branded her, in the currency of right-wing judgment, as one more *liberal*. (Italics mine)

So *The Outsiders* has taken its lumps over the years from censorship-bound citizens. In the days to come, it will probably remain popular and thus subject to further episodes of vilification. Despite past, present, and future challenges, it has hung in there, truly a landmark young adult novel, and will probably prevail as a favorite of students, teachers, and teacher educators. And the attacks leveled against it can justifiably be construed as compliments. Books of substance have often received such attention. In a certain sense, it's a reflection of their quality.

WORKS CITED

Dunning, Stephen A. *A Definition of the Role of the Junior Novel Based on Analyses of Thirty Novels.* (Unpublished doctoral dissertation) Tallahassee: Florida State University, 1959.

Freedom and Discipline in English. New York: College Entrance Examination Board, 1965.

Hassan, Ihab. *Radical Innocence: Studies in the Contemporary American Novel.* Princeton, NJ: Princeton University Press, 1961.

Howells, William Dean. "Review of The Story of a Bad Boy." *Atlantic Monthly* 25 (Jan. 1870): 124-125.

Jennings, Frank G. "Literature for Adolescents, Pap or Protein," *English Journal*, 65 (Dec. 1954): 526-531.

IS *RUN, SHELLEY, RUN* WORTH FIGHTING FOR?

Gloria Treadwell Pipkin

When censors attack works of established literary merit— especially those sanctified by the passage of time and admitted to the canon— teachers, librarians, and other citizens who defend the books against removal or restriction usually have a broad array of resources at their disposal. Critical reviews abound, tradition and widespread practice support the use of the books, and a large segment of the public recognizes titles and authors' names. Even the illiterate know that enlightened societies do not ban Shakespeare.

But what happens when the censors target contemporary literature, particularly so-called young adult books? As John Simmons points out elsewhere in this collection, the young adult novel as we know it today didn't even exist until little more than a generation ago. Few adults outside schools and libraries have ever heard of Robert Cormier or Gertrude Samuels or Norma Fox Mazer, and their first exposure to the writers' work may be in photocopied passages taken out of context and circulated throughout the community, for shock value. Within the schools themselves, some teachers and librarians may oppose the use of contemporary or controversial works. For readers whose experience with books for adolescents ended with Nancy Drew, the themes and language of many current books for teenagers may well be shocking.

Since its publication in 1974, Gertrude Samuels' *Run, Shelley, Run* has drawn the fire of those who wish to limit schoolchildren's reading to happy songs. In its treatment of a teenager's odyssey through the New York state juvenile justice system, the novel graphically portrays how Shelley Clark is "fucked up...by all these goddam institutions." Along the way Shelley encounters rape, drug use, prostitution, and enforced lesbianism. How, then, our critics ask, can responsible teachers and librarians defend their use of this book with adolescents?

Because my own experience has been as a middle school teacher and because books used in the classroom are often subjected to closer scrutiny and held to higher standards than library books are, my focus will narrow to those questions a good teacher will consider in choosing to use—and defend if *necessary—Run, Shelley, Run.*

One of the best means for clarifying and articulating the value of any book used for common reading in the classroom is a written rationale. The form recommended by Burress and Jenkinson in the National Council of Teachers of English's publication, *The Students' Right to Know*, is widely used throughout the country and is the basis for my own rationale for Samuels' book.

Throughout this rationale, I will deliberately avoid using the term "teach" to describe how I use a novel in the classroom. When we say we *teach* a novel, story, or play, we imply that a particular reading or interpretation is privileged, and I find that conception inaccurate and counter-productive. My students and I read and study many texts together, but I do not "teach" books or stories.

RATIONALE FOR *RUN, SHELLEY, RUN*

I recommend this novel for use with mature middle school and general high school readers. It should be considered for government, sociology, and interdisciplinary courses as well as for English classes. In *Run, Shelley, Run (RSR)*, Gertrude Samuels asks her readers to consider the question of how we treat our unwanted teenagers, through the perspective of a sixteen-year-old girl who has been in the juvenile justice system since she was ten. The issues that Shelley's story bring into sharp focus deserve attention in the form of analysis and serious discussion. What better place for that than in the classroom? Samuels' fast-paced, riveting narrative will engage a wide range of readers, and its style and vocabulary are accessible to most. Vigorous debate inspired by the novel will lead to closer reading and to lively writing.

OBJECTIVES

This novel is rich enough to lend itself to an indefinite number of literary, psychological, and pedagogical purposes. The listing which follows should be considered as a pool from which teachers might select and to which they would most certainly add.

—To explore historical and contemporary forces or attitudes which have influenced the economic, political, and ethical development of our society

—To motivate students and teachers to examine their own attitudes and behaviors and to consider their duties, responsibilities, privileges, and rights as citizens

—To develop, articulate, and respect individual responses to the text; to analyze these responses; and to examine their interaction with the text

—To emphasize and develop the reader's active role in meaning-making

—To identify and assess effectiveness of author's technique

—To inspire further reading and writing.

PROCEDURES

Run, Shelley, Run can be profitably read in small groups or by whole classes. Some students will benefit from short reading assignments agreed upon each day and followed by immediate discussion, while others will choose to read the entire book first. All readers will be encouraged to maintain journals in which they record their questions, observations, impressions, objections, etc. as they read. Reading journals also serve as a place for directed entries consisting of responses to questions or issues posed *by* other readers, including the teacher. Readers might also be asked to record unfamiliar words and phrases whose meaning cannot be deduced from context, with these to be shared in small-group sessions.

Whenever appropriate, students will dramatize selected portions of the narrative, through reader's theater and improvisation. Most of each class period will be devoted to discussion, in a variety of formats, ranging from voluntary sharing of reading journal entries to simulations in which class members assume the parts of various members of the criminal justice system. As interests dictate, outside speakers or panelists might be included (social worker, juvenile judge, public defender, guardian *ad litem*, foster parent, etc.).

Because of reforms in the juvenile justice system since *RSR's* publication in 1974, interested students might do independent research on the current status of the system in their home state, with findings presented to the class. Students' responses to the novel will suggest many other possibilities for writing topics and forms, including the following:

1. personal or formal essays on alternative or innovative approaches to the problems unwanted children face, on the state's role, on the responsibility of parents, etc.

2. epilogues showing what Shelley is doing ten years later

5. screenplays of crucial scenes (e. g., Shelley's encounter with Sister, her transfer to state school, placement in solitary confinement)

4. photo essays on child welfare issues

5. abstracts or summaries of magazine articles on juvenile justice issues.

PROBLEMS OF STYLE AND THEME

Those who believe, as one parent in my school district wrote, that "students have the right to be inspired and encouraged by classroom literature—not depressed or disturbed" may object to specific language and situations (rape, drug use, and lesbianism, for example) in *RSR* as well as to its general indictment of the juvenile justice system. Depending on the age and experience of the students involved, the teacher may choose to address these issues directly with parents, inviting them to read the book for themselves, providing a copy of the rationale, and informing them of their right to an alternative selection. I would also encourage students to decide for themselves as they read whether or not the language Samuels uses is appropriate to the characters and situations, or if its use is gratuitous or sensational. As part of their final assessment of any novel we read together, I often ask students to respond in writing to this specific issue as well as to the general appropriateness of the book for their age group. Written responses to questions such as these can be powerful tools in defending a work under attack. Although our severest critics often do not believe that children's opinions should be considered in such matters, many parents will find them enlightening and persuasive. With other controversial books I have also solicited parents' written responses and published them anonymously, with permission, within the classroom community. Parents may also be invited to attend class discussions.

ALTERNATIVE SELECTIONS

Students and their parents who find *RSR* objectionable for whatever reason should be given other choices. Some thematically related possibilities follow. This list may also be used to suggest related reading for all students.

1. *No Kidding* by Bruce Brooks—In a futuristic society in which two thirds of the adults are alcoholic, children reach legal majority at age thirteen.

2. *Up Country* by Alden Carter—Teenager is sent to live with relatives when his alcoholic mother is forced into treatment.

3. *The Pinballs* by Betsy Byars—For younger readers, this novel focuses on the experiences of three children in a foster home.

4. *Jane Eyre* by Charlotte Bronte—This classic provides one answer to the question of how unwanted children fared in another time and place.

5. *To Take a Dare* by Paul Zindel and Crescent Dragonwagon—Thirteen-year-old girl runs away to escape abusive father, befriends homeless boy, tries to understand her troubled family.

6. *Homecoming* by Cynthia Voigt—Four children make their way to another state after their mother gets too sick to take care of them.

Parents should be encouraged to make suggestions, too, with the final choice acceptable to everyone. Procedures for the independent reading must also be discussed freely. Working together, teachers, students, and their families can decide where and how the reading will be done and how the reader will interact with other members of the class. Although I have heard suggestions that children who choose another book will be ostracized by their peers, in practice I've never seen that happen. In a classroom where individual choices and values are consistently honored, it simply doesn't occur to students to question anyone's right to make her/his own choices.

REVIEWS AND OTHER CRITICAL RESPONSE

A touching, poignant story about the absolutely unbelievable strength and beauty of human beings caught in the most shameful of our social failures. An indictment of our outmoded laws, rotten prison system and lack of decent human resources for abandoned children is important and necessary, but it becomes so much more when dealt with through a background theme that children matter and are beautiful—even when treated beyond endurance.

Eda LeShan, family counselor

This is patently a message novel...The substance of the novel is the callousness of our courts, especially toward young people, and the horror of our penal treatment of youngsters. There is no blinking the fact, and if Gertrude Samuels' book opens a few mare eyes she will be doing a great service. She has slanted everything in her heroine's favor, but the facts she deals with are inescapable and form an indictment of us as a society .... She has done a great work with this brief, attractive, hard-hitting book...."

W. B. Hill in *Best Seller*

"Ages twelve to sixteen"—Dale Carson, *New York Times Book Review*

There are sordid elements in the story: an attempted rape by her stepfather; the suicide of a fellow run-away; a stint at a dope ring hangout; and lesbian encounters in the detention center. The language is also rough, but Samuels intends to show the grimness of Shelley's life and make her problems seem real. Although the girl is not as full-blooded a character as the young heroine of *Go Ask Alice*, her story still has impact.

Peggy Sullivan in *Library Journal*

This is an important human document. In the midst of all the statistical analyses of mass society, it reminds us that these numbers represent one human being at a time. We must not lose our concern for the individual. We have all known Shelley; sometimes she frightens us, sometimes we feel superior, virtuous, often we are intrigued, usually we are puzzled. Rarely do we help. Shelley needs help. Her life is important. Here is a chance to understand. When we understand her, we will be concerned for her. Concern translated into action will give her a chance for a decent life, for personal fulfillment. Only through such understanding and concern can America hope to prevent crime. This book will help us see the truth...."

Ramsey Clark, former U.S. attorney general

WORKS CITED

Burress, Lee, and Edward Jenkinson. *The Students' Right to Know*. Urbana, IL: National Council of Teachers of English, 1982.

Clark, Ramsey. *Run, Shelley, Run* (book jacket). New York: Crowell, 1974.

Hill, W.B. *Best Seller* 34 (1974): 7.

LeShan, Eda. *Run, Shelley, Run* (book jacket). New York: Crowell, 1974.

Sullivan, Peggy. *Library Journal* 99 (1974): 1232.

PENANCE AND REPENTANCE IN *THE SCARLET LETTER*

Richard Gappa

It comes as a surprise to many Hawthorne scholars that *The Scarlet Letter* is a work often attacked and banned at the secondary level. That this work which has been more responsible for acquiring Hawthorne's fame than any other of his works should be under attack by censors indicates how serious the problem of censorship is in our secondary and elementary schools. It is a problem that teachers must seriously address if we are to truly educate our students. *The Scarlet Letter*, I feel, has been attacked as an immoral book that mocks religion, glorifies adultery, dabbles in the occult and generally negatively influences young readers because, as is often the case in attacks upon great and complex pieces of literature, the attackers misread the work.

While Hawthorne does examine organized religion, the possibility of satanic influences in the world, the complexities of adultery and the cancerous effects of hypocrisy upon an individual, he does so in a mature and fair-minded manner. He is not, as is often thought and taught, the creator of a shallow one-sided attack upon Puritanism and a defender of the rebellious Hester Prynne. What he is, is an artist. And as an artist he shows life, its problems and temptations, and most of all its people, in all its complexities and ambiguities. Hawthorne is, after all, a master of ambiguity. In "The Custom House" Hawthorne describes Hester Prynne for the first time as a woman who "gained from many people the reverence due to an angel, but, I should imagine, was looked upon by others as an intruder and a nuisance" (Letter 32). This insistence upon seeing both sides of a person's character is inherent in Hawthorne's novel. It is, in fact, that which makes the work a success. The work survives because it does not preach, because it does not provide an easy answer to the thorny moral problems we all encounter in our life.

The more often one reads *The Scarlet Letter*, the more one sees the multiplicity of meanings in the actions of the characters, the setting, and the symbols used by Hawthorne to develop the tale. The first chapter amply illustrates the richness of Hawthorne's art. In setting up the story through a description of the prison, he notes with irony that all founders of "whatever Utopia" must create cemeteries and prisons. To the Puritan, of course, this was a necessity based on man's sinful nature, his imperfect and imperfectible nature. This view of human nature also necessitated the creation of laws and beadles to enforce those laws. To the romantic, however, law was a restriction of man's freedom—it restricted his right to achieve personal happiness. Society and its laws were the source of evil, whereas man was naturally good. Hawthorne, of course, had direct experience with the pantisocratic thinking of his generation during his "wild, free days on the Assobeth" (Letter 25). He also had spent time with the "dreary brethren of Brook Farm" (25), and "talking with Thoreau about pine-trees and Indian relics" (25), Nature, for Hawthorne, included both roses in June and ugly weeds such as "burdock, pig-weed and apple-peru" (48). The forest, in its natural and untamed state, could be both a refuge from the laws of civilization (freedom to the romantic), or it could be viewed as a naturally evil place (by the Puritans), a place where old mistress Hibbins meets the Black Man. This conflict of interpretation is at the heart of not only the novel but also at the heart of life itself. Is Hester a sinner, or is she a saintly woman following the path of Anne Hutchinson? The reader must decide; there is room for both views because Hester is a mixture of both. When she emerges from the prison, she exhibits both a "burning blush" and a "haughty smile" (52). Her elaborately embroidered "A" had "the effect of a spell, taking her out of the ordinary relations with humanity and inclosing her in a sphere by herself" (54). Singularity and isolation are attributes not only of mystics and saints but also of miltonic devils. One old dame calls her a "brazen hussy" (54); another (a younger woman) pities her and sees that Hester feels pain and stitches "in her heart" (54).

During her first appearance on the scaffold, Hester steadfastly refuses to reveal the name of her child's father. This act, whatever the motivation, is viewed by Arthur Dimmesdale as the "wondrous strength and generosity of a woman's heart" (68). This strength and generosity are consciously developed by Hester after she is released from prison. Much of her time she spends "in making coarse garments for the poor" (83). Her reward for this is "bitterest scorn" (83) and a reviling of "the hand stretched forth to succor them" (84). We are told further that "she was patient—a martyr, indeed" (85). Her suffering and shame at the hands of society become a continual way of life for Hester. Whenever she enters a church to share "the Sabbath smile of the Universal Father" (85), she finds herself the text of a discourse. She soon learns to especially fear children since they pursue her from a distance with shrill cries "and the utterance of a word" (85). One cannot deny the suffering of Hester during this period of her life. Hawthorne, without question, depicts society and its cruelness in a light of criticism. However, Hester herself is presented in a manner not totally admirable. Why she chose to stay and suffer the scorn of the public is treated ambiguously by Hawthorne. We are told that two reasons exist in her head. One is that she wishes to remain where "there trode the feet of one with whom she deemed herself connected in a union, that, unrecognized on earth, would bring them together before the bar of final judgment, and make that their marriage-altar, for a joint futurity of endless retribution" (80). The other reason is her belief that here "had been the scene of her guilt, and here should be the scene of her earthly punishment" (80). Either (or both) of these reasons is partially true. As a reader, we are never given certitude as to a single, unambiguous motive behind her choice to stay in the village.

In addition to the dual reasons for her choice of residency, we also find two different interpretations in regard to the bright red dresses with which Hester clothes Pearl. Certainly Pearl has become a symbol in the village. The question of interpreting the symbol adds to the tension of the various parties in the story. Mr. Wilson, who, along with Master Bellingham, desires to remove Pearl from Hester's care and instruction, fears that Hester has "no better thought than to make a mountebank of her child!" (114) Hester, and later Dimmesdale, argues that Pearl is dressed in red because "she is my torture, none the less! Pearl keeps me here in life! Pearl punishes me too! See ye not, she is the scarlet letter..." (113).

Hester, of course, does keep Pearl and slowly manages to win over the minds and hearts of even the most sour and wrinkled of the society. She helps troubled households in "all seasons of calamity" (161). In fact, she becomes a self-ordained "Sister of Mercy" to the villagers. Their admiration becomes so deep that she is not looked upon as a sinner but as a saint; the scarlet symbol ceases, in their minds, to stand for adulteress but rather means "Able" (161).

But though Hester conforms to the norms of society for seven years, she still remains a revolutionary at heart. "It is remarkable," Hawthorne tells us, "that persons who speculate the most boldly often conform with the most perfect quietude to the external regulations of society" (164). Her most radical speculations would "undermine the foundations of the Puritan establishment" (165). She continuously examines the relationship between men and women and reaches several conclusions. "As a first step, the whole system of society is to be torn down; and built up anew. Then the very nature of the opposite sex, or its long hereditary habit, which has become like nature, is to be essentially modified, before woman can be allowed to assume what seems a fair and suitable position" (165). We are never told what "system" is to be torn down; nor are we told what "nature" of men is to be modified; nor are we given any specific information on the "hereditary habit" of men. Neither is there any detail about the "fair and suitable position" for women. We are, again, free to speculate and argue. We can, however, reach one conclusion about Hester; that is, she is a complex, deep, mysterious woman. As such, she defies simplistic interpretations that would make her either a singular saint or a singular sinner.

The previous seven years of "outlaw and ignominy" (200) prepare Hester for her meeting with Arthur Dimmesdale in the woods. She learns, from an estranged point of view, to criticize all human institutions and "whatever priests or legislators had established" (199). "Shame, Despair, Solitude" become her teachers and make her strong, but "taught her much amiss" (200). This strength enables her to decide for Arthur that he will seek a new life of freedom—"of breathing the wild, free atmosphere of an unredeemed, unchristianized, lawless region" (201). To reinforce the decision, Hester removes her scarlet symbol, throws it across the brook and states, as a true romantic, that "The past is gone! Wherefore should we linger upon it now?...I undo it all, and make it as it had never been!" (202) This flush of joy is short-lived, however, for Pearl soon after rejects both Hester without her symbolic "A" and the kiss tendered by her father.

It is an easy thing to read this chapter as a beautiful illustration of two lovers who are reunited in purpose and love. Hawthorne, however, is not so certain that the compact in the woods is rooted in love and truth. In a heavily symbolic journey from the woods back to the village, Arthur encounters what to him is a series of temptations: to blaspheme the Eucharist, to scandalize an ancient widow, to speak obscenely to a young maiden and a group of children, and finally to utter oaths with drunken sailors. He finally encounters Mistress Hibbins, or perhaps imagines it, because Hawthorne tells us this encounter, "if it were a real incident, did but show his sympathy and fellowship with wicked mortals and the world of perverted spirits" (222). Arthur even goes so far as to reexamine his meeting with Hester in the woods as a meeting with Satan. "Am I mad? or am I given over utterly to the fiend? Did I make a contract with him in the forest, and sign it with my blood?" (220) To a Puritan the answer would be a firm "yes." It is possible to see Hester as a satanic figure—*if* we view her ideas from the Puritan perspective of Dimmesdale; and it is precisely this juxtaposition of elation and temptation that creates the conflict within Dimmesdale and the reader.

In contrast to the romantic rejection of the "dead" past by Hester, Arthur flees to his study (next to the cemetery) and books (voices of dead authors), especially the Bible with Moses and the prophets (all long dead) "speaking to him" (223). It is at this point that Arthur realizes that "another man had returned out of the forest; a wiser one; with a knowledge of hidden mysteries which the simplicity of the former never could have reached" (223). But the question remains—is the new man one who will reject his religion and people for Hester or one who will reject Hester for his religion and beliefs? He merely tells Chillingworth that he is going "to another world" (224) within the next year. What "other world" he has in mind could be seen variously as a new country or a spiritual world (death).

The theme of a resurrected Dimmesdale is brought to fruition in the third scaffold chapter. At his moment of death he appears as a strong, honest person. He admits that "the law we broke!—the sin here so awfully revealed!—let these alone be in thy thoughts! I fear! I fear!" (256) In answer to Hester's desire to spend eternity together, Arthur replies, "God knows; and he is merciful! He hath proved his mercy, most of all, in my afflictions" (256). To Dimmesdale, tribulation is treasure; it is redemptive. His perspective is that of a Puritan believer; it is a perspective that Hester rejects throughout the novel, and which makes the gulf between them all the more distant with Dimmesdale's final "Praised be his name! His will be done!" (257)

Hester, unlike Arthur, never does repent. Her perspective remains that of a woman warring with the world and its institutions. After departing with Pearl and her inheritance, Hester remained removed from the Puritan village for "many years" (261). Why she returned after many years is never made clear by Hawthorne. It is important, however, to note that the return is of her own free will and for purposes of *penitence* (not repentance as in Dimmesdale's case) (263). She soon becomes a comforter and counselor to women, assuring them of her firm belief that "a new truth would be revealed, in order to establish the whole relation between man and woman on a surer ground of mutual happiness" (263). Hester further acknowledges that earlier in life she "had vainly imagined that she herself might be the destined prophetess" (263). She further recognizes that the new woman will demonstrate "how sacred love should make us happy, by the truest test of a life successful to such an end! (263) She, of course, is not happy, for as the narrator tells us, "so said Hester Prynne, and glanced her sad eyes downward at the scarlet letter" (264). The incomplete comparison of the "surer ground of mutual happiness" never tells us "surer" than *what*. It is, as so much that appears earlier in the novel, ambiguous and unstated.

The death of Hester many, many years later results in her burial near another grave, "an old and sunken one" (264). Almost everyone reads this as Arthur's grave, but the novel doesn't state this. It could just as easily be Chillingworth's grave. A case could be made for either interpretation, but whether the grave belongs to Roger or Arthur, Hester still remains a singular woman, for there was "a space between, as if the dust of the two sleepers had no right to mingle" (264). Thus, Hawthorne ends the novel as he began, with a graveyard.

As a reader it is extremely difficult to find evidence for a justification of Hester's or Arthur's actions. There is no glorification of the act of adultery, no denial of the consequences of rejecting societal and spiritual norms. I can cite one unbalanced and biased passage in the novel, but it is *critical* of Hester, not supportive. If Hawthorne ever dropped his narrative mask for an instant, I suspect it was on the final scaffold scene. Here, as Dimmesdale lay dying, Pearl kissed his lips, and "as her tears fell upon her father's cheek, they were the pledge that she would grow up amid human joy and sorrow, nor forever do battle with the world, but be a woman in it" (256). The same can not be said about Hester. Therein lies the real sorrow of the novel.

WORK CITED

Hawthorne, Nathaniel. *The Scarlet Letter*. Ohio State University Press, 1962. All references are to the Standard Centenary Edition.

A RATIONALE FOR READING JOHN KNOWLES' *A SEPARATE PEACE*

David G. Holborn

It is hard to imagine a book that has more to say to youth about to enter the conflict-ridden adult world than John Knowles' *A Separate Peace*. *Huck Finn* and *A Catcher in the Rye* come immediately to mind as forbears of this novel of maturation, and if Knowles lacks the range and dramatic intensity of Twain, he at least provides more answers than Salinger to the vexing problems of adolescence.

The novel is set at Devon, a small New England prep school, during the Second World War. The details and atmosphere of such a school are realistically rendered in the dormitories and playing fields, the lawn parties and the truancies. Accuracy of fact and mood makes this an interesting and gripping story. But it is more than just a good story because it has at least two other dimensions. From beginning to end little Devon is impinged upon by the world at war, so much so that the ordinary round of prep school activities takes on a militaristic flavoring. Along with the outward pressures exerted by the war are the internal pressures, particularly in the narrator Gene, which lead to self-discovery and an acceptance of human ideals and human frailties. It is the integration of these three focuses that makes this such an effective and satisfying novel.

The novel opens with the narrator's return to Devon fifteen years after the action of the story he is about to tell. He presents two realistic scenes that later become associated with important events in the story: the First Academy Building, with its unusually hard marble floors that cause the second break in Phineas's leg; and the tree, that real and symbolic tree which is the place of Finny's initial accident and the presentation of lost innocence. These detailed places occasion the narrator's meditation, and suddenly through flashback we are transported to the idyllic summer of

1942, This framework narrative and flashback technique is important because it sets up a vehicle for conveying judgments to the reader about character and action from two perspectives: sometimes we are getting Gene's reaction at the moment and other times we are receiving the retrospective judgment of the mature man.

I mention this narrative technique not merely as a matter of literary style but as an indication of the serious, thoughtful quality of the novel. The author wishes us to see the growth of Gene and at the same time experience an exciting story, not a philosophical or psychological tract. This is deftly accomplished by means of the dual perspective. The following comment on the important motif of fear illustrates the mature man reflecting on the entire experience at Devon:

> Preserved along with it, like stale air in an unopened room, was the well-known fear which had surrounded and filled those days, so much of it that I hadn't even known it was there. Because, unfamiliar with the absence of fear and what that was like, I had not been able to identify its presence.

> Looking back now across fifteen years, I could see with great clarity the fear I had lived in, which must mean that in the interval I had succeeded in a very important undertaking: I must have made my escape from it. (2)

This statement is more philosophical and judgmental than most later reflective statements, since at this point the story proper has not even begun. But the mature man is heard at intervals throughout the novel, as in this analogy of war to a wave:

> So the war swept over like a wave at the seashore, gathering power and size as it bore on us.... I did not stop to think that one wave is inevitably followed by another even larger and more powerful, when the tide is coming in. (101)

Comments such as these encourage the reader to pause in the story and reflect on the significance of events, certainly an important thing to do with any novel but particularly with a novel of maturation.

The story proper begins in the summer of 1942. It is the calm before the storm, the storm of course being the world at war. For these boys—primarily Gene, Finny, and Leper—the war is still a year away. Even the faculty at Devon treat the reduced summer school class with a bemused tolerance. This summertime Devon is like Eden: the sun always seems to shine, the days endlessly filled with games on the playing fields. This Eden also has its tree and, like the original, this is the tree of the knowledge of good and evil. At first, however, it is just a tree, something to jump from into the clear cool waters of the Devon River. As idyllic as this summer and this particular game of jumping from the tree are, hints of the impending war keep creeping in. Jumping from the tree becomes a test of courage, a kind of boot camp obstacle. So, taking a cue from war literature, the boys call their jumping group the Super Suicide Society of the Summer Session. Always the consummate athlete, Finny jumps first with fluid grace and without apparent fear. Gene is reluctant, but cannot refuse the challenge. The two close buddies cement their friendship in this test. Leper, at least on this first occasion, does not jump. This foreshadows his later inability to cope with the pressures of the war. Already the superficial harmony of the summer is disrupted by this competition which separates the boys according to those who possess the particular skills and temperament necessary in the world of war and those who don't. The scene is a preparation for the key event of the book where Finny breaks his leg, and an early reminder that Eden cannot really exist in this world.

Certainly not all generations have had to face impending world war, but this fact does not lessen the relevance of this book for young readers today. Until recently, the nuclear threat was very much on the minds of our youth. While that threat has been greatly reduced, instant communications have made regional conflicts a part of the average family's daily viewing. Though this vicarious experience is not the same as Gene's and Finny's virtual certainty of going to war, most of today's young readers fear war and have a similar sense of a demon lurking in the woods beyond the playing fields, threatening at any moment to swallow them in their innocent play.

In *A Separate Peace*, however, Knowles plumbs more deeply than the war on the surface. We get hint after hint, culminating in Gene's and Finny's awareness of what really happened in the tree, that the war is also within, its battles waged in the individual breast and then subsequently between bosom buddies.

Gene and Finny have a special relationship but it is not immune—at least on Gene's part—from the petty jealousies that infect most relationships. In Gene's own words, Finny is "too good to be true." He plays games, like the blitzball he invented, for the sheer joy of exhibiting his remarkable athletic skills. He is a natural. One day he breaks the school swimming record in the hundred yard freestyle, with Gene as the only witness, but has no desire to repeat it in an official meet. The idea of having done it is enough. And because of his affability, he can talk his way out of almost any jam, as he did the day he was caught at the headmaster's lawn party wearing the school tie for a belt. One side of Gene admires Finny for these feats, while another, darker side envies him for his ability to glide through life unscathed. As Gene says about Finny after the party at the headmaster's:

He had gotten away with everything. I felt a sudden stab of disappointment. That was because I just wanted to see some more excitement; that must have been it. (21)

The last statement is a rationalization, and a weak one at that. Knowles lets the rationalization stand without a direct statement of truth from the older man's perspective, but the irony leaves no doubt as to Gene's true feelings. Surely any reader, and particularly the youthful one, can identify with this ambivalent reaction to a friend's success. In the end Gene comes to understand and accept these feelings, and the book as a whole makes the statement that only by becoming conscious of these feelings, and coming to terms with them, can a person grow toward maturity. Refusing to face up to jealousies leads only to tragedies such as the one that occurs in this book.

Gene's envy of Finny comes to a head when he concludes wrongly that Finny is keeping him occupied with games so that his grades will suffer. Gene is the best student in the class and Finny the best athlete, but

Gene thinks Finny wants him to jeopardize his supremacy in academics so Finny can shine more brightly. It is at this juncture in the book that the boys go off to the tree for what turns out to be the last meeting of the Super Suicide Society of the Summer Session.

The basic facts concerning Finny's fall from the tree that results in his broken leg are revealed in the first narration of the event, but the reader has to wait for the corroborating evidence presented by Leper months later at a mock trial, along with his peculiar emotional and artistic perception of the event. The facts as presented by Gene are that his knees bent and he "jounced the limb." It is impossible to know how much, if any, forethought was involved in the disastrous movement itself. What is clear from the juxtaposition of this event and the commentary that precedes it is that Gene reacts in some recess of his being, not, as we might have expected, to get back at Finny for hampering him in his studies, but out of a sudden awareness that Finny was not jealous of him, was not competing. It goes back to the statement that Finny is too good to be true. This is a particularly keen insight into the human heart; namely, that we often strike out at others not because of the harm they have done us but because their goodness sheds light on our own mistrustfulness.

In the case of Finny, his goodness is of a peculiar kind. He is not good from the faculty's point of view since he does not study very hard and breaks as many of the rules as he can. His is a kind of natural goodness, a harmoniousness with the sun, the earth and its seasons, and his fellow man—so long as his fellow man preserves his imagination and participates in Finny's rituals of celebration. It has justly been said that Finny is not a realistic character, yet he is an interesting one, and something more than a foil for Gene. Most readers have probably had childhood friends with some of the characteristics of Finny; it is in the sum of his parts that he deviates from reality.

Finny is a character fated to die, not because of anything he does, or anything anyone does to him—though Gene's action against him is significant—but because of what he is and what the world is. If the idyllic summer could have lasted forever, then Finny could have lived a full life. If winter Olympic games could have taken the place of fighting troops on skis, then Finny's leg might have been made whole again. But the world is at war and the first casualties—Leper and Finny—are those whose beings are antithetical to the disruption that is war. Finny's harmoniousness cannot coexist with the dislocation of war. Gene humorously acknowledges this when he says:

> "They'd get you some place at the front and there'd be a lull in the fighting, and the next thing anyone knew you'd be over with the Germans or the Japs, asking if they'd like to field a baseball team against our side. You'd be sitting in one of their command posts, teaching them English. Yes, you'd get confused and borrow one of their uniforms, and you'd lend them one of yours. Sure, that's what would happen. You'd get things so scrambled up nobody would know who to fight anymore. You'd make a mess, a terrible mess, Finny, out of the war." (182)

To Finny, the war was like blitzball, a free-flowing, individualistic game, with no allies and no enemies. To Gene, though he doesn't like to admit it, the war was all too real before he even got to it, so much so that his best friend became his enemy.

Leper, the character third in importance in the book, is the one most directly affected by the war and the one whose testimony at the mock trial seals the truth of the tree incident. Leper returns to Devon after having a nervous breakdown in boot camp. He is the most sensitive of all the boys, a loner and a lover of nature. His testimony not only confirms what actually happened in the tree, but also, through descriptive imagery, places the event in the context of the war. Leper's distracted mind remembers all the concrete details of the scene. Finny and Gene were in the tree and Leper was looking up, with the sun in his eyes, "and the rays of the sun were shooting past them, millions of rays shooting past them like—like golden machine-gun fire." And when the two in the tree moved, "they moved like an engine." "The one holding on to the trunk sank for a second, up and down like a piston, and then the other one sank and fell" (166-168). Leper, who previously saw the world in terms of snails and beaver dams, sees the action in the tree in terms of engines and machine-guns. This is because of what the war has done to him, and more subtly, it is a commentary on how a game in a tree has become a wartime battle.

All three boys are pummelled by the machine of war, because, as the book seems to tell us, war is a condition of the human heart and soul.

The ultimate meaning of this book, and its universal message, is in this idea about war being something that is within us. Of the three characters discussed here, the war within is really only dramatized in Gene, but Gene is the representative boy; Leper and especially Finny are exceptions. Gene is our narrator and it is he with whom we identify. The war may flare out at various times and take on form in France or Germany, Korea or Vietnam, but when we look for the causes we should look first within. This concept ties together all the strands of the novel.

But as much as this is a book about war—within and without—it is also a book about peace. The human heart stripped naked to reveal its pride and jealousy, is a cause for sober reflection. But the title, *A Separate Peace*, encourages the reader to pass with Gene through the sufferings of war to achieve a peace. This peace is based upon understanding and the growth that follows such understanding. Finny achieves one kind of separate peace, the peace of death; it is left to Gene to achieve a separate peace that will allow him to live with himself and others in the adult world, chastened and strengthened by his mistake. His words at the end show us that he has succeeded:

> I never killed anybody and I never developed an intense level of hatred for the enemy. Because my war ended before I ever put on a uniform; I was on active duty all my time at school; I killed my enemy there. (196)

This growth in awareness that leads Gene to his separate peace makes the ending of this book an optimistic one. Some readers seem to feel this book is another *Lord of the Flies*, a novel that depicts human nature when stripped of social institutions as reverting to a frighteningly depraved state. This is not the case in *A Separate Peace*. Once recognized and accepted the war within is tamed.

Furthermore, Knowles does not describe the weakness within as evil, but rather as a form of ignorance. After the mock trial, Gene tries to tell Finny what it was that caused him to jounce the limb: "It was just some ignorance inside me, some crazy thing inside me, something blind, that's all it was" (183). One chapter later war is described in the same terms by the narrator: "Because it seemed clear that wars were not made by generations and their special stupidities. but that wars were made by something ignorant in the human heart" (193). Most ignorance is not invincible; Gene proves this.

A Separate Peace is a novel that should be read by adolescents and adults alike, and it should be discussed openly. Jealousy, misunderstanding, and fear do indeed breed violence when they are kept within. Or they can be liberated, not once and for all perhaps, but over and over again if they are seen for what they are in the light of day. This is all we know of peace in this world.

WORK CITED

Knowles, John. *A Separate Peace* 1960. New York: Bantam, 1966.

AUTHENTICITY AND RELEVANCE: KURT VONNEGUT'S *SLAUGHTERHOUSE-FIVE*

Peter J. Reed

What makes *Slaughterhouse-Five* unusually interesting or gives it any particular merit? Its interest lies first in the authenticity of its being based on actual experience. Then there is the interest of seeing how a man who has undergone such trauma comes to terms with it and interprets it over the next twenty-five years of his life. More than that, we see how he finds relevance in the experience not just for himself but for us all. He sets his experience in the widest possible context—both real and imagined—of time and space. *Slaughterhouse-Five* becomes not just a book about the author's experience, but about *our* experience, the *human* experience, not alone in the extremes of war but also in the mundanity of "ordinary" death and the daily round of life. The freshness of style, which dares anything, mixing reality and science fiction, tragedy and slapstick, certainly commands attention. The merit lies low in how this is done—and in the book's moral scrupulousness. Kurt Vonnegut tries to avoid being overbearing or didactic, but the moral commitment in what he writes is unwavering.

Much of *Slaughterhouse-Five* is fact, some of it autobiographical. Mixed in with history and autobiography is fiction, some of it rather far-fetched science fiction. These "made-up" parts of the story do not conflict with the factual parts, however; in fact, they often help underline the meaning or consequence of actual events. And oftentimes even the science fiction elements seem no more fanciful or perplexing than the factual parts.

Kurt Vonnegut is a veteran. He served with the U.S. Infantry in the Second World War and was captured by the Germans in the Battle of the Bulge. On February 13, 1945, while he was being held a prisoner of war in

Dresden, that city was bombed heavily by Allied aircraft. These air raids created a huge firestorm, similar in effect to a nuclear explosion, which destroyed most of the city and left tens of thousands dead. Vonnegut survived in an underground shelter—the meat storage locker which gives the book its title. The horrors awaiting him on emerging from the shelter were compounded when he was put to work digging corpses out of the rubble.

Understandably, these events—war, capture, the raid and its aftermath—deeply impressed the young Vonnegut. The irony of being an American of German stock who is nearly killed first by his ancestral kinsmen and then by his own comrades does not escape him. After the war, as he went from journalism to public-relations work for G. E. to short story writing to creating novels, he kept trying to come to terms with this experience and to write about it. He found it extremely difficult; many, many stories and five other novels came first, but in 1969 the "Dresden novel" was at last published. The book, and the film version which followed it, drew large audiences and won acclaim.

One factual element of the novel, then, is that much that happens to its main character, Billy Pilgrim, as soldier and P. O. W., really happened to Kurt Vonnegut. He even worked in a factory making malt supplement for pregnant women and was punished for eating some (he lost 35 pounds while imprisoned). Besides drawing on experience, Vonnegut uses the most authoritative study of the Dresden raid, David Irving's *The Destruction of Dresden*, as the source of additional information. Other factual material in the novel is both personal (the O'Hares are real people; so was the soldier who was shot over a teapot) and historical (the Children's Crusade of 1213, *Dresden: History, Stage and Gallery* by Mary Endell, material relating to Hiroshima, the biblical accounts of the destruction of Sodom and Gomorrah).

While *Slaughterhouse-Five* has a foundation in history and fact, that does not make it a "realistic" novel in the usual sense. The story is that Billy Pilgrim, a G. I., gets lost behind enemy lines in 1944. He meets other American scouts, is taken prisoner, marched miles in a steadily growing stream of American captives, then finally put on a train and shipped to a prison camp. This involves days of shock and privation, and Billy's mind

wanders. In fact, we are told, he becomes "unstuck in time." At any
moment he will flip out and visit various points in his future or his past.
This continues to happen to him for the rest of his life. Furthermore, in his
future, he is taken by extraterrestrials to a zoo on their planet, Tralfamador,
and mated with a movie starlet called Montana Wildhack. As the story
follows the life of Billy then, it does so not chronologically but as he sees
it himself, full of fits and starts, of jumps from one time or place to another,
across a lifetime and a galaxy. So we see his postwar married life, his space
travels, his becoming a preacher, even his death, before we get to the
chronologically earlier climax, the Dresden firestorm.

This unusual organization of the book is perhaps its most unique and
significant stylistic element. It can be said that on the one hand this
connects the parts in an unusual formation to give them added power,
while on the other hand it scatters them in a disordering fashion. The way
in which the parts of the story are mixed, out of order, like playing cards
shuffled out of suit and sequence, makes the book resemble a collage or
montage. In these the many pictures looked at one at a time may seem to
have no connection; looked at together, connections begin to emerge and
we see a pattern of relationship. But the "chopping up" of the story
prevents its becoming too easy and rational and explanatory; the chaos,
arbitrariness and senselessness of what happens are reflected in their
portrayal.

Telling connections occur because Vonnegut can juxtapose things
which chronologically might be remote; Dresden with the destruction of
Sodom, Hiroshima, the Tralfamadorian version of the end of the world,
even the sacking of Dresden in 1760. Vonnegut details the firestorm's
unique horror, yet also connects it with a timeless, universal pattern of
destruction. This was an awful thing, he seems to say, hideous beyond
imagining, and yet it is actually like others throughout history, a recurring
horror that we must stop—and yet seemingly *cannot* stop. Viewed this
way, the novel is an attempt to deal with the Dresden experience rationally,
to make it mean something, even if it only stands as a symbol of
meaninglessness, of the great indecipherable forces in life. He even
connects it with the deaths of all people and things around us. Each one
is punctuated with a "So it goes." Death is part of daily living, as

inescapable as breathing, but that does not make it easier to bear.

Viewed the other way, the fragmented, chopped-up form of the book looks like an effort to resist rationalization. Narrative, the telling of a story, by its very nature tries to make sense of what it relates. It pre-supposes beginning and end, cause and effect, progress, revelation, resolution. It tries to make order out of chaos. Vonnegut experiments with the opposite; a fragmented text that does not falsify the nature of its content. This firestorm, this explosion of a city, he says, was a moment of disintegration; he will not reconstruct it, as it were, by a narrative that makes everything explained and rational. In the story, Billy Pilgrim at one point sees a war film forwards and then backwards. Viewed backwards it shows planes sucking bombs up from the ruins, which then leap up as complete buildings, and so on. That is what narrative does, in effect, and a story which makes sense out of Dresden has it backwards.

These aspects of how *Slaughterhouse-Five* is written help make it a unique and moving book which tries to match itself in form to the nature of the experience it portrays. *The Red Badge of Courage*, another American classic on war mentioned in *Slaughterhouse-Five*, centers on a blood stained bandage which should be a symbol of bravery and which in fact comes to instill courage. Meaning grows. Dresden's disintegration is the center of this novel which refuses to explain, justify or find meaning in mass destruction. The book ends with a bird poised over the rubble and corpses asking, "Poo-tee-weet?" No answer; just a question in an incomprehensible language.

This is a recent kind of fiction, often called "post-modernism" (as running counter to earlier twentieth century modernism which did try to find meaning or significance at the center of seemingly meaningless existence). Its freshness and invention can be exciting, offering vivid new ways in which to see things. Flying saucers in a book about a major human disaster and perhaps the most traumatic event in its author's life? It may sound flippant, yet it provides rare possibilities. Billy's extraterrestrial love nest with Montana offers a cozy escape from a cruel reality: we come to share his yearning for a more comfortable place away from the horror of a world where teenáged girls are boiled alive in a water tower. Or, to illustrate another characteristic of this technique, Vonnegut's freedom to pop himself into the story and say, "That was me, I was there," gives the ultimate label of authenticity.

In the first chapter, Vonnegut recalls being asked by Harrison Starr if this is an anti-war novel and answering, "I guess." To this Starr responds that he might as well write an anti-glacier novel, because wars would always come and "were as easy to stop as glaciers." He writes the book anyway, less, perhaps, in the hope of "stopping" war than of making us think about it, and about "plain old death." *Slaughterhouse-Five* is provocative as a war novel; it carefully avoids categorical thinking about nationalities, for example, cutting through jingoism and stereotypes to emphasize common bonds of humanity. Above all, Vonnegut emphasizes the helplessness of those caught up in war. There are no characters in war, he says, only pawns, victims. Lots of victims are children and, indeed, even the combatants seem like children swept up in events beyond their control. The urgency and compassion of Vonnegut, who experienced war as little more than a child, who saw children dead in the hundreds, who fathered three children and adopted more, shows through.

The concern for children runs so strong partly because this book emphasizes the nature of *modern* war. Perhaps soldiers have always been young, little more than children, but modern, aerial warfare has shifted the highest death tolls of war to civilian cities, to women and children. Billy Pilgrim, like his creator, survives the muddle of the battlefield to almost perish in just such a setting. *Slaughterhouse-Five's* examination of that kind of warfare is almost unique. It is also very forward looking; the Dresden firestorm closely resembles a nuclear apocalypse.

Yet even while Vonnegut seeks to de-romanticize war, insists on its horrors, and rejects jingoistic nationalism as a rallying cry for war, he is not unpatriotic nor simply what is often dismissed as "a bleeding heart." The book is not un-American, nor anti any other nationality, come to that; nationality appears mostly an accident of birth. The novel is staunchly pro-human, however, and insists on the tragedy of human suffering and death regardless of nationality. But even about this it is not mawkish or demonstrative. Death by war may be particularly callous or unnecessary, but death, "plain old death," will be there anyway. This sense of inevitability imparts an almost stoical tone to the book. It leads toward the idea that, given that we all must die anyway, often cruelly or prematurely or nonsensically, surely that makes it the more imperative that we treat each other with understanding and dignity. The commonness of death does not trivialize it; it makes life the more important. "So it goes" after the deaths of Robert Kennedy and Martin Luther King and Vonnegut's own father becomes a cry of half-resigned grief, not of dismissal.

It is here, then, that we see the moral core of this novel. It is one to which the author commits himself, opening his heart in the opening and conclusion of the novel to talk of his struggle to write it and of the griefs in his own life. He invests himself; this is not a detached, third-person novel where the author simply disappears behind the backdrop of his drama. The word "crusade" in the subtitle seems apt: Vonnegut extends himself in a moral commitment.

One last point. Objection has sometimes been voiced to a profanity used by one of the soldiers in this story. That may be a little like the executing of Edgar Derby over a teapot amidst the destruction of a city. The soldier's uttered profanity is as nothing beside the obscenities of war we are shown. This emphasizes one of Vonnegut's points, that we are constantly indignant over the wrong things and righteously irrelevant. Besides this, Billy Pilgrim is explicitly likened to Jesus Christ in this novel, and like Jesus he is reviled and crucified. His is a contemporary reviling, in language undeniably common among American soldiers.

Slaughterhouse-Five, then, is socially relevant, talking not just about one war, or war in general but about society and about the human condition in a more universal timeless way. It seems conspicuous in recent writing not just in showing a moral center of any sort but an extraordinarily powerful one. It is fascinating as an example of contemporary fiction showing the possibilities of applying science fiction, fragmented narrative, a mix of fact and fantasy, cinematic techniques and radio comedy to the serious novel. And it surely teaches important lessons about the possibilities of integrating autobiography into a sharable art form, or of building from personal experience to a broader human understanding.

But this novel seems important not just in its ideas, or its morality, or as an example of modern fiction, or for what it might teach about how to write, but for its lesson in thinking. It is provocative, even maddening to some, because of its irreverence. It challenges sacred cows, set ideas, merely traditional ways of thinking. And it does not do this irresponsibly, but from the foundation of a moral human decency. This kind of invitation to openness is surely the essence of education.

Finally, if one would know what Kurt Vonnegut has written in defense of his own writing, one should read the first chapter of his later book, *Palm Sunday*.

CENSORING JUDY BLUME AND
THEN AGAIN MAYBE I WON'T

Mel Krutz

1. Who is the most popular children's author in America today?
2. Who is the most censured?
3. Which of her books are most frequently in question?

Numbers one and two are obviously rhetorical. In order of frequency in a list of the top fourteen of the "most frequently censored titles" between 1985 and 1990, the answer to number three is: *Deenie, Forever, Blubber,* and *Then Again Maybe I Won't* (Weidt 23). *Are You There God? It's Me, Margaret* cannot be far behind.

The answers to these questions open the proverbial Pandoric box. Out of the box comes a cacophony of rackety controversy. People for the American Way identify three of her books in the *top ten* most censored between 1982 and 1989. These are: *Deenie,* number seven; *Then Again Maybe I Won't,* number eight; and *Forever,* number nine (Woman's Day 26). These same books reappear in other People for the American Way surveys, and always in the top numbers. In their list of the top fourteen books challenged between 1982 and 1987, *Blubber* is added as well (People 75). A list of forty-eight books most frequently challenged in 1982, reported by Karolides and Burress in *Celebrating Censored Books,* includes *Forever* and *Then Again Maybe I Won't* as challenged and censored. Blume censoring is extensive. Some schools have even blanket-censored all of her books (Survey).

Clashing with these censorings is a plethora of accolades for Judy Blume books. Some are: She received the first Golden Archer Award presented by the University of Wisconsin—Oshkosh, "a selection made without a pre-selected list, by the students themselves" (Weidt 17). In

1982, *Booklist*, the magazine of the American Library Association, in their poll of thousands of children, found that four of the top five of the "fifty most popular children's books in the country...were Blume titles" (18). In 1982 The Assembly for Adolescent Literature asked "nearly 3,500 students in grades four through twelve to list up to three of the best books they had read on their own in the previous two years." Her works topped the list in *every* grade (19). The conductor of that poll, Dr. Donald Gallo, past president of the Assembly on Literature for Adolescents, stated, "There probably hasn't been any writer in history who has been that popular" (20).

Sales figures of her books accentuate their acceptance and value to young readers. While juvenile books generally "sell only ten to fifteen thousand copies in four or five years," by 1983 more than a million copies of her books had sold in hardcover and around twenty-seven million in paperback. By 1987 paperback sales reached thirty-five million. *Superfudge* alone "sold over a million copies in hardcover within four months, and over a million and a half in paperback in six months (14).

The reasons for these statistics and the censoring are the same. Gallo stated it succinctly, "She is popular because what she writes about and how she writes it make her characters and their actions more real than anything anyone else writes—or perhaps has ever written for preteenage and younger adolescents" (20). The authors of *Literature for Today's Young Adults*, Kenneth L. Donelson and Alleen Pace Nilsen state that Blume's books are popular because of "their refreshing candor about worries that young people have," and "that physical development is not treated separately from emotional and social development," making "Blume's books more fun to read (and more controversial) than are factual books about the development of the human body" (113). Children can face their realisms "through a character when it would be too painful to laugh at themselves directly," says Barbara Oliver of the Santa Fe, New Mexico Public Library, who points to Blume's ability to mix humor with issues (Weidt 21). It is this candor, realism and levity which raise the ire of the censors.

Blume is her own best defense. Rather than moralize and dictate solutions to the realities of reader's lives she stimulates their thinking and problem solving (27), which leads to the development of mental growth and to emotional and social confidence and security—to stability in response to life. While this is a major goal of education in a democratic society, it is anathema to many conservatives, fundamentalists, and general followers of the ProFamily Forum, Citizens for Excellence in Education (an irony), the Moral Majority, the Eagle Forum et. al. (24 & 26).

Blume says, "Censors think that by burying the issue they can control their child's thought. If I don't expose my child to this, they think, then my child is not going to think about this. That is not the way it works.... Every idea is insulting to someone. Certain books make me cringe, too...but I would never forbid my child or anyone else to read them. I would just make them aware of what else is available. Children are their own best censors. What matters is that they have a choice. It is up to us to provide them with a balanced diet. But if reality is removed from that diet, if they are not encouraged to face it as children, how can we expect them to cope as adults?" (27-28)

Her readers verify the value of her books by sending her some 2000 letters a month (Letters 22). They say things like: "I like Judy Blume because every book she writes about a kid with problems concerns a little bit of me.... It's like she knows me and is writing about me." "She brings out more of me when she writes." "She knows what I am like." "Her books are about life the way it really is." This is not to say that the experiences of her characters are the experiences of every reader. I find a touch of "east coast" specificity in her stories, but nonetheless there is also constant universality, and, as one reader wrote, "She writes about people I would like to know" (22). She shares with us that which is human.

Tony, in *Then Again Maybe I Won't*, typifies these characteristics. He personifies some of all of us, and Blume puts us into his head to see ourselves. Many of Blume's books are written through the eyes of the protagonist, as this is. Like Joyce and Faulkner, she uses a type of stream of consciousness. The thoughts of Tony (Anthony Miglione) flow through sequences of sensitive and generally sensible logic, topics and ideas which develop and unravel the plot. It is more than a first person point of view. It is a merging of reader/character minds.

Tony is initially a seventh grade paperboy in Jersey City who finds solutions to: how to respond to a cranky customer; how to be himself in the shadow of an impressive older brother, Ralph; how to live up to the image of another older brother, Vinnie, killed in Vietnam; how to be at ease with the situation his grandmother faces because of throat surgery leaving her unable to speak; how to understand a father who seems to him to be working on a secret project; how to adjust to a different social situation in the family move to Long Island; how to resolve his infatuation with an "older" neighbor girl, whom he fantasizes about and ogles from his bedroom window—all of these, and more, instances of his reality in the process of growing up.

His major concerns are how to adjust to and survive his father's major career change and resulting rise in social status, in the move to Long Island, and how to handle friendship with a rich, superficial, kleptomaniac neighbor, Joel Hoober. Tony isn't at ease with this new "rich" role and is embarrassed by his mother's eagerness to climb. He misses his good friend Frankie from the old neighborhood, and life as it was. Sensitive, honest, and genuine, Tony is caught in the middle of Joel's transgressions, and takes it out on himself.

Tony strives to avoid superficiality, as does Blume whose writing is not shallow, but moves beyond the surface to express what many seventh grade boys deal with in the climb toward adolescence, including "it" going up and having wet dreams, which are realistically though briefly and tastefully included, giving credence to the realities of maturation and life.

In real ways *Maybe I Won't* is the metaphoric state of mind of insecurity in youth, but usually Tony "will" when the doing is rational, and he is in inner conflict when it is not. He represents and brings out the best of the reader while struggling with human issues real to all. Weidt says of Blume's characters that "they appear to be simple, one-sided; but their simplicity is that of childhood: honest and complex (22). Tony is a well-rounded character who changes, develops, matures and rises to challenges, realizations and truths. Not narcissistic, he cares so much about others that his health is at stake. It is a story about confronting reality, breaking through simplicity and superficiality and maturing in the process. It is a story of a boy's epiphany, like John Updike's Sammy in

"A & P," or Jackie's in Frank O'Connor's "First Confession," or the boy's in James Joyce's "Araby." It is a story of holding onto one's values. Weidt recognizes in it the need to belong, seeing it as also the story of isolation. Youth often feel outside of things; Tony and his grandmother both personify separation. Neither is part of the family's major decision making (67), nor does Tony easily feel a part of his new environment at school or in the neighborhood. Powerlessness goes hand-in-hand with isolation as does transplanting and the clash of societal class levels (65 & 67). But Tony does have the strength of family ties to withstand his disequilibrium, and that theme also matters (82). In his epiphany he becomes more sure of who and what he is regardless of the world around him. As Margaret prays in *Are You There God? It's Me, Margaret*, "Oh, please, God. I just want to be normal" (100). Fortunately Tony finds his normalcy. His readers will be secure in theirs because of it.

WORKS CITED

Blume, Judy. *Are You There God? It's Me, Margaret*. Englewood Cliffs, NJ: Bradbury, 1970, Dell 1972.

Blume, Judy. *Letters to Judy: What Your Kids Wish They Could Tell You*. New York: Putnam, 1986.

Blume, Judy. *Then Again Maybe I Won't*. New York: Dell, 1971.

Donelson, Kenneth L. and Alleen Pace Nilsen. *Literature for Today's Young Adults*. Glenview, IL: Scott Foresman, 1989.

Karolides, Nicholas J. and Lee Burress. *Celebrating Censored Books*. Racine, WI. Wisconsin Council of Teachers of English, 1985.

Lee, Betsy. *Judy Blume's Story*. Minneapolis, MN: Dillon, 1981.

People for the American Way. *Attacks on the Freedom to Learn: Annual Report, 1986-1987*.

"Survey of Nebraska Public and School Libraries." Lincoln, NE: Civil Liberties Union, 1982.

"They Ban Books Don't They?" *Woman's Day*. (Jan. 16, 1990): 26.

Weidt, Maryann. *Presenting Judy Blume*. Boston: Twayne, 1990.

IN DEFENSE OF *TO KILL A MOCKINGBIRD*
Jill May

The critical career of *To Kill a Mockingbird* is a late twentieth century case study of censorship. When Harper Lee's novel about a small southern town and its prejudices was published in 1960, the book received favorable reviews in professional journals and the popular press. Typical of that opinion, *Booklist*'s reviewer called the book "melodramatic" and noted "traces of sermonizing, but the book was recommended for library purchase, commending its "rare blend of wit and compassion" (23). Reviewers did not suggest that the book was young adult literature, or that it belonged in adolescent collections; perhaps that is why no one mentioned the book's language or violence. In any event, reviewers seemed inclined to agree that *To Kill a Mockingbird* was a worthwhile interpretation of the South's existing social structures during the 1930s. In 1961 the book won the Pulitzer Prize Award, the Alabama Library Association Book Award, and the Brotherhood Award of the National Conference of Christians and Jews. It seemed that Harper Lee's blend of family history, local custom, and restrained sermonizing was important reading, and with a young girl between the ages of six and nine as the main character, *To Kill a Mockingbird* moved rapidly into junior and senior high school libraries and curriculum. The book was not destined to be studied by college students. Southern literature's critics rarely mentioned it; few university professors found it noteworthy enough to "teach" as an exemplary southern novel.

By the mid-sixties *To Kill a Mockingbird* had a solid place in junior and senior high American literature studies. Once discovered by southern parents, the book's solid place became shaky indeed. Sporadic lawsuits arose. In most cases the complaint against the book was by conservatives who disliked the portrayal of whites. Typically, the Hanover County

School Board in Virginia first ruled the book "immoral," then withdrew their criticism and declared that the ruckus "was all a mistake" (*Newsletter* 1966, 16). By 1968 the National Education Association listed the book among those which drew the most criticism from private groups. Ironically it was rated directly behind *Little Black Sambo* (*Newsletter* 1968, 22). And then the seventies arrived.

Things had changed in the South during the sixties. Two national leaders who had supported integration and had espoused the ideals of racial equality were assassinated in southern regions. When John F. Kennedy was killed in Texas on November 22, 1963, many southerners were shocked. Populist attitudes of racism were declining, and in the aftermath of the tragedy southern politics began to change. Lyndon Johnson gained the presidency; blacks began to seek and win political offices. Black leader Martin Luther King had stressed the importance of racial equality, always using Mahatma Gandhi's strategy of nonviolent action and civil disobedience. A brilliant orator, King grew up in the South; the leader of the SCLC, he lived in Atlanta, Georgia. In 1968, while working on a garbage strike in Memphis, King was killed. The death of this 1965 Nobel Peace Prize winner was further embarrassment for white southerners. Whites began to look at public values anew, and gradually southern blacks found experiences in the South more tolerable. In 1971 one Atlanta businessman observed, "The liberation thinking is here. Blacks are more together. With the doors opening wider, this area is the mecca..." (Book 56). Southern arguments against *To Kill a Mockingbird* subsided. *The Newsletter on Intellectual Freedom* contained no record of southern court cases during the seventies or eighties. The book had sustained itself during the first period of sharp criticism; it had survived regional protests from the area it depicted.

The second onslaught of attack came from new groups of censors, and it came during the late seventies and early eighties. Private sectors in the Midwest and suburban East began to demand the book's removal from school libraries. Groups, such as the Eden Valley School Committee in Minnesota, claimed that the book was too laden with profanity (*Newsletter* 1978, 31). In Vernon, New York, Reverend Carl Hadley threatened to establish a private Christian school because public school libraries contained such "filthy, trashy sex novels" as *A Separate Peace* and *To Kill a Mockingbird* (*Newsletter* 1980, 62). And finally, blacks began to censor the book. In Warren, Indiana, three black parents resigned from the township Human Relations Advisory Council when the Warren County school administration refused to remove the book from Warren junior high school classes. They contended that the book "does psychological damage to the positive integration process and represents institutionalized racism" (*Newsletter* 1982, 47). Thus, censorship of *To Kill a Mockingbird* swung from the conservative right to the liberal left. Factions representing racists, religious sects, concerned parents, and minority groups vocally demanded the book's removal from public schools. With this kind of offense, what makes *To Kill a Mockingbird* worth defending and keeping?

When Harper Lee first introduces Scout in *To Kill a Mockingbird*, she is almost six years old. By the end of the book Scout is in the third grade. Throughout the book events are described by the adult Scout who looks back upon life in the constricted society of a small southern town. Since it is the grown-up Scout's story, the young Scout Finch becomes a memory more than a reality. The book is not a vivid recollection of youth gone by so much as a recounting of days gone by. Yet, Scout Finch's presence as the events' main observer establishes two codes of honor, that of the child and of the adult. The code of adult behavior shows the frailty of adult sympathy for humanity and emphasizes its subsequent effect upon overt societal attitudes. Throughout the book Scout sees adults accepting society's rules rather than confronting them. When Scout finds school troublesome, Atticus tells Scout that they will continue reading together at night, then adds, "you'd better not say anything at school about our agreement" (34). He explains away the Maycomb Ku Klux Klan, saying, "it was a political organization more than anything. Besides, they couldn't find anybody to scare" (136). And when he discusses the case of a black man's word against a white man's with his brother, Atticus says, "The jury couldn't possibly be expected to take Tom Robinson's word against the Ewells'.... Why reasonable people go stark raving mad when anything involving a Negro comes up, is something I don't pretend to understand" (84). The author tells us that Atticus knew Scout was listening in on this conversation and purposely explained that he had been court appointed, adding, "I'd hoped to get through life without a case of this kind..." (84). And when the jury does see fit to try and condemn Tom Robinson, Scout's older brother Jem and good friend Dill see the white southern world for what it is: a world of hypocrisy, a world burdened with old racist attitudes which have nothing to do with humanity. Jem says, "I always thought Maycomb folks were the best folks in the world, least that's what they seemed like" (197). Dill decides he will be a new kind of clown. "I'm gonna stand in the middle of the ring and laugh at the folks.... Every one of 'em oughta be ridin' broomsticks" (198).

The majority of white adults in Maycomb are content to keep blacks, women and children in their place. Atticus's only sister comes to live with the family and constantly tells Scout she must learn how to act, that she has a place in society: womanhood with its stifling position of prim behavior and wagging tongues is the essence of southern decorum. Even Atticus, the liberal minded hero, says that perhaps it's best to keep women off the juries of Alabama because, "I doubt if we'd ever get a complete case tried--the ladies'd be interrupting to ask questions" (202). By the end of the book Scout has accepted the rules of southern society. The once hated aunt who insisted upon Scout's transformation into a proper young lady becomes an idol for her ability to maintain proper deportment during a crisis. Scout follows suit, reasoning "if Aunty could be a lady at a time like this, so could I" (217).

The courtroom trial is a real example of Southern justice and Southern local color storytelling. Merrill Skaggs has analyzed the local color folklore of southern trials in his book *The Folk of Southern Fiction*. Skaggs comments that there is a formula for court hearings, and he suggests that local color stories show that justice in the courtroom is, in fact, less fair than justice in the streets (94). He discusses justice in terms of the black defendant, saying, "Implicit in these stories...is an admission that Negroes are not usually granted equal treatment before the law, that a Negro is acquitted only when he has a white champion" (96). During the trial in *To Kill a Mockingbird* Tom Robinson says he ran because he feared southern justice. He ran, he says, because he was "scared I'd hafta face up to what I didn't do" (182). Dill is one of Lee's young protagonists. He is angered by the southern court system. The neglected son of an itinerant mother, Dill is a stereotype of southern misfits. Lee doesn't concentrate upon Dill's background; she concentrates upon his humanity. The courtroom scene is more than local humor to him. It is appalling. When he flees the trial, Scout follows. She cannot understand why Dill is upset, but the notorious rich "drunk" with "mixed children" can. He sees Dill and says, "it just makes you sick, doesn't it?" (183). No one, save Jem and his youthful converts, expects Atticus to win. The black minister who has befriended the children warns, "I ain't ever seen any jury decide in favor of a colored man over a white man" (191). In the end Atticus says, "They've done it before and they did it tonight and they'll do it again and when they do it--seems that only children weep" (195). And Miss Maudie tells the children, "as I waited I thought, Atticus Finch won't win, he can't win, but he's the only man in these parts who can keep a jury out so long in a case like that." Then she adds, "we're making a step--it's just a baby-step, but it's a step (197).

In his book, Skaggs points out that obtaining justice through the law is not as important as the courtroom play in southern trials and that because the courtroom drama seldom brings real justice, people condone "violence within the community" (96-99). Atticus realizes that "justice" is often resolved outside of the court, and so he is not surprised when the sheriff and the town leaders arrive at his house one night. The men warn Atticus that something might happen to Tom Robinson if he is left in the local jail; the sheriff suggests that he can't be responsible for any violence which might occur. One of the men says, "--don't see why you touched it [the case] in the first place.... You've got everything to lose from this, Atticus. I mean everything" (135-136). Because Atticus wants courtroom justice to resolve this conflict, he tries to protect his client. On the night before the trial Atticus moves to the front of the jail, armed only with his newspaper. While there, the local lynching society arrives, ready to take justice into its own hands. Scout, Jem, and Dill have been watching in their own dark corner, but the crowd bothers Scout and so she bursts from her hiding spot. As she runs by, Scout smells "stale whiskey and pigpen," and she realizes that these are not the same men who came to the house earlier. It is Scout's innocence, her misinterpretation of the seriousness of the scene, her ability to recognize one of the farmers and to talk with guileless ease to that man about his own son which saves Tom Robinson from being lynched. The next morning Jem suggests that the men would have killed Atticus if Scout hadn't come along. Atticus who is more familiar with adult southern violence, says "might have hurt me a little, but son, you'll understand folks a little better when you're older. A mob's always made up of people, no matter what.... Every little mob in every little southern town is always made up of people you know—doesn't say much for them does it? (146). Lynching is a part of regional lore in the South. In his study of discrimination, Wallace Mendelson pointed out that the frequency of lynchings as settlement for black/white problems is less potent than the terrorizing aspect of hearing about them (144). In this case, the terrorizing aspect of mob rule had been viewed by the children. Its impact would remain.

After the trial Bob Ewell is subjected to a new kind of Southern justice, a polite justice. Atticus explains, "He thought he'd be a hero, but all he got for his pain was...was, okay, we'll convict this Negro but get back to your dump" (228). Ewell spits on Atticus, cuts a hole in the judge's screen, and harasses Tom's wife. Atticus ignores his insults and figures, "He'll settle down when the weather changes" (228). Scout and Jem never doubt that Ewell is serious, and they are afraid. Their early childhood experiences with the violence and hypocrisy in southern white society have taught them not to trust Atticus's reasoning but they resolve to hide their fear from the adults around them. When Ewell does strike for revenge, he strikes at children. The sheriff understands this kind of violence. It is similar to lynching violence. It strikes at a minority who cannot strike back, and it creates a terror in law-abiding citizens more potent than courtroom justice. It shows that southern honor has been consistently dealt with outside of the courtroom.

Harper Lee's book concerns the behavior of Southerners in their claim for "honor," and Boo Radley's presence in the story reinforces that claim. When Boo was young and got into trouble, his father claimed the right to protect his family name. He took his son home and kept him at the house. When Boo attacked him, Mr. Radley again asked for family privilege; Boo was returned to his home, this time never to surface on the porch or in the yard during the daylight hours. The children are fascinated with the Boo Radley legend. They act it out, and they work hard to make

Boo come out. And always, they wonder what keeps him inside. After the trial, however, Jem says, "I think I'm beginning to understand something. I think I'm beginning to understand why Boo Radley's stayed shut up in the house...it's because he *wants* to stay inside" (208).

Throughout the book Boo is talked about and wondered over, but he does not appear in Scout's existence until the end when he is needed by the children. When no one is near to protect them from death, Boo comes out of hiding. In an act of violence he kills Bob Ewell, and with that act he becomes a part of southern honor. He might have been a hero. Had a jury heard the case, his trial would have entertained the entire region. The community was unsettled from the rape trial, and this avenged death in the name of southern justice would have set well in Maycomb, Alabama. Boo Radley has been outside of southern honor, however, and he is a shy man. Lee has the sheriff explain the pitfalls of southern justice when he says, "Know what'd happen then? All the ladies in Maycomb includin' my wife'd be knocking on his door bringing angel food cakes. To my way of thinkin'...that's a sin.... If it was any other man it'd be different" (250-251). The reader discovers that southern justice through the courts is not a blessing. It is a carnival.

When Harper Lee was five years old the Scottsboro trial began. In one of the most celebrated southern trials, nine blacks were accused of raping two white girls. The first trial took place in Jackson County, Alabama. All nine were convicted. Monroeville, Lee's hometown, knew about the case. Retrials continued for six years, and with each new trial it became more obvious that southern justice for blacks was different from southern justice for whites. Harper Lee's father was a lawyer during that time. Her mother's maiden name was Finch. Harper Lee attended law school, a career possibility suggested to Scout by well-meaning adults in the novel. *To Kill a Mockingbird* is set in 1935, midpoint for the Scottsboro case.

Scout Finch faces the realities of southern society within the same age span that Harper Lee faced Scottsboro. The timeline is also the same. Although Lee's father was not the Scottsboro lawyer who handled that trial, he was a southern man of honor related to the famous gentleman soldier, Robert E. Lee. It is likely that Harper Lee's father was the author's model for Atticus Finch and that the things Atticus told Scout were the kinds of things Ama Lee told his daughter. The attitudes depicted are ones Harper Lee grew up with, both in terms of family pride and small town prejudices.

The censors' reactions to *To Kill a Mockingbird* were reactions to issues of race and justice. Their moves to ban the book derive from their own perspectives of the book's theme. Their "reader's response" criticism, usually based on one reading of the book, was personal and political. They needed to ban the book because it told them something about American society that they did not want to hear. That is precisely the problem facing any author of realistic fiction. Once the story becomes real, it can become grim. An author will use first-person flashback in story in order to let the reader live in another time, another place. Usually the storyteller is returning for a second view of the scene. The teller has experienced the events before and the story is being retold because the scene has left the storyteller uneasy. As the storyteller recalls the past both the listener and the teller see events in a new light. Both are working through troubled times in search of meaning. In the case of *To Kill a Mockingbird* the first-person retelling is not pleasant, but the underlying significance is with the narrative. The youthful personalities who are recalled are hopeful. Scout tells us of a time past when white people would lynch or convict a man because of the color of his skin. She also shows us three children who refuse to believe that the system is right, and she leaves us with the thought that most people will be nice if seen for what they are: humans with frailties. When discussing literary criticism, Theo D'Haen suggested that the good literary work should have a life within the world and be "part of the ongoing activities of that world" (4). *To Kill a Mockingbird* continues to have life within the world; its ongoing activities in the realm of censorship show that it is a book which deals with regional moralism. The children in the story seem very human; they worry about their own identification, they defy parental rules, and they cry over injustices. They mature in Harper Lee's novel, and they lose their innocence. So does the reader. If the readers are young, they may believe Scout when she says, "nothin's real scary except in books" (254). If the readers are older they will have learned that life is as scary, and they will be prepared to meet some of its realities.

WORKS CITED

Book, Simeon. "Black Business Is Top in South." *Ebony.* (Aug. 1971): 56.

D'Haen, Theo. *Text to Reader: A Communicative Approach to Fowles, Barth, Cortazar and Boen.* Amsterdam: John Benjamins Publishing Company, 1983.

Lee, Harper. *To Kill a Mockingbird.* New York: Harper & Row, 1961.

Mendelson, Wallace. *Discrimination.* Englewood Cliffs, NJ: Prentice Hall, 1962.

Newsletter on Intellectual Freedom. Mar. 1966: 16; Mar. 1968:22; Mar. 1978: 31; May 1980: 62; Mar. 1982: 47.

Rev. of *To Kill a Mockingbird,* by Harper Lee. *Booklist* 57(Sep 1, 1960): 23.

Skaggs, Merrill. *The Folk of Southern Fiction.* Athens, GA: The University of Georgia Press, 1972.

FINDING HUMOR AND VALUE IN *WHERE THE SIDEWALK ENDS* AND *A LIGHT IN THE ATTIC*

John M. Kean

Sometime in the late 1950s, when I was an undergraduate student at Ohio University, I attended a poetry reading session by Robert Frost. After a delightful hour or so of his reading his poetry, he asked for questions. Someone asked him about the meaning of one of his poems. Frost stared out a window for at least a moment, turned his head and said "It means what I wrote when I wrote it" or words to that effect. I'm sure that he expressed it more eloquently than I remember it, but at the time it struck me as one of the most profound statements I had ever heard. As an undergraduate English major, struggling to figure out why my professors and I never agreed as to what a poem meant, it delighted me to have a poet remind me of what poetry is. Poetry is what it is, imaginative writing which needs to be expressed, lived, not something which is converted into essays in order to decipher the hidden messages. Shortly after this experience, I read John Ciardi's *How Does a Poem Mean?* through which I came to a better understanding of the relationship between poetry and performance. Even more significant for my future career as a teacher of children and children's literature, I came to understand better why young children like poetry. "[They have] a good time with the poem. The poem pleases and involves [them]. [They] respond to it in an immediate muscular way. [They] recognize its performance at once and want *to act with it"* (Ciardi, 669; italics are Ciardi's).

Shel Silverstein in his two anthologies *Where the Sidewalk Ends* and *A Light the Attic* invites the child to act, to walk, to bounce, to dance with his poetry. He conjures up images which tickle a child's imagination, which speak directly to children's fantasies, their fears, frustrations, everyday experiences. Many of his poems are written from a child's point of view. Others invite/demand physical involvement. Silverstein begins *Where the Sidewalk Ends* with an "Invitation" (9).

> If you are a dreamer, come in,
> If you are a dreamer, a wisher, a liar.
> A hope-er, a pray-er, a magic bean buyer...
> If you're a pretender, come sit by my fire
> For we have some flax-golden tales to spin, Come in!
> Come in!

Only readers who are ready to play with language and ideas can enter into Silverstein's world.

Children genuinely enjoy the verse of Shel Silverstein. They don't know why they like it. They just do. They laugh when they listen to it; they enjoy reciting it. They memorize it. They imitate his style when they write their own poetry. They listen to it for long periods of time. Teachers delight in reading it to children. Children delight in reading it to each other. They don't particularly care about its themes or its meanings, (although the teacher does). His poetry is absurd, weird, sick, gross, gooey, odd, obscure, scary, ridiculous, rule breaking, confusing, impossible. It is repeatable, suggestible, understandable and fun.

Silverstein's poetry is for those with imagination and humor, not those who treat all poetry and fiction as a non-literary reference manual for behavior. Silverstein plays with the everyday world of the children with word pictures that provide them with a constantly moving horizon of images that distort reality like the mirror in a circus fun house. Peggy Ann McKay couldn't go to school because she was so sick until she found out it was Saturday. Sarah Cynthia Sylvia Stout would not take the garbage out and thus met an awful fate, Jimmy Jet turned into a TV set and poor Hungry Mungry ate everything including himself until "Nothin' was nothin' was / Nothin' was left to eat" *(Where* 161).

The literalist sees doom in every poem. The child sees drama. Some parents have been so concerned about the makeup of Silverstein's poetry that they have asked that his anthologies be banned. The poem "Little

Abigail and the Beautiful Pony" evoked such a response in Hoffman, Texas, which resulted in *A Light in the Attic* being banned in the second grade. Abigail wanted "...that pony...if I don't get that pony I'll die". / And she DID die--/ All because of a pony / That her parents wouldn't buy. / (This is a good story / To read to your folks / When they won't buy / You something you want.)/" (120-121). Silverstein says that he made up this poem, but children and their parents will recognize the exaggerated emotional behavior, calculated or not, that often accompanies children's and adolescent's desire for things they cannot have or cannot do. Because the situation is so familiar the children and their parents laugh at the exaggerated accuracy of the image, not the horrors of suicide seen by the literalist in Texas.

Silverstein uses humor in "ma and God" not to mock God as some have suggested but to highlight the too familiar scene in many houses when adult views of hygiene and propriety differ from those of children: "God gave us fingers—Ma says, 'Go wash 'em' / But God gave us coal bins and nice dirty bodies. / ...Either Ma's wrong or else God is" (*Where* 119). Both the parents and the children share the joke with no lack of respect to God.

Complaints have been lodged against "Dreadful" because "Someone ate the baby, / It's rather sad to say" allegedly deals with cannibalism (*Where* 141) and "The Planet of Mars" in which the verse "And they have the same heads, and same faces... / But not in the very same places," is accompanied by an illustration of a side view of a clothed male figure with a head growing from the buttocks (*Where* 93). The latter is apparently in bad taste.

Poet Myra Cohn Livingston summarized what reviewers have said repeatedly: "Mr. Silverstein's genius lies in a new way to present moralism, beguiling his child readers with a technique that establishes him as an errant, mischievous and inventive child as well as an understanding, trusted and wise adult..." (qtd. in Hopkins 135). His use of contrasts with what adults perceive of as positive behavior only underscores his wit and his oneness with children. In "How Not to Have to Dry the Dishes" he concludes "If you have to dry the dishes / And you drop one on the floor / Maybe they won't let you / Dry the dishes anymore" (*A Light* 12) should not be perceived as an invitation to break dishes but rather as way to let children know that adults know that children know there really are rules to getting along in social relationships. That "Mrs. McTwitter thinks a baby-sitter's supposed / To sit upon the baby," (*A Light* 14) does not suggest disrespect for adults but perhaps may deal with those unconscious fears that some children develop about people other than their parents. The "Prayer of the Selfish Child" who says "I pray the Lord my toys to break / So none of the other kids can use 'em..." can help children articulate some of those frequent possessive feelings that they do have about their toys (*A Light* 15). And although his poetry is directed at children, the humor that children find and the humor that adults find may be of different kinds. In the following example from "They've Put a Brassiere on the Camel" the child sees the surface silliness of animals wearing clothes while an adult might find a subtler poke at those who would try to protect society by reverting to some misguided notion of Victorian prudery. "The camel had nothing to say. / ...They say that she looks more respectable now. / Lord knows what they've got in mind for the cow, / Since they've put a brassiere on the camel" (*A Light* 166).

The 1988-90 volumes of the *Newsletter on Intellectual Freedom* chronicle a host of complaints against these two volumes of poetry: child abuse, cannibalism, behavior abusive to women and children, suicide as a way to manipulate parents, mockery of God, behavior that is selfish, disrespect for parents, drug use, the occult, violence, disrespect for truth, disrespect for legitimate authority, sexual innuendoes, demonic overtones, subliminal and antiparent material (36.1, 2; 37.2, 51.67-68, 38.3, 80; 39.6, 210).

Most adult readers make guesses about how children will respond to literature. Some make guesses based on many years of teaching, living and working with children and the literature that they hear or read. Sometimes adults make assumptions about children and the literature that *do* not seem warranted on the basis of the evidence available about what children do with the literature. The accusations about these anthologies noted above have never included any reference to children's having actually been moved to exhibit anti-social behavior as a result of their reading. Critics have made unwarranted assumptions about children and their responses to Silverstein's poetry. They assume that children take everything literally, that they have no understanding of the ironic, satirical or other form of literary humor. The nonsense of Silverstein's poetry amuses only if the reader sees its absurdity. Silverstein actually helps children develop intellectually because he invites comparisons of reality and absurdity. Children take the meaning beyond its literal, explicit senses beyond the meaning of any one word, line, verse, poem, or sequence of poems to a fresh somewhat iconoclastic view of their everyday lives. And Silverstein always challenges the child's imagination. Although he does not seek to overthrow traditional mores, children delight in images and ideals that adults take too seriously. It is possibly true that a child who would answer the question, "How do we tell if a window is open?" by "Just throw a stone at it" (*Where* 147) and then do it is not ready for this poem. But the child who would laugh at the rest of the poem "Does it make a noise? / It doesn't? / Well, it was open. *Now* let's try another... / Crash! / It wasn't!" is ready.

WORKS CITED

Ciardi, John. *How Does a Poem Mean?* Riverside Press, 1959.

Livingston, Myra Cohn. "The Light in His Attic," *New York Times Book Review*. March 9, 1986, cited in Lee Bennett Hopkins *Pass the Poetry Please*, revised edition. Harper & Row, 1987. 135.

Newsletter on Intellectual Freedom 36.1(1987): 2; 37.2(1988): 51, 67-68; 38.3(1989):80; 39.6(1990):210.

Silverstein, Shel. *A Light in the Attic*. Harper and Row, 1981.

Silverstein, Shel. *Where the Sidewalk Ends*. Harper and Row, 1974.

ABOUT THE CONTRIBUTORS

ROBERT M. ADAMS is a literary critic who has written, edited or translated more than twenty books on several of the major literary figures of the Western world. He is a regular contributor to such periodicals as *The New York Review of Books*.

RUDOLFO A. ANAYA's novels include *Bless Me, Ultima* and *Heart of Aztlan*. He has lectured and written extensively on Hispanic literature. He is professor of English at the University of New Mexico.

FRANK BATTAGLIA has written more than 90 articles on a variety of literary and cultural topics, ranging from Anglo-Saxon literature to twentieth-century authors and twentieth-century politics and the environment. He is professor of English at the College of Staten Island.

ROBERT BECK is interested in American culture. He has been a member of the English Department at the University of Wisconsin-River Falls for thirty years.

TERRY BECK is writing a dissertation on rhetoric. He is professor of English at the University of Wisconsin-LaCrosse where his interests include writing across the curriculum and computers in writing.

RICHARD H. BECKHAM is from Mississippi where he lived through the Civil Rights controversies of the fifties and learned of the importance of freedom of expression for a democratic society. The co-author of a forthcoming book on southern culture, he is professor of English at University of Wisconsin-River Falls.

SUE BRIDWELL BECKHAM's most recent book is *Depression Post Office Murals and Southern Culture: A Gentle Reconstruction*. She is at work with Richard Beckham on another book on southern culture. She is professor of English at the University of Wisconsin-Stout.

JAMES BERTOLINO has published eighteen books of poetry and numerous articles. He has won several awards for his poetry and for his activities in small press poetry books.

NORBERT BLEI is the author of fourteen books of fiction, non-fiction and poetry. His writing has appeared in *Chicago Magazine, The New Yorker,* and *The Kenyon Review.* A recent book, *The Chronicles of a Rural Journalist in America,* includes a discussion of censorship.

ROBIN F. BRANCATO is the author of many books for young adults, including *Blinded by the Light, Come Alive at 505, Sweet Bells Jangled Out of Tune* and *Winning.*

SUE ELLEN BRIDGERS writes young adult fiction including *Home Before Dark, All Together Now, Notes for Another Life,* and *Permanent Connections.* She has won numerous awards including The Boston Globe Horn Book Award for Fiction.

LEE BURRESS has written several books on censorship including *The Battle of the Books: Literary Censorship in the Public Schools, 1950-85,* as well as a number of articles on censorship and other subjects. He is professor emeritus at the University of Wisconsin-Stevens Point.

JAMES E. DAVIS has written extensively on the subject of censorship. He edited the book *Dealing with Censorship* (NCTE, 1979). He is professor of English at Ohio University and is past-president of the National Council of Teachers of English.

JOAN DELFATTORE is the author of *What Johnny Shouldn't Read: Textbook Censorship in America.* She is professor of English at the University of Delaware.

JAMES DEMUTH joined the English Department at the University of Wisconsin-River Falls in 1975, specializing in American Literature. He directed the American Studies program, and was awarded Fulbright fellowships in 1981 and 1987. He died in 1988.

IMOGENE DESMET is currently writing a book on love in Chaucer's poetry. She has written various articles and lectured on Chaucer. She is professor of English at University of Wisconsin-Stevens Point.

WALTER C. FARRELL, JR. has written a number of articles on various aspects of American culture and American literature in such publications as *Melus, Minority Voices,* and *Contemporary Literary Criticism* (1985). He is professor of Educational Policy and Community Studies at the University of Wisconsin at Milwaukee.

GILBERT P. FINDLAY has written a number of articles on adolescents in autobiography and teaching adolescent literature. He is currently at work on a book entitled *The Alien Song,* a book exploring the nature of the self as described in autobiography theory. He is a professor of English at Colorado State University.

PAULA FOX is the author of more than twenty children's and young adult books, including *Blowfish Live in the Sea, The Slave Dancer* (1974 Newbery Medal), *One-eyed Cat, The Stone-faced Boy,* and the *Moonlight Man.* She has received many awards for her work, including the Hans Christian Andersen Medal.

RICHARD GAPPA is currently working on an edition of Yao and Zhung folk tales which he collected from Guangxi Province in China. He is professor of English at the University of Wisconsin-LaCrosse.

MARYEMMA GRAHAM is an associate professor of English and African American Studies and director of the Project on the History of Black Writing at Northeastern University. She has written extensively on African American writers and their work. She has coordinated an international symposium on Richard Wright and co-edits the Newsletter of the Richard Wright Circle.

HARRY HARDER is professor of English at the University of Wisconsin-Eau Claire and teaches, among other courses, Shakespeare and American drama. He has presented papers on the plays of Arthur Miller.

DAVID G. HOLBORN is a literary critic who has written several articles on nineteenth and twentieth century literature. He is currently co-editor of the interdisciplinary writing journal *Issues in Writing,* and professor of English at the University of Wisconsin-Stevens Point.

LEE BENNETT HOPKINS' poetry for children includes *When I Am All Alone, Girls Can Too* and *Circus.* He is also the author of *Books are by People,* and compiler of *Don't Turn Back: Poems by Langston Hughes.* His work has been honored by many organizations including the American Library Association, the International Reading Association, and the National Council for Social Studies.

ANGELENE JAMISON-HALL has written a number of articles on Black literature and Black women writers for such publications as *The Western Journal of Black Studies, Sage: A Scholarly Journal on Black Women, Journal of Negro History,* Mari Evans' *Black Women Writers;* 1950-80 and William Robinson's *Critical Essays on Phyllis Wheatley.* She is a professor in the Department of African American Studies at the University of Cincinnati.

EDWARD B. JENKINSON has written books on a variety of subjects including the *Bible* and censorship (*Censors in the Classrooms: The Mind Benders*). He has written and lectured extensively on these subjects. He is professor of English Education, Indiana University.

NICHOLAS J. KAROLIDES, editor of the text *Reader Response in the Classroom: Evoking and Interpreting Meaning in Literature,* is the author of *The Pioneer in the American Novel, Focus on Physical Impairments* and co-author of *Focus on Fitness.* He has published many articles on English education and over 100 book reviews. A former editor of the *Wisconsin English Journal,* he is professor of English and associate dean of the College of Arts and Sciences at the University of Wisconsin–River Falls.

JOHN M. KEAN has been a member and chair of the NCTE Committee Against Censorship, a member of the Conference on English Education Commission on Intellectual Freedom, and the International Reading Association Advisory Committee on Intellectual Freedom. He has published extensively on English education, literature for children and young people. He is a professor in the Department of Curriculum and Instruction, University of Wisconsin-Madison.

MEL KRUTZ has written various articles on censorship and is a member of the NCTE Committee Against Censorship. She teaches English at the Platt campus of the Central Community College at Columbus, Nebraska.

JILL P. MAY has written over 70 articles published in various professional journals and two books, most recently *Lloyd Alexander* (Twayne Children's Authors, 1991). She is professor of literacy and languages at Purdue University.

NORMA FOX MAZER is the author of many books for young adults, a few of which are *Trissy, A Figure of Speech, The Solid Gold Kid, Up in Seth's Room, Taking Terri Mueller,* and *My Name Is Emily.* Her works have received many citations and awards.

WILLIAM MCBRIDE has held various offices in NCTE and in the Assembly on Literature for Adolescents. He is professor of English at Colorado State University.

JAMES A. MICHENER is the author of many well-known books of historical fiction including *Hawaii, Chesapeake, Texas, The Source,* and *Tales of the South Pacific.*

ARTHUR MILLER is known world-wide for his plays, *Death of a Salesman, All My Sons,* and *The Crucible.* He has also written such novels as *Focus* and *The Misfits.*

ARLENE HARRIS MITCHELL's doctoral dissertation was on *The Adventures of Huckleberry Finn.* Her teaching experience includes 16 years in classrooms from grades 7 through 12. She has been a manuscript review editor for *The Journal of Reading,* and she is a co-editor of the forthcoming Scholastic publication *Anthology of Black Literature.* She is professor of literacy and English education at the University of Cincinnati.

OPAL MOORE has published short stories, poetry and essays in various periodicals and collections. Her work is an exploration of the Black experience in America. Two forthcoming books are *I Ain't No*

Stranger...I Been Here Before and *Mildred D. Taylor: Moral Teacher.* She is professor of English at Radford University.

JIM MULVEY's doctoral dissertation was on Ernest Hemingway. His research and publications deal with modern American fiction and children's literature. He is professor of English at the University of Wisconsin-River Falls.

RON NEUHAUS has written critical essays on T. S. Eliot, F. Scott Fitzgerald, and other writers, as well as his own poetry and fiction. His work has appeared in *The Antioch Review.* He is professor of English at the University of Wisconsin-River Falls.

ALLEEN PACE NILSEN, professor of English at Arizona State University, has written extensively on literature for young people, including her book *Presenting M. E. Kerr.* She is the co-author of *Young Adult Literature for Today's Young Adults,* now in its 3rd edition.

MARGARET ODEGARD has taught courses in Chaucer and the literature of England for a number of years at the University of Wisconsin-River Falls.

ZIBBY [ELIZABETH] ONEAL has written a number of books for children, including *The Language of Goldfish, A Long Way to Go, In Summer Light, War Work,* and *A Formal Feeling.*

ROBERT M. O'NEIL is a lawyer and scholar who has specialized in the First Amendment. He has published a number of articles in law journals and several books including *Classrooms in the Crossfire.* He is currently founding director at the Thomas Jefferson Center for the Protection of Free Expression.

KATHERINE PATERSON is the author of many children's and young adult books, including *Bridge to Terabithia* (1977 Newbery Medal), *The Great Gilly Hopkins, Jacob Have I Loved* (1980 Newbery Medal), *Come Sing, Jimmy Jo* and *Park's Quest.* Her work has received many awards from such organizations as the American Library Association, National Council of Teachers of English, Parents' Choice Foundation and the National Council for Social Studies.

DOUGLAS A. PEARSON, JR. has written articles on English instruction for the *Wisconsin English Journal.* He is professor of English at the University of Wisconsin-Eau Claire.

GLORIA TREADWELL PIPKIN was a middle school teacher and target of the censors in the Bay County Florida schools during the 1980s. She has written a number of articles on this experience. She was the editor of *Florida English Review* for five years. She received the 1989 Courage Foundation award for her efforts in protecting intellectual freedom in Bay County, Florida.

FREDERIK POHL is the author of many science fiction books including *Man Plus, Gateway, Jem* and *The Years of the City.* He has edited many collections of science fiction short stories.

LAURA QUINN has published numerous articles and book reviews in academic journals as well as an article in *Reader Response in the Classroom.* She is currently at work on a book on Ann Petry. She is a professor of English at Allegheny College.

PETER J. REED is a literary critic whose work includes *Writers for the Seventies: Kurt Vonnegut* as well as various articles. He is professor of English at the University of Minnesota.

JEAN P. RUMSEY has published articles on Kantian moral philosophy, medical ethics, and other aspects of philosophy. She is professor of philosophy at Clarion University, Clarion, Pennsylvania.

THOMAS SCARSETH came to intellectual freedom activities from a widely varied background as farmer, lumberjack, apprentice to Korczak Ziolkowski on the Crazy Horse Monument in South Dakota and as jet pilot in the Navy. He currently teaches adolescent literature at the University of Wisconsin-LaCrosse.

JOHN S. SIMMONS is the author of 10 books and 75 articles on the teaching of English and reading. His most recent book is *Teaching Literature in Middle and Secondary Grades.* He is the immediate past chair of the NCTE Committee Against Censorship, and is professor of English, Education and Reading, Florida State University.

PAUL SLAYTON is a long-time member of the NCTE Committee Against Censorship. He is currently involved with the Lithuanian Ministry of Education working with Lithuanian teachers of English. He is professor of education at Mary Washington College in Virginia.

WILLIAM SLEATOR is a science fiction writer for both children and young adults. His books include *The Angry Moon, Blackbriar, Among the Dolls, Interstellar Pig*, and *Singularity*. His work has received numerous citations from the American Library Association, International Reading Association, and Horn Book, among many others.

ROBERT SMALL, JR. has written a number of articles for the *English Journal, Language Arts, Kappan* and other journals. He is co-author of *A Casebook for English Teachers: Dilemmas and Decisions* and he is co-editor of *The Alan Review* published by the Assembly on Literature for Adolescents. He is Dean of the College of Education and Human Development at Radford University.

JACK STARK has doctoral degrees in English and in law. He has written about 50 articles and several books, including *The Literature of Exhaustion: Borges, Nabokov and Barth, Pynchnon's Fictions* and *An Almanac of British and American Literature.* He is currently an attorney for the State of Wisconsin.

MARY STOLZ is the author of many novels and short stories for both children and young adults. Her works include *The Bully of Barkham Street, A Wonderful Terrible Time, Go and Catch a Flying Fish, The Noonday Friends*, and *Storm in the Night.* Her work has received numerous awards from such organizations as the American Library Association, Association of American Publishers, and the International Reading Association.

MARSHALL TOMAN has published articles in *Studies in American Literature, Studies in Contemporary Satire, Studies in American Jewish Literature*, and elsewhere. He has recently completed a study of Joseph Heller's novels, entitled *Nonsense and Sensibility.* He teaches English at the University of Wisconsin-River Falls.

GENEVA T. VAN HORNE is a professor of English at the University of Montana where she teaches a variety of subjects including children's literature. She is a member of the NCTE Committee Against Censorship and is a member of the YALSA Intellectual Freedom Committee of the American Library Association.

GLADYS VEIDEMANIS has written more than 40 articles and reviews for a variety of publications including the *English Journal* and *Media and Methods*. She was one of four authors of *Language: Structure and Use* and one of three authors for *England in Literature* . She wrote the introduction to *Shakespeare for Students* . She has been a high school English teacher in Wisconsin for many years.

JERRY W. WARD, JR. has written a number of poems and essays for *The Southern Quarterly, Black American Literature Forum, New Literary History, and Freedomways.* He is co-editor of the MLA book *Redefining American History.* He is Lawrence Durgin professor of literature at Tougaloo College.

JOHN A. WILLIAMS has written twelve novels including *Jacob's Ladder* and *The Man Who Cried I Am;* he was editor or co-editor of six collections of writings and wrote seven non-fiction books including biographies of Richard Wright and Martin Luther King, Jr. He is Paul Robeson professor of English at Rutgers University.

FRANK ZIDONIS has written a number of articles on literacy education, particularly in middle and secondary schools. He is professor of English education at Ohio State University.